Fire in His Heart

Fire in His Heart

**Bishop Benjamin Tucker Tanner
and the A.M.E. Church**

William Seraile

65

The University of Tennessee Press • Knoxville

Frontispiece: *Benjamin Tucker Tanner, c. 1890. Courtesy of the Archives Division, General Commission on Archives and History, the United Methodist Church.*

The paper in this book meets the minimum requirements of the American National Standard for Permanence of Paper for Printed Library Materials.

∞   The binding materials have been chosen for strength and durability.

♻   Printed on recycled paper.

Library of Congress Cataloging-in-Publication Data

Seraile, William, 1941–
    Fire in his heart : Bishop Benjamin Tucker Tanner and the A.M.E. Church / William Seraile. — 1st ed.
        p. cm.
Includes bibliographical references and index.
ISBN 1-57233-027-9 (cloth: alk. paper)
    1. Tanner, Benj. T. (Benjamin Tucker), 1835–1923. 2. African Methodist Episcopal Church—Bishops—Biography. 3. African Methodist Episcopal Church—History. I. Title.
BX8449.T36 S47 1998
287'.8'092—ddc21   98-9095

xiv

242

99.3-57

To the memory of Octave Seraile Sr. (1905–1995)

and

to my wife, Janette, for her winning spirit

and

to my children, Aden and Garnet, with the hope
that their generation may find the racial harmony
that eluded Tanner's generation

Contents

Illustrations

Preface

My interest in Benjamin Tucker Tanner developed while I was researching the life of Theophilus Gould Steward, the subject of my last book (*Voice of Dissent: Theophilus Gould Steward [1843–1924] and Black America*). Steward contributed essays for the *Christian Recorder* edited by Tanner from 1868 to 1884. Tanner was a major figure in the African Methodist Episcopal Church who served the church as a clergyman for nearly ten years, edited the *Recorder* for sixteen years, and was the founder and first editor of the *A.M.E. Church Review,* the literary organ of the church, from 1884 to 1888.

By his numerous editorials in the church's publications, Tanner accomplished much toward developing an educated ministry, a goal that he shared with Bishop Daniel A. Payne. It was his contributions to scholarship and his strong advocacy for mission work that elevated Tanner in 1888 to the bishopric, a position he held until his retirement in 1908. Tanner was not an agitator, preferring instead to point out problems and offer suggestions for actions rather than issue rhetorical challenges. Tanner, a strong advocate of self-reliance, eschewed self-denigration, which unfortunately was common among the freedmen, who were taught to hate their kinky hair and distinctive African features. Tanner achieved distinction as an editor and a bishop because of his determination to "push or be pushed." Many of Tanner's views were compatible with those enunciated by Booker T. Washington, but while he admired the educator, Tanner did not subscribe to any single racial ideology. Tanner was a militant integrationist who supported emigration to Canada in his youth and, at times, advocated black cultural nationalism even though he abhorred racial separatism. Like so many of his contemporaries who were discriminated against and dismissed by lesser men who had to strain their necks to look down upon them, Tanner had to "wrestle with the problem of a dual identity; struggling to excell as both learned professional and racial leader, . . . as [an] American . . . who could never transcend the restraints of responsibilities of his blackness."[1] He advocated black teachers for black schools, not out of racial chauvinism but because he believed that as long as American communities maintained separate schools it was better to employ black teachers, who generally had more affinity for their charges than did their white counterparts. For the same reason, he was a member of a black denomination because white prejudice eliminated him and his race from their pews. Yet he was not comfortable with racial labels, which he deemed anti-Christian and a denial of humanity. Tanner married a black woman, Sarah E. Miller, but he did not oppose the interracial marriages of friends nor that of his son, Henry, because he asserted in 1884 that the American geography would create a distinctive American race that would combine the best of the European, African, and Asian components to form a new American who would be seven-eighths white and one-eighth African, "with a motley of yellow."[2] However, Tanner was not a utopian; he understood that racism would not end unless challenged in the courts and at the voting booth. Tanner advised people to "aim high, and while coming to it, learn to endure . . . snubbing at the hands of empty heads." Tanner also suggested that people should "learn to endure [their] own company, rather than seek to the company of those who require as the price of it, fine dressing. Learn to endure even a pang of hunger for a principle. Be simple livers [and] know no such word as fail."[3]

Bishop Tanner and many of his colleagues in the nineteenth century were the pioneers who built churches and conferences, who fought for civil and political rights, and who guarded the church's doctrine and discipline.[4] In recent years historians have begun to examine the lives of clergymen who were previously overlooked as newly unearthed mines of information in church newspapers, diaries, and other unpublished materials have illuminated their role in politics, education, social welfare, and race advocacy.

This is a welcome signal that Bishop Reverdy C. Ransom may have been too pessimistic when he observed in 1916 that "races, peoples and nations and the times in which they lived are like a mountain sunk to the bottom of the ocean without leaving a trace of the fact that once their mountain peaks were uplifted to the clouds."[5] Tanner, who was a prodigious writer, inexplicably did not write an autobiography. Fortunately, most of his diaries for his earlier years, from age fifteen until his early thirties, have been preserved. This was an important period in his life, as he questioned his lack of religious zeal, which convinced him to leave pulpit preaching in 1868. None of his diaries for the period after 1868 have survived; precious little of his personal correspondence is extant, nor do we have any of his voluminous correspondence as editor or bishop save for those pieces printed in the *Christian Recorder*. For these reasons, I chose to write a general biography depicting his life as a preacher, editor, and bishop instead of concentrating on any one role.

Tanner's life spanned the period from 1835 to 1923, a time when African Americans struggled for freedom and equality. During this period they went from a national identity of "colored" to "Negro" and "Afro-American." Tanner cared little for the appellation "Negro," which was advocated by militants in the last two decades of the nineteenth century. His preference was "American," for he believed people of African descent in the United States were shaped by geography, religion, and culture to be Americans and were neither Africans nor Negroes. This is not to say, however, that he lacked race pride. Tanner, indeed, was one of the earliest advocates of Africans' prominent presence in the Bible.

He viewed slavery both as a voracious reader who closely followed the growing debate over the slavery question in the 1850s and as an eyewitness to the "peculiar institution" as a boat barber near Louisville, Kentucky. Tanner was not merely a silent witness to this nation's most calamitous periods—the Civil War, Reconstruction, Southern brutality against former slaves, and American imperialism on the western frontier and across the Pacific. He addressed these and other issues as editor of the *Christian Recorder* and the *A.M.E. Church Review*. Tanner authored hundreds of essays and editorials, and ten major theological studies, which put to lie the general assumption that African American religious leaders did not reflect upon or address the important theological issues of the day.

While Tanner's contributions to the development of African Methodism and an educated clergy were significant in themselves, his greatest contribution, in my opinion, was his devotion to scholarship and historical truth. He understood the psychological value of race uplift. All of Tanner's writings showed other persons of color that they, too, had the capability for intellectual greatness, for he believed that all races had the potential for scholarly attainments. His challenge of white scholars who arrogantly assumed that they alone were the interpreters of history was a major contribution to black cultural nationalism that spawned a generation of researchers and scholars whose intellectual descendants continue to challenge similar racist assumptions. This great defender of the church and the race has been obscured for too long because his active advocacy on behalf of his people declined measurably after he stopped editing the *Christian Recorder* in 1884. Although he labored on behalf of the A.M.E. Church as a bishop, Tanner's pen wrote less on racial issues and more on religious subjects, which no longer garnered him national attention. He increasingly turned his thoughts and action to preparing ministers for the role of shepherd of wandering souls and was virtually a recluse during the last years of his life. Still, this does not negate his earlier efforts on behalf of integrated schools, political enfranchisement, and racial equality—issues that dominate the civil rights agenda of the twentieth century.

During the past decade biographies have appeared on Alexander Crummell, Daniel A. Payne, Theophilus G. Steward, Henry M. Turner, and other nineteenth-century black religious leaders that raise the question: "Where is Bishop Tanner's story?" Since his death in 1923, Tanner has been overshadowed by the prominence of his son Henry Ossawa Tanner, the famous artist. Hopefully, this book will restore him to the prominence that he richly deserves.

Acknowledgments

The research and writing of this book covered a period of three years. During that time I incurred debts to many individuals. At the risk of leaving out some names, I wish to thank Rae Alexander-Minter, the great-granddaughter of Benjamin T. Tanner, for encouraging me to, first, accept the project of chronicling the life story of a significant voice from the past. Rae provided valuable information pertaining to her family's history as well as research leads. Special thanks to Dale Harger for his hospitality while I was examining Tanner's papers in the Library of Congress. Jonathan Zimmerman and other faculty members at West Chester University offered useful suggestions and helpful criticism during a productive work-in-progress session when I was still trying to focus on the direction of my research. Dennis C. Dickerson, the historiographer of the African Methodist Episcopal Church, graciously shared with me his knowledge of source materials pertaining to African Methodism. I owe a major debt to Kenneth E. Rowe for his immense knowledge of Methodist history and for his collegiality in suggesting leads.

All scholars owe a major debt to the staffs of libraries and historical societies. I wish to thank the staffs of the Schomburg Center for Research in Black Culture; the Library of Congress, Manuscript Division; the University of Pennsylvania Archives and Records Center; the Methodist Center at Drew University; the Robert W. Woodruff Library at the Atlanta University Center; the Union Theological Seminary, especially Betty Bolden; Columbia University's Butler Library; the New York Public Library; and the Library Company of Philadelphia.

I wish to honor posthumously Bishop J. P. Campbell and other African Methodists who saved copies of the *Christian Recorder* and the *A.M.E. Church Review*, which were indispensable for the completion of this book. I profoundly acknowledge the guiding spirit of Benjamin Tucker Tanner.

Finally, I have praise for my children, who again had to put up with their father's "ways" as I sifted through my research notes and spent hours away from them. Thanks to my son Aden, for convincing me that I was not too old to learn how to operate a word processor. As anyone who has undergone the process of learning to manipulate a computer knows, mistakes are frequent and pages do get lost. A profound thanks to Jeremy Grey for his assistance, and a huge thank you to Sam Jones for retrieving material that I thought was permanently lost. And to Jane, my wife, I acknowledge with deep love and respect your encouragement and support during a time when research and books were secondary to your health concerns. My father, Octave Seraile Sr., died before this manuscript was published, but he was aware of its progress, and his encouragement and guidance sustained me during times when the project appeared too challenging. Thank you, Dad, for your support.

Chapter 1

Youth and Early Ministry

Pittsburgh, while cut off from the majority of the Keystone State's residents by the Allegheny Mountains, was no sanctuary in the antebellum years for the city's small African American population, who were victimized periodically by racists. "Debarred by economic inequality, by race prejudice, and by political discrimination from participation in matters of general interest," and numbering only 473 in 1830, or 3.76 percent of Pittsburgh's population, the African American residents cooperated to develop educational, religious, and civic institutions. In 1831 the Rev. Lewis Woodson established a school in the Little Bethel African Methodist Episcopal Church. A year later black residents organized the African Education Society at John B. Vashon's home. The two schools combined in 1833, followed by the state opening a segregated public school for black children in 1838. Despite their poverty, the city's African American inhabitants established in 1831 the Thebian Literary Society to educate adults informally. Pittsburgh's white population, composed primarily of immigrants of German, Irish, Welsh, English, and Scotch extraction, looked unkindly upon their black neighbors. The close proximity of Irish to blacks in the sixth ward often led to racial friction. In 1834 the mayor sent the Duquesne Greys, a white militia, into Hayti, a black section, to disperse a white mob. Similar racial attacks occurred in 1839 and, again, in 1843.[1]

It was in this social and political milieu that Benjamin Tucker Tanner was born in late December 1835, one of twelve children of Hugh and Isabella Tanner. His exact birthdate is a source of confusion; he celebrated December 22 and 23 during his youth, and sometime after 1860 he claimed Christmas Day as his birthday. Benjamin saw little of his father, who was employed on river boats. Taught by Hugh to be responsible, nine-year-old Benjamin contributed to the family's finances by delivering Martin R. Delany's newspaper, the *Mystery*. Denied employment opportunities by Pittsburgh's immigrant community, young Tanner apprenticed as a barber and traveled to other cities in search of work. Without the luxury of a happy childhood, compelled to cut hair or shave men in unsavory places, and pushed to gain an income in a competitive society, Benjamin learned to appreciate independence. The experience taught him to avoid the easy way but rather to "work and win." Small in stature (he was only five feet, two inches tall in adulthood), Benjamin was not averse to physical or mental challenges. It is not known when he began as a barber, but his first diary entry—

for January 28, 1851, shortly after his fifteenth birthday—indicated that he worked for Barney L. Ford, a barber and hairdresser at 13 Clark Street in Chicago.[2] It is not clear how long Tanner had lived in Chicago or why he strayed so far from Pittsburgh. He evidently lived alone, grabbing a meal whenever he could. The man-child, working hard to support his mother, was not deterred from pursuits of pleasure. He enjoyed bird hunting and attended the theater weekly, pronouncing *Romeo and Juliet* "a fine play." Throughout the early spring of 1851, Tanner was also a frequent guest at evening parties, which he enjoyed very much.[3]

Ben attended church when he felt like it. His father was not openly a professing Christian, although Ben had heard him pray privately. It was his mother, Isabella, who conducted the family prayers, and it was she who would later shape his religious perspective. In Chicago, Ben attended a Baptist church. On February 9 he attended church and Sabbath school and diligently recited ninety-one verses from memory. He bid his Sabbath teacher farewell on March 9 as he prepared, for unknown reasons, to depart for Pittsburgh, where he arrived on March 17 after stops in Detroit, Cleveland, Buffalo, and Rochester.[4]

Tanner had a keen interest in current affairs. His succinct diary entries for 1851–53 show an unusual awareness for one so young of the nation's tumultuous times. He commented favorably on a judicial decision that fined and imprisoned two white men "for kidnapping a colored man in Philadelphia." Tanner was concerned that the Fugitive Slave Law of 1850 would lead to the unlawful enslavement of free persons of color. The odious law prevented the accused from receiving a jury trial; the presiding United States judge or commissioner received ten dollars if he found the African American to be a fugitive or five dollars if he did not. Many Americans of both races refused to cooperate with the authorities and assisted fugitives in their escape. Tanner's diary entry for April 12, 1851, noted, "Much excitement prevails in Boston from an attempt to execute the provisions of the Fugitive Slave Law." The reference was to the arrest of Thomas M. Sims, an escaped slave from Virginia who was returned aboard the *U.S.S. Acorn*.[5]

The determination of the federal government to return fugitives, the increase in racial hostilities, and the influence of Martin R. Delany and other emigrationists caused Ben to lose faith in his native land. Racial codes, which prohibited people of color from congregating without the presence of whites, denied them voting rights, encouraged economic discrimination, limited educational opportunities, and imposed other proscriptions, led Tanner to write in March 1851, "I never want to die in the United States." His support for emigration caused him to invest hoarded savings in a land development deal in Canada, which hoped to attract African American families from the United States, but by 1858 it had gone bust. Then, he wrote to his brother Andrew, "That man for whom I bought [the farm] failing and all his property and effects being seized . . . , I have written to [black abolitionist] Mr. Alfred Whipper in Chatham [Ontario], requesting him to sell my place. Tell our parents not to worry about Canada if I lose that place." In 1878 Tanner disavowed his youthful "rabid emigrationist" viewpoint and deemed his step to Canada as an "egregious mistake."[6]

Despite his criticism of the United States and his purchase of property in Canada, in 1851 Tanner was not ready to emigrate. Instead, he sought to further his education by enrolling in the Allegheny Institute (Avery Institute), established by the Rev. Charles Avery in 1849 as a training school for black youth. Tanner began classes on September 8. He refused Avery's offer to pay his tuition, preferring to let his barbering wages support him. Tanner matriculated at Avery Institute for only one year of the prescribed five in the college department. Later, he completed a three-year course at Pittsburgh's Western Theological Seminary. One of thirty-eight graduates in 1860, Tanner "had to war with poverty, with [bad] habits, business complications, ignorance and sin."[7]

Tanner had to work to pay his tuition, but he had difficulty in bowing to his employers' authority. His entry for June 9, 1851, stated: "Last w[ee]k I shaved 104 men[;] cut 16 h[ea]ds of hair." On June 12 he quit after his boss, a Mr. Curtis, slapped him. Yet he returned the next day after receiving a raise of fifty cents per week. He cut hair every day, including Sundays after church service ended. An argument with Curtis on July 15 resulted in Tanner again quitting. Needing money, he returned the next day but left Curtis permanently on August 16.[8] He began working for a Mr. Pulpreys on August 20, then departed on September 6 to enroll in school, but returned to him for Saturday work, which earned him one dollar.[9]

Since he had trouble accepting authority, or perhaps simply because he resented scrubbing the floors of the barbershops, Benjamin opened his own establishment on November 8 after his mother purchased for him a stand and four shaving mugs. He immediately experienced difficulty in attracting customers. He worked on Wednesdays and Saturdays, and his earnings for three weeks—$1.23, 60¢, 20¢, $1.05, 35¢, and $1.60—were so disappointing that he wrote on November 29 that business was dull.[10]

At times the high-spirited adolescent sought escape from the routine of work and school. He frequently missed Sunday church services.[11] On January 14, 1852, a victim of Benjamin's well-aimed snowball soundly kicked him in retaliation. Often mischievous, sometimes obnoxious, Tanner was frequently tardy to school and at times was kept in detention for laughing in class. Yet the inquisitive mind, sharpened by the hardships of his youth, began to show promise. He wrote poetry and essays, which teachers "criticized good." Despite his early academic difficulties he would be recognized in later years not only for his poetry and essays but also for his Latin translations.[12]

Like many of his contemporaries, regardless of age or race, Tanner questioned the failure of the United States to live up to her principles of equality. For a young man, he watched the political scene with unusually close attention as the events of the early 1850s precipitated the nation toward conflict over the slavery question. He avidly followed the presidential election of 1852, noting that Franklin Pierce's victory meant "again has slavery triumphant in America." Tanner's petulance was abated somewhat when a New York judge decided the innocence of five accused of being fugitives from slavery.[13]

His attention to electoral politics impressed upon him the importance of verbal skills. While at Avery he helped formed the Avery Literary Debating Society. The subject of the first debate, November 26, 1852, was "Are the colored people capable of self-government?" Tanner and his partner lost in December when they declared that the African suffered more at the hands of whites than did the American Indian. Years later, a classmate, the Rev. James A. Hubbard, recalled that Tanner "was first in study, first in manly sports and first in the hearts of his schoolmates." These were exciting and educational times for the young man, who had the opportunity to hear dignitaries such as Horace Mann, the educator, and Martin Delany.

However, the classes, the debating society, working in the barbershop, and reading history and philosophy late into the night all taxed his health. Illness forced him to leave school temporarily on February 10, 1853. He soon returned, but a month later was "tolerably sick" and barely able to walk down the stairs in his home. His poor health made him reflective. "O God man knows not the blessing he enjoys when he has health. Were I but blest with a learned mind and could write page[s] many of my days would be spent in writing pieces which might induce people to learn to protect their health and after being blest with it give God the praise," he proclaimed.[14]

Recovered, Benjamin decided to travel to Cincinnati after his brother William sent for him. He arrived at the Ohio city on April 3, 1853, and took up work as a barber for four dollars weekly on a river boat traveling between Louisville, Kentucky, and Wheeling, West Virginia. Removed from the comforts of home, Benjamin toiled among gamblers, drunkards, and the godless. On April 8, he noted, "I [am] looking at the wickedness. It is no wonder that so many get destroyed." He was amazed that gambling and other sinful activities were committed on Sundays, and he believed that God would judge the wicked for their blasphemy. It was during these faith-testing times that Tanner decided to save his soul. He confided in his mother, an "unusually religious" woman who "with Spartan coldness" said, "My son, if it is your purpose to be faithful and adorn your religion, join the church but if you are going to trifle about it, you had better stay where you are."[15]

Tanner pondered his mother's words as he traveled on the Ohio River. He was captivated by the diversity among the people who stocked the boats with cotton and other cash crops, but despite the informal education of river travel, he longed for the formal structure of the classroom. Between boat runs, or when the swollen river made travel impractical, Benjamin attended classes at the Ohio

Manual Laboring School.[16] River travel afforded him an opportunity to see slaves traveling in company with their owners. Being so close to his brethren in chains, Tanner was the more disappointed when he learned that free black George Wright's plot, allegedly involving about one hundred whites and twenty-five hundred slaves, had been thwarted by the authorities in New Orleans.[17]

It was too much for the seventeen-year-old Tanner to bear. Homesick, he lamented on June 4, 1853, "I wish I were at home in Pittsburgh." By June 14 he had saved ninety-five dollars for his tuition; he took the train to Pittsburgh on June 25, arriving the next evening. Tanner left June 30 for Pomeroy, Ohio, en route to Albany, New York, where he arrived July 4. He found lodging with a Mrs. Condit and began school on July 5. Lonely, Tanner informed his family of his unhappiness, and they urged him to return to Pittsburgh. But, lacking travel funds Ben remained in Albany throughout the summer, using his spare time to study Latin and algebra and to review arithmetic. Tanner regularly attended church and Sunday school, opened a barbershop (where his wages were frugal— he only earned ten cents on August 15), joined the Sons of Temperance Society, and busied himself with attending anti-slavery meetings.[18]

With the exception of a single entry for 1858, Tanner's diary for the period 1854–59 no longer exists. As he did not write an autobiography, and few of his personal letters for this period are extant, little of his life is known for this period. In 1856 he converted to the African Methodist Episcopal Church. Also in 1856, he met his future wife, Sarah Elizabeth Miller, who was born May 18, 1840, in Winchester, Virginia, to a slave mother and a free black father. Jesse Tanner, Benjamin's grandson, believed that Charles Miller, Sarah's father, voluntarily took the family to Pennsylvania in 1846. Jesse was born in France and probably heard a sanitized version of his ancestors' travels to the North. Sadie Tanner Mossell Alexander, Benjamin's granddaughter, revealed that Sarah's mother, Elizabeth, was a slave and that some of her children were fathered by Charles, who was free, and the others by her owner. Charles was unable to purchase her, as the owner kept increasing the price; therefore, Elizabeth sent Sarah and the other children north via the Underground Railroad. The Pennsylvania Abolitionist Society divided them among families, with Sarah being sent to Pittsburgh. Sarah attended Avery Institute but left after her father's death to teach public school. Later, she returned to Avery as an instructor. Away on a trip, Benjamin professed his love for Sarah in a letter dated June 5, 1857. He asked her not to turn to another if they faced a "maelstrom." He signed the letter "yours now and forever and no one else." The couple married August 19, 1858, and their union produced nine children, seven of whom lived beyond infancy.[19]

The 1850s were a precipitous time for the nation as the slavery question intensified sectional rivalry. Harriet Beecher Stowe's *Uncle Tom's Cabin* (1852) stirred up southern denials of slave mistreatment. The Kansas-Nebraska Act (1854), which repealed the 1820 Missouri Compromise, led to civil war in Kansas. In the Dred Scott decision (1857), Chief Justice Roger B. Taney ruled that black men "had no rights that white men were bound to respect." Tanner closely followed other events that would soon hurl the United States into civil war.

In July 1856 Tanner angrily assessed America's injustice to her enslaved population.

> O muse of Justice hear my plaintive song
> of Afric's wrongs, of Afric's grief untold
> O aid one while I sing of blood and wrongs
> wrought by . . . America
> And let thy . . . condemnation . . .
> fall heavily on her who boasts of right
> falsely declare all men upon her soil
> with claims for freedom.
>
> Millions of souls are groaning neath the tyrant's blood stained lash,
> Daring to ask what they profess to give
> But, ah the world sees this hypocrisy
> This base deception in fair freedom's name
> This sin fore God this outrage upon man (slaves untaught of God)
> They're heathens in a Christian land
> To liberate would be to loose a band of savages
> Great God of justice hear my plaintive song
> of Afric's wrongs, of Afric's grief untold
>
> Let thy wrath of justice, avenging heaven
> fall heavily on her who . . .
> falsely declares upon her . . . with claims
> to freedom, all happiness, all men are born.[20]

This denunciation of America was reflective of Tanner's views, a perspective that would identify his writings for more than fifty years. In an undated essay, "The Fugitive Slave Law," Tanner condemned the nation for punishing those who sought freedom from tyrants. He referred to the denial of habeas corpus or the right to a jury trial as an act of barbarism, something that even the "savages of the Sandwich Islands would not tolerate." Hungarians, who were widely perceived as victims of Austrian mistreatment, were treated ten times better than slaves were treated by their owners, he noted. "We ask," he demanded, "for liberty! Would to God that the iron fetters . . . would be broken and we permitted to go free."[21]

These unpublished writings reveal Tanner as a writer of force and eloquence, attributes not seen in his terse diary entries, albeit at this time he was his sole audience. He astutely observed in 1858 that European immigrants, in their endeavor to escape poverty, were willing to flock to American cities to work as bootblacks, porters, barbers, waiters, ferry-boat hands, cleaning ladies, and laundresses for a pittance—just enough to provide for shelter and food. Their willingness to work for low wages deprived African American men of employment. Unlike black men who craved nice homes, new furnishings, and servants, foreigners were humble, Tanner declared. Humility coupled with a greater prejudice against African American workers led to Irish and German workers' vertical economic progress. Tanner understood the dynamics of racism; therefore, he urged black workers to improve their character, to save their earnings, and to engage in self-reliance. These themes, later popularized by Booker T. Washington, defined Tanner's life and were his prescription for racial progress.[22]

Tanner was not a mere theorist for racial progress but one willing to lead the way as an activist. During the spring of 1859 he was ejected from Pittsburgh's Masonic Hall by United States Marshal Bernard Dougherty for refusing to sit in the black section. Ironically, Tanner had come to hear a reading by Fannie Kemble, the anti-slavery advocate. The embarrassed but not meek student filed suit for assault and battery. The *Pittsburgh Gazette* supported Tanner's cause because he was a "young man of good character, [who was] intelligent, industrious, sober." The outcome of the case is unknown because a fire near the turn of the century destroyed the court records of the suit.[23]

Tanner was not only an activist for his race; more specifically, he was an activist on behalf of the African Methodist Episcopal Church. Tanner was still a student at Western Theological Seminary when on December 13, 1858, the Rev. John Tibbs licensed him to preach in the A.M.E. Church. On March 23, 1860, Bishop Daniel A. Payne gave Tanner his pastoral certificate and assigned him to Sacramento, California. On the eve of the American Civil War the western state had a black population of five thousand and offered possibilities for promising missionary work. The Rev. Charles Stewart was the first A.M.E. minister in California, arriving on February 11, 1852. On February 22 of that year, the first A.M.E. meeting house was dedicated. Two years later, African Methodists established St. Cyprian as their connectional church in San Francisco, with other A.M.E. churches in the state soon following.[24]

Tanner faced the difficult task of raising funds before he could embark on his journey: an arduous sea voyage from New York to the Isthmus of Panama, then the challenging trek across the isthmus to the Pacific side, and then another leg by sea to San Francisco. On May 29, 1860, Tanner went to the Pittsburgh press requesting that they print an appeal on his behalf. "They all gave me a kind reception and four out of five gave me very flattering notices previous to which I had gone and received kind recommendations from [my professors]," he wrote in his diary. The *Weekly Anglo-African*, a black New York newspaper, supported Tanner's cause by reprinting a plea from the *Pittsburgh Dispatch* to "kindly and liberally" aid his fundraising effort. On July 2 Professor Daniel Elliot, Tanner's professor of polemic theology at Western Theological Seminary, wrote to Dr. William Anderson in California, "The Lord I trust will make him a blessing to his colored brethren and crown his labor with success." Adding a postscript, Elliot indicated that he erroneously thought that Tanner was ordained but was informed by him that he was only a licentiate. "Please allow him to retain this recommendation," he requested. Tanner had fine recommendations, but he needed funds. On May 30 he went begging, a task he deemed "unpleasant." Initially, he met with "only tolerable success." The enterprising Tanner then printed and distributed tickets for his June 14 lecture on historical testimony to the work of Jesus.[25]

The turnout for the lecture was small. It only drew "ten or twelve men [and] about fifty or sixty women," Tanner lamented. His biggest disappointment was with those boasters who promised support but failed to deliver. "I think our people would learn to talk less and do more," he complained. But "I suppose," he added, "I can raise enough money [for] steerage [passage] at least."[26]

While Tanner understood that sending him to California was not among the priorities of his people, the *Pittsburgh Dispatch* of June 16 severely criticized the African American community for failing to attend his lecture. Consumed with the thought of spreading the gospel in California, Tanner wrote to a Rev. T. M. D. Ward "that the triumphs of the Gospel . . . will not be [stopped] for want of means." The United States government was spending millions on the Pony Express to dispatch mail to California, and Tanner hoped that Christians would expend the same effort to spread the word of God to the far west.[27]

Tanner approached his California mission with considerable doubt. His father had died in 1857, and now, in 1860, Tanner's mother complained to her daughter Hannah that she needed money for support. Torn between duty to his mother and his willingness to serve African Methodism, Tanner called upon God to give his mother patience and him success so that he could do his duty to her, "for she has been a good mother to me; for she [brought] me to Christ." Tanner's allegiance to the A.M.E. Church was weak despite his conversion to that faith in 1856. He wrote in his diary for June 19 that his religious belief was "quite unsettled." Tanner admitted that he needed to study the word of God more, and he called upon God to fill him with the Holy Spirit's teachings so that he could obtain spiritual peace.[28]

In part, Tanner's doubt was caused by theological confusion. Western Theological Seminary was a Presbyterian school, and as an African Methodist selected for missionary work, he was quite unsure about his denominational beliefs. Doubts notwithstanding, Tanner was serious about fundraising, which meant that he would have to leave Pittsburgh. On June 17 W. H. Woodbury, who had met Tanner after speaking in his church, offered to assist him in fundraising. The next day, the two met and agreed to write separate letters to Edward Gilbert, "a great friend of the colored people," in New York City. Gilbert's reply reached Tanner on June 23, instructing him to go to Cincinnati. He did so the next day and remained with relatives until June 29. The coldness of American prejudice struck him with the force of bitter wind as he chanced to sit next to a white person while waiting for a train. The conductor told him to stand on the platform, as black people were not permitted in the waiting area.

Failing to raise sufficient funds in Cincinnati or in a brief trip to Rochester, New York, Tanner decided to travel to New York City on July 9. The day before, he preached a farewell sermon at Wylie Street Church from Mark 16:15, "O what a pleasure it is to be permitted to shed a tear. It is but permitting the soul to expand when filled yea crowded with cares." Tanner bade farewell to Sadie and his infant son, Henry. "A sickening sadness seizes on the soul and makes me feel the power of memory." he wrote. "Shall I ever return again[?]" he pondered. In New York, Tanner met Gilbert and Woodbury. The latter was disappointed that Tanner had failed to bring a letter of recommendation and insisted that he write for one immediately. A Rev. Terry of the Methodist Episcopal Book Rooms expressed his dissatisfaction with Tanner's choosing to leave his wife and child alone while he went to California. Nevertheless, he arranged for Tanner to be interviewed on July 14. "I was now in the highest hopes at this bright prospect," Tanner wrote.

Unfortunately, Terry and Woodbury informed Tanner that they thought he should go to Africa as a missionary for the Methodist Episcopal Church; otherwise, Terry added, he would not provide financial assistance. On July 16 Tanner and Woodbury met; Tanner described the meeting's atmosphere as "cold." Woodbury insisted on seeing the letter of recommendation or he would not be in a position to help. Despite his bluntness, he gave Tanner five dollars and arranged to meet the next day. Tanner brought in the letter of recommendation. Woodbury read it, and then said, "Well, what course now are you going to pursue?" Tanner responded that he was waiting for Woodbury's advice. Woodbury dismissed him with a curt "Well, I am about at the end of my rope and you must try yourself." Tanner wrote in his diary that he was not going to waste time seeing others who would treat him just as coldly as Woodbury. Yet he admitted to himself that Woodbury was not prejudiced but was acting on principle. Later, Tanner apologized to his mentor for his intemperate thought (Tanner had a quick temper, and it would be years before he learned to think before flying into a rage over insults, imagined or real), but Woodbury simply replied, "Ah . . . what I do I am not doing it for you but for God."[29]

Far from his financial goal, Tanner traveled from New York to Baltimore in search of assistance. On July 22 he and Bishop Daniel A. Payne went to Brooklyn's Second Street Church, where they collected seven dollars. Unfortunately, the trip from Philadelphia cost Tanner twelve dollars for the round trip fare and for board in New York City. A week later Tanner preached at

Philadelphia's Bethel A.M.E. Church, which netted him $20.04, far short of his goal. By September 1860, he had raised only eighty dollars.[30]

Tanner decided to forsake the trip to California when he was offered the opportunity to be the pastor of the Fifteenth Street Presbyterian Church in Washington, D.C. Established on November 21, 1841, Fifteenth Street Presbyterian would develop later into one of America's premier black churches. The famed abolitionist Henry Highland Garnet was an early minister, and later Francis J. Grimké used it as a power base for his activist ministry. Hiram R. Revels, the future Reconstruction United States senator from Mississippi, was offered the pastorate in April 1860 but declined the position with its annual salary of five hundred dollars. On October 31, 1860, Tanner accepted the position for six months after Bishop Payne permitted him to accept the assignment on a temporary basis. On September 2 Tanner wrote to Sadie in Pittsburgh that a salary advance would allow him to travel to Pittsburgh. Elated, he added, "I preached for them twice today, and they were much delighted indeed." Restating his earlier doubts, he declared, "My belief always has been with the Presbyterians and from a number of providential occurrence[s] I am persuaded that God designs me to labor here." Tanner informed his wife that "the congregation is the finest and most intelligent in the city and . . . they provided me a boarding house. I am treated here as though I was a prince." In 1860 Washington had two Methodist, three Baptist, four African Methodist Episcopal Zion, and three A.M.E. churches that catered to the black population. Fifteenth Street was the only black Presbyterian church in the city. Tanner was certain that Sadie would be pleased to know that Washington counted among its black population such "first class people as you have been accustomed" to. The city's black elite, who worked in the federal buildings or taught in the segregated school system, included the Cooks, Wormleys, Bruces, Syphaxes, Shadds, Francises, Grays, and Terrells. Edward A. Thomas, a prominent African American resident, reportedly had a private library of over five hundred volumes, some three and a half centuries old, and three thousand autographs of the famous, including George Washington, the Marquis de Lafayette, Oliver Cromwell, and Toussaint L'Ouverture.[31]

Relieved of the anxiety of fundraising, Tanner turned his attention to his pastoral responsibilities and to his study, where he often spent six or seven hours studying Hebrew, Latin, or Greek or reading history, philosophy, or theology. He also managed to find time to be president of the Washington Lyceum, a literary society. Tanner's busy schedule did not assuage his loneliness. His entry for November 3 stated, "I will be most happy indeed to have my beloved wife and boy with me." Tanner was very fond of Henry, who was born on June 21, 1859, and whose middle name, Ossawa, "was derived from Ossawatomie, the town in Kansas where in 1856 the abolitionist John Brown" killed some pro-slavery men. "Ossawa" embodied Benjamin's and Sadie's hope for emancipation. Benjamin was pleased that Henry had good health, because his sister Nancy's boy, Louis, had died in infancy. Not knowing Henry's future as a famous artist, Tanner could only muse: "Whether the preservation of [his] life and health would prove a blessing, the Lord only knows."[32]

Mindful as Tanner was about Henry's future, he and Washington's approximately eleven thousand other free persons of color also pondered their own as well as that of the republic. The rapid rise of the Republican party from its inception in 1854 both excited and repulsed millions of Americans: the anti-slavery faction saw in the new party the possibility of a political abolitionist move to eradicate slavery, and the pro-slavery faction had no doubt of it. Years of compromising over the slavery issue had reached a climax with the presidential election of 1860. Tanner noted that the election was such "great excitement" that he was advised to cancel evening church services on November 7. Later, he regretted his compliance: "The devil deceived us in not having meeting [since] there was no danger at all." As for the election of Abraham Lincoln, Tanner declared, "As far as I can judge it is for good."[33]

Instead of being good, the political situation soon became ominous. The real estate market collapsed in the District of Columbia a week after the election, followed by local banks suspending specie payment. For the moment, Tanner put aside the nation's problems and turned his attention to church matters. The attendance for the November 11 service was a "tolerable fair turn out," which did not satisfy him. "O Lord send people," he prayed. Evening service on the 14th was better, which prompted him to ask God for an increase. "May I live for the outpouring of God's Spirit upon the congregation," he requested. Two days later, a navy chaplain, Mr. Noble, offered him the position of chairman of the missionary board, which he accepted. The Presbyterian Church provided him with a quarterly allowance in advance. "Now I can send for my dear wife," he gleefully wrote in his diary. His joy at her impending arrival was overshadowed by his concerns about her safety during the travel from Pennsylvania. Travel for black passengers was a time of trepidation, as they were often insulted by white passengers and conductors alike. The increasing rumors of secession and war coupled with Sadie traveling through a slave state, Maryland, alarmed Tanner. On November 19 he sent her sixteen dollars with the thought "May God give her a safe and comfortable journey." On November 29, Benjamin and Sadie were reunited in Baltimore. Their mutual happiness was quickly spoiled when they encountered "American prejudice" on the train to Washington, which Tanner left unexplained but probably involved rudeness.[34]

It was good that Benjamin had his family with him, because he needed the love and support of Sadie and the joy of being in Henry's presence to lighten the pressures of his busy schedule. He labored to arrange his time so he could feed or watch Henry while Sadie tended to her chores. The presence of his family provided him with the tenderness and love he needed, but it did little to ease his conflicts over the amount of time he spent in studying, particularly the emotional satisfaction he received from scholarship rather than from preaching. During the next six years Tanner would suffer intense anguish over his decision to devote most of his time to scholarship as he contemplated if his calling was indeed to the church.[35]

For the moment, however, he responded to his official church duties. Tanner was discouraged by the Sunday school situation at Fifteenth Street Presbyterian, where there were only two teachers for the many children, including some very mischievous boys. On November 18 Tanner visited a mission school operated by Mrs. Gordon. He vowed, "I must strive to cultivate that field. It *is called Northern liberties.*" His attention was also directed toward the adults in the church, for "when I look at . . . [their] coldness and jealousies—and [their] sins I am ready [in St. Paul's words to say] 'who is sufficient for these things.'" Tanner was disturbed by the presence of too many spiritually dead church members. His diary for November 24 noted, "Alas for the Christian zeal of this people. O Lord contrive to wake this people up to a sense of duty." He feared that the consumption of alcoholic beverages and the use of tobacco were not viewed by people as sinful. Sin was to him a terrible thing. On an earlier occasion, he wrote, "Happy wilt thou be o earth when sin shall be as tho it had not been." Sin was so frightening to Tanner that he believed the death of infants meant that God was showing people "what a horrible thing sin must be."[36]

Tanner's interest in the insolent youth was revealed in his December 4 sermon, taken from Proverbs 22:6, "Train up a child in the way he should go." Tanner was dismayed that church attendance was low, that only a few men came to prayer meetings, and that so many did not realize the intoxicating effects of wine. He called upon God to remove the veil from the people so that they might see "the sin of famishing their souls." On December 29, after spending six hours in his study, Tanner implored God to "look upon this church." "Come here," he urged, "for the sake of the scenes of Calvary . . . to vindicate the glory of the spirit. Come here . . . ever quickly." December 30 was the last Sabbath for 1860. Rain kept the attendance low. "May the Lord encourage my heart" was his sentiment on the eve of the new year.[37]

While Tanner genuinely believed that his congregation suffered from a lack of religious zeal, his anxiety was due in part to his growing awareness of his own lack of commitment to preaching, a concern that would soon engulf him. Meanwhile, he struggled to shore up his own faith. He attempted to make his sermons both interesting and zealous, for he understood that with God's help preachers had the ability to make sermons profitable to the people. He believed that ministers should "have wisdom . . . to present the gospel in all its beauty and in its true light" and should possess sufficient zeal "to make [their] preaching be felt upon every faculty *of the souls of those who hear.*"[38]

Tanner clearly understood that people needed God's word for their spiritual nourishment, but he also wanted to feed the whole person. Therefore, he encouraged Washington's black population to attend the debates held at the Washington Lyceum, of which he was president. A typical debate topic was "Which has the most influence over the human mind, the hope of reward or the fear of punishment?" Scientific lectures on topics such as "Meteorology or the laws of storms" were popular with the invited guests.[39]

Interjected into his efforts to save souls and to enlighten minds were his thoughts of secession and the threat of war. When South Carolina passed an ordinance of secession on December 20, 1860, Tanner noted, "The country is all in agitation." On Christmas Eve, he wrote that slavery had brought the nation to the brink of war. "I pray to God to rule and oversee all to his own glory and the good of man," he noted in his day book. Shortly after New Year's Day he wrote, "May God defend the right" as "the cry is war—war."[40] Reflecting upon the end of 1860, Tanner considered the year "the most eventful of my life." The minister hailed 1861 with prayer and praise but was disturbed by the presence of a fair and games of chance in church for he deplored the "sinful" music played in the house of God, which caused the cancellation of the weekly meeting. Tanner was pleased, however, with the attendance and spirituality displayed at the January 6 service when he preached his New Year's sermon on the text "For in thee is the fullness of life."[41]

Tanner's life was full. He prepared sermons, assisted Sadie with Henry's care, visited sick parishioners, and diligently attended to his studies. He spent six hours daily in his study, often arising at 5:00 A.M. to review Latin, Greek, and Hebrew and to prepare sermons. The impractical schedule led to compulsive eating followed by intense efforts to avoid gluttony. "May I receive grace to have my *appetite to be my slave*," he wrote. Later, he defeated the eating urge by making food something to sustain life without becoming a pleasure in itself. Tanner began to eat only fruit and cereal and to drink tea and/or milk in the morning. He often took lunch at 2:00 P.M. to avoid interrupting his study, for he believed that "if he stopped to eat, his mind would become dull because the blood previously supplying his mind would be used to help the stomach take care of the food."[42]

Despite his rigid schedule, Tanner often procrastinated, which led to moans of time wasted.[43] Tanner's difficulty in managing his time to balance family, church, and scholarship represented a metaphor for life. In his view, one worked constantly because rest would come in heaven. He argued that a man climbing a treacherous mountain does not rest as he approaches its top. Though "his feet [are] sore and blistered . . . tho his clothes [are] all tattered . . . tho he [is] hungry and thirsty," he must forge ahead to the mountaintop before he can stop to muse over the magnificent view. Similarly, he argued that man should develop muscles, stronger nerves, and a healthy and active brain to sustain him on his journey toward the goal of rest in heaven.[44]

Tanner's devotion to the his parishioners paid dividends. On February 27, 1861, he was reappointed pastor of the Fifteenth Street Presbyterian Church.[45] In

October he moved to 248 Fourth Street between J and K streets. Although Tanner had passed through deep waters, he had God's support to guide him. He informed one of his brothers, "I am now treated by my people with the greatest kindness [for little Bennie, who would die in infancy] has received some six or eight dresses." (It was common to dress infant boys in dresses.)[46]

Little is known about his life from 1862 to 1865, for his diaries for those years have not been located. After serving Fifteenth Street Presbyterian Church for eighteen months, Tanner returned to the A.M.E. Church on April 28, 1862, when Bishop Daniel A. Payne appointed him to the Baltimore Annual Conference with an assignment to the Alexander Mission on E Street in the District of Columbia. This was the A.M.E. Church's first effort at domestic mission work during the Civil War. Despite Tanner's preference for the Presbyterian pulpit, he was on loan to that denomination, and it was Bishop Payne's decision that he was needed to fish in Methodist waters. Lacking a viable alternative, Tanner complied. At times the assignment harbored danger; soldiers were posted to prevent ruffians from throwing bricks against the shutters. On May 5, 1863, Tanner pastored a church in Georgetown, and in 1864 Payne appointed him to Frederick, Maryland. While in Frederick, temporarily separated from his family, Tanner lodged with Moses Boon, who before his conversion embraced rituals derived from an African belief system that Tanner deemed "pagan" for its worship of other gods. Like most Americans, Tanner had little understanding of and less patience with African culture. He quickly attributed Boon's former heathenism to slavery.[47]

By the beginning of 1866, Tanner was a rising figure in African Methodism. He and the Revs. John M. Brown, D. W. Moore, M. P. Sluby, James A. Handy, S. L. Hammonds, and J. J. Herbert were selected to plan a celebration of the fiftieth anniversary of the A.M.E. Church for April 16, 1866.[48] On the surface, this was a feat for the then thirty-year-old Tanner, but the recognition could not mask his growing disillusionment with his own religious faith, a faith that he increasingly admired as a scholar but one that was becoming more difficult for him to accept with the zeal demonstrated by others. During the next two years his disillusionment grew stronger. His diary entries from January 7, 1866, to February 21, 1868, were often recorded weeks or months apart, but they revealed his displeasure with his lack of intense spirituality. His facility for languages prompted Bishop Payne to offer him a position teaching Greek at Wilberforce University, which Tanner declined. The thought of relocating his family to Ohio was more than he could take in his emotional state.[49]

As 1866 commenced, Tanner arose every morning at 5:00 A.M. to read, to prepare sermons that he delivered without spiritual fire, and to translate languages. Often, he prayed for the restoration of his religious faith. When a church leader accused of stealing church funds said that "God would make his innocence appear," Tanner was disturbed that an illiterate man had unwavering faith while he, his intellectual superior, had doubts. Tanner wrote that his absorption in his studies caused him to no longer "relish . . . the duties of the pastorate." Deeply concerned, he added, "I have a burning desire to feel as I know a priest ought to feel; but my studies . . . consumed me and I am compelled to it." Tanner asked God for forgiveness "of all the failures of duty," but he still asked for God's blessings in his studies. "O that I was 5 years younger," he lamented.[50]

Clearly, Tanner preferred the life of scholarship, but opportunities for scholars of his race were limited, and the church, if nothing else, offered means to support his ever growing family. The birth of a child on January 30, 1866, added to his woes. The unnamed child, who died in infancy, elicited this response: "Another little girl has been given me and for what o Lord? I already have two [Halle, born 1864, and Mary Louise, born 1865] and . . . I am so poor that I sometimes wonder how I shall meet my responsibilities but I know that God is good and he will continue to provide . . . but o my sweet infant what will be thy faith?" Believing that one day she would read his diary, he offered her this advice: "Love God and never forget to pray [which] distinguishes a man from a brute." He believed that prayer linked people "with the higher spirit who holds continual communication with God. Do this and all duties will be plain to you," he added with irony.[51]

Despite his eloquent defense of the power of prayer, Tanner continued to struggle with his doubts. His entry for February 10, 1866, recorded his desire for an unwavering faith. "I pray for a faith that I can believe without a doubt and recommend without an indifferent spirit," he declared. "Such a faith I have not," he confessed. "O God give it to me lest I die," Tanner cried. A month later, he lamented, "I am so cold in my love to God that I really am frightened at myself." Though he continued to lead his family in morning and evening prayers, Tanner admitted that his heart was "so icy cold." Tanner requested God to revive him and to "let . . . thy rays fall on me." His lack of spirituality, his obsession with his books, and his cry for God's help combined to tax his health. Just thirty years old, his body broke down. "I run the machine too fast" was his succinct observation for March 12, 1866.[52]

On May 2, 1866, Bishop Payne appointed Tanner to the pastorate of Bethel A.M.E. Church in Baltimore, where he was also expected to teach in the church's day school. Tanner approached the assignment with trepidation. "May God give me peace and strength," he implored. Remarkably, in light of his emotional state, he chose for his inaugural sermon Psalms 133:1, "Behold, how good and how pleasant it is for brethren to dwell together in unity." His reception was cordial, but Tanner was apprehensive, tense, and depressed. He indicated in his May 8 diary entry that he would travel to Philadelphia on June 20 and that if he failed to reach that destination alive Sadie should have his real and personal goods and seek a home near Xenia or Wilberforce, Ohio.[53]

Tanner's mental condition was noticed by a correspondent for the *Christian Recorder* who wrote that the pastor's teaching and pastoral duties had stretched him to the point of poor health. An unidentified minister confided to the same correspondent that Tanner should stop teaching if he only wanted money. Instead, he suggested, Tanner should ask the congregation to double his thousand-dollar salary because teaching distracted him from writing out appropriate sermons. Clearly Tanner was worn out. He had written *Memories of Eden,* a twenty-two-chapter Adam-and-Eve story, and was working on *An Apology for African Methodism,* both of which satisfied him intellectually but did little to ease his conflict over his lack of religious faith.[54]

At the end of 1866, Tanner was under stress. His diary entries were now written much less legibly than those of a few years earlier. The new year represented a time of flux for Tanner. He began the year in prayer and with the admission "I really thirst for more holiness." On January 15 he pleaded in his diary, "O Lord wake up . . . the fire of love in my heart . . . lest I . . . die internally. My cry is fire! fire! fire!" On January 26 Tanner added, "Come spirit clear up . . . my heart . . . and let the fire burn for it is cold."[55] During this emotional turmoil, Isabella was born on February 1, 1867. "May God help her" was all he could say.[56] In April Bishop Payne reappointed Tanner to Bethel A.M.E. Church, but he resigned later in the year to return to Frederick as principal of the A.M.E. Conference school. The Freedman's Aid Society used his assistance to organize a common school in the Maryland city. Tanner did much good by informing the freedmen about their responsibilities to their families. Now that he was no longer in charge of a church, he had more time to devote to scholarship, but he admitted that his zeal for knowledge could be "a source of [the] devil" that could cause him to "neglect to comfort my people and become selfish."[57] Tanner had reason for concern. Riled by a colleague, he retorted, "Books and prayers will cause me to triumph" because "the most perfect revenge . . . is to be so read and pray that [others] will be compelled to respect you if not [be] under obligations to you."[58]

Tanner was obsessed with scholarship. It meant everything to him. While not neglectful of his family responsibilities as a father and husband, Tanner devoted most of his energy to writing. On August 13, 1867, at 5:00 P.M., Tanner wrote in his diary "the end" to the writing of *An Apology for African Methodism.* "The end" represented relief at finishing the writing task, but on a greater level, it represented psychic satisfaction. In 1890 Tanner recalled a childhood dream of being enraptured with the thought of power and authority that came from writing a book "that should live." It was a thought that "dominated every other," and it provided an explanation for his compulsion for scholarship at the expense of his religious zeal. It was not without irony that Tanner, who lacked religious zeal, could devote so much time to a book that described the religious faith of African Methodists. Tanner had no problem with studying or writing about theology. The problem that perplexed him was his inability to feel the Holy Spirit emotionally. It was not that Tanner had lost his faith in God's word but that he yearned for a Christian holiness, a concern of many Methodists—

white and black—at that time. As 1867 ended, Tanner busied himself with teaching forty to fifty students in the day school, interacting with his four children, who ranged in age from eleven months to eight years, and rising before dawn to study. No wonder he declared after reading a chapter in the Bible, absorbing forty pages of British history, and translating twenty lines of "difficult Latin," "I have thrown away perhaps one-half the time, o Lord learn me to value time, and be more industrious."[59]

In his last extant diary entry, dated February 21, 1868, Tanner indicated that he had left the day before for Washington to secure funds to pay for the printing of his book. He expected to travel with Bishop A. W. Wayman to the South, where the A.M.E. Church had expanded since the termination of the Civil War. Anticipating possible trouble, even danger, Tanner renewed his life insurance for two thousand dollars and informed Sadie that in the event of his death she should return to Pittsburgh to purchase a small home for twelve hundred dollars and put five hundred dollars into the bank, with the remainder going for expenses. He urged her to persuade the church to put out another edition of *An Apology* and to keep a copy for the children.[60]

Meanwhile, his concern was to print and disseminate copies of his book, an "intellectual and theological account of the schisms between the black and white churches."[61] Tanner put all his energies into promoting *An Apology*, for he was mindful that whites thought little of the African American's intellect. James Lynch, editor of the *Christian Recorder*, shared his concern. "We must have as much intellectual power *inside* of our church as there is *outside* of it," he declared.[62] Lynch praised the manuscript, although he disapproved of the word "apology" in the title. In April 1867 the Baltimore Annual Conference of the A.M.E. Church passed a resolution to order the publication of Tanner's book. (By church law, such approval was needed. This rule was rescinded by the 1868 General Conference.) Daniel Elliot, Tanner's professor of polemic theology at Western Theological Seminary, informed him, "I am happy to know that you are not an *idler* in the vineyard of your divine master but are doing what you can to promote the cause of Christ among your colored brethren." Abel Stevens, editor of the *Christian Advocate*, organ of the largely white Methodist Episcopal Church, requested a copy because he planned to treat the same subject in his fourth volume of the history of that Church. Tanner acknowledged receiving many letters in reference to *An Apology* because "they are anxious," he wrote, "*to see whether, after the mountain has groaned,* [it] *is going to bring forth only a mouse.*"[63]

Despite its title, *An Apology for African Methodism* was a praise song for a race that under the guidance of Richard Allen and Absalom Jones had, in 1787, formed a church where black people could "think, talk and act for self." Tanner denied that the "African" in their name excluded whites as either members or clergy, citing white members in Buffalo and Chicago and an occasional white pastor as proof of their color-blindness. The A.M.E. Church, Tanner argued, was open to all regardless of race or ethnicity who spoke the "Negro language"—"the broad language of humanity." "African" was primarily doctrinal "and only nationally secondarily," he asserted. Tanner and other African Methodists argued that their church's doctrine, which was identical to that of the Methodist Episcopal Church, existed only because of white racism, which limited them, in 1867, to a subordinate position. Tanner further argued that there should be a union of all Methodists because God was color-blind, but as long as some men cherished their whiteness, African Methodists would show them through scholarship that blackness too could be exalted.[64]

An Apology received wide praise from the *New York Tribune.*[65] Henry Highland Garnet, president of Avery Institute, in recognition of Tanner's scholarship, bestowed upon him the A.M. degree; later Wilberforce University granted him an honorary D.D. degree.[66] Nevertheless, in the waning days of 1867, Tanner stood at the crossroads unsure of his choice of paths. A combination of spiritual yearning and an intense drive to read and write caused him to voluntarily withdraw from pulpit preaching, never to return except as a guest minister, primarily after his election to the bishopric in 1888. Tanner left the pastorate because he understood the biblical message "If any man minister, let him do it as of the ability which God giveth" (Peter 4:11). Elisha Weaver, editor of the *Christian Recorder,* visited the Tanners in Maryland on November 13 and noted that they spared "no pain . . . to make [the school] orderly and progressive." Still, Tanner, with his nearly unquenchable thirst for knowledge, would not have been satisfied to continue teaching on a permanent basis.[67]

Tanner was a conscientious person who believed that "all life, save that of God Himself, is but the discharge of a duty."[68] In his own case, duty to the church as an intellectual clashed with his duty to both the church and the ungodly as a preacher. He could preach God's word and believe in His message, but to his distress, he could not *feel* God's spirit within him. He knew the Bible in Hebrew, Greek, Latin, and English; but he yearned for the presence of the Holy Spirit. Like W. E. B. Du Bois, Tanner experienced "in early youth a great bitterness [that] entered [his] life and kindled a great ambition."[69] Tanner's bitterness was his failure to kindle a spiritual fire in his heart. Instead, he wrote about theology, which satisfied him intellectually. It would be in later years, after he was elected to the bishopric, that Tanner would stoke the spiritual fire that had forsaken him.

Under no circumstances could he return permanently to pulpit preaching, which evoked for him guilt about lack of fire in his heart for God's word. His departure from the ministry was timely, for if he had remained in the pulpit, anxiety and guilt would have probably led to a nervous breakdown. There were few viable options for black intellectuals three years after Emancipation. Few of his race could expect to become attorneys or physicians, not to mention bankers, stockbrokers, editors of white-owned newspapers and journals, or other positions limited by class and race to Anglo-Saxons. His future still undecided, Tanner preached on November 10, 1867, in Philadelphia's Mother Bethel A.M.E. Church's 3:00 P.M. service, ironically taking his text from I Corinthians 16:13, "Watch ye, stand fast in the faith. Quit ye like men, be strong." He preached that evening from the pulpit of the city's Union A.M.E. Church. His sermon was from Acts 9:6, "Lord, what will thou have me to do? And the Lord said unto him, arise and go into the city, and it shall be told there what thou must do."[70]

Washington was the city that decided Tanner's fate, because in May 1868 the delegates to the A.M.E. General Conference elected him editor of the *Christian Recorder*. Tanner now had his calling that offered relief from the guilt of pulpit preaching and the tedium of the classroom. The editor's position offered him an opportunity to write weekly on a host of subjects. During the next sixteen years he labored to make the *Christian Recorder* an influential organ for both African Methodists and a general lay audience.

Chapter 2

Christian Recorder, Part 1, 1868–1872
Establishing an Editorial Policy

The 1868 A.M.E. General Conference was an important one for Tanner and the church. He was the conference's recording secretary, which proved significant since Joshua Woodlyn, the book steward, failed to print the minutes. Saving the church from "an irretrievable loss" were Tanner's notes, along with those of A. W. Wayman, Elisha Weaver, W. J. Gaines, and J. C. Beckett.[1] The leadership of the church was confronted with a conference that had grown considerably since its 1864 meeting. Since the end of the Civil War in 1865, zealous missionaries had spread African Methodism and formed conferences in South Carolina, Georgia, Virginia, Florida, Arkansas, Tennessee, Mississippi, Texas, Kentucky, and North Carolina. Black southerners came to hear and to vote, but church law granted voting rights only to those conferences that had a minimum of eight hundred laymen reported at the previous quadrennial. None of the new conferences met the eligibility requirements. Upon motion, however, northern voters decided to rescind the law. "It was a radical motion," declared missionary Theophilus Gould Steward, "but the times demanded it." Later, the southerners would play pivotal roles in deciding the election of bishops and forming church policy.[2]

The General Conference of 1868 that elected Tanner editor of the *Christian Recorder* obtained a worker of energy and passion who for the following sixteen years left his indelible mark on the church organ. Beginning as the *A.M.E. Magazine* in September 1841, the publication effort ceased soon after. In 1848 the church purchased Martin Delany's *Mystery* in Pittsburgh and renamed it the *Christian Herald.* Four years later the *Herald* was published in Philadelphia under a new title, the *Christian Recorder.* Outlawed by slaveholders and condemned by northern bigots, its circulation remained low for years. During the Civil War the *Recorder* followed the Union army with the aid of the Christian Commission, which distributed copies to black soldiers. Still, the *Recorder* was undermined by poorly written articles and lack of popular news. Widespread illiteracy among the freedmen limited readership. In 1853 Bishop Daniel A. Payne estimated that only one of out of every 210 free persons of color could read, equivalent to a 95 percent illiteracy rate. The illiteracy rate among freedmen declined slightly to 81 percent by 1870.[3]

Incompetent or disinterested editors also hampered the *Recorder*'s effectiveness as a church and race organ. The *Recorder*'s first editor was Elisha Weaver, who served from 1858 to 1863, followed by A. L. Stanford, who edited for one year. Weaver took control again in 1864 but relinquished the duties in 1866 to

James Lynch, who in May 1867 was given the pastorate of Bethel A.M.E. Church in Philadelphia in addition to being reappointed editor. These men were staunch believers in African Methodism, but they did not bring to the editor's position any special talents. Lynch's dual appointment was indicative of the little regard the A.M.E. Church gave to its newspaper, as the bishops did not understand that the editor's position was a full-time one. Lynch held the editorship for sixteen months before resigning to help the southern freedmen adjust to emancipation. Elisha Weaver again assumed the editorial responsibilities. In his June 29, 1867, editorial, "Valedictory First—Valedictory Last," Weaver stated, "We were with you first, and we are with you last, in the struggle of the RECORDER." Tanner replaced Weaver because, as his predecessor observed, he was a "man . . . amply qualified . . . and who knows how to sympathize with the many disadvantages our people have to contend with."[4]

Tanner's ascendancy to the editorship raised the hopes of Bishop Payne and others who had long wanted the *Recorder* to rank with the nation's acclaimed religious journals. Tanner was not easily flattered. He understood that the church wanted him to make the newspaper second among religious journals in the United States, but he believed that the bishops did not understand the difficulty of developing a well-crafted journal. Tanner estimated that it would take twenty years before the *Recorder* could match the *Methodist* or the *Independent*, a secular journal, and fifty years before it could even conceivably rank with the *Nation*, then the country's premier journal of opinion. Tanner conceded that the *Recorder* might become a second-class religious journal if it provided readers with a variety of articles and truthfulness. He was confident that a diversity of articles would be submitted by black men and women who had traveled widely and by ministers who had preached in varied American communities. While he assumed that black writers could be as truthful as white ones, he understood that because of slavery, racial proscriptions, and widespread illiteracy his race lacked a literary tradition, which would prevent the *Recorder* from being competitive for years.[5]

During the next sixteen years, Tanner labored to provide readers with editorials, book reviews, poetry, and serialized novels in addition to messages from the bishops and other church news. He himself was a voracious reader who disciplined himself to read snatches during busy periods, only to return to a more detailed reading during his leisure. In 1868, after President Andrew Johnson signed into law the eight-hour working day, Tanner wrote that people misused leisure time to sleep or stay up late, attend balls, play cards, drink liquor, or patronize indecent dance halls, all of which devout Christians should abhor. Tanner's idea of recreation was to read or reread some "congenial authors" or to engage in conversation with family or friends. Nevertheless, realizing that some could not find decent employment, let alone leisure time for enjoyment, Tanner supported Isaac Myers's effort to organize the National Labor Convention of Colored Men in Philadelphia in 1869 by serving on its thirty-four-member committee.[6]

Tanner viewed it as part of his editorial responsibilities to interpret the news for readers, who often lacked his insight. An astute observer, Tanner introduced to his readers commentary on the secular world of politics and class consciousness, topics that many previously saw only in narrow religious terms. He warned the newly emancipated slave in mid-July 1868 to avoid the false promises of the Democratic party. Radical Reconstruction had yet to be fully implemented, and southern whites were warning their former bondsmen to ignore the northern carpetbaggers while remaining loyal to those who truly understood them. It was rumored that some freedmen supported the presidential ambitions of Horatio Seymour, who as governor of New York opposed the recruitment of black troops in the Empire State. Tanner facetiously wrote that since some black men were thieves or drunks, some might as well be Democrats. Seriously, however, Tanner warned the freedmen not to be deceived by the "pretentious smiles of the southern Democrats [for] they are deadly foes to the black man." In Philadelphia, he added, Democrats "mock us" with the words "This is a white man's government." Tanner urged his southern brethren to cast their first presidential vote wisely for Ulysses S. Grant, for a vote for the Republican meant that they loved their children, their race, and their country. Tanner reminded readers that it was the Democratic party that supported American slavery and harbored racist animosities for the freedmen whereas the Republican party armed them to fight for their own freedom, provided them with American citizenship, and granted the franchise to 700,000 of them in the former Confederacy. Shortly before the election, Tanner suggested that the Republican party should assist the *Recorder* by sending ten thousand copies weekly to Dixie because "the Democrats would give us $10,000 for our influence in the South." "We can't be bribed, but we can be helped," he added.[7]

It was incomprehensible to Tanner that any oppressed people would embrace the Democratic party; therefore, he was baffled when he heard that a "*Jew . . . boasted of being a Democrat.* A Jew—a man [who] stands below the Negro, yet does come to our America [and has] struck hands with traitors and oppressors. Oh . . . read thy own history and blush; and then cease trying to put thy flat foot upon the neck of a brother man," Tanner wrote. He understood that Jews were a persecuted group in Europe, and it angered him that members of an oppressed group failed to aid another despised race. For this reason Tanner severely faulted Judah P. Benjamin, formerly a Confederate cabinet officer, for owning 140 slaves. He found it abhorrent for the Jew "who is . . . a football to all people . . . persecuted of men, and accursed of God" to play master of others. In 1882 Tanner condemned two Jews, Representative Perry Belmont of New York and Senator Benjamin Jonas of Louisiana, both Democrats, for supporting anti-Chinese sentiment in Congress. He was particularly upset with their decision because pogroms in Russia followed the 1881 assassination of Alexander II. If American Jews wanted aid and sympathy for their brethren who were exiled to Siberia, Tanner advised them they should stop giving aid and sympathy in the United States to oppressors of blacks "while pleading to be free from it abroad." Later, Tanner tempered his view, observing, "Having our downs with [Jews] may we not hope to have our ups?" On May 5, 1890, he was one of the speakers at Philadelphia's Academy of Music who protested the outrageous treatment of Russian Jews, for "if black is not to give to white, how can white be expected to give to black?"[8]

Like Jews, Catholics were severely criticized by the editor. Catholic influence among Americans attracted his attention. In this respect, he shared the view of most Protestants. Many agreed with Samuel F. B. Morse's 1835 assessment that Catholic immigrants in the United States would be encouraged by their priests to be anti-democratic. "Can one throw mud into pure water and not disturb its cleanness?" Morse argued.[9] On November 29, 1866, Thanksgiving Day, Tanner delivered a sermon, "Paul and John vs. Pius IX," in Baltimore's Bethel A.M.E. Church. Taking his theme from Galatians 1:8, "But though we, or an angel from heaven, preach any other gospel unto you than that which we have preached unto you, let him be accursed," Tanner expressed his opposition to Catholics praying to the Virgin Mary. He also feared that the freedmen might be dazzled by the pomp of Romanism. "This is the church," he claimed, "that hopes to lasso the negro." Steeped in anti-Catholic bias, he added, "We bid our people beware if they would not become . . . rum [sellers] and rum [drinkers] as are the Catholics as a general rule of today."[10]

Others in the church expressed similar fear. In 1869 a Wilberforce student called upon the A.M.E. Church to challenge Catholic priests who sought to convert freedmen. Tanner echoed the student's appeal by calling upon the church to arise "and march to victory . . . over Romanism." Tanner's concern, while overblown, was based on Catholic efforts to convert former slaves. In 1871 four members of an English Catholic missionary society arrived in Baltimore for the purpose of preaching among freedmen. Unfortunately for their cause, the death of Archbishop Spalding on February 7, 1872, dampened the experiment. Anti-Catholic bias bordered on hysteria. In 1875 Tanner wrote two essays for the *Independent* that elucidated his bias. In "The Fruits of the Caste in the Church" and "A Remedy Worse than the Disease," Tanner wrote that it would be race suicide for black people to flee from caste discrimination into the arms of Catholics, because white northern Catholics voted against the African American's interest. He asserted that it would be foolish to seek an alliance with Catholics, since white Protestants practiced individual caste but "papal caste is both individual and official." He noted that while caste in America would one day end, the triumph of Romanism would be America's death knell; Catholics did not tolerate independent or democratic thought, and wherever Catholics ruled there existed darkness and ignorance. This last point was underscored for Tanner when the *New York Times* reported that a Mexican mob, after hearing a priest's incendiary sermon, had killed a Protestant missionary, the Rev. John L. Stevens.[11]

Tanner's anti-Catholic feelings were moot, for Catholic efforts at conversion among blacks were generally unfruitful. By 1888 there were approximately 140,000 segregated black members of the American Catholic church, who received the Eucharist after all whites had finished. Though the St. Joseph Society of the Sacred Heart for Foreign Missions (Josephites) built churches and schools for southern blacks, they were viewed as stepchildren. Three Congresses of Colored Catholics met from 1889 to 1892 to assist the clergy "in the conversion and education of [blacks] in the United States." Even though the Catholic church ordained in Europe three brothers—James, Patrick, and Alexander Healy, the children of a mulatto slave mother, Mary Elisa, and an Irish immigrant, Michael Healy—and all three achieved success in the United States, with Patrick becoming president of Georgetown University, James attaining a bishop's position in Boston, and Alexander teaching in that Massachusetts city, none was visibly identified as "black." Augustus Tolton, who was born a slave in Missouri, was also ordained a priest in Europe, but it was not until 1891 that the American Catholic church ordained a black priest, Charles Randolph Uncles. Four years later, there were approximately 200,000 black Catholics in the United States.[12]

Despite the earlier opposition of Tanner, he and others began toward the end of the nineteenth century to show tolerance and even respect for American Catholicism. A.M.E. Bishop J. M. Brown attended the first Congress of Colored Catholics (1889), and the Rev. Levi J. Coppin, editor of the *A.M.E. Church Review*, addressed the delegates in 1892. Clearly African Methodists had begun to understand that the Catholic Church was incapable of converting but a few. Though Catholics had a mixed record on issues of racial equality, some African Methodists saw in them less rigidity than previously. The Rev. Theophilus G. Steward concluded that "in Catholic countries the Negro sees more of the church in Christ than he can in Protestant America." And Tanner, who opposed praying to the Virgin Mary, acknowledged in 1896, "The Roman Catholic Church is altogether too venerable an institution for any to malevolently approach it or its phases of worship. It is . . . too learned and wise to be despised." The architect of anti-Catholic hysteria cautioned African Methodists not to be malevolent, because the Roman Catholic Church's only concern was "Are you a child of the church?"[13] Tanner's spirit of ecumenicalism resulted from an 1881 trip to France, Ireland, Scotland, and England, where he met Catholics who harbored neither anti-democratic nor racially biased thoughts.

Jewish and Catholic Democrats were only symbolic of a larger issue. Would Americans support the efforts of the Republican party to extend civil liberties to freedmen, or would they reverse those efforts by electing Seymour, who had branded the preliminary Emancipation Proclamation "a proposal for the butchery of women and children"?[14]

"The issue before the people," as Tanner aptly titled an editorial, was whether the nation's future would be in the hands of its friends or under the control of belligerent enemies. Tanner feared that a Seymour victory would lead to the undermining if not overthrow of Radical Reconstruction, the expulsion and possible murder of American Missionary Association teachers and missionaries, and the reenslavement of thousands. Tanner demanded that the denial of the franchise to freedmen should not be the price of political peace. "If loyalty cannot be honored and rebellion restrained without making a man of the dark skinned lover of his country, then let the . . . rebels of the South take back the reins," he proclaimed.[15]

Tanner's fear of violence was punctuated by the assassination of Benjamin F. Randolph, a former chaplain of the 26th U.S. Colored Infantry and a member of South Carolina's legislature. Tanner asserted that despite this atrocity, God had proclaimed the dark night of the Negro to be over. "Everywhere," he insisted, "the chains are being [removed and] his shame wiped away." Believing in divine providence, he added, "Cursed will be the man, or the party who says, nay. God will reign, His truth will prevail."[16] Grant's election was proof to Tanner that God's will indeed prevailed. Tanner described the Republican's victory as "the day of burial . . . *of the demon of American prejudice* against the negro."[17]

The victory of Ulysses S. Grant in 1868 and the Radical Republicans' gaining control of Congress the previous year offered no guarantees for racial equality, as the Ku Klux Klan and unredeemed Southerners sought to deny citizenship rights to the freedmen. Bishop Daniel A. Payne informed the delegates to the National Convention of Colored Men meeting in Washington, January 13–16, 1869, that the black man was mistreated in the South (although he possessed the vote since the passage of the Act of March 2, 1867) and was denied the franchise in the East except for five states and in the West except for two states. The ratification of the Fifteenth Amendment to the United States Constitution in 1870 granted the suffrage to all eligible black males in the nation. In Tanner's view the amendment represented more than a political device to aid the agenda of the Radical Republicans. Clearly he viewed it as a religious amendment that would define the nation's future. When calling for its ratification, Tanner had asserted that the black vote would settle the question of whether or not America was a Christian nation. He was confident that blacks would vote to amend the Constitution so that "the name of God and Christ will appear," he asserted. The black vote would offset the immigrant Catholic vote and keep America free of Romanism, he added. Tanner was pleased with ratification. "Rejoice ye parents of . . . colored children . . . for [they] have a future," he exclaimed. So moved was Bishop T. M. D. Ward upon hearing that the amendment had been ratified that he wrote to Tanner on May 12, 1870, "for the first time . . . I write as an American citizen and not as heretofore, an alienated American."[18]

Political integration represented for Tanner a recognition that black people were constitutionally Americans. Politics aside, Tanner desired a religious integration of Methodists, North and South, black and white. Despite the "African" in the A.M.E. Church's name, Tanner was not a separatist, and he longed for the day of Methodist if not Protestant union. Beginning in the late 1860s, he advocated strongly for unity among the African Methodist Church, the African Methodist Episcopal Zion Church, the Methodist Episcopal Church, North, and the Methodist Episcopal Church, South. After the 1870 formation of the Colored Methodist Episcopal Church, he added that branch to his plea for unity. While most of both races felt comfortable in their separate churches, a minority questioned the wisdom of such practice. Daniel Curry, editor of the *Christian Advocate* in New York, suggested in 1867 that since no fundamental difference existed between the white M.E. church and the black A.M.E. and A.M.E.Z. churches, it was time for the mother church to return black Methodists to the fold as well as use its abundant resources to elevate the freedmen. This view concurred with a resolution passed by the Baltimore Annual Conference of the A.M.E. Church in April 1867, "The ruling idea . . . is the absolute worth of man, and not of any particular race." The delegates resolved to have union with all the Methodist branches.[19]

Editor Curry did not speak for the Methodist Episcopal Church, North, which was unwilling to broach the subject. Tanner became upset in 1869 when he learned that four years earlier the bishops of the M.E. Church, North had met to inform their counterparts in the M.E. Church, South that since slavery—the cause of their split in 1844—had ended, there no longer was an obstacle to prevent their reunification. Tanner was disturbed that their call for union did not include African Methodists. He wanted unity because "Methodism . . . destroys the irrepressible nature of the Negro." "Take him by the hand," he urged, "you need the warm fervor of his heart. Discard it and a purely intellectual religion will follow. Unitarianism if not downright paganism will be instituted," he warned. In 1870 Tanner repeated his call for unity as he sharply rebuked the Rev. Theophilus G. Steward, an A.M.E. missionary in Georgia, for his demand that Tanner keep the color question before the readers. Tanner responded that northern and southern Methodists should become friends over the question of the "maltreated Negro," who should be the glue to unite them. "Come," he admonished Steward, "let us close ranks and have but one army." In the spring of 1870, Tanner, A.M.E. Bishop J. P. Campbell, and other notables met in the Philadelphia home of Robert Wilson to decry all separate organizations as denial of "the humanity of men." They called for union with the M.E. Church "upon equitable and Christian terms."[20]

Tanner saw in Methodist unity a chance for common schools, colleges, newspapers, magazines, home and foreign missions, and support for beneficent works. He conceded that for now the branches would retain their separate clergy and bishops. The Methodist Episcopal Church was unwilling completely to erase the color line. *Zion's Herald*, organ of the New England Conference of the M.E. Church, North, frankly admitted its willingness to accept A.M.E. Bishops Daniel

A. Payne, A. W. Wayman, and J. P. Campbell, who were of "equal culture and character," but none other. The M.E. Church refused to have unity with African Methodists, who had too many bishops for their two hundred thousand members. In the 1890s, after it was clear to Tanner that color prejudice would prevent unity, he suggested a confederation, which would allow for "ecclesiastical states' rightism, and yet will bring together in some general body the representation of all to legislate for all." Even this was not acceptable to the Methodist body. The white Methodists were unwilling to extend ecclesiastical leadership to its black members. Instead, they ordained Francis Burns in 1858 to be a missionary bishop solely for Liberia, and ordained his successor, John Wright Roberts, in 1866. But neither had the authority to minister to either blacks or whites in the United States. At the end of the nineteenth century, they had three black ministers in their northern conferences, and they failed in 1904 and 1908 to elect a black bishop. It was not until 1920 that two, Matthew W. Clair and Robert E. Jones, were elected by a separate ballot formed for that objective. In fairness to white Methodists, not all opposition to unity came from their camp. The *New National Era*, a black weekly, reported in 1871 that some black members of the M.E. Church opposed unity because they feared the talent that merger would bring from their black sister churches. In later years, unity among black Methodists was nearly achieved, but differences over a name and other matters outweighed other considerations.[21]

While the issue of unity whetted his spiritual and intellectual appetite, Tanner and the publication department faced two major challenges: providing the *Recorder* with adequate finances and attracting readers. For different reasons, both were unattainable during his sixteen years of editorship. The A.M.E. Church, influenced by Bishop Payne's demand for an educated ministry, sought through the *Recorder* to be a font of information, yet the paper had only a limited number of literate people to appeal to. In 1870 the school enrollment rates for blacks of both sexes amounted to 9.9 per 100 compared to 54.4 per 100 for whites of both sexes. In that same year, 79.9 percent of blacks were classified as illiterate compared to 11.5 percent of native and foreign-born whites.[22]

In March 1868, several months before Tanner assumed the editor's duties, the *Recorder* suspended publication, partly because a fire in the printing plant added to the church's financial problems. The *Recorder* was thousands of dollars in arrears because subscribers were either late in payment or refused to pay at all. Upon assuming his duties, Tanner urged the ministers to solicit subscribers. Do this, he declared, and the paper would grow from six or seven columns to fifteen or twenty (a feat never accomplished in his lifetime). Adding to the publication department's woes was the insufficient amount of cash received from advertisers, particularly from white-owned businesses. "We . . . remind [the public] that the *Recorder* is . . . read by thousands [who] eat, drink, wear clothes, get sick and die, just like other folks," Tanner proclaimed. The editor called for five thousand new cash subscribers by January 1, 1869. Realizing that some in the South did not receive the paper because postmasters refused to make deliveries, Tanner promised to emulate Jewish editors who sent their publications folded so that the publication's name was not visible.[23]

In 1869 Tanner searched for new funds. The bishops failed to heed his suggestion to merge the *Recorder* with the A.M.E.Z. *Zion Standard* to save expenses.[24] In June, Tanner and A. L. Stanford, the book steward, altered the masthead. Now, beneath the name, THE CHRISTIAN RECORDER, was an outline of Africa with the inscription "Ethiopia shall soon stretch out her hands unto God." The print was larger and more readable, but the paper was reduced from four pages to two by removing some useless ads and a page and a half of excerpted matter. Bishop Payne declared his approval. "I can now feel proud of it, before I could not. I can now take a lively interest in it, before I could not. We can now call it our paper, before we could not," he noted.[25]

Payne's praise notwithstanding, the subscription rate failed to increase. The Rev. Theophilus G. Steward, concerned that the *Recorder* faced disaster unless clergy submitted readable articles, asked, "Have we no authors?"[26] Tanner concurred with Steward's remark. The editor argued that the *Recorder* would never reach its potential until the clergy submitted thoughtful articles and not mere rehashings of camp meetings or revivals. Believing that he could write more erudite editorials that would attract readers, Tanner requested from the connection library funds, since his office had few reference books. He compared this oversight to a "revolutionary flint lock . . . liable to miss fire."[27]

A. L. Stanford, the book steward, promised in October 1869 to double the printed pages if five thousand new subscribers were enrolled by January 1, 1870. Inducements for new subscriptions ranged from copies of the new A.M.E. Church discipline, hymn books, and Tanner's *Apology for African Methodism* to cash rewards. In December 1869 Stanford offered a ten-dollar-value silver-plated pitcher to those who obtained by March 1, 1870, twenty subscribers; a fifteen-dollar ice pitcher for thirty-plus subscribers; a fifty-dollar American Waltham watch for fifty-plus subscribers; and for those who recruited one hundred or more subscribers, Stanford offered a hundred-dollar solid gold American Waltham watch, or a full-jeweled patent leather hunting case. Unfortunately, few clergy showed enthusiasm; worse, many did not subscribe themselves.[28]

Despite failure to add new subscribers, good news came in December 1869 when the Union Printing Association provided Stanford with a printing press, which meant the *Recorder* could be printed in-house for the first time.[29] The resulting elation, however, was dampened by Tanner's dissatisfaction with Stanford. In April 1870 he considered resigning but changed his mind because he was "ardently attached" to the *Recorder* and "loved the whole church too well to impede her progress by silly squabbles." Tanner did not state the source of the conflict, but it probably dealt with Stanford's inability to increase subscribers, which undermined the editor's desire to improve the paper's contents. Church law limited Tanner's responsibilities to editing all books, papers, and periodicals published by the A.M.E. Church, whereas the book steward was responsible for subscriptions, sales, and billings. By May the Book Concern was close to five thousand dollars in debt. Tanner hoped that the *Recorder* would increase in size because he wanted to introduce columns on domestic and foreign news, agriculture, and commerce and a ladies' and children's department.[30]

Beginning with the September 24, 1870, issue, the *Recorder* increased from four to six columns and resumed its four-page spread. Subscriptions still remained low. Stanford threatened resignation because only the sale of hymnals and other books subsidized the *Recorder*, and he lacked two thousand dollars to purchase the building housing the publication department. In July 1871, Stanford announced the suspension of the *Recorder* for several weeks so that he could settle with the creditors. Five hundred dollars was needed to improve the press room, but fifteen hundred dollars was owed by delinquent subscribers, and twenty-four hundred dollars was owed by subscribers who no longer received the newspaper. The good news was that the first August issue would come from their own press.[31] Although the paper appeared infrequently during the summer and fall of 1871, the editor of the *National Monitor* was pleased that the *Recorder* was entirely printed by black workers, because it provided black youth with an entry into printing.[32]

Stanford's announcement in November that eleven hundred dollars was still owed by subscribers and that the *Recorder* would publish twice a month instead of weekly failed to overshadow the rumor that he had mismanaged the Book Concern. An examination of the books by the General Committee of the Book Concern found them to be in order. Nevertheless, in early January 1872, the *Recorder* reported the abrupt departure of Stanford. Bishop J. P. Campbell informed Tanner in a January 15 letter that Stanford had embezzled funds and had fled Philadelphia, leaving his wife for a young woman who was an A.M.E. bookstore clerk. This accusation was denied by Stanford, his wife, his father-in-law, and the father of the young lady. Stanford eventually turned up in Jackson, Mississippi, where he joined the M.E. Church. Upon hearing this, Tanner wrote that the M.E. Church would soon know of his incompetence and dishonesty. After serving a jail sentence in Canton, Mississippi, Stanford emigrated to Liberia, where he died.

Stanford's departure left the publication department in a mess. He had the clerks and agents under his influence. No one could understand his bookkeeping, but it was soon clear that there was a deficit of $3,632.54 without any account of payment for type, press, or rent on the books. (Later, the General Committee of the Book Concern successfully recommended that the publication department be under the control of the Bench of Bishops, with the business manager, editor, and executive committee of three appointed by the bishops and the treasurer appointed by the bishops, managing editor, and executive committee.)[33]

The financial situation certainly hampered Tanner's efforts to make the *Recorder* the type of paper that he believed would bring pride to African Methodists. Nevertheless, he labored throughout his dispute with Stanford to bring topics of both church and secular interest to his readers. One church topic that he kept before the people was the issue of mission work. The biblical prophecy of Ethiopia stretching her hands unto God was a challenge to African Methodists to "help bring on the day of the awakening of the black, brown and yellow peoples who are descendants of Africa." Daniel Coker, an A.M.E. minister, went to West Africa in 1821 under the auspices of the American Colonization Society, but there is no record of him establishing an A.M.E. church there. In 1827 the Baltimore Annual Conference of the A.M.E. Church sent the Reverend Scipio Beanes to Haiti, which began the church's active foreign mission work. Former slaves who had run away to Canada requested A.M.E. pastors in the 1820s.[34] Later, as bishop, Tanner would have more direct involvement with the church's mission efforts in all those areas, but now, in 1868, he would wield his editorial pen in support of African Methodism mission outreach.

Heeding the command "And the ransomed of the Lord shall return, and come to Zion with songs and everlasting joy upon their heads" (Isaiah 35:10), Bishop Daniel A. Payne, while recognizing that funds were limited, believed it to be the duty of the church "to evangelize the world and prepare it for the coming of its Lord and Head." Similarly, the *Methodist*, organ of the M.E. Church, North, and the M.E. Church's Freedmen's Aid Society deemed it the duty of Ham's children to Christianize Africa because she "pleads for help."[35]

The American Missionary Association afforded tremendous assistance to African Methodist missionary endeavors in the former Confederacy by providing half the salaries of missionary teachers. On May 13, 1865, Theophilus G. Steward, James A. Handy, James H. A. Johnson, and Bishop Payne arrived in Charleston, South Carolina, to begin the work of bringing the freedmen to Christ, a glorious work that would see African Methodism spread throughout the South.[36]

While the generosity of the Missionary Association was appreciated, Tanner and some others in attendance at the 1868 A.M.E. General Conference objected to an offer of three to four thousand dollars from the Unitarians to assist in southern mission work. The offer represented a boon to the financially strapped church, but dissenters faulted the Unitarians for dismissing the deity of Jesus as dogma. Tanner did not want the Unitarians' money, as he deemed them unchristian. He warned, "We are Methodists . . . , we cannot be Unitarian. None of our young men must study at the seminaries. In no way is the purity of our faith to be endangered." The Reverend C. B. Ferry dismissed the Unitarians as "mere theists" who believed more in science, politics, and education than in religion. It is not known whether the Unitarian offer was accepted by the delegates, but in January 1869 Tanner reported that the Unitarians had agreed to establish fifty to sixty libraries with a minimum of forty books (approved by Payne) in each one of the principal A.M.E. churches. Bishop Payne also sought financial support from the Unitarians for Wilberforce University.[37]

Saving souls for Christ was Tanner's chief concern, but the decision to accept Unitarian funding was not his to make, as the editor did not create policy. Nevertheless, Tanner was interested in the establishment of a sustained mission endeavor. He was pleased when Bishop Nazrey of the British M.E. Church announced in September 1868 his intention to sail in the spring "to plant the banner of the British M.E. Church" in the Caribbean. Wishing him well, Tanner added, "Let Zion, and Bethel, and British be effaced, and let them be but one grand African Methodist church on the American continent; and let it be war on the ranks of the devil in Africa proper." On September 26 Tanner declared that the B.M.E. Church should incorporate the blacks of the Caribbean, while the A.M.E. Church would take their southern American cousins, and the two branches should meet at Moro Castle "and demand the surrender of that citadel of sin." Undoubtedly he spoke on this subject, since he was a delegate to the B.M.E. conference that began on September 7 in Hamilton, Ontario. Tanner had paternal feelings for the B.M.E. Church, which was formed in Canada in 1856 by African Methodists; he considered it like a child that had permission to leave home.[38]

African Methodists were driven to proselytize not simply by denominational pride but by a strong belief that providential design had brought them from Africa to face the hardship and humiliation of enslavement, later to be redeemed in Christ to fish for the souls of African people throughout the diaspora. The black American, according to the editor, was the agent who could transform the supposedly heathen African into the bearer of Christ's gospel. Neither appreciating nor understanding the diversity and richness of West African culture, Tanner dismissed it as well as its New World hybrids as inferior to the Anglo-Saxon culture of his native land. He curtly dismissed the slaves in Brazil and the Spanish Caribbean as the "lowest of our race on the American continent" because "they have never thrown off [Africa's] barbaric usages." The descendants of Africa in the Danish West Indies, British Caribbean, and Haiti represented progress, but they did not in his estimation compare to their counterpart in the United States, who "has been the pupil of the cool, aspiring, all conquering Anglo Saxon and . . . has partaken of all the greatness of his master." Surrounded by a republican form of government, civilization, and Protestantism, the American black was on the road to rivaling his teacher, Tanner argued. He believed that "God lit the candle in the great house of Negro darkness and barbarity . . . [in order] to lighten the whole house [so] that . . . Negroes in all parts of this great house may see."[39] The saving of the heathen soul was so important to Tanner that he claimed in 1868 that the most vital question facing his race was not the vote "but . . . how are . . . our folks to be saved?" Until Africa is redeemed, he argued, Europeans would view the black American as "a civilized Negro" or a dressed-up monkey. In 1869 he called upon African Methodists to remove the burden of heathenism from Africa or "drop the prefix 'African'" from their name.[40]

Others echoed Tanner's view. Joseph Jenkins Roberts, an emigrant from the United States who served as Liberia's president for eight years, addressed the fifty-second annual meeting of the American Colonization Society on January 9, 1869, with the plea that missionary societies would continue to Christianize "poor degraded Africa . . . from her present state of cruel barbarism." Alexander Crummell, a classical scholar, educator, intellectual, and pan-Africanist who first emigrated to West Africa in 1853, urged black Americans to come to mother Africa as civilizers and evangelizers. "This is . . . according to God's will," he proclaimed. "What a hallucination . . . to see them sailing to China . . . Japan . . . India or the Sandwich Islands" but not to Africa, he added.[41]

Tanner understood that it would take men and women of dedication and strong faith to work in Africa far removed from the support of loved ones, but he did not believe God would have to do more "to save the black race, than he did to save the white race." Tanner expressed gratitude upon hearing in 1869 that Dr. Livingstone had found the source of the White Nile, for he represented God's instrumentality for African spiritual redemption. (He ignored the colonization possibilities of Livingstone's travels.) No wonder he was upset in 1872 when he learned that the M.E. Church was considering withdrawing from African mission work after expending money and lives with little evidence of success. If the hundred thousand black members of the M.E. Church were silent on this matter, Tanner stated, the A.M.E. Church would gladly take control of the Liberian Conference, but this was forbidden by the M.E. Church. We can do the work and they cannot, he asserted. If the heretical Unitarians could assist the African Methodist mission work in the South, why cannot the M.E. Church assist us in Africa? Tanner asked.[42] Even if they had the spiritual blessing of the mother church, African Methodists lacked the financial and human resources to establish African missions. That work remained nearly thirty years in the future.

Meanwhile, opportunities for United States economic advances in Liberia beckoned. Believing that the Americo-Liberians who ruled the African republic desired annexation, Tanner strongly endorsed the idea in a March 1870 editorial. Tanner declared that annexation would introduce American business interest to Africa. Why let Europe reap all the benefits of exploiting Africa's resources? Profits should flow to New York, not London, he noted. Tanner believed that annexation would benefit both Liberia and the United States because "Africa would give her treasures to America, America would give her institutions, her religion, her spirit, her life to Africa." While Tanner assumed that annexation would help to spread the gospel of Jesus Christ to Africans, he naively believed that colonizers or annexers had an altruistic interest in the continent. An unidentified correspondent's letter from Monrovia published in the July *Recorder* (when Tanner was out of Philadelphia) understood the problem of annexation better than Tanner. The gist of the letter was that annexation would diminish the self-respect of Liberians and that it would be foolish not to let pure Negroes build a Negro nationality in Liberia.[43]

The United States had no intention of annexing Liberia, nor was the A.M.E. Church prepared in 1870 to embark on an expensive mission endeavor in West Africa. The Caribbean, however, whetted the appetites of both the A.M.E. Church and the American business community. Tanner rejoiced when Queen Isabella of Spain was overthrown in 1868, because she was a defender of slavery. He called upon the free blacks of the Caribbean to liberate Cuba from slavery. Tanner's militant sentiment was primarily motivated by his commitment to spreading African Methodism. To him, the Spanish Caribbean, ostensibly Catholic, was more pagan than Christian. Tanner urged the United States Department of State to purchase Cuba and open it up to Protestant missionaries. He hoped that the descendants of Africans who were exposed to Western civilization would be God's instrument in spreading His word throughout the Caribbean.[44]

Thus, Tanner was elated in February 1869 when a joint resolution in Congress called for the United States to accept Santo Domingo (Dominican Republic) as an American territory, providing the people of that land requested such action. "God speed the annexation day," he wrote, because it meant an opportunity for mission work. Save in the business community, annexation was not popular among Americans. Many, including some in Congress, agreed with the *New York Times* that they did not want to hail "200,000 dark skinned Dominicans as fellow citizens."[45]

Tanner urged President Grant to annex Santo Domingo; Haiti would follow, ensuring the island's regeneration. "Annex that island," he exclaimed, "and it will become an ally to our Protestant faith[;] a free Bible and a free school will assure this." He called upon Spanish-speaking African Methodists to be in the vanguard to missionize Cuba and Puerto Rico. President Grant recommended to the Senate that it ratify the Santo Domingo treaty—passed by the House of Representatives on November 29, 1869—but that body rejected it on June 30, 1870. Still, Tanner hoped that Congress would reconsider. Tanner's editorial of January 7, 1871, "Blow the Trump," declared that annexation would open to African Methodism "the first great missionary door."[46] Tanner's enthusiasm for mission work was fueled by his belief that unless people or races accepted Christ they would pass away rapidly. He illustrated the demise of the American Indian as a case in point.[47]

The United States had no interest in annexing Santo Domingo, but this did not prevent some merchants in January 1873 from seeking an agreement with the Dominican government for a one-hundred-year lease for control of the Peninsula and Bay of Samana. Tanner supported this endeavor, for it would bring the Catholic land "within the influence of our goodly institution." His faith in future mission work in Santo Domingo was lifted when he received a letter from a resi-

dent begging the A.M.E. Church to send a missionary until they could build a
church "capable of supporting him." He was pleased to learn of the February 8
resignation of King Amadeus of Spain because progressive forces represented by
Don Emilio Castelar, Spain's secretary of state, wanted Cuban slavery abolished.
Again, freedom to that island meant greater mission opportunities for African
Methodists.[48]

Tanner's lofty goals for Caribbean mission work were temporarily thwarted,
but events would unfold that would see African Methodism in Haiti, Bermuda,
British Guiana, Liberia, Sierra Leone, and South Africa within a few years. Meanwhile, other issues captured the attention of the energetic editor. Chief among
them was the fate of Wilberforce University, the connection's premier educational asset, located three miles from Xenia in southwest Ohio. Wilberforce was
established in 1855 for blacks by the Methodist Episcopal Church, North, with
the cooperation of the A.M.E. Church, purchased by Bishop Daniel A. Payne in
1856, destroyed by fire in 1865, and partially rebuilt by 1868. Tanner urged the
laity to support Wilberforce financially so that it might be their Drew University
(a Methodist theological seminary in Madison, New Jersey) "whence will proceed
a band of Methodist preachers that will do much to redeem the Negro character
the world over." It was in this vein that he suggested that the A.M.E. Church
should be represented at the November 17–20, 1868, National Christian Convention to show the orthodox churches that African Methodists stood by the recognized truths of Protestantism.[49] In May 1868 the delegates to the A.M.E. Church's
quadrennial decreed that every church member must contribute twenty-five
cents to help rebuild Wilberforce. This was absolutely necessary, insisted Tanner,
because too many of their clergy were trained by Lutherans, Congregationalists,
Episcopalians, Presbyterians, or other denominations, which led to confusion in
doctrinal interpretation. "Methodists for the Methodists should be our rallying
cry," Tanner wrote in December 1868. Bluntly, he added, "Either finish [build-
ing] Wilberforce, or let it disband." When help came from the Freedmen's Bureau, which sent twenty-five thousand dollars, Tanner was pleased by this generosity but demanded that African Methodists be more supportive of their own
institution. He urged people to value their dollars more and not waste them on
unnecessary gratifications. For illustration, Tanner declared that Germans who
earned ten dollars monthly became richer than black men who earned five times
as much. Sales boys on trains, he stated, preferred a car full of poor black folks to
rich Rothschilds because the former did not husband their money.[50]

Wilberforce University represented to Tanner a place for spiritual awakening whereby graduates would be on the road to civilization with all its appurte-
nances of land ownership, economic development, education, and modesty in
dress, economy, and morals. While he exaggerated the benefits of higher education, Tanner encouraged young ministers to study the Bible in addition to history, math, astronomy, and grammar to "improve their minds or they must give

way before the moral pressure that is to come against them." Notwithstanding his own doubts about his religious fervor, Tanner suggested that ministers develop a pulpit eloquence so powerful that they could "preach a living Christ to dying sinners!"[51]

Tanner was also concerned about the morality of young women. While he saw racism in the YMCA for overlooking black men in their effort to save men from the ruination of urban life, he saw in the formation of the YWCA in late 1868 hope for black women. Tanner urged the YWCA to be a truly Christian organization, because black women would not "come for a generation" unless specially invited. Not inviting them would deny them an opportunity for salvation, which would allow "sin and Satan [to reap] a harvest."[52]

Tanner had witnessed much sinful behavior aboard the river boats of his youth, and he was horrified by the fear of God's wrath. This fear caused him to issue some absurd warnings. In 1870 he denounced theater attendance as representing danger to the soul and body: he declared that over one thousand lives had been lost to theater fires in Europe over the past half century. The assassination of Abraham Lincoln in a theater, he noted was a warning to the church not to be silent about theatergoing. To prevent souls from falling into hell's clutches, the A.M.E. Church already prohibited members from gambling or attending circuses, horse races, and minstrel shows.[53]

Tanner was equally outspoken in his opposition to liquor consumption, which he deemed the nation's curse. The editor called upon ministers and congregations not only to refrain from liquor but to advocate a legal embargo on whiskey and a social one on wine. To support his analysis, he printed a report by the New York State Penitentiary noting that of 20,514 incarcerated, 17,804 were intoxicated at the time of arrest. Tanner cited figures to show that Americans in 1870 spent six hundred million dollars on liquor, of which blacks spent approximately seventy-five million. In 1872 he reported that the *New York Commercial Advertiser* estimated that Americans spent 250 million dollars annually on tobacco. Tanner estimated that blacks accounted for twenty-seven million dollars of tobacco consumption themselves. He questioned, "How can preachers or Christians . . . partake of this great iniquity?" Abstain from liquor and tobacco, he wrote, and use the savings to buy land, horses, or cattle, build schools and colleges, and send missionaries abroad.[54]

Tanner tempered his criticisms of the race's tendency for profligacy with the reminder that they were God's instrument not only to regenerate Africa but also to make America live up to her declared principle of "liberty and justice for all." He believed that God gave the black man the responsibility to represent truth in America, "and it is for him to realize the high honor, and be true through fire and blood." Tanner believed that abstinence from tobacco, liquor, and other vices would restore the African race to a perfection it had before its fall from grace. He, along with black nationalists Martin R. Delany and Henry Highland

Garnet, forthrightly believed that the first civilization was in Africa but that white contemporaries had denied the greatness of the African past in order to justify enslavement. Tanner was clearly influenced by scholars who insisted that civilization came from Ethiopia to Egypt and then to Rome via Greece.[55] Tanner took exception to Buckner H. Payne, who in 1867, writing under the pseudonym "Ariel," suggested that blacks lacked a soul because they were formed before Adam as "a separate and distinct species of the genus homo." Robert A. Young, a black man, wrote in *The Negro: A Reply to Ariel* that Africans had a soul and could be enlightened as well as brought to Christianity. In 1869 Tanner wrote two pamphlets—*The Negro's Origin* and *Is the Negro Cursed?*—to prove that Ham came from Africa and that since Canaan, not Ham, was cursed, "the Negro is free, the recipient of the common blessing pronounced not by Noah under doubtful circumstances, but by God Himself." Like Rufus Perry, a black Greek scholar, Tanner believed that Africans should have pride in their blackness, for they had once excelled in science, philosophy, and the arts. These attributes could be attained again if blacks learned to save their money and to refrain from the tempting vices of the devil. Excel again, Tanner argued, and whites would accept them as equals. That day would come sooner if "whites shall become [truly] Christianized . . . then [they] will see the meaning and feel the force of fatherhood in God and brotherhood in man whether he be white, yellow or black," Tanner asserted.[56]

Tanner was a race man concerned with the progress of African Americans. He defended their strength as well as criticized their vices. During his first four years as editor of the *Recorder* he berated them for their indulgence in tobacco and liquor, for their slowness in supporting Wilberforce, and for their straying ways. Still, he was quick to defend them from what he perceived to be scurrilous attacks on their heritage or character. The key word in understanding his reaction is "perceived." Sometimes Tanner perceived slights when none were intended. This fault caused bitterness and even retaliation from others. One such rivalry existed between him and Frederick Douglass, arguably then the preeminent race leader in America. In later years the two would become close friends, but during the early 1870s they were bitter foes.

Douglass upset Tanner in 1870 by allegedly stating that the late Haitian President Silvain Salnave was "a fine representative of our race [having the] brown and velvety complexion of an Indian, with hair black and silky." In an editorial, "Our Weakness," Tanner classified Douglass's remarks as "pitiable, if not contemptuous," because the African race is black. Essentially, he accused Douglass of color prejudice. A proud man and one not to suffer fools lightly, Douglass denied authorship but added that even if he wrote it, it did not imply race hatred, since "black" is the extreme description of the African race. But not satisfied with a simple refutation, Douglass insisted that Tanner admit that he was deceived in his source of information or had "willfully and wickedly borne false witness against FREDERICK DOUGLASS." He demanded that Tanner recant or "wear the broad brand of Reverend liar." Douglass accused Tanner of wanting to replace him as *the* race leader when neither his deeds nor his devotion to the race was equal. Douglass advised the A.M.E. Church to find an editor who could write plain English and who could tell the truth, since Tanner was "scandalously unfit for the place." Soon after, Douglass wrote that Tanner's silence probably meant that his remarks hit home. Gratuitously, he added that Tanner's editorials looked improved. Not easily cowed, Tanner advised readers in the August 3, 1872, *Recorder* to boycott Douglass's paper, the *New National Era,* until he ceased insulting people.[57]

Tanner's trouble with Douglass was not motivated by any desire to replace the former slave as a race leader; nor was it charged by Tanner's desire to create publicity for himself or for the *Recorder.* Instead, he did not care to stand idly by while anyone, white or black, unfairly attacked his race.

Tanner's four-year term of editing the *Recorder* was at its end as he journeyed to Nashville, Tennessee, to attend the Fifteenth Quadrennial Session of the General Conference of the A.M.E. Church, May 6–24, 1872. On May 10, Bishop John M. Brown, speaking on behalf of the bishops, requested that the church join those trying to save Africa from heathenism. He called for an effective missionary society to develop mission work in Brazil and Cuba as soon as those lands emancipated their slaves. Haiti beckons, Brown added. The Caribbean republic became the subject of a successful resolution, introduced by the Reverend Theophilus G. Steward, to have the church open a mission in that troubled land.[58]

Tanner was proud of both the church and the *Recorder.* To facilitate dissemination of the General Conference's news, Tanner published a triweekly edition of the paper during the May session, which received the delegates' commendation.[59] The delegates decided to keep the Book Concern in Philadelphia despite efforts to relocate it. The *Recorder* was enlarged to eight pages, and ministers were made responsible for collecting one dollar from each church member, the monies to be used in part to support bishops and the managing editor and business manager of the church's publication department. William H. Hunter, a former Union army chaplain who was Tanner's choice, assumed the duties of business manager. Tanner, whose editorials were praised by an unidentified man as "witty, pithy, [and] brilliant," and whose labor to present an intelligent and intellectual publication earned him praise outside the church, was reelected editor by acclamation with a salary of fifteen hundred dollars annually, which enabled him to purchase for thirty-five hundred dollars an eight-room residence at 2708 Diamond Street (later known as Park Avenue) in Philadelphia, where he resided for nearly fifty years.[60]

Chapter 3

Christian Recorder, Part 2, 1872–1876
Advocate for the Church and the Race

T anner's second stint as editor paralleled years of false hopes and broken prom-ises for the black community. The Fourteenth and Fifteenth Amendments to the Constitution offered citizenship and voting rights; black men were members of both federal and state legislatures; schools and universities were established for their training and education. Still, many were relegated to a state of near-slavery as sharecroppers and the Ku Klux Klan intimidated them throughout the former slave states, the Supreme Court began to rule against their interests by narrowly interpreting the new amendments, and northern politicians who had supported their cause died or succumbed to the lure of business interests. These topics were addressed by Tanner and many prominent race leaders, including Frederick Douglass, whose relationship with Tanner worsened between 1872 and 1875.

In June 1872, Tanner challenged Frederick Douglass's statement "If you want to put a Methodist to sleep, put a book in his hand." He urged ministers not to be overly concerned about their daily sustenance. Tanner insisted that ministers should study and that their congregations should demand preachers who pre-pared sermons based on solid scriptural readings. Like the Rev. T. H. Jackson, who estimated that two-thirds of young black men did nothing to elevate the race, Tanner declared that manhood came from within and not from believing that fancy cigars, clothes, or walking canes were superior to education.[1]

On November 9, 1872, Tanner wrote that Douglass "claimed" when a white minister shouted the biblical injunction "Servants obey your masters," there was always some black would-be minister to groan out an amen! Again, Tanner in-terpreted this statement as an example of Douglass's prejudice toward darker-complexioned people. "Come Frederick, no more of your 'velvety brown' ca-pers," Tanner admonished. Douglass responded in the *New National Era* that if Tanner had quoted the entire sentence instead of the portion he objected to, he would know that Douglass "recognize[d] the possibility of a black minister of the gospel," since "one who says amen to his own degradation, is hardly more than a would-be minister." More important, Douglass was a humanist who believed that a future America would be a composite or mixed-race nation, a belief that Tanner later adopted. Douglass challenged Tanner the scholar to "answer his Bible successfully" and explain why it said that the black cannot change his color nor the leopard his spots. Do this, he noted, and then Douglass would "have some patience with [your] reference to us on the black question." Tanner responded by defending Jeremiah for stating a fact and for not condemning the Ethiopian's color with his observation "They who are accustomed to do evil, can no more do good, than can the Ethiopian change his color."[2] Of course, Tanner, who could read Hebrew, understood that the ancient Ethiopians were a mighty people who had no desire to change their color.

While photographs and contemporary descriptions suggest that both were identical in complexion, as a humanist, Douglass chose to identify himself less with race and color, whereas Tanner, despite his integrationist views, felt a deep commitment to his racial heritage. Thus, their differences were fueled by both a concept of race and religious differences. Tanner accepted the scriptures as the literal word of God, whereas Douglass alienated clergymen with his irreverent comments. In 1870 Douglass praised the ratification of the Fifteenth Amendment with thanks to the effort of politicians and abolitionists but with no acknowledgment to God's role in securing the vote for black men. Douglass addressed the final meeting of the American Anti-Slavery Society on April 26, 1870, where the former slave angrily stated, "I dwell here in no hackneyed cant about thanking God for this deliverance."[3]

In 1875 Tanner vehemently criticized Douglass's and John Mercer Langston's July 5 remarks in the Hillside section of Washington, D.C. Douglass demanded for his race a "fair field to work in, and [for] the white man to leave us alone." Langston called upon the black man to manage his own institutions and to stop playing second fiddle to others. Disturbed by what he perceived to be a call for racial separatism, Tanner lashed out at both leaders but particularly condemned Douglass's remarks. Tanner said that blacks could not afford to be let alone. They were left alone in Haiti, and look at the mess. Tanner accused Douglass of being assisted by whites but not wanting the masses to have the same benefits. Tanner expressed hope that white philanthropists would ignore Douglass's cry for separatism. He went on to say that they would understand that Douglass "never did represent the American Negro [because] lacking his sincerity, his religion, and his common sense, it was impossible for him to speak definitely and truly; nor has he spoken." Defending Douglass, the *Louisianian,* a black New Orleans weekly, wrote that he always desired a level playing field and an opportunity for the race to enjoy freedom without prejudice. The editor added that Tanner's quarrel with Douglass stemmed from their religious differences, which was unfair since Tanner wrote for the *Independent,* a New York paper that berated orthodox religious views. The *Louisianian* suggested that Tanner stop criticizing Douglass and instead use his talents "in defense of those principles . . . Douglass . . . has so abundantly displayed."[4]

Within a few years, not only did the antipathy between the two men disappear but a genuine admiration developed between the two as each came to see sterling qualities in the other. Neither man left any records that would shed light on the reason(s) for their friendship, but evidently both men came to the conclusion that each in his own way advocated racial advancement. Douglass, who was noted for disliking his enemies and for being kind to his friends, wrote a letter of introduction for Tanner in 1881 to the Rev. Russell Lane Carpenter, who resided in England, where Tanner traveled to observe the proceedings of the Methodist Ecumenical Conference. Douglass informed Carpenter that he read the *Christian Recorder* not because he was in unity with its "theological opinion but because of its tendency to educate and elevate its readers in all their moral and social relations." On January 2, 1883, Tanner visited Douglass at the Recorder of Deeds office in Washington and attended a banquet for his former foe on the occasion of the twentieth anniversary of the Emancipation Proclamation. Douglass informed Tanner in 1883, "I think of you as lifting on high a standard for our people. I am only afraid that it may be at times too high to be visible to all. Still I would not have you hold it one inch lower. You may depend upon me for any help I can render you and the cause you so manfully advocate [as editor]." In May 1883, after Richard T. Greener, Harvard's first black graduate, had criticized Douglass for being a tired and outdated leader, Tanner called for the young men to give Douglass his due. "Get all the treasures out of the ship before she goes down—or in this instance, we trust, before she goes up [to heaven]."[5]

Tanner believed that Douglass had earned the right not to be criticized after so many decades of service to the race. In 1884, about a year after the death of his wife, Douglass shocked Americans of both races by marrying Helen Pitts, a white woman who was about thirty-five years his junior. While the marriage represented Douglass's "commitment to assimilationism, integrationism, and a composite American nationality," it elicited hostility from many black editors who saw his marriage as a rejection of his own race. Yet Tanner saw the marriage as consistent with his friend's decision to recognize neither white nor black but humanity. Intermarriage was compatible with Tanner's view, expressed in 1870, that since there were "so many *white* black people and *black* white people, . . . each one must be allowed to go where God's irresistible cords may draw."[6]

After Douglass's death in 1895, Tanner recognized his former critic as a man of moral greatness in his business affairs, in his abstinence from alcohol and tobacco, in his domestic affairs, and particularly in his politics as he refused to compromise with the issue of slavery. Even in religion, where Tanner had previously faulted him, Tanner saw moral greatness. "He believed in Christianity . . . but with the shams and hypocrisies of the white church he had no time," Tanner said of Douglass in 1900. Tanner was close to the Rev. Theophilus G. Steward, pastor at Metropolitan A.M.E. Church in Washington during the late 1880s. He undoubtedly knew of Douglass's July 27, 1886, letter to Steward in which he replied to the pastor's curiosity as to why Douglass frequented his church when he had a reputation for religious skepticism. Douglass replied forthrightly that while he did not accept religious dogma he truly believed that "God is good! God is light! God is truth! God is love!" By the early 1890s, Tanner had venerated his former foe as he believed that no parent could err in naming a son Frederick or a daughter Fredericka. Tanner gently scolded John Edward Bruce, a journalist who wrote under the pen name Bruce Grit, for naming a book *The Elliott Reader* after former Reconstruction politician Robert B. Elliott when it would have been more appropriate to name it *The Douglass Reader*.[7]

The evolution of Tanner's relationship with Douglass reveals much about his personality. Tanner often became quite testy with those with whom he disagreed philosophically; he had strong beliefs and was not inclined to accept direct criticism. Two notables, Alexander Crummell and Edward Wilmot Blyden, who visited the editor at his home or office, publicly challenged Tanner's views on race, religion, and emigration and were heirs to his venom. Alexander Crummell, a black Episcopalian priest, had spent many years in West Africa before returning to the United States in the early 1870s, a victim of frail health and Liberia's intraracial politics between the black party and the mulatto party. An advocate of black self-reliance, Crummell confused some while angering others with his constant shifts on issues. By 1876, Tanner believed that Crummell had maligned the race by declaring that it was "pernicious and unscriptural" for black people to establish separate churches, conventions, or dioceses. Crummell was assigned to Washington's St. Mary's Chapel, which was attached to St. John's Protestant Episcopal Church. The parish was "neglected by whites and despised by the [city's] colored aristocracy" because its members were mainly the servants of Washington's white elite. Tanner became incensed when he learned that Crummell was quoted in the *New York Tribune* stating that the District of Columbia's schools had raised a student body that had outgrown the "crude and tumultuous religious system of a former day" and therefore "it is nothing but mercy for the [Episcopal] church to step up front now with her chaste, sober, yet warm and elevating system to . . . satisfy the stimulated cravings of these trained and anxious minds." A slander against Methodist education among black youth, thundered Tanner. Crummell denied in a January 23 letter to Tanner that he had called the A.M.E. Church a "crude and tumultuous religious system." He cautioned Tanner to speak the truth. Tanner replied that once before Crummell had criticized him for his words about an Episcopal dignitary although his words were not as "naked" as Crummell's. "Of course," noted Tanner, "that dignitary was white; but we are loath to believe that this fact would weigh aught in the mind of so intense an African." Again, in a letter dated February 5, Crummell demanded an apology. "Do you intend to cram your outrageous libel down my throat?" he responded. Recant, warned Crummell, or the people will regard you as a slanderer. Tanner replied that Crummell libeled black Methodists and Baptists and was not a race leader because he was raised by [white] Episcopalians.[8]

Edward Wilmot Blyden was another illustrious correspondent and visitor who, at times, received the brunt of Tanner's cutting remarks. Blyden, who was born in the Danish West Indies, spent most of his adult life in Liberia, where he advocated black emigration to West Africa. His intense dislike of mulattos (which he considered Tanner) alarmed the editor and others who saw in him a despicable color chauvinism. During his fourth visit to the United States in May 1874, Blyden declared at Hampton University that there were major differences in the physical makeup of blacks and mulattos. Believing that the latter were genetically inferior, Blyden urged that only true Negroes—dark-complexioned with full Negroid features—should emigrate to Africa. He denied that they could find true manhood in America, where they were viewed by whites "as an underling, an imitator and parasite of the Anglo-Saxon." Tanner agreed with a Hampton student who informed the Liberian that he (the student) was an American and his preference was to remain in the land of his birth. "That sentiment," Tanner wrote, "is the sentiment of our whole people." "How long," he added, "do the professed friends of Africa intend to make it impossible for the American colored man to do aught for the redemption of Africa?"[9]

Tanner opposed wholesale emigration, although he believed that American black men needed to redeem Africa from heathenism, and under no circumstances would he advocate emigration of so-called pure Negroes only. Fellow African Methodist Henry M. Turner, who claimed direct descent from African royalty, despite his mulatto looks, was an ardent supporter of Blyden's emigration proposals. In 1875 Tanner called upon Turner to "stop your nonsense about emigration to Africa. We have nothing to go on. Little money, less education, and not a whit more religion than could save us from lapsing into idolatry!" Even though Tanner eschewed emigration, he urged in 1876 that black American businessmen should go to Liberia to cultivate coffee and cotton because "to content ourselves with crumbs [in America] is alike dishonorable to us and to our family." In 1877 Tanner agreed with Blyden that only those "whose strong arms are accustomed to wield the axe and the hoe" should emigrate.[10]

While Tanner approved of selective emigration to Africa for commercial reasons, his major interest in that continent was the opportunity for the A.M.E. Church to open up mission fields, an objective that would have to wait for both money and volunteers. Yet, in 1872, contradicting an earlier belief, he questioned whether black Americans were robust enough to stand up to the tropical heat. Tanner's judgment was based solely on Crummell's failed health, which caused the editor to bluntly write that the missionary's return to Africa would result in death. Despite the problems of poor health associated with the pioneer experience, Tanner saw in the redemption of Africa a moral crusade to save millions from the clutches of eternal damnation. The devil was everywhere, warned Tanner. In 1871 he called for Christians to spread the gospel among India's 140 million Hindus. "May the time speedily come when they will dash their images to the moles and bats, and learn to worship the God and Father of the Lord Jesus," he declared. Tanner was disturbed to hear that a Hindu temple was being constructed in London. In 1873 he called upon Christians to support the fledging Japanese mission effort regardless of the cost, because "to buy Japan at a great cost of tears and prayers, and even life itself [is better] than [to] offer it to Christ as a gift that cost nothing."[11]

Tanner saw in the 1873 Ashanti war with the British an opportunity to advance civilization and Christianity, although he sympathized with the Ashanti because he did not want to "see the strong . . . pounce on the weak." Early in 1874 he emphasized the urgency of mission work among the Ashanti, who were described in Edward Blyden's newspaper, the *Negro*, as wearers of necklaces of teeth and finger bones. Ashanti warriors also reputedly drank the blood and ate the hearts of their enemies.[12] The Methodist Episcopal Church had missionaries in Africa, but Tanner was not encouraged by what the M.E Church bishops' message in late 1873 had to say about mission fields. "Everywhere, save Africa," lamented Tanner, who understood that the omission involved all blacks; if the M.E. Church neglected Africa, he asked, what could one expect of her treatment of her one hundred thousand black American members?[13]

In early 1874, Tanner's call for an active missionary presence led A.M.E. Bishop J. M. Brown to request that the bishops' wives involve themselves in arousing favorable sentiment for that objective. Tanner urged in a February 26 editorial, "Let the women move . . . [for] we want constant drops; and not uncertain floods." He recommended the establishment of a woman's missionary society to advance the church's cause.[14] A flood of support for Tanner's call galvanized the church. A reader encouraged the editor to "keep the ball rolling till the society . . . is an accomplished fact." A woman correspondent declared that because of Tanner's challenge women could soon do more than pray or cry. "Your letter has awakened me that I may arise and struggle into light; and may all women consider how to do good," stated Mattie V. Holmes. On May 14, 1874, all the bishops' wives informed the church that women should cooperate with the Board of Missions in the effort to evangelize the world and that the wives of ministers should organize mite missionary societies in their husbands' churches to assist the mission work. On May 21 Harriet Wayman, wife of Bishop A. W. Wayman, accused some ministers of being uncooperative. She thought it strange that people left everything to women. "What are the gentlemen doing?" she demanded. "We have been waiting on them. Will they loan the use of our churches, will they call the people together and make known the objects of meeting?" Mrs. Wayman added, "If so, we are ready, and we will 'push the battle to the gate.'" Tanner suggested that each woman invite six guests to discuss the mite society. He urged pastors to cooperate by reading to their congregations the society's constitution and exhorted readers to use their mites for the mission society instead of purchasing rum and tobacco.[15]

Bishops J. P. Campbell and J. M. Brown added their support. In a letter to the society's organizers, dated May 25, Campbell praised them for doing what men had failed to do for forty years. He called upon men to organize themselves and the children into mite missionary societies or aid the ladies in their effort. "Let the word . . . be organize! organize! organize! for one grand assault upon the kingdom of sin," Campbell exclaimed. Bishop Brown urged women across the land to organize, for "souls are perishing for lack of knowledge." Before his words were published, sixty women in Clarksville, Tennessee, were organized. An enthusiastic reader called for female missionaries to go to Liberia, two to teach and two or three others to plant coffee, ginger, and cotton. "Who will volunteer for Africa?" Tanner cried. Excited, Tanner suggested that the women needed to emulate the female Muslim missionary in Sierra Leone who told Africans that Mohammed came of Abraham through black Hagar while Jesus Christ came through white Sarah.[16]

James A. Handy praised Tanner, the architect of the women's missionary society, as nobler than Moses for his role in inspiring women to assist the A.M.E. Church in its evangelization effort.[17] Now thoroughly motivated, in early August the women met in Pittsburgh to organize the Woman's Parent Mite Missionary Society. Sarah E. Tanner was named to the thirty-member Board of Managers.[18]

The euphoria over the establishment of the Mite Missionary Society declined during the winter of 1875. "Drops of rain" failed to turn into a "flood" to float the "missionary ark." On March 4 Tanner wondered if the Mite Society was on the verge of dying. "What is needed," he declared, "is faith in God, and heart in the work." They needed a leader who "can fire [the preachers'] hearts," he noted. Tanner asked, "Where is Amanda Smith?" Smith, who had labored briefly among blacks but more extensively among whites in Europe and North America as well as among subcontinental Indians and Liberians, was needed at home among her own people, he declared. Come home, Amanda Smith, he pleaded. "Let her not prefer the riches of Egypt. Her own sisters need her," he noted. After returning to the United States in 1890, Smith informed the Rev. John T. Jenifer two years later that, in response to God's question, "What have you done for your people?" she established the Amanda Smith Home for Poor and Penniless Colored Children in Harvey, Illinois. Tanner's fear of an inactive Mite Society dissolved when its president, Mary A. Campbell, informed him that they were raising funds for a missionary to go to Haiti.[19]

Haiti was an interesting choice for several reasons. Before it was lost to the French, it was their jewel in the Caribbean that would be their base to develop their large holdings in North America. But the successful 1801 Haitian Revolution led by Toussaint L'Ouverture forced Napoleon to sell the vast land to the United States in the 1803 Louisiana Purchase transaction. From 1859 to 1863, a heated debate divided black America as Haiti's government offered free land and other amenities to black emigrants from the United States. The several thousand who took advantage of the offer were soundly criticized for deserting those at home who remained to agitate for an end of slavery and for equality among the races.[20]

As early as 1867, Tanner asked who would "evangelize the Negroes of the greater and lesser Antilles, if it be not" African Methodists. Haiti had been a major concern to African Methodists since the summer of 1873, when the Rev. Theophilus G. Steward was sent there to reestablish the church organized in 1824 by emigrants from Havre de Grace, Maryland. All, however, were not interested in establishing a mission in Haiti. Bishop Daniel A. Payne, while supporting mission work, understood clearly that the church lacked the finances, which motivated him to decline a request in 1862 from James Redpath, chief agent of the Haytian Emigration Bureau, to go there as a missionary. Nevertheless, most African Methodists enthusiastically endorsed Steward's resolution, approved at the 1872 General Conference, to open a mission in that Caribbean land. Tanner reported in the *Recorder*, "When Bro. Steward introduced his resolution, the heart of the whole body seemed to throb with renewed life."[21]

On March 13, 1873, the missionary board appointed Steward as missionary to Haiti, a glorious day for African Methodism. Steward arrived in Port-au-Prince on June 13 but returned after staying a month, victim of homesickness, poor health, an inadequate command of French, and severe lack of funds. Steward was unwilling to return to Haiti with his wife and three young sons without guarantees of financial security for two years. His refusal to return embarrassed the Parent Home and Foreign Missionary Society and caused others in the church to label him a "quitter." Tanner was upset that the apathy of the Missionary Society prevented Steward's return to the mission field. James A. Handy asked the A.M.E. Church to appoint a replacement from among the church's two hundred most competent ministers.[22]

Tanner was disturbed by the church's apathy. He saw in the Mite Society the instrumentality to assist in the evangelization of Haiti, but he realized that the bishops had the final say. Still, Tanner believed that if members avoided the vices of rum drinking, tobacco chewing, and fancy dressing, they could contribute to the Mite Missionary Society funds to send a missionary to Haiti and perhaps one or two to Africa. In February 1875 the *Recorder* printed an open letter to the bishops calling for a missionary. "Our church in Hayti was the first branch of our mother church in a foreign country and we might have been by this time a large branch" if not for lack of funds and interest. Did the church have a missionary for Haiti? Bishop J. M. Brown informed Bishop J. P. Campbell in a March 29 statement that there was no candidate. Other bishops, however, claimed that there were four willing volunteers. The Rev. Thomas H. Jackson added to the confusion by declaring in an April 22 letter to the *Recorder* that the Mite Society had funds, the people were pleading for a missionary, and the lack of action was due to disharmony in the church.[23]

A month later, Bishop Brown forwarded to Tanner a letter from Haiti expressing hope for Steward's return. "Propositions are made to us by other denominations to supply us with ministers, but we [would] much rather [have one from] our mother church," the letter emphasized. Citing funding problems, he added, "Had I the money a missionary should be in Hayti in thirty days."[24] The silence of Bishops Payne, Wayman, Ward, and Shorter concerned Tanner, who inquired why the bishops could not meet, select a missionary, and send him to Haiti. Caving in to popular pressure, the bishops appointed Charles W. Mossell on June 19, but he had not left for Haiti by September. An incensed Tanner accused the missionary board of apathy, because Mossell was ready to depart and funds were available. "We are simply making a laughing stock of our selves . . . while earning the disgust of the Haytians," fumed the editor.[25]

In November 1876 Tanner reported that Brown would sail to Haiti the following spring. (The trip was canceled due to the bishop's illness.) While the news brought hope, Mossell was still stateside. Near the end of 1876, Bishop James A. Shorter, chairman of the Parent Foreign and Home Missionary Society, announced that Mossell would leave for Haiti once a thousand dollars was raised to support him and his family for one year. Mossell hoped to depart by February 1877 but did not leave until April 14, nearly four years after Steward's return from Haiti. Tanner applauded the church for finally sending a missionary to the Caribbean. Bishop Campbell saluted the Mite Missionary Society. "The women! the women! [They] have saved us . . . [W]hen the men . . . failed the women . . . resolved that the work should go forward," he exclaimed. Soon after arriving in Haiti, Mossell informed Tanner that the church was right in sending him because "the gospel of Christ is needed . . . here"; the people practiced voodoo daily and engaged in card playing and other entertainment on the Sabbath.[26]

Tanner's editorials provoked an awareness in the church about the importance of mission work; later, as bishop of the First Episcopal District, which included Bermuda, Haiti, British Guiana, and other fields, he would provide more valuable assistance. This dedication to a cause illustrated his love for the church. This same devotion was applied to the advancement of the recently emancipated slaves. While at times Tanner joined the crowd in supporting issues that were important to the race, he often was a maverick who declined to respond to a herd instinct in the name of racial solidarity. A case in point was after the reelection of President Ulysses S. Grant in 1872 but prior to his inauguration, when the *Washington Chronicle* suggested that the president should appoint John Mercer Langston to his cabinet. While others exulted in the possibility of having a black man in the cabinet, Tanner dismissed the idea as "bad taste" because cabinet officers were generally "trusted friends" who advised the president; therefore, Grant should appoint Langston to a non-cabinet position. It was not that Tanner thought lightly of Langston's qualifications; rather, he knew neither the president nor the nation was ready for such a radical move and it would be a waste of effort to pursue the matter.[27]

Tanner eschewed black nationalist dogma and was particularly critical of those who used race solidarity for their own aggrandizement. He ridiculed the proposal of black New Jerseyans to meet in 1873 to protest their lack of civil and political rights in the Garden State. Tanner declared that four-fifths of black men's conventions benefited only ax grinders and that they were organized by men who were unfit to lead "and too ambitious to follow [and who] tend to compromise our interests with the nation." He considered politicians to be the worst leaders. He believed that the race's survival depended upon black people being "molded as honest and happy yeomanry." What Tanner advocated for a race less than a decade removed from bondage was a strong community of "whom no demagogue [could] say, *if I don't look after their interest, they will be lost.*"[28] His idyllic image of southern freedmen working their farms, of course, could not exist in a nation where many believed in the innate inferiority of over four million of African descent and sought by fraud and physical violence to keep them subjugated.

Tanner's aversion to race conventions and his suspicion of politicians did not extend to legitimate organizations or protest, for he strongly supported the enactment of the national civil rights bill as presented in 1872. It called for an end of racial discrimination in public accommodations as well as for integrated public schools, although by the time of its adoption two years later, the latter clause was removed. Tanner sharply criticized segregated education. "We want schools for Americans . . . not for Chinese . . . negro . . . German . . . Irish . . . nor English Americans, but simply Americans," he wrote. Tanner warned the people not to tolerate the building of separate schools because it would lead to "separate teachers, . . . separate superintendents, . . . separate academies, [and] colleges." He was pleased that Toledo, Ohio, had abolished racially segregated schools in 1871. While Tanner abhorred the concept of separate schools, reality provided him no choice but to denounce the presence and, in many cases, the dominance of white teachers in colored schools. In 1860 he wrote, "Let every child receive his instruction from a colored teacher." And seventeen years later, he declared that he opposed race-centered schools but that those in existence must have black teachers or close. He deplored the practice of employing white teachers in colored schools, thereby denying employment to members of his race. Tanner's sentiments were echoed in Washington, New York, Baltimore, Cincinnati, and St. Louis, where the cry during the seventies was "Colored teachers for colored schools."[29]

Unlike some of his contemporaries who believed that advanced education unsexed women, Tanner advocated universal education. He expressed his solidarity with women's demands for education by printing in 1873 Clara Bell Anderson's assertion that while an educated woman was man's intellectual companion, uneducated she was a hindrance to him. Concurring, Tanner noted that women possessed intellectual force, "but where is she allowed to expend it? She has moral force, and she has religious force but what can she do with either; save let them rot and rust?" Tanner's strong advocacy for educating women was perhaps nurtured when he witnessed how his mother, a woman of great intelligence, was deprived of a formal education. In addition, his wife had attended classes at Avery College but had left upon her father's death without a degree, and he had daughters whom he wanted to be well acquainted with languages, literature, and love of books.[30]

His support for equality in public accommodations was not merely academic, for he had experienced discrimination on several occasions. In 1870, while traveling throughout the South, he bought a first-class ticket in Kentucky, only to be assigned to an inferior car where he sat amid spilled whiskey, inhaled tobacco smoke, and had his ears burned by profane language.[31] Two years later he was refused accommodations in the best cabin of the Baltimore Steam Packet Company's steamer *Adelaide* and instead given a dark deck cabin. He told the clerk that he was going to publish his dissatisfaction and received shameless profanity in return. Like others of his race, Tanner strongly objected to the huddling together of black people regardless of their station, education, or refinement. Whites had railroad cars that separated the refined from the ruffian, but black people had no choice except to petition for a civil rights law to guarantee equality.[32] On January 10, 1872, a delegation of black elite representing the communities of Washington, Philadelphia, and Richmond, Virginia, presented a petition to President Grant requesting his support for the supplementary civil rights bill pending in the Senate. On December 19, 1873, a memorial was presented to Congress from the National Civil Rights Convention praying for civil and political equality.[33] The petitioners were hopeful that Congress would heed their request because earlier in the year the state of New York had adopted a civil rights law prohibiting discrimination in public facilities based on color or race.[34]

Tanner demanded in 1874 that Congress pass the equal accommodation provision of the bill, citing discrimination in New Orleans against Ebenezer Bassett, a United States diplomat assigned to Haiti. This, wrote Tanner, was an insult to Bassett and the United States government. What if Milton Turner, United States minister to Liberia, came to New York City? Turner asked. "Can the government afford to have [him] sent to the back door of the Astor House[?]"[35]

Tanner became outraged in May 1874 when Republican leadership agreed to remove the call for integrated schools from the bill. "We would prefer to see [the bill] utterly fail, than be compelled to witness this mischief framed into law," he declared. Tanner argued that compromise had not settled the slavery issue, nor would withdrawing the school question bring peace to the nation. By June it was rumored that neither the administration nor Republican congressional leadership wanted the bill enacted. Tanner swiftly reacted by vowing that the bill's failure meant that "800,000 colored voters will be more patriotically American, than they are subserviently Republican which . . . may be a gain to them, and the country at large." As for Grant, Tanner wrote that if the president was wavering in his support for the bill, then black men would "defy him to destroy our manhood."

Bitter, he called upon the race to abstain from liquor and tobacco while pursuing education, money, and service to God. This and not law would make them free, he noted. Congress failed to pass the civil rights bill before adjourning for the summer. An incensed Tanner cried out, "Black men . . . have only *some* rights which white men are bound to respect; others may be trampled under foot."[36]

Tanner was annoyed with Republicans for not showing more leadership, and he called for black voters to deal with the dissenters. Fortunately, Congress enacted in the winter the Civil Rights Act of 1875 that prohibited discrimination in public accommodations based on color or race. Tanner did not expect the South to comply with the law, as he agreed with Frederick Douglass that "we need the measure, not so much for its literal execution, as for *its moral effect*." Reiterating his call for abstinence, Tanner noted that instead of laws the race needed houses, land, money, culture, and religion. "Without these," he stated, "the meanest and lowest [white] can do us harm." This view would later be given international prominence by Booker T. Washington, but now it separated Tanner from black politicians and editors who advocated more inclusion. Tanner believed that his people's strength rested in their strong right arms and not in congressional enactments. "Fall back on [thy] neighbor, fall back on sand," he warned. In a way, Tanner was suggesting a type of racial separatism, a position that was clearly in opposition to his belief that America represented the best hope for African American advancement. That this utterance developed from Tanner's frustration with racism was soon revealed when a thoroughly disenchanted Tanner wrote in the December 30, 1875, *Independent* that America wanted those of African descent to build up an *imperium in imperio* where separatism would define the relationship between the races. This concept of an imposed nation within a nation, he observed, was not the way to provide the country with "unity in peace and strength in war."[37]

Tanner was a foe of all racial separatism, be it imposed or voluntary, for he believed that God had determined boundary lines between nations, not races. Tanner advocated the commingling of all races, particularly because he believed that all races, all colors, all languages had the potential to become Christians. Although he believed in the solidarity of the American black man as a way for racial advancement, he was quick to chastise people of his own race whenever they practiced racial chauvinism. In 1873 the *Elevator* and the *Appeal,* black-owned California newspapers, earned his wrath for their support of the state's efforts to deny Chinese immigration. (According to the 1870 census there were nearly 50,000 Chinese and only 4,272 black residents in the Golden State.) "Let the yellow man stay despite the protests of [white, black, and American Indian] until they shall learn that all colors are equal," wrote Tanner. He emphatically declared that it would be better for blacks to leave California rather than "help persecute the Chinese." He urged Christians to protect the Chinese from mob action; silence on the slavery question had cost the church her brains, he noted, and silence on the Chinese question would cost the church her heart. In 1882, after the state passed a law suspending Chinese labor for twenty years, Tanner asserted that seven million black people opposed the measure.[38]

Tanner spoke from the heart because he understood fully the emotional pain prejudice inflicted upon people. As one who had been insulted and cursed three times in Princeton, New Jersey, because he was in the presence of one whom others "thought to be white; but who in the eyes of American law [was] as black as the blackest Congo," he was ashamed that some black men treated the Chinese as pariahs. Richard T. Greener, a former editor, college professor, and dean of the Law Department of Howard University, bluntly declared that it would be wiser to exclude Chinese than to permit a million to come only to have them send their wages back home.[39] As late as 1901, the lack of African American representation in the American labor movement caused some to scapegoat the Chinese. The Washington *Colored American* newspaper, edited by Edward Cooper, declared that the "disease breeding, miserly, clannish and heathen 'chinee' drove blacks out of valet, cook, waiter and barber positions" and that they represented "a menace to American labor" with "their cheap method of living." In the midst of this bias, few, perhaps, agreed with John P. Green's observation that the race needed to emulate the Chinese for their "industry, economy and quiet habits."

Tanner believed in social equality—not to be confused with the white fear of racial mongrelization and a forced mixture of unequals—because he believed that persons of like culture and refinement should associate and because, like whites, he wanted access to education, decent housing, desirable employment, and respect. Clearly Tanner was a man of considerable intellect and talent, but he was judged by too many whites as an anomaly more suited for a display case or simply dismissed as unimportant because of his color. This he rightfully resented.

In two essays written for the *Independent* in November 1874 and February 1875, Tanner outlined his critique of American race relations. He offered three suppositions to inform white readers of the evil nature of racism. First, he asked white males to consider a life where they were denied pursuits in mechanical, mercantile, sales, and clerking positions but had abundant access to sweeping, dusting, and other menial positions. "Thus doomed to menial poverty, how can they hope to rise?" he inquired. "And how can the nation demand them to rise?" he pointedly asked. Second, he stated that if white women were restricted to washing, ironing, or kitchen work despite education, talent, and aptitude, the nation would not expect them to possess "womanly culture or wifely refinement." Third, he asked readers to suppose that gifted white men and women were denied contact and friendship with their natural peers and "compelled to live and die among those who recognized nothing but hard facts [which] have no sympathy with ideas." With these burdens, he added, only those who possessed an abundance of moral courage would succeed. While these suppositions were meant to educate whites about the daily economic and social problems of his people, Tanner still encouraged black women not to shun "white people's kitchens" because "all work is honorable" and good workers are indispensable and thus independent.[40]

While Tanner readily admitted that two and a half centuries of enslavement placed the freedmen in an unequal social position with whites, he understood that America could not lay claim to racial harmony until notions of white superiority and black inferiority were erased. He conceded that too many whites accepted the belief of white superiority because they knew black men only as "the trustiest of coachmen and the fanciest of waiters." The oratorical powers of Frederick Douglass or the political acumen of Pinckney Benton Stewart Pinchback, former acting governor of Louisiana, and the political contributions of John Mercer Langston and Robert Elliott were viewed as exceptions by whites, but Tanner noted that brains in the cotton, rice, and sugar fields were overlooked. He believed that whites underrated blacks while blacks overrated whites. A balance was needed, but that awaited the lifting of the racial fog that limited a vision of equality to integrationists in both races.[41]

Tanner's eloquent defense of the race, and particularly of its men, did not deter one woman reader from requesting that the *Recorder*'s editor address the question of women's suffrage. The unidentified writer challenged Tanner to "unfurl the banner of WOMAN'S RIGHT TO THE BALLOT." The correspondent urged all bishops, elders, deacons, licentiates, and laymen to fight on behalf of the women's suffrage movement. Significantly, this request came after the Fifteenth Amendment had been approved by Congress in 1869 but before it was ratified by the states in 1870. In response Tanner urged his readers to read Carlos White's book, *Ecce Femina,* a plea for women's rights, and Eleanor Kirk Ames's (a.k.a. Eleanor Maria Estabrook) *Up Broadway, and Its Sequel: A Life Story,* a call for more liberal divorce laws to assist women who were in abusive relationships or who had philandering husbands who abandoned their families for mistresses. His recommendation of the two books was all the more interesting because he thought it silly to permit women to vote and he opposed divorce. Equally significant in light of his opposition to female voting was Tanner's serialization in 1877 of Frances E. W. Harper's *Sowing and Reaping,* wherein a daughter tells her mother that it would be dreadful for women to go to the polls and be in the presence of men with tobacco-and-rum breath who foul the air with curses. The mother replies, "I want however to possess power as well as influence." She adds that women voters would make society holier because they then would be able to protect their homes from "the ravages of rum." Tanner opposed divorce on the charges of abuse, incompatibility, or desertion because it was God's will to keep couples together. His only exception was made for adultery, which he deemed abominable in God's eyes.[42]

In contrast to Tanner's disapproval of women voting, the Rev. Theophilus G. Steward suggested in 1870 that church law be amended to allow women to vote in all church meetings, especially in the election of trustees. Five years later, Methodist Episcopal Bishop Gilbert Haven presided over the Seventh Annual Session of the American Woman's Suffrage Convention and declared that women voters would make politics decent and respectable. By 1881 Tanner made a distinction between women voting in church matters as opposed to state matters. A correspondent informed him that women in Wyoming had all the rights of men and asked whether electing women trustees would violate A.M.E. law; Tanner responded, "The fact that the civil law makes no distinction between the sexes is not sufficient to warrant the election." But Tanner clearly understood that women, like black men, needed the vote to protect their interests. In the December 29 *Recorder* he noted that women would not have protection from an abusive society until voting laws were reformed. In September 1882, while en route to Albany, New York, he observed men reading and women eating on the train. "When will our women cease making play things of themselves?" he inquired. Answering his own question, he concluded, "When we give them the franchise upon which question [I] vote aye."[43] Tanner believed that while women needed the vote to protect their interests in a secular society, they had nothing to fear from the male-dominated A.M.E. Church.

His gender bias aside, Tanner's interest in the advancement of black people could not be questioned. In 1870, after visiting Missouri and Kansas, the editor was so impressed with Kansas's liberal politics and fertile, inexpensive land that he suggested that 10 percent of the black male population stop unsexing themselves by removing the waiter's apron and purchasing farmland in Kansas. A letter from a correspondent echoed Tanner's call. "We as a people fail to see that it is [advantageous] to scatter out, to emigrate, to take chances in investment," wrote the westerner. Tanner's suggestion for westward migration came a decade before the Exodus of 1879, in which forty thousand emigrated to Kansas. Still, his suggestion should not be mistaken as a panacea to racial discrimination or an indulgence in utopianism. Tanner scoffed at Henry M. Turner's 1874 suggestion that the federal government turn over New Mexico Territory to black people. Tanner believed that only a minority would reach their destination; the others would be victims of tomahawks or of lack of medicine, clothing, or basic comforts. Instead, he urged black Georgians to "STAND YOUR GROUND"; "be manly [and] don't run from a white man the moment he frowns."[44] Similar to his views on African emigration, Tanner believed that migration to the West would be successful if practiced in moderation.

Tanner's admonition was due to his pragmatic belief that race advancement would be determined by the ability of black people to purchase land, acquire education, and refrain from pernicious habits. The editor faulted the race for seeking pleasure in food, drink, and fashion. He chastised people who earned two or three hundred dollars annually—the average income of a laborer—for thinking that they could live in the same style as those who earned thousands.[45] Tanner understood in 1871 that those who were only a few years removed from slavery could not afford, literally or figuratively, to imitate the excesses of upper-class whites. He ridiculed their reaction when confronted with their conspicuous consumption. Tanner wrote that they could not reply, "White people do so," because they could not afford "to do the ten thousand things that white people do, be they right or wrong." He urged them to cast aside imitation of the foolish or extravagant ways of white folk and imitate instead their efforts to build homes, schools, and churches as well as save money.[46]

Urging readers to build schools was an indirect appeal for assistance for Wilberforce University, the A.M.E. Church's showcase educational institution. Despite receiving twenty-five thousand dollars in spring 1870 from the Freedmen's Bureau, thirty months later Wilberforce could not pay the salary of teachers. Tanner called for "some of the rich and charitable of the land to endow it." The school was on the verge of closing its doors when it received ten thousand dollars from the estate of Salmon P. Chase, the late chief justice of the United States Supreme Court. The money was timely, for the fiscal year ending June 17, 1873, showed that the university had receipts of $4,547.89 with expenditures of $4,418.28. The balance of $129.71 was humiliating for a university with assets worth $60,326.07.[47] Wilberforce needed money not only to cover the arrears in salaries but to provide accommodations for students. A new hall costing five or six thousand dollars was desperately needed. Readers suggested fundraising from Sunday school classes, special collections, and concerts by Wilberforce singers.[48] Tanner endorsed the call for a new student hall because Wilberforce had only eight students in 1873 studying for the ministry. The perplexed editor could not understand how a religious body with two hundred thousand members could have so few ministerial students while the Presbyterians with an equal number of members supported 608 students in their seminaries.[49]

Tanner wanted Wilberforce to succeed because the church needed an educated clergy to show the people the way of a pious life, to compete with Catholic priests for the souls of freedmen, and to develop mission fields. Tanner understood that as the masses acquired education, they expected their minister to be refined and erudite or they would seek spiritual teaching elsewhere. Tanner insisted that ministers needed the type of education that would make them serious in their pulpit preaching. Above all, he cautioned them to eschew buffoonery by not wiping their brow, loudly blowing their nose, or using poor grammar while preaching.[50] Tanner's thoughtful editorials, his appeals for Wilberforce, and his scholarship led to the university awarding him the honorary Doctor of Divinity degree in 1873.[51]

Tanner derived pleasure in seeing the A.M.E. Church progress because it displayed to all that a maligned people had the capacity to achieve. With this backdrop, he and others sought to push for a monument to honor Richard Allen. The nation's centennial in 1876 marked the sixtieth anniversary of the incorporation of the African Methodist Episcopal Church, and African Methodists, led by Tanner, were determined to raise funds for an Allen monument. In March 1874, Tanner suggested that black Americans and particularly African Methodists should participate in the celebration or face charges that they had contributed nothing to the nation's progress. He further suggested that African Methodists erect a monument in Philadelphia's Fairmount Park dedicated to religious freedom and have it crowned with a bronze statue of Allen. Believing that a ten-cent tax on the church's two hundred thousand members would cover the statue's expenses and that the erection of the Allen statue would enhance race pride as well as attract new members to the church, Tanner encouraged support for the project.[52]

The proposal elicited considerable reaction within the A.M.E. Church. While many supported it, others questioned the approximate ten-thousand-dollar cost in light of limited funds for Wilberforce, churches, schools, and the *Recorder*. Tanner dismissed the concerns as irrelevant since they had until July 4, 1876, to raise funds and erect the Allen statue.[53]

African Methodist optimism for the Allen statute was tempered by the failure of the Centennial Exhibition Committee, as late as spring 1875, to invite black people as a race to participate. Tanner wrote that people must be ready to accept the call. "We will not compromise our manhood," he vowed. He urged people to send in their money for the statue because "if we do not do something *special* the event goes by without so much as the weight of our finger being felt. Shall this be so? We trust not," he declared. In July he admitted that the efforts to build the statue had failed. Disappointed but not defeated, Tanner called on the race to support Wilberforce University.[54]

Talk of the Allen statue's demise was premature. On November 2, 1875, delegates attending the Arkansas Annual Conference of the A.M.E. Church supported a resolution to place Allen's statue in Fairmount Park on July 4, 1876, after A. J. Chambers had persuaded James G. Blaine and others in Congress to appropriate five thousand dollars for their church. In January 1876 the chair of the Arkansas Annual Conference informed Tanner, "The statue is commenced. One payment has been made. We must now sink or swim." More good news followed. In April the A.M.E. Church received permission to erect the statue, but it had to be removed sixty days after the close of the exhibition. The cornerstone was laid in early June, with a dedicatory service planned for September 22, the fourteenth anniversary of Abraham Lincoln's preliminary Emancipation Proclamation. Disaster struck when the train carrying the marble shaft to Allen's memory derailed en route from Cincinnati to Philadelphia. The shaft and the pride of African Methodism descended into the waters of the Susquehanna River. Fortunately, the Allen bust, which was carved in Italy, was not on the ill-fated trip, and it was unveiled before an enthusiastic gathering in Fairmount Park on November 12.[55] Mrs. Frances E. W. Harper, the distinguished writer, read her dedicatory poem "We Are Arising" to an appreciative audience.[56]

While the A.M.E. Church was able to raise thirty-five hundred dollars to pay all the expenses connected with the Allen tribute, the effort clearly showed that the church had spread itself too thin financially. Editor Tanner supported all the church fundraising efforts—Wilberforce, the Allen monument, and mission projects—but the pressing economic problem for him during his sixteen years of editorship was the solvency of the *Christian Recorder* and the Book Exchange. Tanner constantly berated readers to husband their money because he saw a direct correlation between the paucity of readers—there were three thousand when there should have been ten thousand—and the race's spending on what he deemed unnecessary gratifications. In May 1873 he compared the subscription rate of the *Recorder* with that of other religious journals and found it lacking even though the A.M.E. Church had more members than some of the other denominations.[57]

Despite Tanner's hopes that the subscriber base would increase to five thousand, the high illiteracy rate among the former slaves limited readership. Others, plagued by poverty (notwithstanding Tanner's accusation that they were extravagant), had concerns more pressing than reading a newspaper. A reader estimated that only 5 percent of the race supported any paper and that many could not afford the *Recorder*'s two-dollar annual subscription rate. Tanner's standard reply was that too much money was wasted on liquor and tobacco. He cited numerous studies to show that liquor consumption led to arrest and incarceration as well as impoverished families. He noted that the average black male spent about eighty-five dollars yearly on the two drugs.[58]

The lack of funds nearly led to the temporary suspension of the *Recorder* in the fall of 1873. W. H. Hunter, manager of the Book Concern, appealed to African Methodists to pay off the Book Concern's six-hundred-dollar debt so that he could provide boys with apprenticeships, open a book bindery, and "do many things to open the door to the various trades for our people." "We ask help," he begged.[59]

The A.M.E. Church was supposed to receive one dollar from each member collected by the minister to help pay for the salaries of bishops, the *Recorder*'s editor, business manager, and two secretaries, as well as expenses of the Book Concern. Collection of funds was undermined by the indifference of ministers and laymen and the refusal of the bishops to enforce the law. It was an issue that Tanner addressed not solely because his salary depended upon the dollar money but because noncompliance reflected adversely on the ability of the church to support itself. All over the land ministers offered excuses for their laxity in collecting dollar money. Some were cowered by Klan violence, plagued by smallpox outbreaks, or stymied by small congregations. The Rev. A. H. Newton of Pulaski, Tennessee, represented more than a few of the clergy. His congregation confused dollar money with missionary money and therefore did not contribute. Few read the *Recorder,* he remarked, because "the people have no taste for literature." Numerous ministers informed Tanner, "We have not forgotten the dollar money" or "Dollar money is coming soon."[60]

Tanner estimated that the dollar money for the period from May 24, 1873, to May 24, 1874, should have been approximately twenty-five thousand dollars but that some men and conferences thought themselves too big to collect. They "must be made to know that there is a God in Israel," he declared. For the period ending May 1875, the A.M.E. Church with twenty-five conferences, six bishops, 1334 itinerant preachers, 2664 local preachers, and 1642 churches with 206,730 members raised $21,789.98 in dollar money, or just over ten and one-half cents per member instead of the one dollar required by law. In January 1876, Bishop J. P. Campbell stated that the church should have collected annually forty to fifty thousand dollars since 1868 but had not because of lazy and uncooperative ministers. "Shame, shame, bitter shame" upon their souls for robbing the church, he thundered.[61]

Tanner faced the *Recorder*'s financial problem with stoicism. as he sought to make the paper attractive, easily available, and scholarly. He wrote five or six editorials for each weekly edition, but he was easily frustrated when contributors submitted poorly written pieces. "Write short, WRITE PLAIN, WRITE FACTS. . . . Ten facts to one opinion. Lastly, write on one side of the paper," Tanner requested. He asked for book reviews or inspiring thoughts from scripture but not plagiarized poetry. Tanner appealed to their vanity by telling them to write to have their name part of church history.[62] On the eve of the quadrennial of 1876, Tanner declared that the church should make subscription to the *Recorder* obligatory for all A.M.E. clergy, which was common in other branches of Methodism. Believing that "we have the first church of the land, we must have the first paper." Tanner requested a budget to pay for solicited articles.[63]

Tanner's *Recorder* was arguably the most influential black weekly in America during the 1870s, but he did not let his concern for improving the paper's circulation diminish his interest in promoting other race weeklies. He urged Baptists of both races to support Rufus Perry's *National Monitor*, and he was pleased with the April 22, 1876, inaugural edition of the *People's Advocate,* a District of Columbia paper, because its editor, John W. Cromwell, had "brains" and its general agent, Rozler D. Beckley, had "push," a winning combination in Tanner's estimation. Understanding that the black press had the power to lift up the people if only they supported it, he argued that lack of subscribers would make black-owned papers second- or third-rate, and the public would reject them as "nigger paper[s]." Tanner added that these newspapers would become first-rate if more scholarly articles were submitted. He praised his fellow black editors and publishers as "the most laborious and self sacrificing the race has produced."[64]

Tanner needed a respite from the grueling challenge of editing the *Recorder* in the midst of its dire financial situation. Every summer, he spent a few days with his family at the Jersey shore, where the sounds of the ocean invigorated his senses. One such break, while not at the shore, indicates how he valued his rare leisure time. For two days, June 14 and 15, 1874, Tanner visited Gouldtown, a black settlement in Cumberland County, New Jersey, that dated back to the late seventeenth century. There he preached and lectured. "Oh that we could for a fortnight . . . push our papers aside, and lay down our pen and return to its pleasant shades, its cultural and Christian society. But such rare release is not for us—not yet," he wailed after returning to his desk.[65]

Such may have been his thoughts as he departed for Atlanta to attend the Fifteenth Quadrennial Session of the General Conference of the A.M.E. Church, May 1–18, 1876. Resolving an important issue, the delegates decided to keep the publication department, which oversaw the *Recorder,* permanently in Philadelphia rather than transfer it to Washington after the debt was removed as recommended by the 1872 gathering.[66]

Many delegates were pleased that Tanner and Hunter had improved the *Recorder* during the past four years. The Reverend A. T. Carr noted that Tanner provided the *Recorder* with an "intellectual power." Tanner was reelected editor by acclamation, and immediately he called upon bishops and others for help, for "without such . . . [I] can do but little." Weary but delighted, he added, "We begin what in all probability is our last editorial term."[67] Despite Hunter's impressive improvements in the publication department, Henry M. Turner actively sought the position of manager and defeated Hunter by a vote of 81 to 50. Turner's biographer described the manager position as potentially the most illustrious administrative position in the church, but up to May 1876 it was a graveyard for episcopal ambition.[68] Turner would by the force of his personality use the position to espouse his causes, but his constant threats to suspend the paper in order to force debtors to pay would alienate him from many subscribers.

The next four years would be difficult ones for African Americans as the disputed election of 1876 led to the end of Reconstruction. The subsequent removal of federal troops from the South left the freedmen unprotected from Klan violence in the South and political indifference in the North. The rapid increase in European immigration to America would lead to violence between that group and black laborers who competed for menial jobs. For the freedmen, this period began a long descent into an era that by century's end would be known as the nadir in race relations as lynchings, disenfranchisement, Jim Crow laws, and vicious stereotypes demonized Americans of color. Tanner's facile pen would address these and other important issues during the next quadrennium.

Chapter 4

Christian Recorder, Part 3, 1876-1880
The Struggle to Save the *Recorder*

The *Christian Recorder* still faced severe financial problems, in part because some subscribers continued to refuse to pay. Additionally, the publication department still attracted little advertising, save for books published by A.M.E. clergy or quick-fix remedies for hair loss, constipation, or female health problems. Tanner vehemently criticized papers that carried advertisements for fortune tellers and astrologers, a decision that caused conflict between him and Turner. Earlier, in 1874, Tanner directed his anger at Turner when he believed the Southern minister to be associated with the *Tribune,* a black-owned paper in Savannah, Georgia, that in Tanner's opinion permitted questionable advertisements. "Has not [Turner] read the Bible," which forbade the practice of divination, witchery, or necromancy? Tanner asked. Turner replied that he had no connection with the *Tribune,* which was not a religious paper. John H. Devereaux, editor of the *Tribune,* complained that Tanner was attempting to harm a fellow black editor who accepted two liquor advertisements and one for fortune telling. Tanner's reply was terse: if Devereaux allied himself with destructive forces, then the *Recorder* would assist the public in frowning the *Tribune* down. Despite Tanner's sanctimonious attitude, the *Recorder* frequently printed advertisements extolling the virtues of Professor A. C. J. Hamilton, M.D., a celebrated phrenologist and medico-electro-scientific physician, and promoting a host of home remedies of questionable value.[1]

After the bishops replaced business manager Hunter, with whom Tanner was compatible and whom he respected, with Turner, it took time and deep soul-searching before the new colleagues agreed to stop bickering between themselves. The exchange between the men suggested their differences in personality and temperament. Tanner was an intellectual, a gifted scholar who mastered Latin, Greek, and Hebrew and guarded his privacy, which only a few outside his immediate family ever penetrated. Turner was a man of strong emotions and mercurial moods that intimidated others. An admirer described him as having "a Caesar's head on a frame like a sphinx; a Hercules in body and mind."[2] Between 1876 and 1880, despite their differences, the two men worked together for the betterment of the *Recorder.* Turner declared in 1911 that not a harsh word was exchanged between the two during this period although Tanner reprimanded him for using tobacco, a boyhood indulgence that had him addicted, and for saying "confound." This was a remarkable statement because in January 1875 Tanner had called Turner a false leader with a "crack brained theory of an exceptional future for the negro."[3]

Turner was an astute student of politics who understood clearly that since racists had used the pen to promulgate anti-black propaganda, men and women of the race should make the *Recorder* a vehicle to defend themselves against diabolic untruths.[4] For Turner, the paper represented the greatest opportunity to heighten the race consciousness of a maligned people. Believing that good writing would attract readers, Turner declared in his inaugural statement that blacks must write because "a race that cannot produce its own literature [will] hardly amount to a cypher." While his sentiment was admirable and needed, it encroached upon the jurisdiction of Tanner and did nothing to endear the business manager to the editor.

For four years he labored to improve the paper's circulation through bluster and threats, which alienated readers and church officials alike. Upon assuming the manger's position on June 26, 1876, Turner learned that it was common practice to sell weekly several hundred copies of the *Recorder* as waste paper, a practice that he quickly ended.[5] He was also appalled to learn that not one-half of the four thousand copies published weekly were paid for and that fewer than five hundred were mailed to ministers. The manager boldly proclaimed that fifty thousand copies of the *Recorder* should be printed weekly because there were seven thousand itinerant ministers who should subscribe and sell copies. Under church law, ministers who did not subscribe to the *Recorder* could be removed from their jobs by the bishops. However, few took the law seriously, and it was not enforced.[6]

Turner knew how to build churches and conferences, but the bluster that could move ministers and laity in the South was ill suited for a scattered audience that had little motivation to read newspapers when survival was a more pressing issue. Still, wasting no time, Turner informed readers in a July 13 notice that the *Recorder* met only one-third of its expenses. If there were not more subscribers or more advertisers, Turner vowed, he would reduce the paper one-half or one-fourth in size or issue it bimonthly or monthly. Turner noted that he would do this even if it meant ruining his reputation; better his than that of the church. The Rev. Theophilus G. Steward suggested that the publication department issue stock. "Cease heralding your own death!" he advised Turner, for "men don't buy sick horses!" Tanner approved of selling stock to the public, but Turner dismissed the suggestion and defended his harsh words as necessary because he lacked money to improve the paper. Tanner hoped to attract readers starting with the August 10 issue by serializing Frances E. W. Harper's temperance story, *Sowing and Reaping.*[7]

The two titans of the publication department—Turner and Tanner—while maintaining a superficially cordial relationship for the good of the *Recorder*, struggled to keep the tension from bubbling over. During the summer and fall of 1876 significant current events elicited contrasting responses from the two. The nation was abuzz over the death of General George Custer and his troops in the June 25 Battle of the Little Big Horn. On July 13 Turner and Tanner led a discussion about the incident in Philadelphia's Bethel A.M.E. Church. Turner expressed sorrow over Custer's demise but stated that he could shed no tears, since Custer had defended those who killed southern black Republicans. Tanner was more outspoken in his condemnation of Custer. The editor attributed the general's death to revenge for wrongs perpetrated against the Sioux; Custer had delighted in cutting down the "red nagurs" of the West. Tanner noted that black people did not feel sadness over Custer's death. "Does one say he does? He is a fool or a hypocrite" was Tanner's blunt assessment. Tanner, who considered the Sioux to be savages, nevertheless believed that they were right in fighting for their land.[8]

Turner and Tanner also differed over the volatile political issue of the end of Reconstruction and the Republican party's abandonment of support for southern black Republicans. Rutherford B. Hayes, the Republican nominee for the presidency of the United States, impressed Tanner because he was a graduate of Oberlin College, an antebellum training ground for abolitionists. This suggested to Tanner that, if elected, Hayes would support human rights for all. "Let him be elected," wrote Tanner. The election of 1876 was mired in controversy as disputed votes in Oregon, South Carolina, Louisiana, and Florida prevented either Hayes or his opponent, Samuel Tilden, from claiming victory. A compromise led to the election of Hayes, but the price was the end of Reconstruction with the removal of federal troops from the South. While Turner responded with characteristic anger when it was mistakenly believed that Tilden had won the election, Tanner noted that redemption followed suffering. "Only let Hayes attain to the presidency and the wholesale intimidation of the colored voters of the South will cease . . . forever," predicted Tanner. The editor was willing to give Hayes support as long as he protected the rights and lives of the freedmen, but otherwise he vowed to "give him unto the hands of his maker."[9]

Hayes adopted a "let-alone" policy in southern race matters. The federal government moved from nominal protection of the freedmen's rights in 1877 to a complete abdication of responsibility by early 1881 with Hayes's gratuitous hope that the good people of the South, rather than government officials, would uphold the principle of black citizenship and voting rights. A disenchanted Tanner welcomed Republican defeats in 1877 because it was "a necessity to wake the . . . nation up to . . . the danger of . . . Hayes' [southern] policy." By the end of Hayes's presidency, Tanner stated, "He leaves us and the South to our fate. This is as it should be." He advised readers not to put their faith in the United States Constitution, civil rights laws, or politicians but instead to "paddle [your] own canoe" in emulation of the Jews.[10]

Tanner was a strong advocate of self-reliance, but he was also a pragmatist who eschewed a race-first policy simply as a salve for an embittered people. For instance, he did not advocate appointment of a black man to the presidency of Howard University simply to satisfy race pride. Tanner agreed in an October 1876 editorial with John W. Cromwell's assertion that General Samuel Chapman Armstrong of Hampton Institute, who was white, was wise to decline the presidency of Howard. A black man should be president, declared Tanner, because Armstrong's "estimate of the negro is too low." We are the coming men, Tanner added. Yet "we could only vote a colored man president of [Howard] with the understanding that it was . . . independent of all charities." He added this caveat because he feared that whites would not trust black men to handle finances. If a black president meant that Howard's future would be insecure, Tanner preferred to continue with a white administrator.[11]

Manager Turner was less pragmatic. Two months later, he declared that a black man could accomplish more as president of Howard University than could a white one since Congress would listen to the former as a representative of his people. Besides, Turner added, it was difficult to obtain a white man of fame to take the position, and anything less would be a figurehead. Black people needed their own leaders, Turner noted. In February 1877, Tanner suggested that Bishop Daniel A. Payne had the experience (he had been president of Wilberforce for ten years), reputation, and strong moral character to be Howard's leader. A white man, Dr. D. W. Patten of Chicago, was selected several months later to take over the reins of Howard University. Tanner accepted the decision, understanding that many opposed Payne because they wanted a separation between church and state. Still, on a visceral level, he believed that the appointment of a black president would lead to Negrophobia that would undermine Howard. It was not until 1926, with the appointment of Mordecai W. Johnson, that Howard University had its first president of African descent.[12]

Presidential politics and Howard University, while important in their own right, represented a dilemma for Tanner. He wanted to enlighten readers about politics, economics, history, and other subjects, but he and Turner faced an arduous challenge of keeping the *Recorder* financially stable. There were so many demands on the laity for money. Chief among them were Wilberforce University and the mission field, which cried out for funding. Outside of some bishops, few besides the editor and manager had any interest in the publication department's financial situation. Many laymen were illiterate, some focused on feeding their families, and others found the *Recorder*'s topics to be irrelevant or boring. Still, the concerned parties sought to keep the deficit manageable.

Tanner assessed the *Recorder* in an August 4, 1876, editorial, "A Reason." He believed that the paper would have more white subscribers if white publications exchanged material with the *Recorder*. Of the white quarterlies, only the *Methodist Quarterly Review* indulged in this practice, and none of the monthlies obliged except for the *Nation*, which agreed to do so for one year. Tanner thought it shameful that white Americans were unwilling to know the thoughts of their black fellow citizens.[13] The problem was clear. Tanner believed that an intellectually stimulating newspaper would attract readers, although a large and sudden addition of subscribers was unlikely to come from the white religious or secular community. The absence of a large educated black population compounded the situation.

Unable immediately to attract a diverse readership that would add to the publication department's coffers, Tanner suggested that one thousand faithful provide five dollars for five years or that three hundred individuals lend them one hundred dollars for five years. He was pleased with the recommendation of the Rev. W. E. Stiles that all traveling A.M.E. pastors donate one dollar within thirty days to show that they wanted a literary establishment to assist them in improving themselves and their congregations. Tanner suggested that they study geography, arithmetic, grammar, the church's discipline, and Bishop Payne's *Semi-Centenary and the Retrospection of the African Methodist Episcopal Church in the United States* as well as his own *An Apology for African Methodism*. The rudimentary assignments showed the level of ignorance among clergy and laity. Tanner was eager to help the ministers in acquiring knowledge because he believed that uneducated clergy could not preach the gospel in a way that commanded respect; they made "too much noise in the pulpit" or gave little thought to what they said in their sermons.[14]

In contrast to Tanner's appeal to intellect as a way to increase the *Recorder's* circulation, Turner bluntly demanded financial support for the *Recorder*. Turner warned that unless ministers paid for their subscriptions, he would print their names, their congregations' membership, and the fact that few members were subscribers. In September 1876 Turner called those who had not paid for subscriptions or postage "bloodsuckers." He threatened to drop their names from the rolls if they did not pay the two-dollar annual subscription or the twenty-five-cent annual postage. In the October 12 issue, Turner indicated that he meant no disrespect to those he had castigated but that hardly any had responded to the one to two hundred bills he sent out for payment. Pay up, and if the paper does not arrive in time, "then give me 'thunder,'" he volunteered.

To assist him in the office, Turner hired William Steward, brother of Theophilus G. Steward and a resident of Gouldtown, New Jersey, who previously was an American Missionary Association teacher in the South and a cashier in the Freedmen's Bank in Tallahassee, Florida, and North Carolina. Steward would prove to be a welcome addition to the office, as Turner was frequently absent.[15]

Turner's sledgehammer approach to collecting arrears alienated many. The Rev. Theophilus G. Steward urged him to stop sending tenth-rate preachers across the land boring people for money. A reader who paid for and had not received the *Recorder* for six months, not an uncommon occurrence, complained, "I expect you have got like the rest; got up there [in Philadelphia] and is sitting down doing nothing." An enraged Turner replied that no one could decipher the man's address and asked how the writer dared send one dollar and expect to crack the whip.[16]

Turner's intimidating tactics had their effects, but not the one he wanted, for the end of 1876 brought the publication department no closer to reducing its debt. However, things were much brighter on a personal level for Tanner, who in November became the first vice-president of the Literary Association of the Philadelphia Annual Conference. On December 12 he addressed the Historical Society of Bethel A.M.E. Church in Philadelphia and declared that Egyptians were descendants of Ham through his eldest son Mizraim and were black; he added that the rest of the world had been semi-barbarians while Egypt was in her splendor. Bishop Daniel A. Payne remarked that there was no logical reason to believe that others than blacks built the pyramids.[17]

This type of intellectual stimulation was exactly what Tanner wanted to print in the *Recorder*, but to find space for that *and* reports of the annual conferences, bishops' messages, and church news called for an expanded paper, which took funds that were difficult to obtain. Part of the problem in raising public funds was the mistaken belief of many that whites primarily were the arbiters of truth. This legacy of slavery was noted by Tanner in December 1876 when he spoke at Philadelphia's Union A.M.E. Church and the pastor failed to get the dollar money from the parishioners. Soon after, a white man spoke and the congregation gave him five dollars in quarters, which prompted Tanner to write, "As long as our people *generalize* their quarters, but little will be done." His last editorial of 1876 deplored the practice of others using A.M.E. churches to raise money for causes not pertinent to the advancement of African Methodism. "Until the *Recorder* is made self-sustaining, no countenance should be given to others," he wrote. Despite this admonition, Tanner suggested readers subscribe to a new publication, *Frank Leslie's Sunday Magazine,* and the Vineland (N.J.) *Independent* because both supported the advancement of black Americans.[18]

Tanner hoped to appeal to the reader's intellect, but he depended on Turner to improve the paper's circulation. To expedite that matter, Turner announced on January 11, 1877, that William Steward would be in charge of the office while he toured the South in search of revenue. During January 1877 the publication department was printing six thousand copies of the *Recorder* weekly, far short of the manager's goal of ten thousand copies by April. By badgering and threatening, Turner returned to his office in mid-February with funds to print the desired ten thousand copies for the February 15 issue. Nevertheless, snags in delivery persisted, undermining confidence in the publication department. The postmaster at Tuscumbia, Alabama, regularly returned two ministers' papers with the words "no such negros here" written on the envelope. An outraged Tanner declared that he was going to send the returned newspapers to the Postmaster General of the United States and demand that he replace the bigot with "a gentleman" or "one at least who has studied . . . the Webster speller."[19]

Trying to improve the *Recorder*'s circulation forced Tanner, at times, to soothe the feelings of inexperienced writers whose articles were rejected or heavily edited. "We [are] resolved to take ... denunciations ... rather than make a paper that you yourselves would be ashamed of," he wrote on April 5. "Be a little patient," he begged. Tanner was concerned not only with the quality of articles but with the appearance of the *Recorder* as well. Tanner was extremely pleased with the April 12, 1877, issue. Set in a new, smaller type, which allowed more to be printed on a page, it had been reduced from eight pages to four. Ministers who had previously complained that their articles appeared on inside columns were happy, too, with the change. A major change in the masthead showing a hand holding a torch with the inscription THE CHRISTIAN RECORDER. GOD OUR FATHER. MAN OUR BROTHER. received enthusiastic praise. Despite the new look, some things had not changed; Turner notified readers that five thousand dollars was still in arrears, as some had not paid their debts for two or three years. Uncharacteristically optimistic, though, he wrote, "Look forward, look upward, let the motto be *Excelsior.*"[20]

Tanner's optimism was based on hope that African Methodists would see the wisdom of supporting the publication department, but neither Tanner's intellectualism nor Turner's bluster convinced the masses of African Methodists to contribute their dollar money to support the publication of the *Recorder.* Some ministers understood the importance of dollar money and sought to inform their congregation of their need to comply with church law. Others, either misinformed or indifferent, did little or nothing to assist the editor and his manager. In May 1877 the Rev. J. T. Jenifer informed Tanner that the *Recorder* was well received in Little Rock, Arkansas. "I find," he wrote, "but little trouble to collect my DOLLAR MONEY ... from those who read the RECORDER," because they saw the paper trying to elevate black people. Others were not as encouraging. The Rev. E. W. H. Andrews of Springfield, Tennessee, informed the editor that most of his congregation was illiterate. He requested ten copies weekly so that children could read to their parents. One minister indicated that the dollar money declined because people did not see their names or contributions listed in the conference minutes; some refused to give or in protest donated five cents.

Even the bishops were in disagreement over the dollar-money policy. In 1878 five of the six bishops recorded their views on the subject. Bishop J. M. Brown stated that the dollar-money idea was received with lukewarm indifference by the laity. Bishop A. W. Wayman felt encouraged that people were intelligent enough to support the dollar-money system. Bishop J. A. Shorter believed that despite heavy debts, churches were encouraged by the people's growing interest in supporting the policy. Bishop T. M. D. Ward concurred, but Bishop J. P. Campbell argued that paltry contributions were a reflection of the nation's dismal economic conditions. Like five blind men feeling an elephant, the bishops could only describe what they experienced. Their diverse reactions to the dollar question did not bode well for the dreamers who wanted the *Recorder* to compare well with white religious newspapers.[21]

Throughout June and July 1877, Tanner and Turner, acting like good cop and bad cop, appealed to subscribers. Deep in debt, in July Turner reduced the wages of the printers. Exasperated, he threatened to reduce the *Recorder* to the size of a letter sheet or postcard. He pleaded that unlike his predecessor, William H. Hunter, he was unable to put up twenty-six hundred dollars of his own money to keep the *Recorder* in print. Numerous suggestions for raising funds were sent to Turner along with a few precious dollars. Tanner reported in the July 12 issue that the paper was barely alive, because June had brought in six hundred dollars less than previous months. The publication department was still five thousand dollars in the red and could hardly pay the weekly expenses of the *Recorder*. Some readers were angry that Turner had dunned them. One sent in his two-dollar payment late with an irate comment: "Sir, your insolent demand . . . comes to hand. Send an acknowledgment . . . and immediately discontinue the paper."[22] Turner dismissed them brusquely with the statement that he had spent twenty-one dollars in postage for billings only to receive nine dollars of an expected thirty-five hundred.[23]

To set an example for others, Tanner personally sold seventy-five copies of the *Recorder* weekly because the paper represented to him the salvation of his race and African Methodism. He urged the church to support the *Recorder* or "pass the reins to white men and take a back seat." This latter point was picked up by the *People's Advocate* in Washington, D.C., which recommended support for the *Recorder* because the A.M.E. Church "has the grandest opportunity to prove the fitness of the American Negro to maintain himself in the high civilization of the age."[24] We forget today how momentous it was in the late 1870s for men and women of color to proudly identify with achievements of the race. Failure meant not simply incompetence on the part of an individual but rather the inability of African people to produce, manufacture, or in the case of the *Recorder* sustain a newspaper. Bigots were inclined to discard their efforts as incompetent or, when success was met, to dismiss their achievements as similar to that of mediocre whites.

Some African Methodists refused the *Recorder*—as they told Turner, who was traveling out west—because Tanner's "editorials have no life in them." Bruised, Tanner feebly dismissed the charge. "Possibly not," he replied, "but they are of the kind we have been writing for the last ten years."[25]

Even worthy suggestions to assist the publication department were met with indifference. The August 30, 1877, issue printed the suggestion of Rev. Dr. J. H. A. Johnson of Annapolis, Maryland, that approximately twelve members of each of the one thousand church boards donate one dollar in October, the money to be presented November 1 at Philadelphia's Bethel A.M.E. Church with spectators paying twenty cents to witness the offering. His plan would have easily satisfied the publication department's debt, but no one complied.[26]

Meanwhile, shocking news demoralized supporters of the *Recorder* when William H. Hunter, former publication department manager, sued in January 1878 for payment of debts that he contracted while in office. White creditors gave the *Recorder* time, but Hunter demanded payment immediately. Tanner notified readers in the February 14 issue that Hunter had threatened to put the sheriff on them, an act that if carried out would wipe the publication department out of existence. William Steward, deputy manager of the publication department, hoped to raise funds by establishing an illustrious roll of donors whose names would be prominently displayed in the *Recorder*.[27]

In February 1878 Turner returned to his desk after spending five months in the South. He quickly seconded Steward's proposal, because printing names would save him the expense of sending receipts, and he offered ministers an opportunity to sell the paper for five cents and send him three, earning a tidy profit for themselves if they sold a substantial number of copies. Still strapped for cash, Turner warned that he might have to dismiss all but two employees and print a paper the size of a letter sheet. By March 14 Turner announced that funds from ministers and a decision of employees to accept only one-half of their wages until the financial situation improved had prevented the paper from being reduced by half. Some questioned Turner's blunt scare tactics, but the irascible manager retorted, "If I die I will die hard. The truth is, I have not told half the story yet, and shall not unless driven to it." He denied that he was using the manager's position to seek a higher office; therefore, he admonished those who threatened to block his ambitions, "When my time is up, I will leave and go to Africa."[28]

Of course, Turner was bluffing, as he had no other recourse. While this tactic had served him well in early years as a builder of churches in Georgia, it had little effect in journalism. His pleas alienated many, but some understood the necessity of his bark. A reader informed him that he sold forty copies of the *Recorder* weekly although "I have complained a little about the manner in which you have pitched into the brethren." Despite its money woes, the *Recorder* had a fine reputation. The April 1878 *Methodist Quarterly Review* considered it the leading black paper in the nation. Philip A. Bell, editor of San Francisco's the *Elevator,* referred to the *Recorder* as "a representative of our race as well as of the A. M. E Church" and said, "We cannot afford to let it die." From within, Tanner described the *Recorder* "as a tongue to the church by which it lets its wants and wishes be known." "Shall the church be dumb?" he asked.[29]

Hoping to increase readership, the *Recorder* forged an agreement with black Masons to devote several columns to Masonic matters. It appeared to be a brilliant move. Many African Methodists were Masons, and Tanner believed that if they could be influenced to support the church's needs, the alliance was justifiable.[30]

Unfortunately, this outreach had little immediate impact on the *Recorder*'s deficit. Once again, after several months of quietude, Turner bombarded readers with more harangue. The May 30 issue heralded his plea in bold letters: READ! READ THIS! The embattled manager reported that his request to the publication department to release him from his duties had been refused. Turner reported a week later that at his request Theodore Gould was appointed deputy manager and would be in charge during his absences. Turner's biographer considered Gould's appointment Turner's "finest accomplishment as manager . . . because he found someone with talent that complemented his; . . . whereas Turner was flamboyant, Gould was low key." The appointment of Gould had immediate results, as he donated one thousand dollars of his own money to help the cash-starved publication department.[31]

The August 29 issue of the *Recorder* carried Gould's plea for funds to reduce the seven-thousand-dollar debt. It cost $150 weekly to print the newspaper, but receipts had averaged only $69.55 for several weeks. In spite of Tanner's eloquence, Turner's bluster, and Gould's competence, receipts remained low. Only one out of every sixty-five church members subscribed, and only one out of every twenty-two ministers took the *Recorder*.[32]

Notwithstanding the dismal figures, several months later Turner asked for eighteen hundred additional subscribers to reach a total of ten thousand. Accomplish this goal by New Year's Day, he declared, and "I will proclaim a year of jubilee, pardon all faults and remit all debts not owed to me, and restore all lands for which you have good deeds and titles." To alleviate the debt, all six bishops pledged one thousand dollars, Tanner and Turner promised seventy-five dollars, and some ministers affirmed gifts of twenty-five dollars each, while clergy in eighteen of the twenty-nine annual conferences of the A.M.E. Church pledged lesser amounts.[33]

Men in the church failed to support the *Recorder* just as they neglected to finance the mission field. Once again, women took the initiative. In mid-November Fannie M. Jackson, principal of the Institute for Colored Youth in Philadelphia, decided with the help of friends to organize a bazaar or fair to aid the publication department. Her plan was to hold the event in February 1879 and to have participants transform a cigar box into "a pretty little work box, or comb and brush box" or display products such as preserved fruits, rice, cotton, tobacco, or sweet potatoes. Meanwhile, Theodore Gould took responsibility for twelve hundred dollars' worth of notes on the debt.[34]

Christmas did not bring in cash. On December 26 Turner asked, "Shall Our Paper Suspend[?]" He complained that too many "big men" in the church refused to pay the forty to one hundred dollars they owed. Receipts for the past week amounted to a paltry $15.03. Thoroughly distressed, Turner lamented, "I fear our effort to issue a weekly paper is a failure." A few weeks earlier, Turner had quietly submitted his resignation, but Bishop J. M. Brown, chair of the publication department, refused to accept it while advising the manager that the ten-thousand-dollar debt was small. The *Recorder* is a monument to African

Methodism, so "retrench or die, retrench or close up," suggested the bishop. Turner, who had been in North Carolina, returned to Philadelphia to find that William Steward and Theodore Gould had also tendered their resignations. Gould was persuaded to withdraw his resignation, and W. C. Banton was brought in to act as chief clerk.[35] The financial situation was a mess, and the bishops—unwilling to take any positive initiatives—relied on an increasingly frustrated manager to make the publication department solvent.

There are no extant copies of the *Recorder* for 1879. Theodore Gould reported in the January 8, 1880, issue that the black ladies of Philadelphia, irrespective of church or denomination, had organized themselves into a National Union Bazaar Association to sell items for a week or ten days commencing November 19 to benefit the publication department. Editorial support for the paper's solvency came from the *Christian Index,* which declared, "The *Recorder* cannot die as long as Dr. Tanner wields the pen in its defense."[36]

Although Tanner devoted much of his time in the late 1870s to the *Recorder*'s dire financial situation, as editor and intellectual numerous issues competed for his attention and ultimately for his pen. One such topic that aroused a passionate response was the controversial issue of African emigration, which had divided the race since the founding of the American Colonization Society in 1816. The ACS supported the repatriation of former slaves to Liberia, first a colony and then since 1847 an independent republic. While approximately fifteen thousand men and women of color would emigrate between 1820 and 1870, the prospect of emigration was a hotly debated subject. Tanner and Turner held opposing views on African emigration. Tanner opposed mass emigration; Turner saw in emigration the salvation of an exile race. The subject was widely discussed, and not only in the black press. The editor of the *New York Times* asserted in 1875 that African emigration was impractical: "We have brought Sambo here. Such as he is, he means to stay." Black Americans, a decade removed from slavery, expressed mixed views on emigration. John W. Cromwell, editor of the *People's Advocate,* criticized Turner for defending the efforts of the American Colonization Society to arouse interest in repatriation. Shortly after Turner assumed the manager's position, Cromwell wrote, "If Mr. Turner would just go to Africa, take all his family with him, stay there, his sincerity would be stronger argument than he now makes, while accepting a position which honor bound keeps him four years longer in the United States." By 1877 Turner and Tanner had both moderated their voices on the African emigration question. Edward W. Blyden praised them for their ability to work together and for Tanner's ability to "put down the 'brakes'" when Turner "puts on the steam."[37]

Tanner's blood pressure rose whenever anyone suggested that the United States was a white man's country. Such a view in the January 1878 *African Repository,* written by the Rev. D. A. Wilson, elicited a denunciation from the *Recorder*'s editor, who considered the sentiment the voice of Satan because the future of the nation depended upon the welding together of the two races. J. A. Newby, a subscriber to the *Recorder*, believed that emigration was a scheme "to get rid of the newly enfranchised race and supply their places by foreign elements for political purposes . . . or race hatred." Former United States senator Blanche Kelso Bruce warned that Liberia did not need multitudes of ignorant emigrants. Only a few will go to Africa, Tanner declared, because "Africa calls for brains [and] brains are scarce, while America calls for muscles." Tanner, however, was willing to endorse limited emigration, which would not deny the right of black Americans to remain in the land of their birth. Turner agreed with him on this latter point, which caused Tanner in April 1878 to write, "We find greater harmony than we thought to exist between us." But soon the harmony between the two was strained; in May the Philadelphia Annual Conference's committee on emigration, chaired by Tanner, condemned emigration "as a speculative movement of thoughtless men." The decision of committee members Tanner, Theophilus G. Steward, Theodore Gould, and Leonard Patterson to oppose the effort of the Liberian Joint Stock Steamship Company in South Carolina to take people to West Africa distressed Turner.[38]

In mid-May James Green wrote to Tanner requesting information about Liberia. Tanner declined to reply because "Africa is not the place to which ignorant people ought to go. They who go should be intelligent, and well-to-do, for only such Africa needs." Mary Ella Mossell, an A.M.E. missionary in Haiti, stated that Africa would profit more from a Bible in the hands of intelligent Christians than an influx of thousands of ignorant and superstitious emigrants. James Milton Turner, a former United States consul in Liberia, sought to discourage emigration by painting Liberia as a land of miasmatic fevers.[39] Much of the anti-emigrationist view was fueled by a fear that widespread interest in Africa emanating from the black community would assist the foes of racial equality who decried the inclusion of blacks into the American family.

The venerable Daniel A. Payne, the senior bishop in the church, stirred emotions with a series of published letters to Charles H. Pearce of Tallahassee, Florida. Pearce believed that the A.M.E. Church should send missionaries to Africa. Payne informed him in a reply dated June 27, 1878, that the South Carolina exodus movement was instigated by "disappointed political ambition" in South Carolina and Georgia. Payne predicted that in fifty years, after science wiped out diseases, more of Africa would be home to Europeans. He advised Pearce, "*Be wherever the white man be. Don't fly from him, but stand by him* . . . until he feels your excellence and acknowledges your equality." An offended Turner declared in late July that he believed Payne's "disappointed political ambition" statement was a reference to him, as he was the only member or former member of Georgia's legislature to advocate emigration. An advocate of African missions since 1849, Turner expressed sorrow over Payne's low estimation of blacks' intellectual and moral worth.[40]

Tanner declared in October that there was no truth to the accusation that white men were unsuited for the tropics. Let them go and repair some of their wrongs, he suggested, because "the great principle of repentance is the principle of restitution." He believed that white America's antipathy toward black people kept the nation out of Africa while Europe was developing the continent's resources. Tanner suggested that the government should send the man-of-war *Ticonderoga* to West Africa to explore the possibility of American commercial development. Perhaps to forestall the charge that he was in alliance with imperialists, Tanner suggested that Martin R. Delany, a black American who had explored the Niger River valley, be part of the expedition.[41]

Africa's strongest voice for emigration from America came from Edward W. Blyden, who in 1880 informed a reporter from the *Philadelphia Record* that blacks had to "emigrate . . . or remain . . . to 'creep and crawl.'" Tanner denied that this was the only viable choice; he believed that race caste was doomed. Such faith in American justice led Blyden to cite the editor as an example of "a man of mixed blood who used his influence to hinder the progress of Negroes."[42]

Although he approved of the word "African" as part of the title of his church, Tanner eschewed its use for those of his race who resided in the Americas. As early as 1846 opposition to the name "African" in the A.M.E. Church divided members, and again in 1870 and in 1876 official requests were made that "American" be substituted for "African" in the church's name. Tanner declared in 1875 that Richard Allen selected "African" instead of "Negro" in 1816 because he wanted to "link irrevocably their religious destiny with the continent whence their forefathers came." Tanner and T. H. Jackson presented a resolution to the 1880 General Conference to retain "African" in the church title. The resolution was adopted with one dissenting vote.[43] By 1884 Tanner was of the belief that the welding of the races in America was inevitable. Therefore, he stated that the designation "African" in the church's name must be buried, "but not until the church is . . . perfectly willing to have it so." He added that "African" would be dropped once black people became completely Americanized.[44]

The acceptance of the nomenclature "African" represented a political stance then much as the term "African American" today defines those who feel a special spiritual, political, or cultural connection to the continent. While Tanner was willing to use "African" in the name of his church affiliation, he strongly denied that he and others were culturally Africans since enslavement and acculturation had robbed them of that claim. Nor did he take kindly to the suggestion that he was a Negro, for it was a term that he seldom used; when he did it was in reference to black-complexioned people in Africa or to those inhabitants of ancient African kingdoms. Tanner opposed capitalizing "Negro" because it was not in his estimation a proper noun. In 1872 Blyden started a publication in West Africa, *Negro*, to "serve the race purpose." In 1873 he stated that "Negro" was approved by race thinkers in the diaspora to be an acceptable race designation. Still, few in the United States agreed, preferring "colored." In 1877 Blyden informed Tanner that he should capitalize "Negro" because several white American editors had complied after reading Blyden's rationalization. "Surely the leading editor in the United States will not be indifferent to it," he wrote to Tanner.[45] Impressed with Blyden's flattery, Tanner responded in 1878 that "we are not negroes any more than those who came to America in the Mayflower . . . are Englishmen." Believing that the descendants of enslaved Africans were colored people and "neither Africans nor negroes," Tanner advised readers to reject "Negro" because "it has the smell of the horrors of the middle passage about it. It must not be tolerated." He added that as there was "no virtue in being white," there was "no condemnation in being colored." This last point was a criticism of Richard T. Greener, who was president of the Negro American Association of Washington, D. C. Tanner dismissed Greener's assertion that "colored" was a weak euphemism that meant nothing.[46]

The *People's Advocate* in Washington, D.C., accused Tanner of rejecting "Negro" because he relied too much on dictionary definitions instead of ethnological or anthropological evidence. In response, Tanner charged the editor, John W. Cromwell, with relying on white authorities. Cromwell makes Greener a "Negro," but "we make him a simon pure American," he concluded.[47]

Tanner had not studied African cultures, languages, or history (except for the African presence in the Bible) and was nearly ignorant of the most elementary aspects of the diversity of the African continent. Thus, to Tanner, "Negro" meant literally black in complexion and unmixed in racial stock. By his definition, clearly few in America could answer to the name. But on a deeper level, Tanner ascribed to Negroes a primitiveness that was undeserved, as he, like so many, white and black, equated greatness with the achievements of the Anglo-Saxon. Unable to see anything modern in African culture, Tanner simply dismissed it as "primitive." In later years, however, he would have a better understanding of African culture as African Methodists missionaries to West and South Africa returned home with fascinating tales of the regions' cultural richness.[48]

The acceptance of a proper race designation involved more than semantics in Tanner's estimation. He believed that the black people in the United States lacked self-respect, and therefore respect from whites, because they could not decide if they were Americans, Africans, or "simply blacks without a habitation and a name." From October 1880 to early February 1881 the pages of the *Recorder* revealed the diverse opinions of contributors on the name question. Tanner declared, "Plainly the work of the hour is to settle this question." The Rev. John D. Bagwell argued that "American" would suffice; therefore, he advised, get rid of "African, Negroes, Negro-American, American Negro, black and colored." Many sided with Bagwell, but others supported the nationalist thesis of Martin R. Delany that "African" sounded "sweeter than . . . 'American.'" Tanner held that the capital *N* in Negro implied citizenship in one of the Negro governments of

West Africa. He insisted that the race had to determine who they were before they could declare "what we are." "Are we weak or strong, foolish or wise, ignorant or learned, excuses for men, or men prepared to take whatever responsibilities providence throws upon us?" he asked.[49]

The debate over a proper race designation did not abate by the end of the nineteenth century and still has not been completely resolved as we approach the dawn of the twenty-first century. When Alexander Crummell organized the American Negro Academy in 1897, some intellectuals and race leaders criticized the "Negro" in the title. Timothy Thomas Fortune, editor of the *New York Age* and supporter of the term "Afro-American," berated "Negro" as a term meaning "unmixed" whose acceptance would exacerbate tensions over color questions between blacks and mulattos. Tanner, one of the founding members of the American Negro Academy, objected to the position of "Negro" in that organization's name because "we are Americans. Let negro be the adjective and not the noun," he stated; "we who are of African descent should rate ourselves precisely as people of European descent." Tanner failed to realize that while the descendants of the British, Irish, Germans, and other Europeans who migrated to the United States considered themselves Americans, they were unwilling to shun their cultural legacies or disavow an emotional allegiance to the land of their parents. Tanner could not understand that people could both be loyal to their cultural past (even if they had to invent one) regardless of how many years they had been removed and still consider themselves Americans. Tanner's opposition was so strong that in his book *The Dispensations in the History of the Church and the Interregnums* (1898), he identified himself as one of the bishops of the A.M.E. Church and a member of the "Negro American Academy" because he wanted "American" and not "Negro" to be the noun.[50]

Despite Tanner's aversion to using "Negro" as a proper noun, he quickly defended pure Negroes from slanderous comments. When James Parton declared in the November–December 1878 *North American Review* that no pure Negro had ever achieved distinction in the arts or professions or displayed any signs of extraordinary intelligence, Tanner responded in the *Recorder* that since most Negroes in America were not of pure blood, Parton's statement was "grossly libelous . . . if he simply means a black . . . [person]." In defense of those with pure blood (as much as could be visually determined), Tanner cited the illustrious careers of Bishop James Theodore Holly of the Protestant Episcopal Church in Haiti, attorney and former Reconstruction politician Robert Elliott, and numerous others who made names and fortunes.[51]

Tanner's point was well taken, because by the late 1870s more young people, both black and mulatto, sought to elevate themselves by enrolling in colleges and universities. Literary societies were formed in major American cities to accommodate the black elite who prided themselves on their taste in literature and their ability to converse in German and French. In spring 1878 Tanner, along with Bishops Wayman, Brown, Campbell, and Shorter, the Rev. Theophilus G. Steward, and others supported in concept the formation of a Literary Congress of the A.M.E. Church where great minds could meet to discuss the moral, literary, and scientific questions of the day, devise ways to further the race's interest in literature, scholarship, and missionary enterprise, and develop closer bonds between laity and ministers and between the geographic sections in the connection. A reader in Mobile, Alabama, informed Tanner that a literary society "would reflect undying glory upon ourselves and the church if we could arouse our people to a love for the sciences." It was announced in May that the Literary Congress would meet in August in Baltimore with one minister and one layman from every church in the connection. Unfortunately, the plans for the Literary Congress were abandoned after a consensus could not be reached on the ways to determine representation.[52] Despite the failure to establish the Literary Congress, Tanner was sowing seeds for a literary journal that would bear fruit in 1884 with the advent of the *A.M.E. Church Review.*

Tanner's diligent work on behalf of the church and race warranted him special attention as the 1880 General Conference approached. His name, of course, was mentioned for reappointment to the editor's position, but some suggested that his contributions deserved an election to the bishopric. Seven months before the May meeting, John W. Cromwell praised Tanner's editorial skills as "one of the finest specimens of the Negro in journalism." He added, "The 'Recorder' is the place for Bro[ther] Tanner and the General Conference will be wise in keeping him there." Cromwell understood that Tanner's effectiveness would be undermined by removing him from the editor's chair, and he was dismayed that the 1876 General Conference had made a mistake. "Let it not make two," he warned. Presumably the election of Turner as manager of the publication department was the "mistake" that Cromwell meant.[53]

Delegates to the General Conference heard Turner's report of the publication department's financial woes. The situation was so bad that before he could obtain credit to buy supplies, Turner had to swear out an affidavit that he had a personal estate valued at six thousand dollars and have it certified by Tanner and Bishop T. M. D. Ward. While the period from 1875 to 1879 was a time of failed businesses, including the demise of eighteen publication departments, Turner's blunt threats to debtors did little, despite some initial optimism, to sell the *Recorder.* For a while Turner increased weekly subscriptions of the *Recorder* from 1309 copies to 8000, and for a few weeks he printed 10,000 copies, but by May 1880 the circulation was 5400 weekly. Turner's biographer noted that "a less outspoken man than Turner was needed at the helm . . . before [reform] could be implemented." During Turner's tenure the publication department brought in receipts totaling $50,142.27 and had expenses of $50,123.99, for a profit of $18.28.[54] Clearly the paltry profit during Turner's tenure indicates that while it was necessary for the publication department to implement a system to efficiently collect subscription dollars, Turner's personality was utterly useless in attempting to develop permanent readers for the *Recorder*.

The other pressing point facing the delegates was the need for more bishops. The church had grown considerably, both geographically and numerically, since 1876. In that year two bishops lived close to one another and three lived within 150 miles of each other. Clearly, as suggested by Tanner, "a bishop should be in speaking distance of his people [for] an occasional visit does not suffice." There was a definite need for three or four more bishops to supplement the existing six, with particular assignments to the South. In 1880 two of the bishops were nearly incapacitated. There was a complaint that bishops stayed up north (the exception was Payne, who wintered in Florida) and were "like the wild geese that come from Canada . . . during the rich harvest and gather and return home again!" Although Tanner believed that the unidentified writer misrepresented the bishops, he agreed that half of the bishops should reside in the South or there would be no peace.[55]

John W. Cromwell decried the selection process, which was based on regional muscle or individual popularity. In a critique of B. F. Lee, president of Wilberforce University, Turner, and Tanner, Cromwell pointed out that their positions alone did not warrant elevation to the bishopric. He emphatically stated that Tanner gave character to the editor's position and that he could wield more influence there than as bishop.[56] The delegates agreed, giving Tanner thirty-six votes for the bishopric on the first ballot, far short of the necessary 103. Tanner's vote declined on the following three ballots as Henry M. Turner, Richard H. Cain, and W. F. Dickerson were elected, victors of the South's electoral muscle. Cromwell praised the election of Dickerson while criticizing the elevation of Turner, who he believed was better suited for the manager's position. Cromwell was contemptuous of Cain's election, dismissing him for suggesting a lottery drawing as suitable for a fundraiser for the proposed Metropolitan A.M.E. Church in Washington and for his belief in the maxim "Let the end justify the means."[57]

Years later, in 1911, Turner stated that Tanner was better fitted than himself in 1880 to be bishop but that the only office the editor then wanted was the one he already had. Despite their differences, Turner added, he and Tanner got along because their differences were "of opinion only, and not of malice; for a more perfect gentleman I have never been associated with, nor do I ever covet the association of a better."[58]

Tanner's then twelve years in the editor's chair warranted praise. His advocacy of self-reliance and his bold challenges to prejudice placed him in a leadership role historians have overlooked because the bulk of his writings appeared in the *Christian Recorder*, a newspaper that failed to attract the attention of historians save those of the church. Instead, historians have examined with care the writings of Timothy Thomas Fortune, editor of the *New York Age*, or Monroe

Trotter, the militant editor of the *Boston Guardian,* because of the secular nature of those publications. Nevertheless, Tanner's love of race made him an activist journalist, which, as Cromwell understood, made him more valuable to the church than a bishop's appointment could do. It was this commitment to social justice that gave the *Recorder* a larger circulation in 1880 than any other black-owned newspaper in America. For the next four years Tanner and Theodore Gould, who succeeded Turner as business manager, continued the struggle to improve the *Recorder* by increasing the advertising revenue. The charge would prove challenging.[59]

Chapter 5

Christian Recorder, Part 4, 1880–1884
Europe, Africa, and Tanner's Departure from the *Recorder*

The departure of Turner from the manager's position provided no immediate relief for the cash-strapped publication department. Theodore Gould called for ten thousand agents to canvass the land and sell the *Recorder*. He wanted fifty thousand copies sold weekly, an ambitious but not extraordinary goal, since he expected assistance from the wives of the connection's two thousand ministers. Gould offered a two-cent commission on each copy sold, with the hope that each wife would sell five copies weekly. The expected fourteen thousand dollars earned in commissions would support eight missionaries under the auspices of the Mite Missionary Society headed by Sarah E. Tanner. Gould additionally hoped that five thousand boys and girls plus three thousand young ladies would duplicate the effort of the ministers' wives, thereby reaching the targeted goal. Do this for four years and the publication department would be debt-free, Gould asserted. While Gould, like Turner, would experience difficulty in collecting funds, Turner's detractors found Gould's personality pleasing and thus provided him with more breathing space. By August 1881 Turner praised his successor for making additions and improvements in the manager's office and for enlarging the size of the *Recorder*.[1]

In July 1880 Tanner excited African Methodists with his announcement that the *Child's Recorder,* which had appeared in one volume in 1873, would be issued again commencing in August. The inaugural issue was widely hailed. One reader exclaimed that it was "just what the church needs. It is a compliment you have given to the church." Twenty-five thousand copies of the *Child's Recorder* were printed monthly by November 1882.[2]

Interestingly, people were willing to encourage their children to read but still disinclined to readily support the *Recorder*. Gould still struggled by August 1880 to get the connection to "Read! Read! Read!" During that month, he sent out bills amounting to $771.56. Lacking Turner's vehemence but not his diligence, Gould, too, threatened to print the names of delinquent bill payers. "The church has placed me here to guard her interests and I will do it regardless of the smiles of friends, or the frowns of foes," he warned. In May 1881 the local news column of the *Recorder* asked why "the colored citizens of Philadelphia" did not "do more to help sustain the only colored paper that has been able to live in their city." The columnist continued, "This is unjust not only to us but to yourselves."[3]

The dire money situation certainly hampered the publication department's effort to increase circulation and limited Tanner's ability to present to readers a newspaper of exceptional literary quality, but it did not deter him from attempting to provide subscribers with an informative journal. In many respects the *Recorder* of the early 1880s was a national newspaper. While there were numerous black-owned newspapers in the country, few then had a national circulation. Frederick Douglass's *New National Era* was no longer published, and Timothy T. Fortune, who in later years would become the dean of African American journalists, was just beginning his journalistic career at this time. Tanner hoped to have the *Recorder* assist the race to succeed. A successful race, insisted Tanner, must learn to aim higher intellectually, not to pat themselves on their collective back for knowing that two plus two equals four. He believed that too many blacks were satisfied with a mere smattering of Greek, Latin, or Hebrew when whites were motivated to learn Sanskrit for a better understanding of classical grammar.[4]

Editor Tanner had no restrictions on fodder for his editorials save his own good judgment. His thoughts roamed widely across the nation's landscape of politics, economics, race relations, and religion. A prolific reader, he often culled from other publications themes for his own essays or editorials. At other times he leaped ahead of others to present his thoughts on issues that would later captivate them. One such issue was his support for Methodist unity, an anathema for many. Tanner, more than most in the A.M.E. Church, sought unity among Methodists, because he believed that true Christians should put aside differences of color, race, and nationality and embrace each other as children of God, a sentiment not shared by most white clergymen, many of whom proudly wore the badge of superiority. Once, Tanner rode fifty miles in a railroad car in silence because the white ministers who were his fellow passengers, and who knew his calling, said nothing to him. To his dismay, white Episcopalians who by his observation would spit at a Methodist ordination gladly exchanged pleasantries with white Methodists while the same Methodists ignored him. "It wouldn't be true," he noted, "if a white R[oman] Catholic met a fellow black R[oman] Catholic," but the motto of a white Protestant was "I'm white and . . . you [are] a niggard." In 1883 Tanner declared that the racist behavior of white Methodists caused black people to prefer Rome or the devil to them. He accused white preachers of having stronger feelings about stopping sales of cigars on Sunday than about snuffing out the sin of caste.[5]

Tanner would become exasperated when whites accused African Methodists of belonging to a race-exclusive church. In 1875 he argued that the A.M.E. Book of Discipline did not limit membership by race or color. Angrily he wrote, "We have scores of 'white' members, we have 'white' pastors, 'white' presiding elders, and will possibly have a 'white' bishop per inter paris sooner than will the M.E. Church have a 'colored' one." For instance, he cited an 1882 visit to W. B. Derrick's Israel A.M.E. Church in Albany where two-thirds in attendance were white—and not riffraff, as he noticed. Tanner believed that ultimately ignorance and not color separated

Christians and that whites would join A.M.E. churches that employed educated preachers. Churches should serve neither white nor black but penitent souls, Tanner declared, for he deemed it just as obnoxious for A.M.E. churches to remain "colored" as it was for white churches to remain "white."[6]

For others, a more immediate concern was unifying the A.M.E., African Methodist Episcopal Zion, and Colored Methodist Episcopal churches. In October 1875 Tanner published an open letter in the *Recorder* to Daniel A. Payne, J. J. Clinton, and W. H. Miles, respectively the senior bishops in the A.M.E., A.M.E.Z., and C.M.E. churches, urging them to meet to discuss unity "and in the fear of God, ask what reason is to be given for keeping up the division!" Ironically, the *Methodist* called for the same union of black *Methodist* churches. Unimpressed, Tanner responded that Dr. Wheeler, editor of the Methodist, should first plead for a union of white churches, since charity begins at home.[7]

In 1878, after the Wesleyan Methodists and the Primitive Wesleyan Methodists of Ireland united, Tanner declared that since all Methodists shared the same doctrine irrespective of race, they should unite. Recognizing the power of prejudice, Tanner hoped that by the year 2000 Methodists would no longer care about color or regional differences.[8] Tanner believed that "caste is doomed, its death is simply a question of time."[9]

Tanner's optimism was not shared by white Methodists, as caste prevailed over ethical judgment. Since the M.E. Church did not want union with them, Tanner suggested in 1880 that the African Methodists reunite with the British Methodist Episcopal Church, the Canadian conference of the A.M.E. Church prior to 1860. This would mean a union of Africo-Americans in North America, the British West Indies, and British Guiana, which would provide the A.M.E. Church with the strength to evangelize in the Caribbean and South America, where people "unconsciously await to be with us." A Caribbean and South America in Christ's hold would serve as the base for the long-desired African mission field. September 11, 1880, was a glorious day for African Methodism as the A.M.E. and B.M.E. churches signed articles of agreement for union pending ratification by two-thirds of the annual conferences of each church. The union, completed by September 1884, added to the A.M.E. Church conferences in Ontario, Nova Scotia, Bermuda, and Demerara (British Guiana); seventy-seven ministers; 2,684 members; a newspaper, the *Missionary Messenger*; and a bishop, R. R. Disney. The union, however, had a major dissenter in Bishop Payne, who agreed with Bishop James Theodore Holly of Haiti's Protestant Episcopal Church that the merger represented imperialism, which would bring opposition from Christendom. In 1884 Payne accused Tanner of misleading the public about the benefits of a merger with the B.M.E. Church. Yes, it brought in fourteen million potential proselytes, Payne argued, but union also meant an additional annual expenditure of thirty-one hundred dollars for Bishop Disney's support, money that would be better used for financially strapped Wilberforce University.[10]

Tanner was obviously pleased with the merger, but he still held out for a union of all Methodists—and by extension all Protestants—because it would mean victory in the battle for religious and social equality. He contended that the race question would not be settled until blacks "were admitted into the school, church and parlor everywhere with equal rights." Tanner believed that the future America would be a color-blind nation and that integration would reign in the country's churches. Sooner or later, he argued, race-exclusive churches would be amputated "like diseased limbs." He envisioned an A.M.E. Church comprised of all races, tongues, and colors. Whites would join for cultural reasons, he declared, because of their attraction to black church singing. "Let us charm him by our preaching and our living; and his coming will be to stay," he asserted. Tanner had a glimpse of white Christians casting aside race prejudice at the 1880 A.M.E. General Conference when a delegation of British Wesleyans led by the Rev. F. W. MacDonald described all men as brothers in Christ. Tanner offered a resolution citing their presence as hope for the end of caste prejudice. Upon their return to England, he declared, "they will [not] represent that prejudice which is the characteristic of the American people."[11]

The matter of union with the Colored Methodist Episcopal Church remained unsettled. On April 26, 1882, the Episcopal Council of the A.M.E. and C.M.E. churches met, but no formal business was conducted because only one of the four C.M.E. bishops attended. Two years later Tanner informed delegates at the church's quadrennial that he hoped the time was near for union even though privately he believed that only a fraternal, not an organic, unity was possible, but a strong minority in both church organizations opposed union.[12] Tanner sincerely believed that unity of Methodists was needed, but his belief in racial harmony was belied by the fact that white Methodists in the 1880s were unable to fully accept the black man as their equal regardless of the achievement of men such as Tanner. In their estimation, successful blacks were the exception and not the rule. They were unwilling to permit them to integrate into their society and certainly were not inclined to consider those who were two decades removed from slavery their intellectual or spiritual equal. Tanner also failed to appreciate the fear other black Methodists had in reference to unity with the A.M.E. Church, which by its sheer size threatened to dominate the others. It was in their best interest to remain outside the folds of the African Methodist's skirt.

Tanner's understanding of white bigotry with all of its implications of black inferiority deeply hurt him, for he was a man of culture and intellect. His effort to display before the *Recorder*'s readers the literary contributions of the race severely taxed him physically and emotionally. Sometime in 1879 his nerves were shattered. For ten years, he noted, he had seen every issue of the *Recorder* go to press, but he "broke down as thoroughly, if not literally, as ever glass dashed among the rocks breaks." Sympathetic friends advised him to go to Europe. He planned his departure for June 29, 1881, to represent the publication department at the Methodist Ecumenical Conference. While the trip was for rest and recuperation, Tanner also planned to raise funds in England. He informed readers in the May 26 issue that he would be away for three to four months: "We ask [for] your prayers, first for the cause we go to represent, and secondly for us personally," he wrote. Theodore Gould asked for donations to help finance Tanner's trip, as the church did not include him in its official delegation.[13]

Tanner informed the black exchanges weeks before his departure that he planned to lecture in England on the black press of the United States. He requested two copies of their latest issue, "provided they considered it to be the best issue, a brief description of their paper and their goal for publishing and their photograph so English people could see the fraternity of colored editors."[14] A lonely Tanner bade farewell to his family on June 17 as he left for New York to board the steamship *Greece*.[15]

The two-week ocean voyage provided Tanner with ample time to discuss religion and race with some of his fifty-four fellow passengers, who were Danish, Russian, English, French, and American. The second day at sea, Tanner listened to an Englishman describe the rapid decline of aborigines in Australia who could not adjust to the ways of the country's white inhabitants. Tanner proudly noted that "the American Negro alone of all the dark races can withstand an assault of these mighty forces." He was particularly pleased when other Americans recognized him simply as an American. "We are not African," he declared. "Certainly to designate us as Negroes is a fraud. We are Americans [and] the sooner we recognize it the better," he added. On July 9 Tanner intensely discussed the United States' caste system with the four other clergy aboard the steamer. Despite the nation's abhorrence of miscegenation, Tanner boldly predicted that within fifty years race intermixture would be common. Tanner's optimism was due to his unyielding faith in the potential of his race to completely adapt to the ways of Anglo-Saxons, unlike the North American Indian, who could accept the white man's vices but not his concept of modern living. While Tanner clearly believed that he was an American, which meant that the principles of a democratic society would offer no barriers to friendship and even marriage across race lines, others were disinclined to respect the message or the messenger. It was impractical for him to assume that by 1931 the nation would openly accept intermarriage between whites and blacks when in 1881 the better class of whites severely frowned upon the thought of licit interracial relationships and coarser white men routinely lynched black men for simply looking provocatively at white women. Even his fellow African Americans disapproved of intermarriage, as witnessed by the hostility displayed by the black press in 1884 to Frederick Douglass's exchange of vows with Helen Pitts.[16]

Tanner arrived in England on July 12 ready for an educational and sightseeing adventure. Four days later the Rev. Marcus Hansen, a Dane and Tanner's stateroom mate, parted company with him. Tanner would have been on "the verge of despair" except for his curiosity to visit more of Europe's sights. After a short trip to France and Switzerland, Tanner spent a week in Belfast, Ireland, attending a convention of the Right Worthy Grand Lodge of the World (Good Templars). The city's residents provided him with a warm welcome, which utterly surprised him. "Are these the same race of [Irish] people who in America delight in mobbing colored Americans?" he inquired. Later, upon returning to his editor's desk, he commented: "[I] wish that the Irish kept their warm nature when they came to America." While he had a right to be pleased with his reception from the Irish, Tanner failed to understand two crucial factors. First, the Irish he met in Belfast were not refugees from a depressed economic system who rushed to America dirt poor and determined to let no man stand in their climb to prosperity, let alone black men who were their immediate competitors. Second, Tanner, or any African person in 1881, was an exotic minority who was not perceived as a social, political or economic threat as would be his counterpart from the Caribbean, Africa, or the Indian subcontinent in the late twentieth century. Then, Tanner was enthusiastically received after speaking passionately about America's caste system to Templars from Africa, Europe, Asia, Australia, and North America. Henry Browne, editor of the London *Good Templar Pioneer*, informed Theodore Gould by mail, September 17, that Tanner was special to Templars because of his "fearless and Christian denunciation of 'caste' which would ostracize his entire race from all civilized society."[17]

A rejuvenated Tanner bade farewell to England on September 21 as he boarded the *Erin*, arriving home on October 6. On October 27, he attended a meeting in Connecticut to organize a Good Templars lodge for black members, which was formally done on November 3, with Tanner as an elected officer.[18] Later in the year he was elected a corresponding member of the New England Methodist Historical Society, and on January 26, 1882, he was elected to office in a racially mixed New Jersey branch of the Grand Lodge of Good Templars.[19]

Tanner's acceptance by Templars in Belfast exposed him for the first time in his life to the reality of a world where men were indeed brothers in Christ. He was not viewed with scorn or singled out for his "nigger blood"; he was genuinely accepted for his intellect and character and not rejected for his color or race. He wrote for the October 13 issue of the *Recorder*, "With a better feeling and a higher appreciation of human nature [I] understand that feelings of white supremacy and contempt for people of African descent had not contaminated Western Europe on a scale comparable to that in the United States." In the December 22 *Recorder*, Tanner admitted that he began his essay with thoughts about "a better feeling" because, although the fight against caste had made him cynical and narrow, he had now decided to be more positive and to avoid confrontation with men, races, or the church. In October 1882 he admitted that previously he only read and considered things that related to black people, which made his thinking and information narrow. He vowed now to think and act as an American, not a black man. This represented a major shift in his thinking. Tanner would address himself more and more to preparing his people to emulate the best in American culture or suffer the consequences of the Australian aborigine. He urged black men and women to obtain money and education and to become more pious in order to "lift [themselves] out of the condition of dwarfs."[20]

This proved to be a watershed in his life, for before the trip to Europe Tanner, stung by the contemptuous behavior of racists, sought to arm himself with racial propaganda ammunition to hurl in their faces the achievements of his people. Race and color defined everything in his life. It dictated his choice of intimate friends, the associations he held membership in, and even the church he chose to associate with. For him, to live as an American offered more possibilities than simply to exist as a black man, because if he thought of himself in terms of color others would continue to judge him as an excellent "colored" editor rather than the accolade he preferred: an excellent American editor. As an American, he or anyone else of color would compete with the nation's best. As black people, they were limiting themselves to a small arena where few would glance. This is not to say, however, that Tanner now shunned all things associated with colored society, for he was too much of a realist to believe that racism and prejudice were near extinction. From now on, his editorials urged the race to rise above the status others had placed them in and to make themselves indispensable to the nation not as men and women of color but as Americans.

Tanner suggested that black Americans emulate British Quakers, who with their small population of fifteen thousand wielded influence out of proportion to their numbers. He was concerned that the eight hundred white emigrants who returned with him on the *Erin* would push aside his people unless the latter gave up their cigars, billiards, and liquor. He called for black men to emulate a local black boatmaker who rose above the rigidity of American caste.[21] Tanner feared that many adopted vices or took short cuts because "white people do it." Do not! he admonished, for whites are stronger and wealthier and can do such things without cost to their race, but black people who emulated their actions would be crushed. Instead, he suggested that they emulate the best of white ways and buy homes, obtain education, acquire stocks and bonds, and seek a life of refinement. He urged the southern brethren not to give up the mechanical positions they had to be slaves in the kitchen or cotton field. Stop cursing, he scolded young men, for God curses those who use His name in vain.[22] Tanner knew that most of the race, less than twenty years out of bondage, were not in positions to acquire homes, knowledge, and financial security, but he wanted them to believe that these and more were within reach if only they would learn to stop dressing like peacocks and attempting to impress others with their spending power.

Tanner felt a particular responsibility to warn the race to question the wisdom of sanctioning segregated facilities, regardless of their modern condition. On November 3, 1881, two thousand attended a meeting for the purpose of erecting a black YMCA in New York City, but Tanner challenged the value of black New Yorkers raising fifty thousand dollars for a structure that "proposes keeping apart the white people and colored people of the country." He admitted that American prejudice forced him to remain in a black church. Like Bishop John M. Brown, he would not belong to a black church if he lived in England, where men were not judged by their color.[23]

It was Tanner's insistence that black people master the ways of the technically advanced Anglo-Saxon that led him to castigate Edward W. Blyden, president of Liberia College, in November 1881 for ordering the principal of the college's preparatory department to stop teaching English to any but the younger pupils. Blyden believed that the language degraded blacks by subjecting them to ideas and expressions inconsistent with their self-respect. Tanner responded that slavery caused the enslaved to acquire the language, civilization, and religion of the master race, which made blacks potentially superior to red, brown, and yellow people as well as to Europeans of the Levant. Indeed, he argued, God Himself joined black and white together; therefore, it would be foolish for the black man to break away from the white man, who was destined to rule for centuries.[24]

Tanner's criticism of Blyden overlooked the Liberian's concern with cultural imperialism. A linguist, Blyden clearly understood the power of language, particularly when it was used to elevate Europeans over the supposedly backward races. Unlike Tanner, Blyden recognized that some Africans were rejecting their cultural and racial heritage by adopting European surnames and disdain for indigenous African art, music, or religion. English was simply a manifestation of European imperialism that Blyden feared, and he sought to limit English instruction to young children and was determined not to have the language corrupt older students. In contrast, Tanner, who was blind to African culture, saw nothing uplifting in a land that had not embraced Jesus Christ's teachings. Tanner saw in Africa's millions not lost cousins of African Americans but rather souls to save for Christ, with the instrument being the African Methodist Episcopal Church. Thus he supported the return of the Rev. Santania Francis Flegler, who in 1881 was in the United States visiting with his family. Now a bishop no longer concerned with maintaining harmony with the editor, Henry M. Turner viewed Tanner as indifferent to the church's African mission work. He expressed sorrow that Tanner had not gone to Europe years ago; the church would have benefited from his absence, "for no man is so much responsible for the missionary apathy. . . as you," he accused. Turner criticized the editor for failing to use his pen to drum up support for mission work; in this respect he believed that Tanner wielded more influence than any bishop, including himself. The mission attack was simply a cover for Turner's real concern, which was his disturbance over Tanner's failure to print significant articles about Africa. He urged Tanner to use his editorial power to arouse the church. "Do not try to make me responsible for your sins [of omission]. You, more than any [other,] . . . are culpable for the mission-ary apathy of our church," he thundered.

It was true that Tanner printed few essays about Africa, but he did not re-spond with venom to Turner's harsh indictment. He replied instead with cool-ness. Virtually ignoring the bishop's charges, Tanner once more admitted his pre-vious obsession with caste prejudice by stating that the race needed to respond less to white prejudice and concentrate more on individual and collective devel-opment. He vowed that this would be his last quadrennial as editor, a decision he reached while crossing the ocean. Tanner promised "to pursue the even tenor of life, till we pass from the fatiguing toil below to the refreshing toil above." De-spite his calm response, Tanner was struck by Turner's accusations, and he re-sponded by printing more general-interest articles on Africa, including a letter from President Anthony W. Gardner of Liberia to William Coppinger, secretary of the American Colonization Society.[25]

Once again, the personalities of the two men, Turner and Tanner, caused a rift where none should have existed. A pragmatist, Tanner clearly understood that the church's finances could not sustain a costly missionary endeavor. Despite its 402,636 members in 1882, the A.M.E. Church had to raise fifty thousand dol-lars to construct Metropolitan Church in Washington, D.C. (soon to be the connection's flagship church), collect funds from nonpaying *Recorder* subscrib-ers, fix Wilberforce University's crumbling buildings, and come up with seven thousand dollars in back pay for a patient but long-suffering faculty.[26]

It was wrong for Turner to blame Tanner for the church's failure in the Afri-can mission field, for the latter showed his support with his eloquent delivery of a sermon at the 1880 General Conference. Taking his text from Psalms 72:19, "And let the whole world be filled with his glory," Tanner noted that both Charles W. Mossell in Haiti and Santania F. Flegler in Africa were "doing grandly" but that it was "only for the general conference to *legislate that the good work shall be accelerated* [emphasis added]." Turner's blatant criticism would have been better directed at the church's missionary society, which raised $34,800.41 between May 1880 and May 1884 while spending $36,112.81.[27]

Tanner's failure to write an autobiography and the loss or destruction of his journals make it difficult to completely understand his thinking at this time. His editorials in the *Recorder*, however, offer some insights. These public rather than private jottings reveal a man who while professing his American identity was will-ing to listen to other voices regarding Africa. The truce that existed between Tan-ner and Turner while they labored together on behalf of the *Recorder* was now shattered by Turner's harsh criticism, which led to an exchange of opinions in the *Recorder* involving them, Blyden, and the subject of African regeneration. Blyden wrote to Tanner on January 24, 1882, that "Turner's view about Africa and as to the work [emigration] to be done here are astonishingly correct." He warned Tanner to be selective in what he wrote about African regeneration because his words might "indirectly influence millions now destitute of your high Christian principles." Tanner was so impressed with Blyden's declaration that whites must learn to respect the Negro, capitalize his name, and eschew the epithet "nigger" that he expressed hope that the exchanges would carry his letter. Tanner believed in Liberia's development, but not at the expense of sending to her 250,000 of America's best Negro blood. He publicly defended the character of the African republic's citizens when a German claimed that the colonists did nothing to regenerate Africa. When it was suggested in 1885 that black Americans donate one dollar each, or one million dollars, to help alleviate Liberia's debt, Tanner wrote, "Agreed. Here is our dollar. Who is ready to receive it?"[28]

Tanner's dollar support for Liberia underlined the dilemma that he and others of African descent faced. They were Americans by birth, culture, and values, but they recognized that they were also children of Africa if not inheritors of the continent's cultural and religious ethos. While Tanner aspired to be accepted by American whites as simply another American, he could not deny his color and features, which despite their dilution reminded all of his African ancestry. The August 17, 1882, *Recorder* contained a remarkable Tanner editorial, "The Blood That Is in Us," which attributed the lack of race harmony to "the humble and broken spirit of the Negro-African blood which comes through our veins." The multiracial black person was a victim of diversity, argued Tanner. "If only we will allow our Teutonic blood to measurably neutralize our Latin, all will be well," he added. To advocates of pure blood such as Blyden, the editor concluded, "Were we of Negro-African descent pure and simple, then would we expect to find harmony among us." This editorial was remarkable in several respects. First, Tanner understood the fallacy of pure-blood theories; therefore, it was an anomaly for him to even mention the subject. But once he did, it was significant that he accepted Teutonic blood as the arbiter over others. Thus, he believed that national (racial) behavior was determined by blood, e.g., Latins were emotional whereas Anglo-Saxons were rational. His ignorance of Africa made him assume that all Africans, regardless of whether they were from the highlands of East Africa or the rain forests of West Africa, shared a common personality or temperament. He believed that the Anglo-Saxon differed in temperament from the Spaniard or Italian, but he was unable to detect differences in temperament between the Ashanti of the Gold Coast and the Amhara of Ethiopia. Second, Tanner did not like the use of the term "Negro" to represent the black people of the United States, who were, in his estimation, superior to other Africans in the diaspora. While "Negro-African" might serve as the appellation of a race, "individually," he asserted, "let the title that distinguishes us be that of some talent possessed, some culture attained. More than this we do not wish; and more than this we . . . will not have." For this reason, he rejected the suggestion that black Americans were "Americo-Africans." If origin must be mentioned, Tanner preferred "Africo-Americans," because "the former trenches altogether too largely upon our Americanism." He continued to insist, "We are Americans and the sooner we realize it and act upon it, the better for all concerned."[29]

Despite his statement on the disharmony caused by mixed blood, Tanner vehemently disagreed with John Smyth, the United States consul in Liberia, who declared in June 1882 that the race should maintain self-respect by not mixing their blood. Tanner dismissed his comment as "twaddle upon a hot June day." He accused Smyth and Blyden of wanting to remove the black man from Western civilization. Tanner boldly predicted that the cessation of prejudice would sever the black American connection to Africa. Blyden quickly responded to Tanner's "Negro-African" editorial. The mixing of blood, he asserted, may allow the African to cope successfully with a race that in his pure state he differed so much from or it may conversely allow Europeans to have a tool to divide and neutralize "the strength of the whole." He graciously thanked Tanner for writing on a subject that most showed no interest in.[30] Tanner obviously accepted Blyden's first point while rejecting the second.

Blyden's second letter to Tanner, dated September 12, called for Christians to combat Islam in Africa. Tanner concurred with Blyden's call to redeem "Negro Africans from barbarism and superstition," but he rejected his pure-blood theories because Americans had the blood of all races in their veins. Blyden was wrong, he declared, to ask black Americans to "link their destiny to the Negro of Africa." We cannot, he added, for we are "simply black white men . . . who have lost everything that relates to Africa save our color, and have found everything that relates to America save the same; and in both instances this exception is being nullified." Again, he expressed his opposition to a large exodus of black persons to Africa. We will help Africa but not at our expense, he declared.[31]

While Tanner was cool in his response to Blyden's plan for African regeneration, the editor admired the Liberian for his scholarship and confessed it surpassed his own. However, Tanner considered Blyden out of line for wanting to "develop the Negro African on the plane of his color and 'race.'" While Tanner sought to downplay the significance of color and race in determining national greatness, he, too, expressed pride in Africa's glorious past. Tanner in 1882 and 1883 offered praise for African contributions to world civilization. Long before archeologists suggested that our common ancestor came from Africa, Tanner stated that the Western world was "black" because its racial roots were in Ham and its religious roots in Shem. He encouraged people to read Herodotus and the Jewish chronicles to know of Africa's greatness. In his critique of George Washington Williams's pioneer 1883 study, History of the Negro Race in America, Tanner exclaimed that "we must write our own past; we must give our own interpretation and color to its great facts." Evidently, Tanner's choice of the word "color" was deliberate because he believed that white scholars purposefully omitted Africans from ancient history. Tanner urged people to master both Western and Eastern lore, for "that will enable us to more . . . speedily put a right value upon the statements of white historians and white scholars in general." This insistence on Tanner's part to examine and question the Eurocentric domination of historical inquiry made him—along with Williams, and later Carter G. Woodson, who in 1915 founded the Association for the Study of Negro Life and History and in 1916 the impressive *Journal of Negro History,* and W. E. B. Du Bois, to name a few—a pioneer figure in black intellectual scholarship. His criticism of European biblical scholars who ignored the African presence in the Bible would later influence a number of younger scholars whose assertions about Africa's achievements have generated controversy among traditionalists.[32]

Blyden visited Tanner on November 5, 1882. Four days later Tanner wrote in the *Recorder* that he was flattered to think of Blyden as a friend. He still was troubled, however, by Blyden's race theories and considered his influence in the United States as harmful to black people. Tanner saw in the recruitment of T. McCants Stewart, pastor of Sullivan Street A.M.E. Church, New York City, to teach at Liberia College an example of Blyden raiding the country of its best and brightest black talent. On December 14 Tanner wrote that Blyden strained credibility by stating in Richmond, Virginia, that a subordinate race could not rise to the level of a superior race when the two coexisted.[33]

Stewart sided against Tanner with a vengeance that both puzzled and pained the editor. Stewart was disturbed that Tanner, author of "Our Fathers' Church," a popular A.M.E. hymn, advocated Americanization since the hymn suggested "an antidote for the poison of possible miscegenation." Stewart accused the editor of calling for Negroes to shed their race identity "in the sea of amalgamation." Stewart wrote that the moving words of Tanner's hymn, "our fathers' church, our mothers' church is just the church for me," would read "our fathers' church, our mothers' church is not the church for me" if Americanization occurred. Puzzled, Tanner replied that only followers of Blyden would think that he wrote an antidote to miscegenation. He denied that "miscegenation [is] a poison! That is, a black man marrying a white woman. Out, we say, with all such stuff." Pained and irritated by Stewart's accusation, Tanner added that if people believed Stewart's interpretation of his hymn's meaning, "a strong effort would be made to recall the thousand of copies abroad and [burn them]," for he wrote a hymn that could be sung by any Christian who believed in the glory of their fathers' church. Tanner strongly "object[ed] to having to do service either in the interest of unchristian clannishness or unchristian bigotry."[34]

Despite his belief that the destiny of the race was tied to American soil, Tanner continued to be interested in Africa and its development, particularly Liberia, to which thousands of African Americans had migrated before and after the American Civil War. He urged black Americans to take an interest in Africa in order to be in a position to influence their government's economic ventures. "When we shall be able to speak with the authority a million votes will give us Africa will receive more attention than now," he declared.[35]

Tanner continued to believe that American blacks were better off staying in America, where they were needed to develop resources for their own advancement. Therefore, his opposition to African emigration did not lessen. In particular, he objected to the American Colonization Society's effort to influence the secretary of state's selection of a consul general for Liberia. The ACS suggested to Secretary Frederick T. Frelinghuysen in July 1882 that John Smyth, who was replaced by the prominent black abolitionist Henry H. Garnet in 1881, be appointed to fill the vacancy caused by the death of his successor. Tanner wrote that the ACS had no business nominating diplomats. The Pennsylvania branch of the ACS, aware of Tanner's influence, invited him in late 1882 to speak and to suggest six black leaders to meet with them. Tanner invited the Rev. Dr. J. B. Reeve, pastor of Philadelphia's Lombard Street Presbyterian Church and a former Howard University professor; the Rev. Dr. T. Doughty Miller, pastor of the city's Cherry Street Baptist Church; Theodore Gould, manager of the A.M.E. publication department; the Rev. Charles T. Schaffer, an A.M.E. minister; the Rev. Matthew Anderson, pastor of Philadelphia's Berean Presbyterian Church; and the Rev. B. F. Combash. Tanner bluntly informed the ACS delegation that its members accepted the dogma that the United States was a white man's country. He also stated that southern blacks would not desire to leave the country if they were guaranteed their civil and political rights. Bishop Turner objected to three of the delegates selected by Tanner because he did not know them or did not think that they knew the sentiment of the people on the emigration question. Tanner responded that he traveled widely in the country and believed that he knew the mind of the thoughtful, literate people, implying that Turner's supporters were either emotional or ignorant. Again, Tanner accused Blyden of clouding the issue by stirring up problems between the races. We are not aliens in America, Tanner declared. "Go to work, get land, and money and trade and education," was his advice to the disenchanted. Several readers supported Tanner's contention that Blyden and Turner were misleading the public about Africa. Peyton M. Lewis of Baltimore complained that Turner had no African experience, thus no real idea of what Africans needed. The Rev. J. A. Scott of Staunton, Virginia, described Africa as a place for heathens who practice idolatry.[36]

Blyden, the center of the controversy, was traveling in the United States during the winter of 1883. On February 6 he wrote from Washington, D.C., to Tanner with thanks to the editor for not misrepresenting his views, as others had done, and for providing space in the *Recorder,* which contributed to his success in the United States. Blyden emphasized that he did not endorse wholesale emigration, which would damage American race relations. Tanner agreed with Blyden that Africans should control Africa and Americans should control America, but he could not accept Blyden's and Turner's contention that America would always be a white man's country; instead, Tanner argued that the future America would be neither white nor black but bronze.[37] Again Tanner's belief that the near future would witness a transformation in race relations as well as a preference of many for interracial marriages was not justified either by the laws or mores that deemed white women "angelic and pure" and black men "brutes" determined to ravish white flesh.

While Tanner seemed to like Blyden personally, the same could not be said for his relationship with Turner. Tanner printed in the *Recorder*'s February 27 issue Turner's letter from Morrilton, Arkansas, whereby the bishop reiterated his theme of American oppression and African opportunity, which Tanner summarily dismissed in his editorial of the same date. Tanner's lack of respect for Turner's view led to the *Washington Bee* declaring, "Bishop Turner has it in for Dr. Tanner. Look out doctor, you have insulted the bishop."[38]

In mid-March 1883 Blyden, Tanner, and Turner were in Washington, D.C., to attend different events. Tanner spoke on March 13 at Union Bethel A.M.E. Church's Literary Society on the subject "the year 2000 and what of it." The *Bee* described an attentive audience of writers, lawyers, physicians, soldiers, sailors, musicians, artists, and mechanics, precisely the types that Tanner saw helping black people fulfill their destiny in the United States. Two days later, Turner hosted a dinner in his home for Blyden. The impressive guest list included A.M.E. Bishops John M. Brown and T. M. D. Ward; Francis L. Cardozo, former black secretary of state of South Carolina; Major Martin R. Delany, African explorer; James A. Handy; and Francis J. Grimké, pastor of the Fifteenth Street Presbyterian Church. Cardozo expressed surprise that anyone objected to Blyden's suggestion that one hundred thousand or one million black persons emigrate to Africa, because there would still be enough remaining to solve the race problem. Blyden said that he would welcome the day when the formerly enslaved of America brought their acquired civilization and Christianity to rescue Africa from barbarism and degradation.[39]

Several weeks later, Blyden and Tanner had an opportunity to discuss their differences when they were among the twenty guests of A.M.E. Bishop J. P. Campbell in his Philadelphia home. Their conversation was not recorded, but while Tanner refused to yield his position on emigration, he continued to allow Blyden and his supporters an outlet for their message. In 1885, the year after assuming the editor's position of the *A.M.E. Church Review,* Tanner printed the result of a symposium, "What Should Be the Policy of Colored Americans toward Africa."[40]

Tanner's position was clear. America was the destiny of the black man because the future American would be "a happy mingling of the Japhetic, Hamitic and Shemitic blood[;] a oneness in color, if not in character, will be produced," he predicted. Tanner believed that American food, geography, and environmental factors would create a continental race with no physical or racial similarities to Africans, Europeans, or Asians and that amalgamation would be the norm. On May 13, 1884, Tanner presented to the Bethel A.M.E. Church's Literary Society in Washington a paper, "The Coming American Race—What Is It to Be?" with the conclusion that the future American would be one-eighth black and seven-eighths white with "a motley of yellow." He offered no formula for his figures, but presumably it was based on the numerical superiority of the white population. To his credit, Tanner recognized that racial prejudice and European immigration would slow the process, but he believed that amalgamation was inevitable. He favorably quoted "The Problem of Our African Population" by the Rev. Abel Stevens and E. V. Smalley's essay "The German Element in the United States" to illustrate that the American melting pot would in a century or so absorb all her diverse peoples into one. Tanner urged those who insisted on an "African destiny" to read Smalley's article, which described the impending integration of German immigrants as a harbinger of the African's fate in the United States. "There is nothing to do but surrender to an American destiny," suggested Tanner, for in the future America "no one is to rule the other, unless by superior ability to demonstrate its right to rule."[41]

The radical amalgamation theory of Smalley, Stevens, and Tanner had few supporters. One supporter was the Rev. Theophilus G. Steward, who argued in the April 26, 1883, *Recorder* that unless America changed its concept of race, the republic would be nothing but a dream. He recommended the dropping of the term "white race" in favor of "the American people." Steward noted that America had the opportunity to exult "the oneness of the entire species," which would "give to the progress of mankind a contribution not European, Asiatic or African but a contribution blending the best element of all these—the typical American." Another voice of support came from Henry O. Tanner, the editor's son, who married Jessie M. Olssen, a white American, in 1899. In 1914 Henry questioned whether he was a Negro. "Does not the $^3/_4$ of English blood in my veins count for anything? Does the $^1/_4$ or $^1/_8$ of 'pure' Negro blood in my veins count for all?" Although Henry's fractions were reversed, his sentiment was clear: is "race" determined by biology or by cultural choice? Clearly, both Tanners believed that racial classifications should be eradicated.[42]

Many of both races objected to Tanner's assertion that race should be irrelevant. Of course, white racists dismissed as preposterous the notion that the "savage" Negro could ever be assimilated. Late-nineteenth-century social scientists argued that races were either "superior," "inferior," or "decadent," with the Anglo-Saxon heading the list while the African ranked barely above the apes, monkeys, and gorillas in the evolutionary scale. Many believed that blacks with a large admixture of white blood might attain an eminence equal to that of the bottom rung of Anglo-Saxons but would revert to savagery if removed from "civilizing" influences.[43]

Black critics of Tanner's theory included Alexander Crummell and W. E. B. Du Bois. In 1875 Crummell delivered a Thanksgiving sermon, "The Social Principle among a People and Its Bearing on Their Progress and Development," ridiculing the idea that black men should divorce themselves from organizations because they benefited only black men. Crummell urged his audience not to deny their racial identity or to "give up all distinctive effort, as colored men, in schools, churches, associations, and friendly societies." Like Tanner, he believed that caste and race distinctions needed to be eliminated. But unlike Tanner, Crummell urged blacks to "strive for footing and for superiority in this land, on the line of race as a temporary but needed expedient." W. E. B. Du Bois in 1897 specified that "the conservation of the races" was necessary because "the history of the world is the history . . . of races, and he who ignores or seeks to override the race idea in human history ignores and overrides the central thought of all history." Du Bois warned against imitation, which would lead to absorption. He called upon blacks to seek "a stalwart originality which shall unswervingly follow Negro ideals," and he acknowledged that an accident of birth made the Negro an American by citizenship, language, religion, and political ideals, but "farther than that our Americanism does not go." Black Americans were duty bound to "strive by race organization, by race solidarity, by race unity to the realization of that broader humanity which freely recognize differences in men, but sternly deprecates inequality in their opportunities of development," Du Bois asserted.[44]

Tanner's outspoken support for racial amalgamation did not blind him to either the perils or prevalence of racism. He believed that whites would accept those black men and women who improved their economic condition, their morality, and their character. This belief paralleled that of Booker T. Washington, but it was one that Tanner held before Washington was born. Starting with the premise that slavery made the African a servant, Tanner called upon the slaves' descendants to stop their obsequious grinning and seek manlier work, because the jobs that they previously monopolized, such as barbers, servants, and waiters, were being taken by European immigrants. He advised the race to create employment for itself or continue to be "underrail." Tanner was pleased in 1882 to see a black-owned restaurant in Atlantic City. He seconded the call of the *Denver Weekly Star* for a black person to establish in that city a hotel for all, since the 1875 Civil Rights Act, he facetiously noted, provided "white people [with] some rights that we colored people are bound to respect." The West was the place to go, suggested Tanner, advising young men to emulate John Shafer, a black man who owned a fancy-goods store worth a hundred thousand dollars in the Dakota territory.[45] He agreed with the *Weekly Star* that black men had to become business-minded or remain "only fit for a slave to the superior race." Tanner wrote that black people were tired of begging and that whites were tired of giving them money for schools, churches, and projects. Instead, he called for whites to provide more than menial jobs for blacks, who if they had such "white" jobs as packing goods, clerking, and printing would be able to do more for themselves, he declared.[46]

Even though Tanner stressed character as a means of advancement, it was clear to many that economic deprivation contributed immensely to the degraded condition many blacks were subjected to in the early 1880s. The denial of decent employment opportunities coupled with the refusal of labor unions to include them as members made it difficult for many men of color to achieve economic parity with white workers. During this decade, Tanner provided contrasting views on labor's need to strike. As a delegate to the 1882 annual meeting of black editors, he offered the following resolution, which was defeated: "While the industrial ostracism practiced against us both by the trade unions and the great monopolies of the country, especially those of the North continues, the Press Convention . . . proclaims its purpose to favor such a radical change in the tariff and in the direction of free trade as will more easily enable us to bear the onerous expectations it makes."[47] Tanner advocated that black workers caught between capital and labor should stand by white labor only when whites reciprocated: "Strike when they strike, and come to terms when they come to terms." "Look out for yourself," he warned, when white laborers are hostile to you. Get work and do it well "and make that that was intended to be temporary, lasting." To those who complained that blacks were strikebreakers, Tanner strongly suggested that they educate black workers individually and southern whites generally; then the South would be on the same level as the North. Strikes will end once the nation realizes that the interests of labor and capital are one, he asserted. However, by 1887, Tanner stopped supporting strikes because he saw the nation's problem rooted in "the money thirst of southern whites and northern white laborers." Interestingly, he asserted that workers sought higher wages to indulge in liquor, clothes, and tobacco—frivolities that kept them impoverished.

David W. Wills's analysis revealed that Tanner's failure to indict northern capitalists was attributable to the eagerness of black clergy to have a "positive relationship to the labor movement." Benjamin F. Lee, editor of the *Christian Recorder* and a future bishop, praised in 1890 the pastor of Shiloh Baptist Church in Philadelphia for securing positions for one hundred black women in a clockmaking establishment after Russian Jewish immigrants struck. "This is an opening which must be followed by many such openings," Lee wrote. The lack of workers' solidarity extended into the twentieth century as whites generally refused the admission of African Americans into the unions. John E. Bruce, better known by his pen name, "Bruce Grit," complained in 1901 that "the trade and labor unions are the greatest enemy of the Negro . . . and are doing more to encourage race hatred and the caste system than any other agency I know of." Equally discouraged was the editor of *The Colored American,* who noted in the following year that, if a civil war ever plagued Americans again, "the asininity of the captains of industry who oppose Negro labor will have a heavy finger in the provocation." With some exceptions, the black Methodist and Baptist clergy and bishops failed to support African American union organizers in their struggles to integrate the unions or to organize black workers. A. Philip Randolph, organizer of the Brotherhood of Sleeping Car Porters, argued in the 1920s that the black clergy offered his men little support because the Pullman Company gave passes, through the A.M.E. bishops and the National Baptist Convention, to the preachers, enabling them to travel half fare.[48]

Tanner greatly admired Booker T. Washington's philosophy of industrial education and believed that it offered the possibility of economic relief for an economically deprived people; therefore, he was one of thirty-eight signers who called for a conference on industrial schools to be held in New Orleans on January 15, 1885, because he wanted black men and women to "ennoble themselves" by being of "value to the state." Tanner preferred that black workers, instead of securing employment by breaking strikes, become land owners, hotel keepers, mill operators, and professionals, unfortunately positions that required capital or cooperative development.[49]

Parallel with the dire working opportunities for black persons was their general mistreatment on the nation's public carriers, especially in the former slaveholding states. The difference between North and South, noted Tanner in 1882, was a difference between the spirit of Christianity and the spirit of heathenism. Most northern schools were integrated (he had four children in white schools), and black people were accommodated in hotels and generally traveled without discrimination on railroad cars. In the South, however, discrimination was constant despite the passage of the 1875 Civil Rights Act. In spring 1882, seventy-one-year-old Bishop Payne was removed from a railroad car in Florida and forced to walk five miles in oppressive heat while carrying twenty-seven pounds of luggage because he refused to go to the colored coach, where his ears would be assailed by coarse language from drunken whites. On March 30 a large crowd assembled in Bethel A.M.E. Church on Sullivan Street in New York City to protest Payne's ouster. On April 12 a delegation led by Bishop John M. Brown, Frederick Douglass, and A.M.E. clergymen called upon United States Attorney General B. H. Brewster to complain that his deputy for northern Florida failed to enforce the Civil Rights Act of 1875. Similar discrimination marred the travel plans of Bishops J. P. Campbell in Georgia and Richard H. Cain and his wife in Texas. Tanner joined other speakers on March 24 in Philadelphia to protest against the Atlantic and Western Railroad sending Campbell to the baggage car where animals and smokers were relegated. A.M.E. bishops met on April 26 in Baltimore to plan strategy to elicit support from eminent Christians. Soon after, a delegation from the Florida Annual Conference of the A.M.E. Church marched to the railroad office, where they received an apology and refund for the mistreatment of Payne.[50]

The United States Supreme Court ruled in the fall of 1883 that the 1875 Civil Rights Act was unconstitutional, a decision that provoked a storm of dissent. *New York Globe* editor Timothy T. Fortune remarked that the decision was akin to baptizing black people "in ice water." The *Detroit Plaindealer* wrote that the ruling "comes like an avalanche carrying our fondest hopes down the hill of despair." An embittered Tanner thundered that if whites insisted on widening the breach between the races, the day would come when a strong angry group of blacks would respond with action. "The underrail cannot be destroyed without bringing down the upper," he warned. Again, he told readers to "husband . . . resources . . . preserve health, get information [and] know . . . that you must depend upon yourself." This militant statement did not mean that he had lost faith in the republic; Tanner believed that the legal ability of Congress, which enacted the 1875 Civil Rights Act, and of President Grant, who signed it into law, was greater than that of the seven justices who rendered the ruling.[51]

The Supreme Court's decision reflected the nation's changing mood toward civil rights issues as well as the declining influence of black people on white politicians. Most blacks rigidly adhered to the Republican party despite the call of a few mavericks who advised them to become Democrats or support independent politics. By 1880 the reactionary policy of President Rutherford B. Hayes, scientific racism, and desires for economic expansion led to the Republicans treating freedmen as stepchildren.

Although in February 1882 Tanner criticized preachers who proclaimed allegiance to a particular wing of a political party, by July he proclaimed his lack of respect for those black men who advocated breaking with the Republican party in the North and uniting with southern Democrats. To do so, he argued, would make the race prey "to the meanest and most unprincipled party that ever existed in a popular government." Instead, he urged them to improve themselves educationally and financially in order to force the Republicans to take them seriously. When Timothy T. Fortune, George Downing, a Rhode Island caterer and restaurateur, T. McCants Stewart, James Monroe Trotter, a former member of the famed Civil War Fifty-fourth Massachusetts Colored Infantry Regiment, and Peter Clark, a Cincinnati principal, called for political independence, Tanner challenged their logic.

Tanner believed that black independents were dupes of southern Democrats and would take votes away from the Republicans. After Fortune wrote, "We cannot . . . explain the knuckle close policy of" Tanner, the editor responded that independents could not win, that the race needed friends to defend their rights, and that Republicans had not oppressed them as had the Democrats.[52]

Meanwhile, in 1882 Ohio Republicans lost the state elections, which prompted Tanner to credit the defeat to a combination of German Americans' dislike of the state's temperance movement, dissatisfaction with the policies of President Chester A. Arthur, and the decision of black voters to remain home on election day. Tanner added that the old issue of states' rights versus abolitionism was irrelevant and that people trusted democracy to work regardless of which party was in office. He stated that he no longer cared if one party was pro-slavery or not as he vowed to support the party that supported temperance, national education, and free trade. The race needed to be the ally of a strong political party until its members were strong enough to control their own destiny, he wrote after the Republican defeat. This was an amazing assessment that even Tanner did not advocate for long. In 1883 he described Democrats as favoring rum in the North and the Ku Klux Klan in the South. "Let the colored men . . . be prepared to save the nation next year from falling into the hands of a party who . . . stands to steal our rights," warned Tanner.

In early 1884, mindful that many feared that the removal of the Republicans from the White House would lead to reenslavement, Tanner wrote an editorial, "Vote at All Hazards," imploring southern black men to resist atrocities and vote or the nation "will drop us." Although A.M.E. minister J. C. Embry of San Antonio, Texas, dismissed Tanner's comments as foolhardy, Tanner replied that southern black editors agreed with him. It was time, he said, for black roughs to meet white roughs, which he admitted was his most warlike statement since he became editor in 1868. Tanner's philosophy was simple: vote in the South and face scrimmages; fail to vote and face extermination. So confident was Tanner that a voting race would achieve positive results, he beseeched northern black men to "stop hanging around corners and billiard saloons" and go south, where the field was ripe for harvest as teachers and entrepreneurs.[53] In a speech by John E. Bruce on October 5, 1883, the journalist referred to men who did not protect their families as "moral cowards." He advocated "organized resistance" as the "best remedy for the solution of the vexed problem." Even though the black population outnumbered whites in some southern areas, northern militants failed to appreciate the fact that blacks lacked the firepower and overall community support (the white legal and political system) to wage a retaliatory war. The courts would not prosecute white southerners who massacred black men, and lynch mobs had the means to take care of agitators with the full understanding that neither local, state, nor federal officials would interfere.

In early June 1884, Tanner reluctantly endorsed the Republican ticket of James G. Blaine and John A. Logan. He did not care for Blaine's anti-Chinese sentiment, nor did he think that Logan was presidential material, but he considered the Republicans to be a better party for black people. He warned black Democrats to learn to distinguish between persons and parties; otherwise the race would become a cipher. The Democrats, Tanner noted, were "bad in the past, bad in present and would probably be bad in the future."[54]

Tanner's political philosophy was antithetical to that of Timothy T. Fortune, who declared in 1883, "We do not ask the corrupt Republican party for its sympathy. We spurn it with loathing contempt." Few rank-and-file black Republicans supported political independence. Rather, they despised those black men who supported the Democratic party. For instance, when a former Virginia slave died shortly after he voted for the Democrats, the "Negroes refused to attend the funeral, and the service was conducted by . . . a white minister, and he was buried by white men."[55] Others, such as the Rev. Theophilus G. Steward, believed on the eve of the 1884 presidential elections that a Republican defeat would signal a "providential retribution for their indifference and pusillanimity in dealing with the Negro vote." The election of Grover Cleveland confirmed Steward's prediction, but many feared that his victory might lead to their reenslavement. To assuage their fear, the *A.M.E. Church Review* devoted over thirty pages to the meaning of the Democrats' return to power.[56]

Tanner's support for the national Republican ticket did not blind him to the need to support progressive local politicians. In 1881 Robert Purvis and Will Still, prominent black Philadelphians, supported the candidacy of mayoral aspirant Samuel G. King, who won with the help of Democrats, independents, and maverick Republicans. King appointed thirty-five black men to the city's police force, but his progressivism cost him reelection in 1884. On April 4 Tanner and twenty-five other black men expressed their gratitude to him in short speeches. Soon after taking office, Republican Mayor William Smith dismissed most of King's appointees while adding to the police force black officers of his choice. The black politicians who had supported King quickly returned to the Republican fold, chastened.[57]

A month after meeting with King, Tanner attended the Seventeenth Quadrennial Session of the General Conference of the A.M.E. Church. As time drew near for him to attend his last conference as editor of the *Recorder*, Tanner reflected on his sixteen years' service to the church. Often, his health was poor; on several occasions he was forced to his bed by nervous prostration. He had traveled to thirty-two states. The demands of his office made him nearly a slave to his desk. The lack of finances made his office an extremely stressful environment. The *Recorder* was often the battleground for the church's fights. Tanner's judgment was tested. How far he should go with a controversy left him fatigued. Yet he was proud that he had transformed the *Recorder* from "a small yet fiery sheet . . . into a giant in the literary world." Bishop Levi J. Coppin recalled in 1923 that Tanner made the paper one that Christians could read "with profit, without leaving in the minds of the youth suggestions that would not be morally elevating." The *Sentinel* (Trenton, N.J.) critiqued the *Recorder* as favorably, saying that there was "no abler enemy of the flesh and devil in the United States." The Rev. B. W. Arnett declared that Tanner "wields the most facile pen of any man in the country. His pen is sharper than his razor, and his editorial chair is finer than his barber chair."[58]

During Tanner's sixteen-year tenure, the *Recorder* was the most influential black newspaper in the United States. Tanner provided an outlet for the nation's race leaders to express their often contrasting approaches to blacks' social, educational, political, economic, and religious development.[59] Despite the accolades, Tanner did produce blunders, of which he admitted to two. The first was when he joined an unidentified manager of the publication department in money battles, which interfered with Tanner's editorial responsibilities. His second blunder was his failure to "have allowed the parties dissatisfied to have done the same."[60] On a more serious level, Tanner used poor judgment in printing an inflammatory article without reading it first. In 1881, the Rev. J. C. Embry stated that some church leaders had bought and sold appointments, while some traveled to Europe at the church's expense. Tanner considered the publication of Embry's diatribe the stupidest thing he had ever done, for the editor should build up and not tear down. He referred to this incident as his "eclipse."[61]

Tanner went to the General Conference with the hope that the delegates would honor his wish to be relieved of the *Recorder*'s editorial responsibilities. Perhaps as a tease, twenty-four loyalists voted for him to remain editor of the *Recorder,* but that honor went to Benjamin F. Lee on the second ballot. Tanner also received one vote out of 157 cast for the publication department's managerial position, which went to J. C. Embry even though some considered Theodore Gould's administration brilliant.[62]

The prize that Tanner wanted and won was the editorship of the new quarterly church magazine, the *A.M.E. Church Review.* Little did Bishop Richard H. Cain realize in 1883 that, when he wrote that he wanted more church news in the *Recorder* (for "we care nothing about John Wanamaker's old clothes, or Saddall's dirt removing soap. We want, and will have, papers which discuss the great moral, social, educational and national questions of this race, and not quack medicines"), he was echoing Tanner's desire for literary liberty. Tanner was unanimously elected editor of the *Review.*[63]

Tanner's responsibilities to the *Recorder* ended in early July 1884; he held on to the reins while Lee, president of Wilberforce University, completed that institution's commencement exercises. Tanner promised in his valedictory editorial to make the *Review* a "real joy." "God bless the old RECORDER," he wrote. "We never knew how dearly we loved it till we were called upon to enter upon another work."[64]

The Tanner family, c. 1890. Left to right: *Isabella, Halle, her daughter Sadie, Henry, Bishop Tanner, Carlton, Mrs. Tanner, Bertha, Sarah, and Mary. Courtesy of the University of Pennsylvania Archives.*

Tanner c. 1923. Courtesy of the University of Pennsylvania Archives.

Chapter 6

A.M.E. Church Review, 1884–1888
A Literary Expression of a Race

Bishop Daniel A. Payne was the impetus behind the development of the *Review*. Diminutive, ascetic, and eccentric (he would not sleep in a room without a stove), Payne was a strong believer in the liberating power of knowledge, as he believed that blacks were victimized by their ignorance. The bishop mastered mathematics, English, Latin, Greek, and French, and for years he was a staunch advocate of an educated ministry. Payne so intimidated A.M.E. ministers with his scholarly attainments that an associate observed that "many of the preachers [were] so eager to appear literary to [him] that they [ran] and [got] a book and stuck it under their arm when they [saw] him coming."[1]

The *A.M.E. Church Review* had its genesis in 1841 with the introduction of the *A.M.E. Magazine,* which was intended as a weekly but became a quarterly until its demise in 1848. From 1858 to 1864 John M. Brown edited the *Repository of Religion and Literature.* In 1876 Tanner, recognizing that many talented African Methodist writers lacked an outlet for their literary skills, wrote in the *Christian Recorder,* "Let [the] General Conference but give us a 'Quarterly,' and we will show some folks what we really can do." For those who doubted that the church had the capacity to publish a literary magazine, Tanner retorted that he knew the intellectual capabilities of the connection more than anyone else and that the formation of a quarterly would bring credit to the church and to the race. Rufus Perry, editor of the Baptist *National Monitor,* seconded Tanner's call. "Let . . . Tanner's suggestion be adopted . . . that the fruits of that scholarship may be plucked and tasted by the hungry," he exclaimed. The Rev. A. C. Crippen added that the educated ministry was ready for a quarterly and would read it if it contained no quarterly meeting suppers, festival fairs, cake walks, grand rallies, or other superficial reading.[2]

Tanner's call for a quarterly was well received by William Steward, then assistant manager of the publication department, who addressed the 1879 National Conference of Colored Men of the United States meeting in Nashville, Tennessee, on "The Necessity of a National Review Devoted to the Interests of the Negro American." Such a review, Steward declared, would provide more mature thought and more candid opinions than dailies or weeklies. He further noted that a well-edited quarterly would compel quotations in the nation's leading white newspapers. Steward hit on a key point, for too many of the race's great minds utilized the white press as an outlet for their best thoughts. "For them to fill our tiny journals with their rich, ripe treasures of their minds would be worse than casting pearls before swine," stated Steward, because "their thoughts and judgments and opinions would be lost to the world. They must go to the journals of the whites and lose their race identity." Tanner echoed this last point in 1880 with the observation that if Frederick Douglass and other leaders stopped "communicating with any white paper, however liberal it may be," whites would respect black publications more, which would make the people prouder of their race.[3]

A cry for a quarterly was given greater incentive by the support of the outgoing manager of the publication department, Henry M. Turner, who on the eve of the 1880 A.M.E. General Conference recommended the establishment of a quarterly review. "Shame on us if we fail to provide for it," he remarked.[4] Two years later, the church, while not committing to a quarterly, organized a monthly literary and religious magazine under the auspices of the Connectional Historical and Literary Association, which Turner presided over. The editor- and publisher-elect was Benjamin W. Arnett, who hoped to have the first issue by July 1882. The magazine was not published by November, and the first issue was deferred to sometime in 1883 because Arnett was tending to his dying mother. It is not known if the magazine was ever published.[5]

During the spring of 1883, Theophilus G. Steward formed the Theological, Scientific, and Literary Association of the A.M.E. Church (TAWAWA) to promote habits of reading and studying in nature, art, science, and secular and sacred literature in order that knowledge could be acquired by those with limited education. Students would read one hour daily and take annual examinations by correspondence.[6]

TAWAWA whetted the appetite of African Methodists for a literary magazine. The June 14, 1883, issue of the *Recorder* printed Paul Quinn College professor Paul Kealing's hope that Tanner would "gladly accept the position of 'agitator,' a role, as it relates to a magazine, he has been essaying to play in the years past." He added, "The church is about ready to take the work in hand, so manifest is the want."[7]

Tanner reported in December that the magazine was due in January and that it would have submissions from the race's intellectuals in the diaspora because "for years we have taken pains to cultivate an acquaintance with this class of personages." In the new year, a cultured West Indian, upon hearing about the forthcoming magazine, wrote, "Hip, Hip, hurrah for the Negro's first magazine."[8] Tanner was eager to present the magazine to the public, for he knew that newspapers presented news whereas magazines contributed scholarship, which could shape or modify white public opinion. Like others who thought of themselves as no different from whites in temperament and taste in literature, political thought, and refinement, Tanner believed that ignorance about black people more than racism was the factor that kept the better elements of both societies from mixing. It was his belief that racial restrictions would ease once whites recognized that some blacks were their intellectual kin worthy of knowing. While no press date had been set in January 1884, Tanner had in hand articles on church history, Haiti, blacks in science, Greek in the New Testament, and art and literature. Rufus Perry declared, "The A.M.E. Church has within its fold all that is necessary to produce a first class magazine, and that we expect to see." But the public enthusiasm for the quarterly was tempered by the publication department's lacking the hundred dollars needed to print the magazine. At the end of May, however, Tanner declared that the first issue would appear in a few weeks because "negro scholarship must be recognized, not by ourselves, but by the world. To this end was our Review born, and to this end it will devote its energies." The General Conference, meeting in May, ordered the publication of the *A.M.E. Church Review,* which Bishop T. M. D. Ward later nicknamed "the cream jug of the church." Bishop Henry M. Turner offered to pay the printing bill for the first issue, but General Conference delegates raised money for the expense.[9]

The long-awaited inaugural issue appeared in July 1884. True to his word, Tanner received submissions from the race's literary, religious, and political luminaries, who out of respect for him did not request compensation. Among them were Bishops Daniel A. Payne, J. P. Campbell, and William F. Dickerson; former United States senator Blanche K. Bruce; Professor William S. Scarborough; D. Augustus Straker, essayist and attorney; author and clergyman Theophilus G. Steward; and poet Frances E. W. Harper. Accolades inundated Tanner's desk. *New York Globe* editor Timothy T. Fortune wrote, "Judging by the standard of excellence by the contributors to this first number . . . , it would bid fair to accomplish the object intended of affording an outlet for Negro scholarship." Bishop Henry M. Turner was delighted with the *Review,* for "a people, race, country or church that has no history has no literature, and where there is no literature there is no development, progress or respectability." The pride of the race was evident, but, praise aside, Tanner apologized for the "dateness" of the articles, which he had had on hold for up to eight months. He was not pleased with all the entries, but his satisfaction came from knowing that there was "room for improvement." Tanner promised to no longer accept advertisements that did not meet his approval. Perhaps he was speaking of advertisements for future issues, because only one announcement, for William Still's book on the Underground Railroad, ran in the first issue.[10]

Tanner's contacts provided him with numerous pieces for publication, but he was not pleased with all that he selected for print. Six months later, Tanner admitted that he did not endorse the views presented by some of the contributors (he did not identify them) and even felt like combating several, "so opposite are they to [my] views." But he understood that the *Review* should not represent the mind of the editor. "On the contrary," he confessed, "the varied thought of the church and the race should be allowed full scope."[11]

A conservative theologian, Tanner had views that often clashed with those of more enlightened thinkers in African Methodism. One such issue was the question of female preachers, which he strongly opposed. In 1880, on the eve of his election to the bishopric, Henry M. Turner suggested that women be permitted to preach because they could not do a worse job than some of the men. Even though the 1844 and 1852 A.M.E. General Conferences defeated petitions calling for ordination of women, many preached in A.M.E. churches, and some of their allies were imposing men. Bishop John M. Brown licensed Emily Calkins Stevens in 1883 to preach in the New Jersey Annual Conference, and two years later Bishop Turner ordained a woman, the Rev. Sarah Ann Hughes, a full member of the A.M.E. body, to the office of deacon, which led to a reprimand from the 1888 General Conference. Formidable opposition, however, came from Tanner, Bishop J. P. Campbell, the Rev. James H. A. Johnson, and others who argued either that women lacked the physical or mental strength associated with the ministry or that neither God, Jesus, nor the disciples sanctioned female preachers. Tanner's stance pleased his spiritual mentor, Bishop Daniel A. Payne, who believed that the ideal woman was a genteel person who devoted her time to home and family or to acceptable social activities in the community or church. However, it contradicted his assessment that he had offered in his 1867 study, *An Apology for African Methodism*: that women were "zealous souls . . . [who] taught not, yet it cannot be said she did not preach." Apparently he did not object so much to women preaching as to their receiving sanction to preach. In other words, Tanner's objection was to women being members of a group that he believed God had sanctioned for men only. Indeed, in his *Dispensations in the History of the Church,* Tanner declared that, although the scriptures offered contradictory views on female preachers—for example, that women could interpret prophecies but were not among Jesus' disciples—the Bible offered no evidence that women should carry on the "ordinary or regular service of the Most High." He concluded that women could not be ordained to preach because God, Christ, and the Holy Spirit do not "sanction it, or set the examples." Still, he noted that women were eligible to be prophets, evangelists, or helpers.

Contrasting with this orthodox assessment was the enlightened viewpoint projected by others who accused Tanner of quibbling semantically since women in the Methodist connections had been engaged actively for years as lay preachers, evangelists, and missionaries. Notably, Bishop John M. Brown cited the works of Jarena Lee, who was verbally licensed by Richard Allen to preach in the early nineteenth century. Brown declared that Martha and Mary were sent by the angel to spread the word of Christ's resurrection, which was preaching. He and others cited Galatians 3:28, "There is neither male nor female, for ye are one in Christ Jesus," to prove their point. It was not until the mid-twentieth century that A.M.E. women were formally permitted to preach.[12]

The subject of women preachers brought to the pages of the *Review* the schism that existed between the conservative wing and the liberal wing of African Methodism, respectively represented by Tanner and Theophilus G. Steward. While Tanner, Steward, and James T. Holly offered forceful and imaginative views that related "theological argumentation to the realities of black life," other conservative voices up to 1900 added to the interpretative mix. Among them were J. C. Embry, author of *Digest of Christian Theology Designed for the Use of Beginners in the Study of Theological* Science (1890), Levi J. Coppin, who wrote *The Relation of Baptized Children to the Church* (1891), and Bishop Jabez P. Campbell, who argued that Moses authored the Pentateuch and that the Bible's account of creation was valid as was the description of the fall of man; they defended the Methodist position on the nature of episcopacy, infant baptism, the study of Methodist history, and the teaching of Richard Watson's systematic theology. The conservatives demanded that Wilberforce teach these doctrines, and they sought to dominate the ideological and theological essays of *The A.M.E. Review* by controlling the editor's position even while allowing a few liberal interpretative theological essays to be published for "balance."[13]

But it was Theophilus G. Steward who by the sheer force of personality and unorthodoxy forced African Methodists to confront their religious beliefs. His mother, Rebecca Steward, had taught him to challenge the "established truths," and he raised questions about man's relationship with God in *Divine Attributes* (1883) and *Death, Hades, and Resurrection* (1885) that shocked some bishops, clergy, and laity.[14] Steward, who did not believe that science and religion were incompatible, outraged fundamentalists with his assertion that scientists could question the literal interpretation of Genesis while accepting that the mystery of the universe was the creation of God. His statement that the Bible "may have been inspired" alarmed conservative theologians. Steward's alleged heresy was compounded with the publication of *Genesis Re-read; or, The Latest Conclusions of Physical Science Viewed in Their Relation to the Mosaic Record* (1885), in which he suggested that Moses' description of events was more a historian's interpretation than the statement of one who was reflecting God's words. Tanner reviewed the book as representing "the best gauge yet offered from which to estimate the possibilities of the future literary career of the American colored man," but he was disturbed by Steward's suggestion that Moses and, by implication, all prophets were secular historians. Steward's unorthodoxy, heretical as it sounded to some, did not prepare them for his most provocative theological study, *The End of the World; or, Clearing the Way for the Fullness of Gentiles* (1888), which contended that Anglo-Saxons were the retiring men and that after their fall a true Christianity would come out of Africa and Asia. Tanner strongly objected to Steward's thesis that the end of the world meant "simply a change of hands in the work of disseminating the grace of the Kingdom of God," for the world's end was foretold in the Bible to mean resurrection, not a transfer of power. Tanner believed that Steward's description of the consummation of the age as the same as Judgment Day was fallacious; the two were not the same. An agitated Steward privately wrote about his mentor, "I bow to his authority in some other things [but] I cannot say so much for his judgment of what is logical or for his ability to follow a line of argumentation." He accused Tanner of acting "impetuously." Tanner did not believe that anyone other than Moses wrote the Pentateuch or that Solomon wrote songs or proverbs. For him, the Bible was complete, and it was blasphemous for man to add to God's word.[15]

Despite their differences in theological interpretation, both Steward and Tanner connected theology to blackness. As suggested by David W. Wills, Steward showed that African American Christian culture "would not emerge as a subculture within Christian America nor as a gradual result of the colonization and Christianization of Africa."[16] Tanner's command of Hebrew, Greek, and Latin provided him with linguistic clues to the African presence in the Bible, and he used this knowledge to relentlessly criticize scholars for ignoring the contributions of Africans to the origins of Judaism and Christianity. In 1886 he reviewed *A New and Simple Explanation of the Unity of the Human Race and the Origin of Color* by the Rev. J. F. Dyson, a black man. Tanner accused the author of self-hatred for his assertion that Eve was white, thus implying that a white woman was the mother of all humankind. Only a miseducated Negro could declare, Tanner wrote, "What color is more attractive than white?" "Shame," he added.[17]

Tanner had no tolerance for theologians who denied an African presence in the Bible or who doubted the capability of African people to address issues of theology. He criticized the Rev. James T. Bixby's comment that people of color never developed civilizations but rather formed high levels of barbarism and that, lacking innate intelligence, they had never developed "religion to any high range."[18] Upset with the rantings of those he considered false Christians, Tanner declared in 1888 that it was time for "all the colored races of the earth, as these may become Christians, to construct a theology for themselves [because] the white man has twisted and turned theology to suit himself." This important declaration of theological independence, which was so necessary as a weapon against European colonization of Africa, was to a large degree undermined by Tanner's belief in an enslavement theory controversial among non-theologians such as Timothy Thomas Fortune, editor of the *New York Age*. Tanner noted that Providence enslaved Africans, bringing them into contact with Western civilization to enable them to correct false interpretations of secular and spiritual history. His comments were partly a response to the Rev. Joseph E. Hayne's book *The Negro in Sacred History; or, Ham and His Immediate Descendants,* which identified Ham as the youngest of Noah's three sons; he was really the second son, said Tanner, as shown in his own 1869 study *Is the Negro Cursed?*[19]

It was easier for Tanner to believe that God postponed emancipating American slaves to provide them with several centuries of tutelage in Western civilization, which their descendants could take back to Africa as missionaries, than to accept a view that man's cruelty and inhumanity served no legitimate purpose.

This belief cemented his argument that the black man belonged in America. On the other hand, Tanner was pleased that a fellow black man, Rufus Perry, a Baptist minister, remarked in a paper delivered before the Brooklyn, New York, Literary Union in 1887 that God gave Africa, including Egypt (Mizraim), to Ham. This view had been Tanner's for the past twenty-five years.[20]

Unfortunately for black theology, neither Coppin, Embry, Tanner, Steward, nor Bishop Turner, who declared in 1898 that "God is a Negro," continued past 1900 the thesis linking theology to blackness. By then, Coppin was occupied with his bishop's assignment in South Africa, and J. C Embry died in 1897. Steward was a military chaplain (1891–1907) then a professor at Wilberforce University until his death in 1924. Turner was busy with his bishop's responsibilities; Tanner suffered from poor health and chronic depression.[21]

Meanwhile, Tanner sought during his tenure as the *Review*'s editor to entice readers with erudite articles and book reviews. One of the controversial books reviewed by Tanner was Timothy T. Fortune's polemical study *Black and White: Land, Labor, and Politics in the South* (1884), which was heavily influenced by the economic views of Henry George and John Swinton. *Black and White* condemned white bigotry, questioned the value of the United States Constitution to black Americans, rejected and ridiculed emigration to Africa, and called for political independence for blacks. Fortune contended that the struggle in the South would not center around race but rather would be between "capital and labor, landlord and tenant."[22] *Black and White* was favorably reviewed by several white publications.[23] However, its anti-religionist tone disturbed Tanner, who took exception to Fortune's assertion that it was "religious nonsense" to contend that Africans were enslaved to prepare their descendants to return to Africa as Christian evangelists. Tanner believed that because of his youth (he was twenty-eight), Fortune had written a destructive book "of the heart and not of the head." Despite this dismissal, Tanner acknowledged Fortune's ability and encouraged others to reach their own judgment after reading the book. T. McCants Stewart also found Fortune's cavalier attitude toward the clergy troubling, but he praised *Black and White* as a monument that would bear "testimony to the intellectual capacity of the American Negro of the nineteenth century."[24]

Tanner was a voracious reader who supplied readers with reviews of books that many would not have heard of otherwise, even when, as represented by Fortune's book, he vehemently disagreed with the author's thesis. He did this as a service to the *Review*'s subscribers because he wanted them to be well informed about the leading issues of the day. Swift condemnation was reserved for those authors who attacked the capabilities of black Americans or who doubted the wisdom of an integrated society. Tanner castigated Albion Tourgee's *An Appeal to Caesar* in the January 1885 *Review* for the author's contention that the races could never live peacefully together in the South. Tanner's faith in an integrated society was based not simply on an optimistic view of human nature but rather on a belief that a true Christian spirit would "allay and keep in subjection race pride, until the time comes that it shall practically cease to be, or until the natural forces of the continent, [or] . . . the inevitable percent[age] of mixed marriages, shall have given the American continent a really continental race." His conviction that the uniqueness of the American continent would lead someday to racial integration was heartened by a seven-week trip to the South in the spring of 1885 when he traveled to Beaufort and Charleston, South Carolina, to Jacksonville and Ocala, Florida, and then to New Orleans, finding that the area had changed for the better since he last visited in 1867. Still, Tanner feared that integration would not be hastened until whites learned to be more sociable with their black neighbors, who Tanner believed exuded warmth whereas whites were cold, morose, and uncommunicative.[25] Unlike those who believed that only whites could bring something to the integration table, Tanner knew that his people could bring delectable dishes that, if only tasted, would show whites that two chefs could indeed exist in the same kitchen.

This zealous rooting for Americanization sometimes led him to make snap judgments lacking in logic or validity. For instance, he wrote in the April 1885 *Review* that, unlike American Indians or Chinese, blacks would assimilate once they made contact with civilization. The exception was the black who practiced Islam. He added that blacks were susceptible toward Christian missionaries because Africans who believed in animism or witchcraft had no religion. This reflected his bias, because he considered Buddhism, Shintoism, and Taoism as examples of religion even though they did not accept Jesus Christ as their savior. Interestingly, and again a reflection of his ignorance about the non-Western world, Tanner could not accept the beliefs and practices of Africans as anything less than religious heresy even though they were spiritual in their relationship to nature and the universe.[26]

While Tanner diligently sought to have the race's leading clergy, professors, politicians, and scholars submit essays, and he labored to present quarterly his own reaction to events, he was keenly disappointed that most exchanges failed to mention the *Review* in their notice of quarterlies. In July 1885, a year after the inaugural issue, Tanner complained that the other quarterlies had failed to inform him whether he had created a literary magazine or not. "Brethren of the press," he pleaded, "we stand or fall with the quarterlies of the day. In this light be kind enough to recognize us."[27] A major consideration that Tanner failed to address was the reluctance of some whites to acknowledge black scholarship in its diversity. The general white population then was reluctant to look to more than one black spokesperson for the race. In the late nineteenth century Frederick Douglass was listened to; after his death in 1895, Booker T. Washington became the token messenger. All the rest, despite their eloquence and erudition, were basically ignored. Of course, this limited the knowledge that whites had about their darker fellow citizens, and it undermined the effort of men and women like Tanner who believed that social intercourse would lead eventually to social integration on all levels.

Tanner was acutely aware that the African race in America was judged by all its parts: articulate and illiterate, erudite and ignorant. He was particularly concerned that black graduates shine as role models, and he was quick to criticize them when they misbehaved. But he was equally diligent in his support of them when he believed that they were slandered. Such was the case when Alexander Crummell, the rector of St. Luke's Church in Washington, D.C., remarked in a sermon, "Common Sense in Common Schooling" (1887), that 50 percent of black male graduates were "inflated, senseless and sensual" whereas 50 percent of black female graduates were the "easy prey of profligate men." Tanner surveyed the university presidents of colored schools (without attributing the quotes to Crummell) and found that the respondents strongly disagreed with the remarks. President S. T. Mitchell of Wilberforce University estimated that only five out of eighty-five graduates were charged with acts of questionable morality "and not one woman [graduate] has entered the ranks of the dissolute." One president remarked that the author of the condemnation probably considered those who learned to read and write in public schools or those who briefly attended college as representative of college graduates.[28]

Tanner defended the graduates because he believed Crummell's assessment to be incorrect, but also because he feared that whites would misinterpret it to further deny black graduates equal opportunities for employment. Without mentioning Crummell, Tanner wrote that black people were too critical of themselves because they lacked love of race. Black people, he stated, believe that everyone else is better, which explains why too many want to be somebody else. Blacks must cultivate self-love and racial pride, or others will reject them and wish to be anything except a Negro. Tanner believed that "God will continue to punish the race as long as it continues to show disintegrating tendencies." Despite his wish for an integrated society void of racial exclusiveness, Tanner understood that separate race organizations were needed until the day they could be cast aside like chaff from the wheat. Thus, he showed his race pride through membership in race organizations. For instance, notwithstanding his busy and taxing schedule, he served as an officer and director of the Century Building and Loan Association in Philadelphia.[29]

The lack of racial harmony in the nation continued to distress Tanner, as it had since his youth. In large part, he attributed this problem to whites who knew black men and women not as individuals with likes and dislikes similar to their own but simply as servants. "He is colored" in the ears of a saintly priest means the same as "he is a nigger" to a white ruffian, Tanner complained. He believed that white Americans would continue to underrate black people as long as they did not read the *Christian Recorder,* the *A.M.E. Church Review,* or books written by black authors. But he also understood that his own people who read white authors tended to overrate whites.[30]

Tanner had since 1868 labored, first as editor of the *Recorder* and then as editor of the *Review,* not only to bestow upon readers his interpretation of those economic, political, and social events that had an impact on black Americans but also to expose them to the brilliance of other authors. Now, after twenty years of unstinting service, he chose to leave the *Review*'s editor's desk for the Council of Bishops. Perhaps he was tired of the challenge of soliciting articles, or maybe he saw himself better serving the church as a bishop who could build up conferences. Possibly the positive response to his book *An Outline of Our History and Government for African Methodist Churchmen, Ministerial and Lay* (1884) convinced him that the fire for the pulpit he had lost in the 1860s was returning and could best be sustained as bishop. His *Outline* was written after Bishop James A. Shorter convinced him that too few knew the church's history and that by providing a review of questions and answers the book would help those who joined the A.M.E. Church understand its creeds, rules, and regulations. Later, he declared that the *Outline* would help Sunday school teachers instruct their classes and, if studied for one generation, "will put an end to the church broils that threaten to prove our death." This reference was to converts who joined the A.M.E. Church and then questioned why things were not done as they were in the Baptist, Presbyterian, or other denominations.[31]

Benjamin F. Lee, editor of the *Christian Recorder,* considered the last issue of Tanner's *Review* (April 1888) to be better than the first. He credited the editor with bringing literature to the people. "Probably no publication by colored men receives a larger patronage from white men," Lee wrote. No other publication, he added, equaled the *Review* "in disabusing the mind of many Americans of the idea that the colored variety is disinterested in any subject that attracts other peoples." The Rev. W. G. Alexander praised Tanner for giving the race and the church "standing and a name among the refined Anglo Saxons and thinkers of the world that we never had before."[32]

Tanner had much to be proud of during his four-year tenure in the *Review* editor's chair. He published thoughtful essays from the race's leading thinkers, and his introduction of poetry and fiction—much as W. E. B. Du Bois did for the *Crisis* twenty-two years later—helped to attract white readers, although they were not in the numbers that he desired. From 1884 to 1888, Tanner accepted thirty-seven articles devoted to philosophy, theology, church history, and biblical studies. This impressive number declined under Levi J. Coppin's editorship and was down to only seventeen for the same subjects under H. T. Kealing's tutelage (1906–10). During Tanner's reign, the *Review* printed 27,950 copies with an average of 2500 copies for the October 1887 and January and April 1888 issues, more than any other black publication, and even more than most white church quarterlies. For example, the

Methodist Review averaged 4400 copies, the *Baptist Review* 2000 copies, the *Unitarian Review* 1300 copies, *Bibliotheca Sacra* 1000 copies, the *Lutheran Quarterly* 520 copies, and the *Universalistic* Quarterly 500 copies for the period under consideration. Tanner's feat was remarkable considering that the *A.M.E. Church Review* was the youngest of these publications. The editor was also pleased that his subscribers were scattered over the globe, with one each in South America and India, three in England, twenty-eight in the West Indies, fourteen in "British America," and an impressive thirty-four in Africa.[33]

The significance of Tanner's editorial skills was noticed immediately. His successor, Levi J. Coppin, failed to include in his inaugural issue (July 1888) book reviews or a listing of the names and contents of other quarterlies, staples under Tanner; he did provide them in the October 1888 issue.[34]

Tanner was a good editor, as he possessed a solid liberal arts education, was well read, and loved his work. As noted by the editor of the *Recorder* in 1916, both Tanner and Benjamin F. Lee, his successor at the *Recorder,* had the potential to be great editors, but both left to become bishops instead of staying to hone their skills. "A great editor," he noted, "does not want to be bishop. A really good editor ought not to be spoiled by becoming a fairly good bishop." In 1910 Timothy T. Fortune, viewed by many as the dean of black journalists, considered Tanner to have been the *Recorder*'s greatest editor. "Pity he elected to be a bishop rather than editor!" Fortune wrote. Perhaps if Tanner had remained as an editor, he rather than Fortune would have been acclaimed the dean, because before Fortune's rise in the mid-1880s, Tanner was the most recognized if not celebrated journalist of his race.

This is not to say, however, that Tanner did not have his dissenters. In 1909 a review of the contributions of previous editors of the *A.M.E. Church Review* assessed Tanner as the most polemic and controversial editor of the magazine. "Indeed, it is to be questioned whether he did not become over suspicious of alleged Caucasian friendship and over sensitive to plain criticism; but if this was so, it was a failing on the safe side, and made it next to impossible for gift bearing enemies to invade his castle for betrayal." Tanner's style annoyed some who were accustomed to more conventional late-nineteenth-century prose, which was overwritten and stiff. In contrast, Tanner's writing was "crisp, nervous and unadorned. His sentences [were] so sparing of words [that] sometimes . . . they are not even skeletons for a perfect skeleton has all of its bones," assessed the *Review*. At times, Tanner was difficult to read because he presumed that readers knew more than they did.[35]

Tanner did not preserve the lengthy correspondence that he received while editing the *Recorder* and the *Review,* so it is not clear to what extent his writing style alienated readers. Similarly, the lack of a diary leaves unresolved his reasons for leaving a position that he had coveted for years.

Nevertheless, the A.M.E. Church desperately needed more bishops in 1888; the deaths of Richard H. Cain, William F. Dickerson, and James A. Shorter since the 1884 General Conference left the Bench of Bishops undermanned. Numerous articles and letters to the *Recorder* offered names, and among the most frequently mentioned were W. B. Derrick, W. J. Gaines, Benjamin F. Lee, Benjamin W. Arnett, J. M. Townsend, John Turner, and Tanner.[36] Besides specific names, strong suggestions came in for a bishop to represent the West and the South, the church's fastest growing areas. The Rev. Theophilus G. Steward initiated a controversy in 1887 with his argument that men should not be made bishop as a reward for great work or service, for if that were the criteria, then all the future bishops should be female. Bishops, he insisted, should be selected for their piety. "Do they believe . . . in repentance, regeneration and sanctification?" he asked. The Rev. J. H. A. Johnson wrote twenty essays on the bishop question; unlike Steward, he favored the election of more.[37]

The 1888 General Conference in Indianapolis turned out to be a raucous affair as Bishop Daniel A. Payne viewed the delegates as "determined to put into office themselves or to put their favorites in by hook or crook." In his autobiography, Theophilus G. Steward recalled how his pre-conference support for W. J. Gaines caused the Georgian to inform Steward that a gentlemen's agreement was all that was needed to insure that Gaines would be elected bishop, and that Steward had his choice of the bishopric or the editorship of the *Christian Recorder.* Steward declined the offer, but the popular Gaines was elected bishop by an overwhelming margin on the first ballot. Benjamin W. Arnett of Ohio was also elected on the first ballot, with just a bare majority. The South's demands for more authority in church matters led also to the election of Texan Abram Grant, and Tanner, who tried to remain above sectional politics, was well known to southerners from his travels in that region as editor. Although Tanner had chronic poor health and was the feeblest of the quartet, he outlived the others. In his ordination sermon, Bishop Payne called upon the new bishops to "develop your manhood as Christ did and you will act as bishop of His church ought to act."[38]

Tanner, who was elected on the second ballot with two votes above the minimum 123, was victorious, according to Benjamin F. Lee, because of "his indefatigable energy as a student, his . . . tendency to serve and honor the connection . . . and his bold advocacy of the interests of the Negro race." Lee considered Tanner "an African Methodist of the African Methodists" and "a Negro of the Negroes" whose "literary efforts have possibly excelled [all others] in strengthening the character of our people in transition from slavery to full and unquestioned citizenship." In 1896 the Rev. R. C. Ransom stated that Tanner was honored with a bishopric because of his launching of the *Review,* the most successful literary achievement of the race.[39] Tanner's successful transition from editor to bishop started a trend as the church sought to honor her intellectuals by first assigning them to edit the *Recorder* or *Review* and then rewarding them with a bishopric. This tactic successfully worked to attract bright men to the editor's desk who might otherwise have sought less arduous ways to serve African Methodism.

Tanner received numerous letters of congratulations upon being elected the eighteenth bishop in the A.M.E. Church. He was assigned to the Eleventh Episcopal District, which covered the Ontario, Nova Scotia, Bermuda, St. Thomas, Haiti, San Domingo, and Demarara (British Guiana, Barbados, and Trinidad) conferences. The Reverend P. E. Mills was happy that the General Conference followed suggestions to place the entire West Indies under the supervision of one bishop, and the Rev. J. A. Johnson predicted that Tanner's election would "stimulate" the flock "to great endeavor." Tanner was pleased with his assignment. It is the "field which the Lord . . . would have [me] especially work for the first four years of [my] episcopacy," he commented. Along with this episcopal assignment, Tanner was ordered by the General Conference to assume the presidency of the missionary board, which provided him with an opportunity to send Christ's disciples on a holy mission. As assessed by Bishop T. M. D. Ward in his Quadrennial Address in Indianapolis, fifty missionaries were needed for Africa and twice that number for the West Indies and neighboring areas. Fifty thousand dollars was needed for the mission field because rum from Christian nations was devastating Africans.[40]

Tanner's self-imposed mandate was to redeem Africa from sin and heathenism, but limited funds determined that his attention be devoted to areas closer to home, which, of course, led to dissension from Bishop Henry M. Turner. The church's missionary endeavor was nearly nonexistent as there were only two missionaries in the field, the Rev. John Albert Johns of Bermuda and the Rev. H. J. Miller at St. Thomas, Virgin Islands. There were none in Demarara, Haiti, or San Domingo, although American consul H. C. C. Astwood lent a hand until help could arrive. Six missionaries were needed immediately. Tanner asked African Methodists to "take the West Indies in your heart, in every prayer remember it, and God will wisely make our ears to tingle with success." He repeated the need for mission support at the June 6, 1888, meeting of the Philadelphia Annual Conference.[41]

For the next twenty years, until his retirement, Tanner would bring to the bishop's office the same degree of scholarship, diligent leadership, and love of church and race that characterized his devotion to his editor's desk. However, the pen that so eloquently defended the race from savage attacks and urged men and women to aim for the stars in their self-elevation would write less on racial issues and more on issues of spirituality. In a full sense, Tanner was at the crossroads for the first time since he had decided with anguish in 1868 to leave the pulpit for his editorial responsibilities. Ironically, then he had to escape from the pulpit in order that he might live physically, removed from the guilt that racked him when he no longer felt God's presence in his preaching. Now, it appeared that he needed to return to a closer affiliation with the church in order to feel spiritually alive. He was at peace with himself, as he had restored to his heart the religious fire that he desperately needed in his youth. This transformation made him now more than ever a valuable asset to African Methodism, but even though Tanner would use his formidable skills to continue addressing secular or racial issues, the bishop's position tended to marginalize him as his views became more parochial and limited to conference members. Still, Tanner was happy, for like Saul, who traveled the dusty road to Damascus and emerged a new man in spirit, Tanner, too, understood the need to let God control his destiny. It was a choice that he made gladly, and the passion that motivated his pen to write on behalf of the race pushed him forward to labor for Christ. From now until his death in 1923, Tanner knew that God's spirit was in his presence, and he rejoiced in the knowledge.

Chapter 7

Establishing a Mission Field, 1888–1892

Tanner embarked on a new career at an age when most men would think of slowing down. But his fifty-three years had accustomed him to arduous work, first as a teenage barber who labored under unpleasant conditions for meager wages, and then for two decades as an enterprising editor. Now Tanner's new responsibilities brought him more into daily contact with the members of the connection as his duties called for him to preside over conferences, encourage pastors and parishioners alike, investigate charges of pulpit misconduct, and attend bishops' councils. He brought to the bishopric the same attitude toward hard work, preparation, scholarship, and accountability that over the years had defined his work ethic and earned him respect from others. The trustees of Wilberforce University praised him for his intelligence and agreeable manners, which brought him "the confidence of all with whom he [came] in contact." But Tanner was successful largely because of a willingness to sacrifice pleasures of food and sleep to have long hours for reading, reflecting, and writing. It was this commitment to sacrifice that he wanted to instill in the clergy and laity of the Eleventh Episcopal District. Tanner knew that the A.M.E. Church had succeeded due to the sacrifice of its founder and early leaders, and he insisted that African Methodists deny themselves and take up the cross to spread the gospel. He called upon six dedicated souls who were willing to absent themselves from family and friends, risk their health, and suffer deprivation in order that the mission field would be served. Interested parties were urged to contact him at his Philadelphia home.[1]

Between July and early October 1888, Tanner sought to shore up support for African Methodism in eastern Canada and the West Indies. In his "Missionary Notes" published in the July 5 *Christian Recorder*, he reported that the Rev. John Albert Johns had returned from Bermuda and a successor had been appointed. The Rev. J. W. Skerrett, who had labored for eleven years in Nova Scotia, wanted to go to Africa or the West Indies but needed financial support. The same was true of a candidate Tanner had for Demarara. Two weeks later, Tanner urged that funds be sent immediately; donors should not wait until their conference met to loosen their purse strings. He also requested that people send in their twenty-five-cent annual subscription fee to the *Missionary Record*, for he intended to personally assist editor John M. Townsend to "make it, if possible, even more interesting than it has been."[2] Tanner's generous offer of assistance underscored the connection's problem: attempting too many projects with a woefully inadequate budget and/or mediocre staff.

From July 12 to 17, Tanner presided over the Ontario Conference. Consisting of Chatham, Hamilton, Amherstburg, Colchester Ct, Bronte, and Oakville, it claimed 174 members and forty-six probationers in six churches but only two traveling preachers. While the twelve in attendance were viewed by him as the apostolic number, the low figures represented trouble to Tanner, who understood that there previously had been some harsh feelings shown to them by African Methodists in the United States. "How glad [I am] and how glad are those for whom [I] speak, that the pursuit is ended; only dear brethren, LET IT BE ENDED."[3] Tanner left Ontario on July 19 for Nova Scotia, a smaller conference with 135 members and eight probationers. On August 13 he joined his family at their seaside cottage in Atlantic City, New Jersey.[4]

Tanner informed readers of the *Recorder* in late August that initiative was a key to success. To illustrate, he described how a black widow inherited her husband's ice business and obtained a monopoly in St. John, New Brunswick, by acquiring a ten-year lease on the lake where the ice came from, building an ice house, buying wagons, and becoming the sole ice dealer in the area. She employed sixty workers in the winter and brought in more than ten thousand dollars annually. He told this story out of race pride but also because he wanted readers to take the initiative to contribute five hundred dollars to assist the mission work in Demarara. He called for a dozen ministers to add to the three already in Bermuda, where the church had established a foothold in 1870 when Bishop Nazery of the British Methodist Episcopal Church visited.[5] In September Tanner and J. M. Townsend issued an urgent appeal for five hundred dollars within six weeks to assist the Rev. J. H. Buckner and his wife, who were scheduled to sail for Demarara. Help, Tanner pleaded, because "souls in Demarara are waiting for the word of life from our hands."[6] Later in the month, Tanner presided over a Philadelphia reception sponsored by the Women's Mite Missionary Society to aid the Demarara mission. He opened the program "with a ringing speech on the unity of the Negro race and the opportunity of the church to organize the race in this country, the West Indies and Africa," reported the *Recorder*.[7]

In early October, Tanner reported that during the past three months he had dedicated a church in Chatham and Amherstburg, put five men to work in the Ontario Conference, and added two members to the Nova Scotia Conference. In an ecumenical spirit, white Roman Catholics provided money and free labor to complete the Amherstburg church. Bethel A.M.E. in Philadelphia aided the mission work with several special collections.[8] But by mid-October only five hundred dollars had been raised for the mission field, as African Methodists were expected to support Wilberforce University and so many other church-related projects. Not sympathetic, Tanner questioned the church's policy of setting aside one day each for special collections for education and Sunday schools but not one for missions.

Less than one-half of the collection on Easter Sunday was designated for missionary activities. Give missions a full day of collection so we can help Africa and the islands, Tanner pleaded. He reminded potential donors that the early A.M.E. Church was based on missionary work and that "no church can expect to be blessed of God that gives any interest precedence [over] the work of soul saving."[9]

Meanwhile, Tanner departed New York on October 11 aboard the steamer *Trinidad* accompanied by the Revs. W. H. Dysett and J. A. Johnson, presiding elders in Bermuda, and a Mr. Woodson, a teacher and preacher. He proudly reported that Charles Burgess, the pilot, was one of "us," a rare position for a black man. Tanner arrived at Hamilton, Bermuda, on October 14 and remained on the archipelago until November 15. He was pleased to find that the black inhabitants were generally well-to-do; many owned stores, cottages, and land, and some were exporters of tomatoes, potatoes, and onions. He was surprised to learn that few had knowledge of the *Recorder,* and he suggested to its editor that an improved distribution system would lead to one hundred new subscribers. Tanner sensed that Bermuda was ripe for African Methodism because the white churches refused to allow black worshipers seats in the front pews or black preachers the right to officiate from their pulpits. Black people were also denied membership in the Bermuda Mutual Life Assurance Society, the Hamilton Reading and Recreation Club, the Sons of Temperance, several of the Masonic lodges, the Ancient Order of Foresters, and the Tower Library and admission to the grammar schools. This discrimination was more appalling considering that out of a total population of 13,948, black people amounted to 8560. Tanner saw much hope for African Methodism in Bermuda but admitted that growth had been slow. He was determined to improve the situation.[10]

Despite the potential for growth, only 8 percent of Bermuda's population belonged to the A.M.E. Church. Some were too old to leave the white-run segregated churches; others were waiting to decide if black men could manage as well as whites. Tanner's 1888 visit and a subsequent one a year later convinced many that something good could "come out of Nazareth." After returning home, Tanner indicated in the December 13 *Recorder* (he would have written sooner, but his right arm was incapacitated) that "Episcopalians and Wesleyans vie with one another in giving [African Methodists] a cordial reception. It is nothing unusual to hear it said: 'while I belong to this or that church, yet I greatly favor your church and will do everything in my power to have it succeed.'" While in Bermuda, Tanner dedicated Bethel A.M.E. Church in Shelly Bay, selecting his dedicatory sermon from I Chronicles 17:11, "Behold I dwell in a house of cedar, but the Ark of the Covenant of the Lord remaineth under curtains." The local Royal Gazette described his sermon as containing "a historical resume, a cluster of practical suggestions and wholesome lessons strongly put by the eloquent bishop."[11]

The New Year, 1889, witnessed Tanner joining Frederick Douglass, Fannie J. Coppin, her husband the Rev. Levi J. Coppin, A.M.E. bishops, and dignitaries of both races on January 2 to celebrate the twenty-sixth anniversary of the Emancipation Proclamation at Association Hall in Philadelphia. Benjamin F. Lee, editor of the *Recorder,* asked, "When again will the American Caucasian listen so attentively to the statements of the American Negro, especially pleadings for the Negro made by the Caucasian?"[12]

Elated by the Emancipation Proclamation celebration, and mindful that black men had helped return a Republican to the White House after Democrat Grover Cleveland had reigned for four years, Tanner was part of a delegation that called on President-elect Benjamin Harrison in late January "to insure [him] of the confidence and loyalty of the people they represent and to remind him that [they] expect the government to be 'of the people, by the people, and for the people.'" The delegates placed their faith in the Republican because they believed that, despite some setbacks, the party represented their interests better than the Democrats, whom many still identified with slavery, lynch mobs, and racial prejudice. Harrison told them that he would resign the presidency if that would lead to the demise of injustice and permanent peace between the races. Tanner reported, "[We all thought,] 'You are not president yet.'" Before and after seeing Harrison, Tanner toured the South until his return on February 11, when he read his mail from Haiti, Samana, Santo Domingo, Jamaica, Bermuda, Ontario, Nova Scotia, and the Turks Island. "Oh, for men! Oh, for money!" he lamented.[13]

The mail was timely, for Tanner had plans to visit Port-au-Prince and San Domingo in February but was deterred by civil war and yellow fever in Haiti. Tanner had deep concern about the Haitian mission. The congregation felt neglected and had discussed leaving the A.M.E. connection because missionary John Hurst was about to depart and his predecessor, Charles W. Mossell, had frequently been absent from his duties. Tanner asked the church to pray for Haiti. "Are not [Haitians] . . . bone of our bone and kith of our kith? Verily so then let them not be forgotten," he requested.[14]

In mid-March, Tanner asked, "Is the African Methodist Episcopal Church really doing missionary work?" He answered his own question with a resounding no, if missionary work meant bringing religion to non-Christians. He dismissed this reply as confirming a narrow definition of mission work. Instead, he ventured the opinion that the church was performing well in an evolutionary sense because African Methodism began in Philadelphia and spread in the United States, then to Canada, the West Indies, and Africa. Tanner compared this to the rise of Christianity, which began in Jerusalem and spread to Judea, then to Samaria and to the uttermost parts of the world.[15]

Psychologically, his explanation justified the slowness of the connection's response to his appeal for funds. But on a spiritual plane, Tanner honestly believed that a quick infusion of money would shore up the church's fledgling missionary effort. In late March, he called upon African Methodists to raise ten thousand dollars by Easter, a few precious days away. He said that a thousand dollars was needed to anchor Bermuda to the church. Editor Lee supported Tanner by informing the laity that their donations represented a token of their "indebtedness to suffering humanity."[16]

Bermuda's political stability contrasted with the volatile political situation that undermined democracy in Haiti throughout much of its history. But Haiti had held a special place for African Methodists since the church's efforts in the early 1820s to proselytize in the republic. Bishop Daniel A. Payne saw historical and ecclesiastical reasons for Haitian mission work. Believing that the nation, with its mixture of African religion and Catholicism, lacked "a strong Christian character" and would remain "heathen" until visited by Protestant missionaries, particularly African Methodists, Payne declared that it should be a primary goal of his church "to aid in making the Haytian nationality and government strong, powerful and commanding among the civilized nations of the earth." Similar views were offered by other black denominations, who took pride in Haiti's successful revolt against France. Tanner turned his attention to Haiti by appointing Solomon P. Hood, a recent convert from Presbyterianism, to that troubled land. Tanner and Hood boarded the *Alisa* on May 9 to sail for Port-au-Prince to relieve John Hurst, making Tanner the first A.M.E. bishop to officially visit the island. During the trip Hood had many deep conversations with the bishop, which convinced him of Tanner's interest "in seeing the islands accept the true faith."[17] The bishop and the missionary arrived at their destination on May 14. As they approached land Tanner jotted down his impression.

> Bluff island of the sea
> As gaze my eyes on thee,
> Through history's lens I look
> And see the blacks who took
> Their right to live and be—
> With none to oversee
> Into their own brave hands
> And drove the foe of lands
> Far off into the sea
> And gained their liberty.

Haitian customs demanded their passports because of anxiety caused by the civil war. Tanner fortunately had one from his 1881 trip to Europe, but he was surprised to have his luggage thoroughly searched. The visit was crucial, for the church had to determine if it could effectively compete with Roman Catholicism, the island's dominant religion. The significance of Tanner's trip was noted by Editor Lee, who viewed it as a trip that would push mission work or hasten its termination because Haiti was "undoubtedly the greatest trophy of our race." He was confident that Tanner's constant care would lead to "unprecedented success."[18]

Lee's optimism was aptly guarded, because Haiti represented for African Methodism a minefield of potential devastation. The obstacles were not minor: French language, African culture, civil unrest, and the leaders' support for the Roman Catholic Church made Haiti a place for only the most dedicated missionary. Even Port-au-Prince with its foreign legations, merchants, and urban environment could provide few Protestants out of a population of forty thousand. The Baptists claimed fifty members; African Methodists had 112 converts; the Wesleyans led with 213 members; and a few professed belief in the Episcopal Church. The Congregational, Methodist Episcopal, and Presbyterian denominations were not represented in Haiti, as they determined that resources would be better used elsewhere, which prompted Hood to fault Protestants for being passive missionaries. General Louis F. Hyppolite, the provisional president, was a Catholic, but he believed that Protestants would do "great things for Hayti and he . . . [promised Hood that he would] do everything in his power for the advancement and success of the Protestant churches," wrote the missionary. Hood called upon African Methodists to bring the "civilizing influences of Protestant Christianity [to] this beautiful island . . . peopled with Negroes."[19] Soon after, Hyppolite was elected president for seven years, and the appointment of John Hurst as secretary of the Haitian legation at Washington indicated to Benjamin F. Lee that the government was supportive of Protestantism in Haiti. Elated, Lee predicted that in 1890 things would be bright for the church's efforts in Haiti. "Already," he wrote, "the star of hope is high in the Haytian heavens, much higher than we are stating."[20]

Despite Hyppolite's support and Lee's optimism, Haiti still represented major problems for the A.M.E. Church. The mission needed one thousand dollars; five Haitian workers had not received money for five years, nor were there any plans to establish mission schools or other signs of an active mission field.[21]

Haiti may have well represented a "trophy" to the race and church for historical purposes, but Bermuda was a prize more easily accessible and receptive. Everyone spoke English, which would facilitate mission work; Bibles and hymnals would not have to be translated, nor would missionaries need to master a foreign language. In April 1889 Tanner sent missionary A. H. Mews to Bermuda to assist J. A. Johnson, George F. Woodson, and W. W. Dyett. Mews had instructions to open a school in St. George, where only 53 of the town's 1605 black residents identified with the A.M.E. Church. The low figure belied the mission effort, because during the past six months Woodson had convinced forty-three, mostly Episcopalians, to join the A.M.E. Church. Prospects looked bright for the A.M.E. connection; J. A. Johnson's church in Hamilton was so small that hundreds were turned away every Sunday evening. Ironically, many were white Americans who would never attend a black church in the States, but outside of the rigid segregated environment of the United States they felt comfortable attending services conducted by a black minister.[22]

For financial and logistical reasons, Tanner's focus was on Haiti and Bermuda to the neglect of the other stations. What about Africa? the Rev. J. M. Henderson asked in May 1889. Supportive of missionary work but ignorant about the continent, Henderson pledged five dollars annually to help J. F. Dyson (who was waiting for funds before departing) "perform my share of the work . . . in that land of fevers, crocodiles and cannibals." Henderson requested that Africa be included in Tanner's district, a view seconded by Lee, who optimistically stated that there were two hundred persons who would gladly donate ten thousand dollars annually for the African mission work "if sufficient effort is put forth. We ought to be ashamed of our lethargy," he added.[23]

The A.M.E. Church had many willing to volunteer for the mission field, and some, like Henderson, offered financial support, but a sustained fundraising effort and even accountability for funds already obtained were missing. A scandal broke out in August 1889 when Tanner reported that the mission treasury was empty. Bishop Daniel A. Payne wanted to know what William B. Derrick, mission secretary, did with the funds. For five months, Derrick and ten bishops were embroiled in a mess that tested patience and Christian forgiveness. Taking no side (but declaring that if Derrick was incompetent or a thief it was the fault of the churches that elected him), Tanner urged them to stop their public quarrel, for it dried up funds needed to support the mission effort. Tanner suggested that money for missions be sent to him if people did not trust Derrick. Defending himself, Derrick stated that Tanner did not realize that he had given Haiti more money in the past four months than his predecessor provided in thirty. Perhaps Derrick was correct, but giving the money in cash may have led to malfeasance on the part of others. Tanner was eager to end the controversy. "Oh for a full comprehension of what [it] means in bringing the isles of the sea and Africa itself to our feet. Certainly . . . it's through us that 'Ethiopia is to stretch out her hands unto God.'"[24] The Rev. Theophilus G. Steward was shocked at the bishops' unwillingness to settle the animosity over Derrick. "Reared from my infancy to venerate your persons and respect your office . . . I . . . invite you to look with me upon the sad spectacle now standing before the church and the world." He pleaded, "On my knees, on the graves of my ancestors who lived and died in the church, I beg of you, remove this sad and serious bone of unholy strife."[25]

The Derrick fiasco underscored the difficulty the church experienced in promoting a systematic mission effort. Both before and after the Derrick diversion, Tanner actively sought to shape the Eleventh Episcopal District. On June 14, 1889, he departed Philadelphia en route to Wilberforce University's commencement with stops in Rochester, Pennsylvania, and Steubenville, Ohio. He arrived in Chatham, Ontario, twelve days later, coming early for his scheduled one-week stay at Amherstburg, the seat of the conference, because he wanted to "rally the choir and the congregation to a daily and punctual attendance upon our session." Clearly he was stamping his own personality on the conference's proceedings.

"Our thought," he wrote, "is that conferences generally give themselves up too largely to the secular side of church life." Tanner felt that he achieved his goal of stirring up the spiritual side, as the first hour of each conference day was devoted to a rousing choir performance before a full house. The conference quickly learned that he did not like solo singing because it often led to singers showing off their voice for personal acclaim and not for the glory of Jesus Christ. He harshly condemned most solos as "an unmitigated nuisance" because few soloists reached the heart and "bore it aloft to God."[26]

From July 2 to August 7, Tanner attended to conference duties in London (Ontario), Montreal, Amherst, Nova Scotia, Halifax, St. John, New Brunswick, and Yarmouth. On August 1, and again on the 6th, he delivered a lecture on "The Negro in the New World." On August 12, he departed for Philadelphia, arriving two days later after an absence of two months. Safe in his residence, Tanner praised God for his health. "It is the best we have had for years. As to our spirits, we are rejoiceful in the Lord," he exclaimed.[27]

The pressing financial situation overshadowed Tanner's episcopal duties. Throughout September, he informed the *Recorder* that he had received letters from the mission fields requesting funds to start projects or to sustain ones already established. He emphatically stressed that they could not wait until Easter 1890 for a collection of funds because the June 22 Board of Missions financial report revealed that $1154.75, or less than half a cent for each of the connection's four hundred thousand members, had been raised. This amount was expected to cover expenses for three missionaries in Sierra Leone, five each in Liberia and Haiti, and seven in Santo Domingo, as well as maintain ten churches and eight schools. Since the close of the 1888 General Conference, thirteen months previously, the Indian Territory (Oklahoma) had received $185, Africa a paltry $300, and the nearby West Indies $1412.90.[28] An outraged Editor Lee angrily complained, "No more rattling figures, no more gushing rhetoric . . . but work" was needed for the mission field. He called for all in the connection to contribute one dollar in sixty days or face the prospect of failure in Haiti.[29] Lee respected Tanner's effort to "keep his wants before the Church. There is not an episcopal district better known to our readers than the eleventh, so little known before." Lee asked readers to help Tanner raise money for a church in Windsor, Ontario.[30]

Unfortunately, Tanner could not concentrate just on Ontario. His far-flung assignments had him in Bermuda again in mid-October, where he remained until November 14. On November 4 he reappointed for the third time the Rev. John Albert Johnson as presiding elder for the Bermuda Conference and pastor of St. Paul's Church in Hamilton. Johnson, who had arrived in Bermuda in 1888, was responsible for increasing St. Paul's membership by 37 percent. The church elected him bishop in 1918 for his outstanding work in the connection. Like Tanner, Johnson was a tireless worker who was troubled by his congregation's superficial faith. "Oh! my Father if we could but have a *deep deep* . . . revival of the blessed Jesus throughout the colony so that men and women would turn away from strong drink, impure commerce, blasphemy and turn unto God by repentance, self denial, and cross bearing. What a transformation! but alas! alas!" he lamented.[31] This pious conviction was representative of the dedication of the missionaries, which highlighted the failure of the A.M.E. church to sustain their selfless efforts.

While in Bermuda, Tanner laid the cornerstone of an A.M.E. church at Port Royal, lunched at the governor's home, and on November 12 delivered a lecture at St. Paul's Church on "The First of August and Its Result," a description of the abolition of slavery in the British West Indies. The *Bermuda Journal* considered it "of a classical tone [but] so paraphrased that it could be thoroughly comprehended by the most illiterate." Tanner argued that the Anglicized African was the only race that could compete with Caucasians; Indians and Chinese could not because they would always be Indians and Chinese, victims of their culture. The adaptable blacks would share the future of the white race while others would be dominated or exterminated, he concluded.[32]

On the eve of his departure, Tanner was pleased that the Bermuda mission had increased its membership from 213 in April 1888 to 351 in October 1889, and its ministers from four to seven during the past two years. Johnson's farewell message to his bishop was "God be with you till we meet again . . . , drive on that Hayti and African work, and let us win some thousands of them to Christ." Once again, Johnson expressed displeasure at the quality of the new members. He admitted that his congregation had increased, but few, he lamented, were true converts. "Oh Bermuda! seek the Lord while he may be found," he confided to his journal. Johnson was concerned with the liquor consumption of his church members, especially during the holidays. He also expressed dismay with the colony's disinterest in educating black youth. "Alas Bermuda," he noted, "better get over your prejudice against the weak people."[33]

The mission debacle did not lessen as 1889 came to an end. Tanner announced in December that a crisis existed within the mission work in Haiti, Africa, and Santo Domingo. The latter site saw only a feeble effort from the A.M.E. Church, which barely attempted to compete with Catholicism. There were no funds in the treasury to send a missionary to Demarara, and while St. Thomas and Bermuda offered bright prospects, they did not represent to Tanner true evangelization. Tanner accused the Missionary Society of indifference. This sentiment was underscored by missionaries sending their complaints to Tanner instead of William Derrick. Missionary J. R. Frederick wrote from Sierra Leone on October 4 with numerous complaints. Chief among them was his claim that he had more support from the Women's Missionary Mite Society than he had from the Missionary Society. Frederick was upset that he could not keep promises made to chiefs to start or maintain schools and missions. Lacking funds, Frederick had rationed his meals to one per day. He requested immediate help or "a crash is inevitable." Tanner asked in the *Recorder*, "What should we do? Are we to abandon Hayti, San Domingo, Africa?" Bewildered and angry, the bishop added, "The fathers planted the church in Hayti. Shall the sons starve it out? The fathers planted the church in Africa. Shall the sons allow it to die?" It was not without irony that Tanner wrote his comments on November 28, Thanksgiving Day.[34]

Editor Lee reacted quickly to Tanner's questions, for they put into perspective the profound indifference of the whole church to supporting the mission field. Lee's blunt editorial revealed the depth of his frustration. He considered Tanner's questions "humiliating . . . in the light of our pretensions, humiliating . . . in the light of our ability, humiliating . . . in the light of our responsibilities . . . humiliating . . . in the light of our pledges, humiliating . . . in the light of excited hopes and expectations, humiliating . . . in the light of the great judgment." He added that the Missionary Society needed a thousand dollars in thirty days and ten thousand dollars invested in the missionary cause.[35]

Two weeks after Tanner and Lee expressed their outrage, the Rev. Theophilus G. Steward offered the practical suggestion that the bishops donate 5 percent of their salary to support foreign missions. This gesture, he believed, might inspire the laity, for "many of us are holding back the Lord's money." Lee, Steward's cousin, viewed the proposal as presumptuous on the minister's part, but he endorsed it because "a movement of that kind would start a mighty missionary movement." The December 26 *Recorder* printed Tanner's declaration that while the financial situation had been dismal for the past four years, the money problem had lessened somewhat during the past eighteen months and Derrick had received word of financial support from the South. "Already money has begun to come in," he reported. "The winter of our discontent may yet be made glorious," he cautiously concluded.[36]

Tanner's effort on behalf of the mission endeavor was temporarily restricted when he and other family members unhappily started the new year as victims of the grippe, which incapacitated him. The only known remedy was a mixture of quinine and whiskey, which presented a moral dilemma for the prohibitionist bishop.[37] Upon recovering, Tanner applied his energies to his mission duties. In February Derrick appealed to the church's membership to raise twenty thousand dollars annually for home and foreign mission work. He urged the four hundred thousand members to donate five dollars each, which would provide eight thousand dollars for home missionaries and twelve thousand dollars for supporting an increase of foreign missionaries to eighteen (two in Sierra Leone, six each for Liberia and Santo Domingo, and four for Haiti). This was one of many good suggestions, but the church lacked the organization, dedication, and discipline to collect dollars from a tax-burdened membership who were asked to subscribe to the *Recorder* and *Review*, maintain Wilberforce University and other colleges in the connection, and give dollar money as well as contribute generously for Sunday school and other special collections. All Tanner could do was urge his fellow bishops at their semi-annual council in Charleston, South Carolina, to make a better effort in Haiti and Santo Domingo.[38]

Adding to his already burdened schedule, Tanner was asked to preside over the Baltimore Annual Conference from April 23 to 29 as a replacement for the ailing Bishop J. P. Campbell.[39] On May 18 he and Sadie observed her fiftieth birthday. It being a Sunday, they did not have a party, but four days later they invited some ministers and their wives to enjoy food, music, and speeches. He was pleased to learn from his son Henry that he had sold a painting for seven hundred dollars; his widowed daughter Halle Tanner Dillon, a senior at the Women's Medical College in Philadelphia, accepted a summer position with the infirmary at West Chester, a nearby suburb. She received her medical degree on May 6, 1891, a proud day in the life of her parents.[40]

In late May 1890, Tanner (substituting again for Campbell) presided over a missionary convention at Kittrell, North Carolina, in the Second Episcopal District, where delegates decided to have a home missionary travel to states where the A.M.E. Church had few members. This missionary was expected to organize churches and Sunday schools, preach, lecture, and distribute church literature. Again, the church ambitiously sought to pursue new projects without successfully completing others or adequately preparing for financial support for any. In June the Board of Bishops ordered Tanner to continue assisting in the administration of the Second Episcopal District's affairs. In an open letter to its members, Tanner told them not to lag. "Get your own bread and water . . . but see to it that the church . . . has its bread and water [too]." "Aim," he added, "for the conversion of souls. Aim for a full treasury." Tanner's advice and assistance were appreciated by the Second Episcopal District. The Rev. R. H. W. Leak, a presiding elder, informed the *Recorder* that Tanner was the first bishop to visit Milton and Reidsville, North Carolina. Presiding elder C. K. King added that Tanner showed himself to be "a great harmonizer of church factions." Editor Lee found it "a pleasure to see the ease with which everything in the [Second] District seems to move along with Bishop Tanner."[41] An upset Bishop Campbell, who was suffering from leg paralysis, complained that Tanner could not be an assistant presiding bishop; this violated church doctrine, because Campbell had not invited Tanner as he had invited others on previous occasions to substitute for him.[42] It appears that a personality difference as well as a misinterpretation of church law caused the problem. Church law called for a bishop visiting any episcopal distract to act alone, if the presiding bishop was absent, or cojointly with him to carry out the duties of his district. It is not clear whether Tanner was invited by the Bishops' Council or by someone in the district; this may have led to Campbell's anger.

Tending to his own episcopal duties, on June 25 Tanner departed for Chatham, arriving the next day. From July 2 to 7, he presided over the Hamilton Conference, then went on to Montreal on July 11 and to Halifax on July 20. Often he preached three times daily, mostly to white congregations in Nova Scotia.

Tanner assessed African Methodism in Canada as "still in swaddling bands." He believed that good work could be accomplished but that the young men in the church were unwilling "to bear the burden and heat of the day, and think nothing of getting an easy appointment." He emphasized that men needed to understand that God must own their work, otherwise "the preaching of the most learned and most eloquent goes for nothing." While in the Nova Scotia wilderness, Tanner pondered "over the passion for domination the white man has. Not content with ruling the weaker races, he haughtily attempts and largely succeeds in subjugating the wilderness and the sea."[43]

While Tanner decried white men's passion for subjugation, he envied their spirit in confronting obstacles, be they races or nature; it was this spirit that he wanted African Methodists to have as they sought to eradicate heathenism among African people. Tanner arrived home on August 3 "somewhat faded [but] in good health," but looking for a rest before sailing in early October for Bermuda with possibly two more missionaries.[44] He visited briefly with Henry, who came from Atlanta en route to Europe for art studies. On September 23 his daughter Mary and Aaron A. Mossell were married in the bishop's residence with Tanner performing the ceremony.[45]

The visit and marriage were a welcome respite that momentarily took the bishop's mind off the pressing mission field financial situation. On October 9 Tanner and missionary Reuben A. Sealy (or Sealey) boarded the *Orinoco* to sail to Bermuda. While en route to the British territory, Tanner's thoughts were about Haiti, where the church had already expended twenty thousand dollars. Now missionary Solomon P. Hood requested that five French-speaking missionaries be sent to secure the A.M.E. presence. Tanner wanted to replace Hood with a native Haitian, the Rev. S. G. Dorce. The situation was even worse in St. Thomas, where the congregation voted to unite with the English Wesleyans after the A.M.E. body was unable to erase their debt of three thousand dollars. Secession talk was in the air in Santo Domingo. Adding to his woes was his disappointment that he was unable to convince six missionaries to sacrifice themselves for Bermuda; however, the mission work there was secure, as limited monetary expenditures had brought good returns.[46]

Solomon P. Hood was disgusted with the situation in the West Indies because the A.M.E. Church could only claim three hundred converts in Haiti and Santo Domingo combined, with a third of that number in Port-au-Prince. Hood emphasized that seminaries were needed in the island to train pastors. He stressed that Haiti, the only black land that threw "off the yoke . . . drove the invaded [away] and stands . . . to-day in defense of the world," should have at least five missionaries and five schools. Hood was dismayed that the bishops tolerated a bare A.M.E. presence when there should be "a living power."[47]

Tanner was disturbed by Hood's assessment. He wanted to send Dorce to Haiti, but lack of funds and then Mrs. Dorce's illness (she died February 13,

1891) kept him in the United States until April 1891.[48] Meanwhile, Tanner attended a conference in Bermuda from October 16 to 18 at which John Albert Johnson described the past year as rewarding due to "a very general growth." By the end of 1890, a dozen had joined Sealy's church, a fair gain in two months of an active ministry.[49] The continued lack of support for mission work angered Editor Lee, who again called upon African Methodists to support the West Indies endeavor or cut it loose. The church would not let it go, because it represented prestige even if the price was bickering and poor organization. Nor was the A.M.E. Church willing at this time to emulate other denominations and assign a resident bishop to each island.[50]

The mission financial mess drained Tanner emotionally, and his effort to finish his book *The Divine Kingdom* so deprived him of proper rest that by early 1891 the bishop was the victim of "nerve and head trouble," which would turn out to be the beginning of years of chronic depression.[51]

By August the situation in Bermuda looked encouraging. The *Recorder* reprinted an article from the *Bermuda Royal Gazette* that delineated the decline in membership among Wesleyan Methodists (9 percent) and Reformed Episcopalians (33 percent), while Roman Catholics and African Methodists increased 44 and 74 percent respectively. While the Catholic increase came from an influx of Portuguese immigrants, the A.M.E.'s rise came via desertion from other Protestant denominations.[52] But the apparent good news was an aberration. A July 27 letter from J. A. M. Johnson in St. Thomas to Tanner described the development of another fiasco. A loan was urgently needed to pay $640 in gold or the church property would be sold. Tanner was helpless to comply unless the church amended its law to permit the Missionary Society to keep 100 percent of the Easter money or stop "scatteration" of mission dollars all over the world. The *Recorder* complained that the church had "a puerile unbusiness like grasp of our spiritual work" and that it was ridiculous to boast of great church edifices when they were unable to send six hundred dollars to Santo Domingo or even supply funds for a bishop to visit the West Indies. At this time there was talk about building or purchasing a building for the publication department, which prompted Lee to protest that he would rather work in a chicken coop if it meant more funds for missions.[53]

Tanner returned to Bermuda in October 1891 to preside over a conference, his last one of the current quadrennial. After his departure, John Albert Johnson wrote in his journal that Tanner was pleased with the work of the missionaries, and the laity reciprocated their pleasure with the bishop by presenting him with a gift of an inkstand, a gold pen and pencil, a blotter, and a paper knife.[54]

Despite the difficulties the West Indian missions faced, the situation was even worse for the A.M.E. Church's efforts in West Africa. Few shared with Turner a desire to emigrate to their ancestral home. Many agreed with the declaration of the Rev. J. M. Henderson that only missionaries, merchants, or tourists had any need to go to Africa. If black people, he noted, could not "thrive in this civilized and Christianized land, how dare we indulge even a hope of success as pioneers in an unhealthy, savage country where beasts, reptiles, nature and men would be our inveterate foes?" Dismissing African Methodist involvement in mission work, Henderson claimed that it would take one thousand years to support a church body even if all migrants who went to Africa worked like a Turk in the jungle.[55] Henderson's belief could be dismissed by many as an irrational one based on ignorance of Africa's peoples and geography, but like all stereotypes, it had a ring of truth to it. In September the *Recorder* printed the Rev. J. R. Frederick's July 22 letter to Tanner whereby the missionary, writing from Freetown, Sierra Leone, revealed that nine white missionaries had arrived in June and that five had caught fever while waiting for the rainy season to end, with three quickly dying.[56]

All news from Africa was not as discouraging. From Millsburg, Liberia, returned to his station after a two-year absence, the Rev. S. Jefferson Campbell happily reported that the government had granted him one hundred acres of land on which he planned to plant three thousand coffee trees in 1891. This profit-making venture would make the mission self-reliant, but he needed immediate funds to purchase hoes, axes, and rakes or donation of the same. From Lower Buchannan, Grand Bassa County, Liberia, the Rev. J. P. Lindsey reported that in twenty-five years his mission would produce fifty thousand pounds of coffee if he had funds for seeds and tools. Frederick wrote in February 1891 that white missionaries from Kansas were trying to establish a presence in Maybelly, but a strong A.M.E. presence would prevent other denominations from succeeding. He had converted eight Temme people but needed more missionaries and money to prevail. Tanner requested in April that readers send in money. "Read the letters from Africa and pray the Holy Spirit moves you to act at once," he wrote. While Bishop Payne sympathized with the missionaries' need for funds, he considered it imperialistic for the A.M.E. Church to invest precious funds and persons in seeking converts in Canada and the British West Indies when England had provided for those residents' intellectual, moral, and spiritual wealth for a century. He questioned the wisdom of going into those areas only "to split their churches in the name of 'organic union.'" Instead, he urged mission activity in Africa. In 1884, after the rush by Europeans to explore the Congo River, Payne directed to African Methodists "on, on on! to the Congo."[57]

The self-reliance ethic of these missionaries was also displayed by Sarah E. Gorman, who left New York in June 1890 with only ten cents. After brief stops in Monrovia and Freetown, she went into the interior and preached in over one hundred villages even though she was not sponsored by the Missionary Society. The courageous missionary survived on fifty dollars from the Women's Mite Missionary Society and small donations from friends, but she requested help, as it cost thirty dollars to make the trip from Freetown to the interior. This devoted and tireless worker died in Freetown on August 10, 1894.[58] Ironically, Derrick, whose office contained new furniture at a time when missionaries were begging for funds, pleased the executive board of the Missionary Society with his May 28 report, which showed that for the past year $5394.90 was spent in foreign fields with nearly $1700 of that allocated to Haiti. Both the executive board and the *Christian Recorder* praised Derrick for the marked improvement. Lee noted that "Derrick . . . has demonstrated his fitness."[59]

The African missionary effort received a psychological boost in October when Bishop Turner sailed for West Africa to survey the mission field and to offer encouragement to the beleaguered missionaries. Before his departure, the bishop asked, "Who wishes to help Africa?" Lee declared that Turner was the best man to represent the church in Africa and that the race had to bring the gospel to the lost souls because blacks, unlike whites, recognized the full brotherhood of Africans. Only blacks, he contended, can kiss and love a black baby as well as tender "all the courtesies of the gentleman as well as all the graces of . . . Christ to a black lad." Lee added that ten men should accompany Turner to Africa. "Money and men for Africa should be the theme," he concluded. Turner's supporters provided him with three hundred dollars for the African missions.[60]

Some who supported the evangelization of Africans adamantly opposed the bishop's undying call for emigration. After Turner called for 150,000 to go and redeem the continent, T. McCants Stewart, who had lived in Liberia, mildly rebuked the bishop for not going sooner nor sending his children. Stewart argued that African colonization on the part of American blacks should be forgotten unless it was backed by brains and money. He added that they should elevate themselves first before they sought to do the same for Africans, since many in the continent were their superiors. As proof, Stewart cited the Mandingoes, who were merchants and could read Arabic literature, and the Veys, who had a literature and schools of their own.[61]

Still, Lee wrote that Turner's trip would show Africans that American blacks had the "ability to cooperate with their best energies, in evangelistic work in the land of our fathers."[62] In November the bishops decided that they would send two missionaries and two assistants to Africa. Significantly, the bishops vowed to raise two thousand dollars to support the four. Interested parties were requested to send applications to Tanner.[63] A word of caution, however, came from Bolding Bowser, formerly of the United States consulate in Sierra Leone. Bowser, who had lived in Africa for sixteen years, fifteen of them in Liberia, predicted that Turner would face difficulty in establishing churches outside of Sierra Leone because few were being converted. He accused missionaries of lying with their glowing reports about conversion and dismissed their begging letters as levers to obtain money from the Missionary Society. He suggested that Turner would see the truth of his statement within twenty-four hours of arrival. To the contrary, Turner spent a month in Africa and wrote fourteen letters praising the people, climate, and agricultural and evangelization possibilities. On November 10, two days after his arrival, Turner organized annual conferences in Sierra Leone and Liberia.

Turner did not care for Frederick and tried to remove him in 1893, but the missionary was too popular with his congregation, and until the death of Bishop Daniel A. Payne the same year, he received one thousand dollars annually. Turner became the senior bishop upon the death of Payne, which gave him undisputed control over mission funds. Compounding the Turner-Frederick dispute was the color question. The dark-complexioned Frederick accused the tan-hued Turner of color prejudice. The sour situation between the two men eventually led the missionary in 1899 to remove himself and two congregations from the A.M.E. Church to join the Wesleyan Methodist Church, where their interest would be "better conserved."[64]

Turner was a man of powerful emotions who evoked strong reactions from others. By the end of 1892, J. M. Henderson, a former critic of evangelization and emigration, wrote, "There is . . . deep wisdom in . . . Turner's ceaseless appeal for the evangelization of Africa. It is disheartening to see that it is misunderstood and unresponded to." Even though Turner did not advocate that all eight million blacks in America emigrate to Africa, many believed that he did. Turner's voice, however, was becoming more strident on behalf of emigration, a cause that hurt the mission effort because people, as noted by J. M. Henderson, saw them as interchangeable. Therefore, the "impracticability of one hides the glorious feasibility of the other." A different perspective on Africa was provided by Mrs. N. F. Mossell, who was neither an African Methodist nor an advocate of mass emigration, when she called upon African Methodists to use the church as an instrument to develop commercial relations between Africans and African Americans.[65]

As early as the 1830s, black missionaries representing the Congregationalists, Methodists, Baptists, Episcopalians, and Presbyterians traveled to their ancestral home to bring "civilization" through the instrumentality of Christianity. By the early 1880s, black Methodists and Baptists went to African independent of white missionary societies. In 1876 the A.M.E.Z. church was sent to set up missions in the "Dark Continent." In 1883 the black Baptist Foreign Mission Convention of the United States sponsored the mission endeavors of six African Americans in Liberia as they agreed with the African Methodists that it was God's design to redeem African "through the instrumentality of her sable sons." In this respect black missionaries, while sharing with their white counterparts a strong sense of social duty to help others, and a belief in African cultural inferiority, did not see them as racially inferior, which troubled westernized Africans in their relationship with European and white American missionaries. Such was admitted by the president of the Baptist Foreign Mission Convention in his annual address in September, 1895. War destroyed their mission work among the Vey in West Africa and in South Africa. R. A. Jackson, the lone representative of the black Baptist church, accused Europeans of using white missionaries to prey "upon the poor, ignorant Africans." Expressing a viewpoint embraced also by African Methodists, Jackson added that only black missionaries could bring the "light and liberty of the gospel" to relieve the continent of her "spiritual darkness." Despite the cost of mission work in funds and health, dividends were achieved when Africans educated in the United States returned home as teachers, nurses, and missionaries. Between 1895 and 1905, A.M.E. schools, Wilberforce and Morris Brown collectively enrolled fourteen students. Livingston College, affiliated with the A.M.E.Z. Church, had four students during this period, whereas Lincoln University in Pennsylvania, founded by a Presbyterian minister, enrolled twenty-seven African students during the same years.[66]

While the mission focus was on Africa, Tanner attended to his episcopal duties in Canada, where he spent several weeks in the spring of 1891. While in Ontario, Tanner suffered from insomnia caused by tension. The hardworking bishop impressed many. Henderson, for instance, wrote, "He is sustaining his reputation for broad and thorough scholarship. Eminently is he fitted for [his position]. He is an excellent judge of men and local needs. It is apparent that there are great possibilities for the A.M.E. Church in Canada."[67]

The popular bishop returned to Philadelphia in early May to learn that the presiding elders in three Arkansas conferences of the Eighth Episcopal District had requested that the Council of Bishops appoint him to succeed the late Bishop Disney, who died April 20, until the General Conference met the following May. The *Recorder* concurred. "Many of [us] will be glad to see . . . Tanner exercise the episcopal office in the states this [coming] quadrennium," Lee stated. Heeding the request, in June the council appointed Tanner to take over the Eighth Episcopal District while still retaining charge of the Eleventh.[68]

During this time, Tanner suffered the loss of his beloved mother, Isabella, who died at the age of eighty-five in Williamsport, Pennsylvania, where she lived with her daughter Mary Tanner Russell. Tanner described Isabella as "unusually religious," "a born leader," and as one "without education [who] was intelligent to a remarkable degree." At her death, Tanner and his wife were at the bedside of a sick daughter. He was unable to attend her funeral, as he was bringing Sadie, exhausted from tending to her sick child, home. Privately, he praised his mother by citing Proverbs 31:16, "She considereth a field, and buyeth it with the fruit of her hands; with the fruit of her hands she planted a vineyard."[69]

Other family issues demanded his attention and concern. During the summer of 1891 Tanner fretted over daughter Halle's chances to pass the Alabama state medical examination, which lasted for ten days. He informed Booker T. Washington that he was concerned that her color and sex would be used against her but was confident that she had the ability to "pass any reasonable and just examination." On September 21 Halle became the first woman of any race to pass the exam, with an average of 78.81. She remained in Alabama until 1894 as the resident physician of Tuskegee Institute.[70] All of Tanner's children were exemplary individuals. Carlton, who graduated in 1891 from the Institute for Colored Youth, was a normal-school professor of math at Huntsville, Alabama; Mary T. Mossell was the wife of attorney Aaron Mossell and lived in Lockport, New York.

On June 14, 1893, his daughter Sarah Elizabeth graduated with a recitation average of 97.8 from the Spring Garden Girl's Normal School in Philadelphia. Henry, the most famous of his children, was studying art in Paris and would develop into one of the world's foremost artists. The *Christian Recorder*'s comment on Sarah Elizabeth Tanner's achievement was applicable to all the bishop's and Mrs. Tanner's children: "This distinction is no less creditable to [her] than to her honored parents."[71]

Tanner went to the 1892 General Conference confident that he had done his best for missions and understanding that the church rotated its bishops among various episcopal districts. He was prepared to go where the church thought his services were best needed. Tanner was assigned to the First Episcopal District, which encompassed New York, New Jersey, New England, and Philadelphia. The bishop of the First was automatically the president of the Board of Publication of the A.M.E. Church. For a brief period in 1893 Tanner again had charge of Nova Scotia and Bermuda when Bishop Turner was in Africa. The deaths of Disney and Campbell and the need for more bishops led to the election of Benjamin F. Lee, Moses B. Salter, and James A. Handy. H. T. Johnson was elected editor of the *Recorder*, and J. C. Embry assumed the responsibilities of the Book Concern.[72]

There are no extant copies of the *Recorder* for 1892. Consequently, little is known about Tanner's episcopal activities during this period except as they were covered by other publications. J. M. Palmer offered a remarkable analysis of Tanner's demeanor at the 1892 General Conference. "He seemed happiest in watching the proceedings . . . with careful scrutiny. His personal appearance and manners were both unassuming and unattractive." He wore "an air with which nature has endowed him, the distinct characteristic of which rather repels than attracts"; still, Palmer said, those who knew him "from an inner . . . standpoint" knew that he made people comfortable. Alluding to Socrates, Bacon, and Plato, Palmer added that Tanner "appear[ed] more at home in the role of Christian philosopher" than in that of bishop. "His countenance," Palmer noted, "alternated between stern frowns and interested smiles. In the heat of discussion he grew fierce and hurled facts with a vengeance as from the ends of his fingers. His eyes flashed the very fire of earnestness, candor and sincerity." Some months later, Palmer declared that Tanner taught as he preached and vice versa.[73]

This rare description of Tanner captures the essence of the man. Tanner was a man of exactness. He had complete control over his appetites; his mind was sharp and inquiring, and he demanded that others refrain from indulgences and use their God-given talents and skills to labor on behalf of Christ and the race. He did not tolerate laziness in any form. For the next four years he urged the members of the First Episcopal District to test their mettle as the A.M.E. Church sought to strive forward in a time scarred by racial intolerance, economic panic, and developing American imperialism.

Chapter 8

Bishop of the First Episcopal District, 1892–1896
A Time of Spiritual Healing

The manner in which the A.M.E. Church made assignments removed Tanner from a position where he had genuine interest in improving the mission situation to immediate charge of overseeing the operation of the financially strapped, poorly managed Book Concern, the nemesis of past managers of the publication department. Tanner, of course, was well acquainted with the problems of funding the *Recorder*, including collecting arrears from indifferent subscribers. Presumably, as bishop he would wield more clout in instilling efficiency in the management of the Book Concern than he could ever muster as editor, but it would take all his skills in organization and diplomacy. Besides overseeing the publication of the *Recorder* and the *Review*, the Book Concern was responsible for selling hymnals, the Book of Discipline, and books written by A.M.E. authors. In 1892 Benjamin F. Lee estimated that not one in five hundred church members had purchased a hymnal in the past four years and not one in three hundred had bought a copy of the Discipline of 1888.

The publication house was in poor condition and needed to be replaced. Critics called for the removal of the Book Concern to Nashville. However, it remained in Philadelphia after a new publication house was built in 1892 and dedicated May 4, 1893. In 1894 an Alabama minister called for the publication department to be separated from the Book Concern and for the reduction of the price of hymnals, Disciplines, and the *Recorder*. While the Book Concern's business manager, J. C. Embry, resented the suggestion, *Recorder* editor H. T. Johnson saw a need for a reconstruction of the publishing arrangement. The ensuing mess severely taxed Tanner's health.[1]

Tanner's mediating skills were called for soon after the end of the 1892 General Conference when trouble broke out at Bridge Street Church in Brooklyn, New York. The itinerant system of the A.M.E. Church replaced the Rev. John M. Brown, who died unexpectedly, with the Rev. Dr. William H. Butler. When Butler pastored the same church previously, many had left because they did not like his scholarly or Presbyterian-style sermons. Now the church was split. Younger, more literate members had no problem with Butler, but the older and less educated members wanted someone like Brown who would stir up their feelings and allow them to shout "amen, glory be to God." Tanner came hoping to solve the problem of disunity, as it interfered with the daily operations of the church during the summer and fall 1892. The *Brooklyn Daily Eagle* reported that the bishop's preaching so moved

Aunty Brice "that she jumped up . . . and begun to shout." Tanner, who eschewed emotional displays, made her keep quiet until he finished his sermon. Brice and friends confronted Tanner after the service with the accusation that he and Butler wanted a high-toned church. She vowed to continue to shout whenever the spirit moved her. Some church members shook Tanner's hand, while most did not. The conflict had eroded church attendance, once overflowing, by half during the past year. Some threatened to remove Bridge Street from the New York Annual Conference and operate it as an independent church unless the Rev. Dr. W. H. Heard was brought in as a replacement for Butler. Tanner decided that Butler should remain for a year. On May 31, 1893, Tanner assigned Butler to Allen Chapel in Philadelphia, a very wealthy church. Many, including his most vocal critics, were moved to tears by Butler's gracious departure.[2]

Tanner's resolve was again challenged by Bridge Street in January 1893, in a fiasco that involved its trustees and its musical director for the past seven years, Dr. Susan S. McKinney, a prominent physician and community activist. The trustees wanted to replace McKinney, who had the support of the choir and the tacit support of Butler, who declined to get involved since he was leaving in a few months. Tanner came on March 1 to restore order after the trustees dismissed McKinney; he viewed their action as illegal, since it lacked Butler's approval. Furthermore, Tanner considered the matter trivial, but he bluntly told dissenters to obey church law or find another church to attend. Church law called for the pastor to declare his desire for a chorister, for the trustees to declare their ability to pay for one, and for the choir to recommend to the pastor the person they wanted to direct them. An upset bishop informed everyone, "I have come here to see that the law is obeyed . . . I have left my sick bed . . . and I want it settled tonight before I begin at once to install a chorister here." After McKinney spoke with the choir, they gave Tanner a name, which he passed on to Butler, who stared at the name for five minutes before announcing the chorister to be John Thompson. Bedlam existed for fifteen minutes as the angry trustees expressed their unwillingness to pay Thompson's salary because he was not their candidate. At this point, Tanner ordered them to accept Thompson and pay him. A clearly irate bishop dismissed the assembly, ordered the lights shut off, and left for Philadelphia. Tanner's Bridge Street experience was not atypical. Although some Baptist and Methodist churches catered to an elite congregation and some ministered to the working class, others, as exemplified by Bridge Street and by Metropolitan A.M.E. in Washington, to name two, had congregations with both elements. Some of the Bridge Street worshippers represented a conservative element—part African, European, Shinnecock or Montauk Indian—who migrated from eastern Long Island. They were "resolute in manner and method," keepers of well-furnished homes and private libraries, fluent in several languages, and were doctors, dentists, skilled craftsmen, schoolteachers, or clerks. They could afford to live in the splendor of Brooklyn, away from the black slums of Manhattan across the East River. Bridge Street's other element was composed of former slaves or their descendants who were employed as cartmen, day laborers, porters, washerwomen, street sweepers, and domestic servants. As noted by Theophilus G. Steward, the pastor of Bridge Street from 1874 to 1877, the two elements' differences combined "to develop a triangular conflict with cupidity, caste and callousness."[3]

There was more to Tanner's bishopric duties than presiding over conferences, ordaining ministers, or settling disputes even though these functions took up an inordinate amount of his time. Tanner was first and foremost a scholar who, like Bishop Daniel A. Payne, understood that the church could not survive without a literate clergy. Thus, he insisted that ministers had an obligation to study science, history, literature, and philosophy as well as the Bible, following the advice presented in Malachi 11:7, "The priest's lips should keep knowledge." Tanner suggested that ministers favor books over most newspapers and magazines, which he considered superficial, and particularly recommended Carlos Williams Larned's *The Great Discourse of Jesus: The Christ, the Son Of God,* Alfred Edersheim's *Jesus the Messiah,* and Henry J. Van Dyke's *The Church: Her Ministry and Sacraments.*[4] While this did not represent light reading, Tanner believed that it was not beyond the realm of understanding for African Methodist clergy.

To encourage more scholarship within the A.M.E. Church, Tanner stressed that the church should promote its own denominational literature, which was the theme of his article in the January 1892 issue of the *A.M.E. Church Review.* Fortunately, the church was not without its writers. H. T. Johnson had written *The Divine Logos; or, Wonderful World of John;* Levi J. Coppin authored *The Relation of Baptized Children to the Church;* J. C. Embry published *Digest of Christian Theology;* Josephine Heard wrote *Morning Glory;* Theophilus G. Steward authored *Theological Works.* Along with himself, they were indicative of a small but productive group of scholars within the A.M.E. fold. While this was remarkable for a race only twenty-five years removed from slavery, Tanner believed in 1892 that the race and the church had the potential to write hundreds of books, particularly about African Methodism's early history when ignorance and slavery had prevented many from writing. Bishop Tanner was disturbed that there were no studies of Richard Allen or William Paul Quinn, early A.M.E. giants, nor any written history of the church's pioneer missionary efforts in the United States. Therefore, he called upon the publication, financial, missionary, educational, and Sunday school departments to decide on the type of literature the church should produce. Always conscious of the need for accuracy in interpretation, Tanner added that it was the duty of Shem and Ham to write about what Japheth had dominated for two thousand years because God and law were on the side of Ham, who "deserve[s] to exist."[5]

Tanner's statement was significant, for he was a witness to the distortions some Caucasians had formulated pertaining to the contributions of African people to world and American civilization and history. Thus, instead of being cowed by the writings of others, Tanner had no qualms about challenging white scholarship.

Paradoxically, he, who often praised Caucasians for their devotion to scholarship and applied learning, was a pioneer figure in what twentieth-century scholars would later describe as an Afrocentric school of Bible historians. In an April 1892 *A.M.E. Church Review* article, "The Negro and the Flood," Tanner questioned the absence of an African flood tradition. After a professor, only identified as Harper, declared in Frankford, Pennsylvania, on March 8 that all races save the African had a flood tradition, Tanner, who was not in attendance, learned that none in the audience challenged this assertion even though among the assembled were Wilberforce president S. T. Mitchell, Levi J. Coppin, editor of the *Review,* and other prominent African Methodists. Tanner responded that Harper, not unlike most white scholars, did not want to associate blacks with Egyptians; but Cush and Mizraim were brothers, added the bishop. Tanner noted that if Theophilus G. Steward, Taylor Lewis, James Strong, Edward Strong, and others were correct, there was no universal flood, but it was his belief that a flood did occur even if the entire world was not covered.[6]

It was Tanner's contention that in time black scholars would earn the respect of their white counterparts, but at present they were proscribed by social bans. Yet he was not willing to accept white respect if blacks were not deserving. Whites should not agitate for removal of signs that read "colored" or "African" if they did not believe that blacks too were men. "If we are men, they should cease making our lives 'hard' by the daily ostracisms practiced upon us," he asserted. Saddened and frustrated by white machinations, he implored, "Oh for some William Lloyd Garrison to make the same holy protest against caste that he made against slavery! Oh for the coming of the day of freedom to the soul!" he declared.[7]

Tanner's lamentation was the cry of the black elite who desired a society that was oblivious to color and other racial distinctions. Of course, the fault was with those whites who would not acknowledge that while some blacks were ruffians and social misfits, there were others who were far superior in education, and social attainments to many laboring whites. They, too, were cultured men and women who cherished tradition, respected the law, and longed for a society of good manners and polite social intercourse. Instead, too many whites judged all African Americans as persona non grata. At best, as a near-white informant confided to Theophilus G. Steward in 1896, the better classes of both races associated "freely in religious, charitable and educational movements," but "such connection is limited, temporary, and bounded by confines." Realizing that racial harmony would never exist nor black men have equal opportunities until the demon of color bias was destroyed, Tanner called upon a higher force to right the wrong.

> Almighty Jesus, change proud Japheth's heart—
> Make him know that thou a brother art
> To Shem and Ham, the yellow and the black

From him thy throne's great force o hold not back
Almighty Jesus, stay proud Japheth's hand—
Upraised and dominant in ev'ry land
He goes but not for love of thee and God
In public he scorns to kiss messiah's rod

Almighty Jesus, thou of Shemitic blood,
Remember, o remember Shem, for good;
Thou priest, like to Melchijedeh, who came
Of Ham, remember, o remember Ham.[8]

On May 31, 1892, Tanner joined Bishops Payne and Wayman, Frederick Douglass, Peter H. Clark, Booker T. Washington, J. C. Price, Albion W. Tourgee, Timothy Thomas Fortune, William S. Scarborough, Frances E. Harper, George T. Downing, John M. Langston, and others in observing a day of fasting and prayer beseeching God to show whites the evils of racial segregation, political disfranchisement, and lynching. They asked for encouragement to "rise to that level of intelligence and virtue which makes the character of a good citizen."[9] Tanner believed that racial segregation would eventually go the way of slavery, and he was heartened that since 1888 Catherine Impey, an English Quaker, had been publishing the *Anti-Caste*, a journal devoted to eradicating racial segregation throughout the world. On her visits to the United States, Impey met with Tanner and other race leaders to obtain firsthand accounts of the pernicious racism in America.[10]

Even though Tanner criticized Caucasians for their unchristian behavior and faulted the exclusionary practices that denied the humanity of his people, he found much to admire in the principles of Western politics and jurisprudence. And while he acknowledged the evils of American slavery, he clearly believed that it was the instrument of capture and enslavement that brought the African to the Americas, where Providence introduced him to Christianity. This reasoning led Tanner to the conclusion that Columbus's voyage to the New World was worth celebrating, for the explorer was God's tool to acquaint Africans with His teachings. Tanner believed that the glory days of Ham and Shem had passed; therefore, the destiny of African Americans was "linked to the destiny of the master race . . . which to us is a 'glittering robe of joy.'" He joined the nation in celebrating the quadricentennial of Columbus's voyage. According to Tanner, it was not only a great navigational achievement but, most significantly for him, brought the "ignorant" African into the midst of a Christian and republican form of government denied to the descendants of Ham and Shem. Tanner's belief, as difficult it is for African Americans a century later to comprehend, was widely accepted by his contemporaries with few, if any, major dissenting voices because Christianity represented for them hope for everlasting life, whereas heathenism meant eternal death in hell. Tanner believed that one day Americans would honor the command of Jesus to love their neighbors as they loved themselves.[11]

While readily admitting that a weakness of Western civilization was its intolerance for racial equality, Tanner knew that oppressed people had much to seek revenge for. However, for personal and theological reasons he eschewed talk of retaliation. When Albion W. Tourgee, a former carpetbagger Reconstruction judge in North Carolina, called upon blacks in 1892 to organize boycotts, sue for their rights, and use force to defend themselves against white oppressors, he delivered a message acceptable to militants bent on confrontation, but to Tanner the message was unpalatable. Even though A.M.E. Bishop John M. Brown called for the hanging of white men to avenge the lynching of black men, Tanner, who joined others at Boston's Faneuil Hall in August 1894 to condemn lynching, refused to advocate that black men massacre white women or children in retaliation, because they were "American Christians not French Catholics." It was his belief that God would administer punishment to lynchers. Despite the atrocities committed against blacks, Tanner declared, the race was not leaving the South nor emigrating to Africa, for "here we intend to remain and . . . win our suit from a people . . . who . . . will be seen gallant enough to put the laurel upon our brow." His views were compatible with Booker T. Washington's social vision, and it was no surprise that he endorsed Washington's Atlanta Compromise speech in which the educator called upon the races to remain separate "in all things that are purely social . . . yet one as the hand in all things essential to mutual progress."[12]

Tanner's racial views evolved dramatically from his youthful days when he considered himself an emigrationist to the early 1890s when he pragmatically evaluated the state of African Americans. Since his return from Europe in 1881, Tanner had been committed to not viewing everything in a racial light. Now, instead of judging every action of whites in racial terms, Tanner was more determined to look at issues and personalities from multiple perspectives. Furthermore, he recognized that patience and faith in God would carry the African race forward. While he was willing to judge men for their misdeeds, he saw no need in punishing government officials, including presidents, for matters they had no control over. When Rufus L. Perry wrote in August 1892 of his decision not to vote for the reelection of President Benjamin Harrison, who had informed some clergymen that he could not protect American citizens in their rights, Tanner, who recognized that the black vote possibly held the balance of power in a close election, faulted Perry for not understanding the limitation of presidential power. He argued that it would be naive and foolish to punish Harrison by voting for the Democrats since the president lacked the power to administer civil justice in the southern states.[13] Still, Tanner saw in the subsequent Republican party's defeat the hand of God, who had used the party as an instrument for emancipating slaves. Now, he reasoned that God brought about its defeat because it had forsaken the cause of humanity and freedom for other gods. Unless the Republicans returned to their original values, Tanner saw them dying without hope of a resurrection. The majority of black editors, unlike Tanner, attributed the Republicans' defeat to forces other than divine intervention.[14]

Despite his interest in national politics, Tanner did not feel compelled to assume the role of spokesperson for his race. His primary responsibility, he believed, was to his bishop's duties. Nevertheless, for both personal and political reasons Tanner, like numerous others in the country, sought support from Booker T. Washington. Unlike many black Americans who criticized Washington's accommodationist approach to the white power structure, and Bishop Henry M. Turner, who considered Frederick Douglass a giant and Washington a pygmy, Tanner generally agreed with Washington's insistence that African Americans become self-reliant as well as strive for control over those passions that devalued them as a people. Both men were in accord that too many black preachers were pitifully unqualified for the pulpit. In 1890 Washington had started a controversy with his assertion that two-thirds of black Methodist and Baptist clergy were mentally and morally unfit. Washington had the support of Bishop Daniel A. Payne, but other bishops and prominent clergy, including Theophilus G. Steward and Benjamin F. Lee, led the opposition. Tanner did not publicly comment on the controversy; however, considering their similar views, it is unlikely that the bishop would have agreed to assist Washington in establishing a Bible school if they were on opposite sides on the important issue of ministerial qualifications. In March 1893 Tanner commenced the first of twelve lectures to students in the newly formed nondenominational Bible School on Tuskegee Institute's campus. He organized three lectures each on four topics: symbolism of the Old Testament; chronology of the Old Testament; harmony of the New Testament; and the ministry of Jesus. Tanner's lectures were published in 1894 as *Theological Lectures* and were widely read and praised. By 1902 Tanner considered Tuskegee's theological department comparable to that of many theological schools but not yet equal to those of Princeton, Drew, or Allegheny.[15]

Tanner was in constant demand to give lectures, but his willingness to comply in addition to his writing and episcopal duties sometimes left him exhausted. In June 1892 he visited with Professor William S. Scarborough at his home at Wilberforce University, where he had "several days of quietude." In September his wife and two daughters accompanied him to Chicago, where he delivered a lecture before the A.M.E. Missionary Congress.[16]

Tanner diligently tended to his episcopal duties, which warranted praise from the *Recorder*. Up to 1893 Tanner increased both membership and dollar money more than any other bishop in the history of the First Episcopal District.[17]

Tanner ranked among the most erudite bishops in the church and arguably had
no peer following the death of Payne on November 29, 1893. While others lamented the loss of their senior bishop, Tanner alone declared that "death has not
robbed us. His work was done . . . and therefore that which belonged to us we
still have—death's doings to the contrary notwithstanding." Tanner added that
an educated ministry would be the best memorial to Payne's memory. Despite
his rather pragmatic commentary upon Payne's passing, Tanner was close ideo-
logically to his mentor, and he was adamant that poor health would not prevent
him from attending the senior bishop's funeral. Tanner's son Henry made a bust
of Payne, with copies available for $2.50.

Henry Tanner, who had gone to Paris in 1891 for study and returned two years
later to raise funds to stay in France, was not yet well known. In spring 1894 the
Philadelphia Item proposed to purchase *The Bagpipe Lesson* to hang it permanently
in the Academy of Fine Arts. The local board of ministers of Tanner's church agreed
to pay Henry one thousand dollars, more than he had received from previous sales,
and then present the painting to the academy on behalf of the black people of Philadelphia. The board planned to recoup their outlay by selling copies of the painting,
but the purchase fell through as they could not raise more than $300. Even though
the concept had the support of the *Item* and many black Episcopalians and was a
sectarian rather than a family effort, its failure weighed heavily on the bishop. Fortunately, Henry was able to return to Paris after selling *The Thankful Poor* in October to the Pennsylvania School for the Deaf. The following month Robert C. Ogden,
a prominent Philadelphia retailer and white liberal, purchased *The Banjo Lesson* and
donated it to Hampton Institute.[18]

Meanwhile, shortly after Payne's death, Halle was ill in Alabama; her mother
went to be with her, returning to Philadelphia in early January 1894. Bishop Tanner, who was scheduled to deliver a lecture at Tuskegee, left for Alabama the following month.[19] In May he traveled to Virginia Normal and Collegiate Institute
in Petersburg to deliver the baccalaureate sermon.[20]

Tanner's involvement in civic affairs and his writing for the *Review* and other
publications did not diminish in any way his commitment to his episcopal duties.
His intimate involvement in so many endeavors reflected his devotion to the spiritual, emotional, and political needs of his people. If anything, his religious devotion
to the people increased during this period, as he was alarmed by the decline of religious fervor among Americans. From May 24 to 28 Tanner presided over the New
York Annual Conference, which met in Jamaica, Long Island. He opened the conference with remarks on "ministerial failure" because of his concern that there were
fewer members than there were twenty years earlier, which meant that less money
was being raised for church causes. He found it alarming that in the conference
there was not one applicant for the four-year ministry course and that the "second
and third year classes had no subjects for examination." Tanner applied his energy

to this matter, and within a year he reported that the New York Annual Conference had "forged ahead . . . in the work of soul winning, money getting and the extension of the work inside her territory." He cited Bethel in Manhattan and Bridge Street in Brooklyn as the leading churches in the conference.[21]

In mid-October 1894 Tanner, substituting for Bishop Turner, presided over the Bermuda Annual Conference. Upon his return, he tended to the duties of the First Episcopal District, including the presidency of the A.M.E. Church Historic and Literary Society.[22] A combination of factors—notably fatigue and too many responsibilities—resulted in Tanner sinking into a deep depression that afflicted him for more than a year. He received some comfort from reading I Peter 5:10, "But the God of all grace who hath called us unto his eternal glory by Christ Jesus, after that ye have suffered, awhile make you perfect, stablish, strengthen, settle you." Bishop and Mrs. Tanner ended his depression by constantly repeating the words "suffering, stablish, strengthen, settle," and one day he felt so comforted that his youngest daughter, sixteen-year-old Bertha, "jumped up and clapped her hands." A joyous bishop exclaimed to his wife Sadie, "Mama, I believe from this time out, I am going to get well." For a time he was better, although periods of minor depression reminded him of the fragility of his spirit. During his recovery, coincidentally, he received a letter in late November from the Rev. Theophilus G. Steward, now an army chaplain, who had decided to send to the Tanners his notes for a sermon pertaining to scriptural references to suffering. He requested that they be passed on to someone in need, not knowing that the bishop himself was such a man. Tanner was so moved by the coincidence that he wrote a poem, "Our Plea," which the *Recorder* published in the December 20 issue.

> To thee, oh Lord, we make our plea
> That human sorrows thou wouldst see
> And human grief; and human tears
> That flow throughout the life—long years
>
> Awake o Lord and speak the word,
> Awake, assert thyself as Lord
> And let the pain of head and heart
> At thy dear comings Lord depart
>
> Awake, and let thy people know
> That from them thou wilt never go;
> And let the world be put to shame—
> If, Lord, it rev'rence not thy name.

Tanner was so relieved that God had heard his cry for relief that he described the intense joy of emerging from his deep depression in another poem, "Darkness."

Presumptuous darkness, hie away
Thou shalt not, shalt not spoil the day,
The night is thine, and thine alone,
Avaunt to blackness all thine own.

Bright is my day, and calm and clear
I love the peace it brings so near
Presumptuous darkness, hie away,
Nor dare break upon my day.

In the final verse, Tanner commands

Away, presumptuous darkness, hie
On thine own wings of blackness fly
Bright is my day, and calm and clear
It is a day to me most dear.

Tanner, a prolific religious poet, was described in 1894 by the *New York Age* as one of the nation's twenty leading African American poets.[23]

Relieved of his depression, during Christmas week 1894 Tanner went to Bridgeton, New Jersey, to lay the cornerstone at Mt. Zion A.M.E. Church's dedicatory services. The *Recorder* acknowledged the bishop's presence with the observation that he "has given ocular proof of his belief in the genius and capacity of the Negro to cope successfully with the Saxon; not only of literature and science, but in art and sciences as well."[24]

Now in excellent spirits, Tanner and his wife entertained as Christmas houseguests Professor and Mrs. Scarborough, who were visiting from Wilberforce University. The bishop's good spirits were reflected in his poem "The Holidays," which emphasized "the humble home now filled with light, the centre now of real delight."[25] Bishop Tanner greeted the new year 1895 in a grand spirit full of love of God. The belief that only God could cure all problems was reflected in the first stanza of his poem "Who?"

If Jesus Lord, I come to thee
And freely thou receivedst me,
Who shall say nay?
Who shall bring up the days of sin?
When earthly passions raged within?

Thirty years earlier, Tanner had questioned the absence of fire in his heart and called upon God to touch him. Now, he felt God's presence, which brought immense joy. In "The Divine Presence," he wrote:

> I sing the praise of my Lord
>
> . . .
>
> Come in, come in, thou guest divine,
> And make my gloomy heart to shine,
> My cold and frozen heart to glow,
> And waters from the rock to flow[26]

In February 1895 he based a *Recorder* essay, "God's Anointed," on Psalms 105:15, "Touch not mine anointed, and do my prophets no harm." The following month, he wrote, "To be spiritually minded is life" because a spiritual person asks God to clothe him in righteousness and sees "God and duty in the incidents of every day."[27] Tanner believed that growth emerged from spirituality. He reminded readers of the *Recorder* that God freely gave the world His only begotten son. "Oh for wisdom to comprehend this world in all its fullness; for grace to accept it, and for faith to practically exemplify it in our lives," he wrote. Tanner displayed this belief in faith in a poem, "All Things Else,"

> How inconsistent, Lord my fears
> How useless all my flowing tears
> If Lord, I believe the word
> Mine ears a thousand times have heard
> I know that thou hast given thy son
>
> . . .
>
> And what besides so dear to thee
> Can be imagined, Lord, as he?
>
> . . .
>
> Naught else, o God, wilt thou withhold.[28]

In another piece, "Depart Not," he wrote,

> Ye saints of God, awake
>
> . . .
>
> Depart not from the living God,
> He only is the Lord.

It was Tanner's belief that God guided man like a rod, assisting him over treacherous pathways, and this knowledge comforted the bishop in the spring of 1895, when both his teenage daughter Bertha and Sadie were ill. Bertha's condition was the worse, as a tooth extraction hemorrhaged long enough to cause considerable anxiety. Perhaps out of concern over Bertha's health and even fear of her possible death, Tanner wrote "Immortality" for the *A.M.E. Church Review.*

In hope I lay me down
Of life beyond the vale;
In sweet assurance of a crown,
And joys that never fail

What if the cold damp grave
Me opens to receive?
Has not the savior pow'r to save
All those who will believe?

And what, if worms consume
Remains already dead—
Worms, fit companions of the gloom
Whence light and life had fled?

In hope, I lay me down
Of life beyond the vale
In sweet assurance of a crown
And glory without fail.[29]

Tanner's poetry was therapeutic, for his faith reinforced for him the belief that God controlled all the forces in the world. It also helped him to cope with the various assaults perpetrated by racists against the intellectual capabilities of Africans in the diaspora. Much of the negative assessment of African aptitude that passed for intellectual discourse regarding the historical achievements of black people was swiftly challenged by Tanner, who took offense at the scholarship that attempted to write the African out of world achievement. While Tanner realized that slavery and deprivation had caused African people to lag behind Anglo-Saxons in intellectual productivity, he took umbrage with the prevailing view that they lacked the innate capacities to compete with Caucasians. For years he had believed that some whites were guilty of falsifying history when it came to the contributions of Africans. For instance, when James T. Bixby declared in the July 1883 *Unitarian Review* that Africans, American Indians, and Australian aborigines never developed higher civilizations, Tanner, then editor of the *Recorder*, retorted, "Did not Egypt receive her civilization from [Ethiopia]? And did not Greece receive her civilization from Egypt? And Rome from Greece?" In 1895 Tanner published *The Color of Solomon—What?* which he dedicated "to the rising scholars of the colored race . . . with the hope that the subject . . . will vindicate the colored races of the earth and save them from the delusion: the leading race in all history has been the white race." Tanner rejected then current scholarship that ascribed Solomon to the white race; instead, he declared that Solomon was of Hamitic and Semitic mixture, which made him Asian or yellow but not white by American standards. Tanner added that Solomon's bushy hair and non-Jewish blood made him a black person. He accused scholars of misinterpreting the Hebrew in the Old Testament. Instead of "my beloved is white and ruddy," it should have been translated "bright and ruddy."[30] Tanner, of course, was not suggesting that Solomon resembled a typical American black man as some did, but certainly, in his view, Solomon did not resemble a typical Anglo-Saxon, either.

The *Christian Recorder* praised Tanner's work, as did T. McCants Stewart, who added that Africans "were the pioneers of mankind in the . . . fields of literature and science." Stewart was pleased that Tanner was following the scholarship of Martin R. Delany, Rufus L. Perry, Edward W. Blyden, Alexander Crummell, and himself, who all insisted that Africans were major players in world civilization.[31] Not all black men were in agreement with Tanner's assessment of Solomon's color. An unidentified reader of the *Recorder* denied that Solomon was "black," since he was a Jew and Jews were not black (evidently he was unaware of black Jews who had resided in Ethiopia for centuries). Besides, he added, the Song of Solomon was an allegorical description of Christ and His bride, the church, and was not to be taken literally.[32]

In a larger sense, *The Color of Solomon—What?* represented Tanner's hope that white Americans would be free of racism if they knew and understood the truth that all people were capable of intellectual gains and that no race had a monopoly on greatness or futility. Tanner believed that if so-called Christians really accepted the truth of Jesus Christ's teachings, they would accept all men as brothers. He contended that "the Christ idea of man has conquered every other idea of Him; whether Jewish or pagan. That idea, is the idea of Fatherhood—largely foreign to the Jew and never dreamt of by the pagan." Optimistically, Tanner believed that acceptance of the Christ idea meant brotherhood and the inevitable reality that government would soon become a government "of the people, and for the people and by the people." However, distancing himself from early militant statements, he called upon the black man and woman to put their cause for equality in Christ and let Him conquer the arm of their foe.[33]

Meanwhile, Tanner labored to continue moving the First Episcopal District forward. At the end of May 1895, the New York Annual Conference met in Albany. Tanner addressed the preachers' meeting in that city and Troy with a message of the shortcomings of American Christianity toward her black citizens. The New York Annual Conference "voted a unanimous testimonial in token of its appreciation of Tanner's services and administration," reported the *Recorder*. On July 30 Tanner requested that the members of the First Episcopal District support Wilberforce University and make the last year of the quadrennium the best one of all. Tanner's farewell admonition to them was from Nehemiah 4:16, "Have a mind to work."[34] Clearly, he was telling them to approach every endeavor with intelligence and not with brute force or reckless disregard for the consequences of their action. He wanted them to maximize their senses for the betterment of the race and for the advancement of Christ's teachings.

Tanner's contribution to the A.M.E. Church and to scholarship was recognized by Wilberforce University, which conferred upon him (and Alexander Crummell) an honorary LL.D. degree on June 20, 1895. What should have been a joyous occasion for the connection was overshadowed by the death of Bishop T. M. D. Ward on June 10. In the Episcopal Address delivered at Wilberforce's commencement, seven of the bishops declared their opposition to African emigration as a solution to America's race prejudice. They believed that while the church could contribute to the missionary effort, only God was capable of redeeming Africa. Bishops Abram Grant and Turner were out of the country, but it was unlikely that their presence would have altered the tone of the message.[35]

Tanner was popular among African Methodists, and many saw in him a model to judge potential candidates for election to the bishopric in 1896. The Rev. J. M. Henderson stated that Tanner possessed such extraordinary gifts that it was remarkable that his successor at the *Review,* Levi J. Coppin, did "not perish by the contrast." Tanner was a man "of an uncompromising fine taste," which determined "his irresistible strength of character." Henderson added that "being a true scholar [Tanner] lack[ed] that robust, bluff manner that . . . is mistaken for strength but he possess[ed] that . . . true strength of character . . . the uncompromising instincts of lofty ideas and refined tastes." People deferred to him because he expected more than ordinary production to please him. "Though prominent and learned, [he is] kindly and friendly," Henderson concluded.[36] The Rev. H. C. C. Astwood added that Tanner was "not a Bible beater, turbulent or boisterous in his eloquence or oratory." Furthermore, he noted that Tanner's "reasoning is so clear and forcible, that you . . . soon become absorbed in the great thought enunciated [and] one often fancies that he is listening to a father admonishing his children." Tanner's supporters admired his sterling character, his unswerving love of the church, and his deep devotion to scholarship, but they should not have overlooked the strong supportive role provided by his wife, who held the family together during his frequent trips over the years, first as editor and then as bishop. It was Sadie who comforted him during the worst moments of his depression. As an admirer of Sadie's observed, the success of the bishop and his illustrious children was "due more to [Sadie's] nobility of character, self-sacrifice, and godly judgment than anything else."[37] Unfortunately, the portrait of Sadie will remain incomplete until further evidence is located. Despite her major contributions to the church's mission work and her support of her husband's duties, little is known about her personal life, as the bishops guarded their privacy.

On the eve of the 1896 General Conference, names were suggested to replace the loss of Daniel A. Payne, John M. Brown, Thomas M. D. Ward, and Alexander

W. Wayman, who had died since the church last met in 1892. Like others who speculated on the need for more bishops, but unlike most who wanted their favorites in office, Tanner called for replacements to fill the void left by Payne in education, Brown in church and conference organization, Ward in solid work, and Wayman in popular preaching.[38]

So many names were suggested to the *Recorder* for the bishopric that Chaplain Theophilus G. Steward satirically recommended himself as "A Most Deserving Candidate" who could among other things walk, whistle, "scratch his head and pat his foot all at the same time." Since he could also walk backward with his eyes shut without stumping his toes, he declared himself a candidate for all the general offices within the church.[39] Satire aside, the church elected three bishops: William B. Derrick, Josiah Haynes Armstrong, and James Crawford Embry, the former business manager of the Book Concern. The General Conference that met in St. Stephen's A.M.E. Church in Wilmington, North Carolina, was in Tanner's estimation the best that he had attended since 1856. Tanner preached the Quadrennial Sermon from Psalms 80:17, "Let thy hand be upon the man of thy right hand. Upon the son of man whom thou madest strong for thyself." Tanner considered the A.M.E. Church the right hand of God and called upon the members not to let the church crumble. He added that they came from strong African stock but now were in need of a virtuous life. He noted that black people were a service people whose job it was to carry God's message but not to add to it nor take away from it. The *Recorder* described Tanner's sermon as "logical, instructive and interesting," a reflection of his reputation as "a pulpit orator and scholar." The Rev. B. W. Roberts described the sermon as "the master effort of [Tanner's] life." Ironically, Tanner, who began the quadrennium responsible for the Book Concern, witnessed the delegates vote to reduce the *Recorder*'s subscription price from two dollars to one dollar per annum as a measure to deter the possibility of the paper folding if paid subscriptions did not increase. Dr. T. W. Henderson was elected business manager of the Book Concern. H. T. Keating, former president of Paul Quinn College, became editor of the *A.M.E. Church Review,* and Henry T. Johnson was reelected editor of the *Recorder.*[40]

It was time for Tanner to move on to his new assignment in the Fifth Episcopal District, which encompassed Missouri, Kansas, Colorado, New Mexico, Montana, and Arizona. Again, during the next four years, Bishop Tanner would challenge the clergy and laity to aim for the heights symbolized by the majestic Rockies.

Chapter 9

Bishop of the Fifth Episcopal District, 1896–1900
Extolling the African Presence in the Bible

The Fifth Episcopal District, made up of both old and new conferences, represented the skill and dedication of hardy missionaries who crossed the Great Plains, formerly known as the Great American Desert because of the absence of trees, combating the forces of prejudice and natural wilderness to bring African Methodism to the West's scattered black population. The Rev. William Paul Quinn introduced the A.M.E. Church into Missouri in the 1830s, and the Rev. Jordan W. Early was one of the pioneer ministers who introduced African Methodism to Iowa and parts of Missouri during the 1840s and the following decade. Bishop John M. Brown organized the Colorado Annual Conference on September 24, 1887. During Arizona's pioneer days an A.M.E. Church was established in Phoenix when N. D. Valentine, Laura Valentine, and a Miss Bell met with the Rev. H. H. Hawkins to develop a mission to foster "family life." Years later, the enlarged property was named Tanner Chapel A.M.E. Church.[1]

Much of the district was in isolated areas where societal restraints were few save for individuals' own judgment. For this reason Tanner was quick to place his personal stamp on the district. In June he informed the clergy and laity of his singular philosophy, which was taken from Amos 3:3, "Can two walk together, except they be agreed?" With typical frankness, he added, "Let there be agreement between us in the things to be done. Let the word be between us: up and at it. Personally I have no use for the lazy and the contentious. Such [will not] be allowed to stand in the way of success." Tanner vowed to do his duty and urged them to do the same. His parting words were "Aim to win souls. Look after the Sunday School. Carry the lambs." Finally, "Improve on last year."[2]

Tanner remained consistent in his challenge to bigotry and racism despite his previous retreat from militant activism. The last years of the nineteenth century were perilous times for African Americans, who were victimized by labor unions, Jim Crowism, disfranchisement, and lynching (122 blacks were lynched in 1897). The Rev. J. G. Robinson of Columbus, Mississippi, attacked American clergy for their silence in light of atrocities committed against African Americans. He urged ministers to speak out against injustices because in their congregations were lawyers, judges, and potential jurors who could make a difference if they lived their lives as true Christians.[3] In an "Emancipation Hymn," the Rev. Joseph Wheeler called upon God for deliverance.

O God of love and grace
smile on our rising race
most graciously
Thou who doth nations bless,
Give to our race success;
Help us when in distress
To trust in thee.[4]

What should blacks do to better their condition? asked the Rev. J. D. Barksdale of Ypsilanti, Michigan. Barksdale believed that they lived under a self-inflicted curse due to an unhealthy racial environment that led them to consider their physiognomy ugly because it was so unlike the white standard of beauty. He urged them to heed Booker T. Washington's words and dignify themselves by not seeking white approval. The Rev. J. I. Lowe said editors and clergymen should seek God's help, wake up, and speak more boldly, adding that it was necessary to put agitators on the lecture circuit, "for our future is gloomy."[5]

In 1897 the question of race pride was addressed by Alexander Crummell, who disdained Booker T. Washington's policy of accommodation. Forty-six of the race's leading scholars, clergy, and activists responded to Crummell's call to a March 5 organizational meeting of the American Negro Academy under his leadership. Among the twenty-nine who took up initial membership were Tanner, W. E. B. Du Bois, John W. Cromwell, editor of the *People's Advocate* in Washington, D.C., poet Paul Lawrence Dunbar, and Professors Kelly Miller and William S. Scarborough. During its early years the ANA "concerned itself with the discovery of working theories for the good of the race" as opposed to literary efforts, which came later.

In contrast, the National Afro-American Council headed by A.M.E.Z. Bishop Alexander Walters fought against the barbarous treatment perpetuated against blacks by setting aside June 2, 1899, as a day for prayer and fasting. Bishops representing the A.M.E., C.M.E., A.M.E.Z., and Union A.M.E. churches were invited to participate. Tanner spoke on June 4 in Philadelphia's Bethel A.M.E. Church, where he urged the race to watch and pray earnestly daily for deliverance from the injustice heaped upon them. There was a motive in every pain people suffered, Tanner asserted, as God in His own way would relieve them of all their burden if people assisted Him.[6]

Despite Tanner's aversion to Crummell's leadership, the American Negro Academy appealed to him. With its emphasis on creating art, philosophy, science, and scholarship—the very things that defined civilization—for blacks as a race, it embodied principles Tanner had been advocating earnestly for thirty years. Unfortunately, his poor health limited his involvement in the organization and finally led to his resignation in 1913.

Tanner's episcopal duties continued to be his priority. Sometimes they even took precedence over important family occasions; his son Carlton married

Frances Serrill in her parents' home in Darby, Pennsylvania, while the bishop and Sadie were attending the Kansas Annual Conference in Topeka.[7]

After completing his first round of conferences, Tanner assessed the Fifth Episcopal District as "all right." The members were Christians to the core, which provided the bishop with immense pleasure. Tanner was so pleased with their promptness and willingness that he challenged the other bishops to pick up the gauntlet, because the Fifth intended to outdo the others. "What say you senior [Turner] leading in the Sixth? What say you junior [Embry] leading on the Seventh? Let us all praise Him for the heritage given, and work it for what it is worth."[8]

The admiration was mutual. In November 1896 the *Recorder* published a letter from C. R. Runyon, a presiding elder in Hannibal, Missouri, praising Tanner for endearing himself to the people by combining religion and business in a way that pleased all. Runyon's observation was all the more telling because Tanner inherited a district that needed a decisive decision maker. After Tanner completed his four conferences, Runyon observed, "no bishop was ever regarded by the people of the district with more solicitude." Tanner's leadership removed from the district's operations the "distrust and timidity" that had previously dominated the Fifth's affairs. The Rev. James H. Hubbard described the bishop as "strict but not unkind." He also had kind words for Sadie, who he thought was an ideal bishop's wife because she was "cultivated and amiable and [had] more than a passing interest in the welfare of the preachers."[9]

Tanner was in poor health at the beginning of 1897. In mid-January Sadie departed Philadelphia to join her husband at 614 Troup Avenue, his residence in Kansas City, Kansas, where he was suffering from pleurisy. During this period, confined to his room for weeks, he suffered poor appetite and had sleepless nights. Understandably, his depression returned. Mail brought hot tears to his eyes. "In these later years," Tanner informed the *Recorder*, "we cry so easily. Time was when we seem[ed] to be as flint." His mail brought him photographs of Sadie and Bertha, a letter from Henry, and a copy of the *Independent*'s art section that contained two references to Henry. "One would think, instead of tears should be smiles but what does unstrung nerves know about smiles," complained the bishop. In October 1898 he took sick at a conference at Carrollton, Missouri, and was confined to his home for two weeks. During these periodic bouts of depression, Tanner wrote poetry to aid in his recovery.

Up

Up, to the ever beck'ning skies
I gladly lift my waiting eyes
The beck'ning skies
Up, to the great white throne of light
Too dazzling for my weeping sight
The throne of light

Up, to the smiling face of God,
The certain rest, the sure abode—
The face of God

Up, up my soul to rea'ms on high
No more to suffer, nor to sign—
The realms on high.

In another poem, "Surrender," Tanner wrote that Christians must surrender to God their head, heart, and hand, for "surrender is [their] offering."[10] Tanner clearly placed his life in God's hands with the belief that someday he would have true peace in Jesus' bosom. Of course, it did not mean that Tanner never complained. However, his complaint was not for himself but rather for the condition that all bishops were subjected to in the A.M.E. Church. It was evident that the bishops were extremely overworked. This sentiment was expressed by the *Recorder* when Bishop J. C. Embry died on August 11, 1897, a victim of malaria contracted on his constant travels. Tanner was in Denver when he heard of his friend's death. His eulogy for his fellow bishop was a blunt criticism that the church had to "stop driving her capable men as with whip and spur." He added that Embry should have had an opportunity to travel abroad or to Nova Scotia or Colorado during the summer instead of to unhealthy South Carolina and Florida.[11]

Between his bouts with depression, Tanner achieved remarkable success in the Fifth District less than six months after taking over the reins. By his own admission, E. W. Lewis of Washington, Missouri, was not an easy man to flatter, but he found Tanner's leadership to be so distinguished "that a statement [about it] may appear as the effusion of a dreamer." Lewis credited the bishop with uniting a fractious group and with developing pride among all for Western University in Quindaro, Kansas. While all understood that Wilberforce was the church's beacon, they appreciated Tanner's efforts to make Western a dominant force in church education. Tanner was lauded for making revivals, dormant for many years, once again fashionable. In October the *Recorder* printed H. B. Parks's evaluation of Tanner, noting he had raised seventeen hundred dollars in dollar money, a thousand over the previous year, and also increased the missionary and educational collection by 10 percent. Parks viewed the bishop's leadership skills as admirable because the Middle West contained "would be political reformers, calamity howlers, and free silver enthusiasts, and [was] dominated by long haired men and short haired women—the advocates of every shade of political creed from women's rights to anarchy." Still, Tanner possessed the skill to lead by "his terse, pointed and practical remarks to the conferences," which impressed even the local press.[12]

Tanner was effective because he had the ability to persuade or compel the members of the Fifth District to adopt his motto, "Up and at it." For instance, shortly after taking charge, Tanner informed those who were not subscribing to the *Recorder* that he had decided to follow the church's discipline and instructed the editor to send the newspaper to every man on the district's roll. Tanner was a skilled administrator who rarely failed to rally the members. He reported in 1898 that the Colorado Conference (Montana, New Mexico, Colorado, and Arizona) had collected one hundred dollars more in dollar money than there were members. But he had a setback when the Missouri Conference did not meet its dollar-money quota, the first time that had happened in a conference under his supervision. He dismissed the fluke with "But there must be a first for everything." Despite this cavalier statement, Tanner was serious about raising dollar money. He informed the elders in the conference, "Remember . . . there must be no failures. To fail is to be incompetent; and incompetent men must go to the rear. Up and at it is the word all throughout the district heard up and at its the call."[13] It was this commitment to discipline that set Tanner apart from many of his fellow bishops who expended little or no effort to raise the necessary funds to support the church.

Tanner had much to be thankful as the heat of summer changed to the cool months of fall in 1897. The district was thriving under his leadership, Western University was attracting students, and the people were pleased with him. But still the dark cloud of depression hung over him. Recognizing this, on October 24 Tanner wrote a poem, "Life's Day," which aptly described his emotions.

How long the day hath been
Since morning sun arose,
The moments and the heavier hours
So slow, how? No one knows

And hot the day hath been
The Sun has simply poured
it rays upon our naked head,
Oft have I cried: help Lord

And full of labor, too,
And full of envious spite
Has been to us this stretched out day
Oft have I longed for night

Oh, peaceful, quiet night
No weary hours, no heat,
No ceaseless toil, no envious spite
Thee, blessed night I greet.[14]

Tanner's toil on behalf of the church could not continue indefinitely. M. B. Sheppard of Pittsboro, North Carolina, noted that the bishop was one of the "elders passing the torch of activism to younger men." Sheppard added that Tanner "has served notice that he will soon lay aside his pen and let those with stronger heads and hands take control." Sheppard believed, however, that many of the younger hands and heads were not as strong as Tanner's.[15]

Despite his periodic depression, tiredness, and willingness to step aside, Tanner was a fighter who worked to his utmost to build the church in the West. He labored hard in 1898 and the following year to make Western University an institution of theological learning. Originally called Freedmen University by its founder, the Rev. Eben Blatchley, it became Western in 1881 after his death. Purchased by the Kansas Annual Conference in that same year, the school suffered from major physical deterioration until March 22, 1898, when Tanner met with its trustees to discuss the school's physical condition. On November 15 they met to hear Tanner tell them to urge the clergy and laity in the Fifth District to support Western the way Wilberforce was supported by leaders in the Ohio area. After Western opened on September 20 for the 1898–99 academic year, the *Western Christian Recorder* editorialized that the presence of Tanner, *Christian Recorder* editor Henry T. Johnson, A.M.E. Church Financial Secretary M. M. Moore, Missionary Secretary H. B. Parks, and Secretary of Education J. R. Hawkins proved that the West was the coming power of the church and that Western University was recognized as good for the church and the race. In late October W. Tecumseh Vernon, editor of the *Western Christian Recorder* and a professor at Western, declared that Tanner was "a safe pilot" to the church and a progressive leader to the race. Mrs. Tanner was praised for her "kindness, prudence, business tact and sympathy," which is "the standard by which a woman's great needs is to be measured."

Tanner became president and dean of Western's theological department, which began classes on November 22. Additionally, he taught courses in the Bible, natural and revealed religion, and A.M.E. history and discipline. Tanner's initial enthusiasm was soon tempered; by December attendance lagged in the theological department. Tanner blamed this on the nearby negligent ministers and renewed his call for an educated ministry. Otherwise, he said, graduates of colleges and universities would leave the pews of African Methodist churches for ones ministered to by a trained clergy. The university's normal, academic, and music departments were crowded, which suggests that the ministers were unprepared for the rigorous theological courses. In the spring of 1899 Kansas governor W. E. Stanley signed into law the Bailey Bill, which appropriated over ten thousand dollars to Western's industrial department. Tanner was close to Booker T. Washington and, while no correspondence suggests it, it is possible that the bishop used his influence to obtain the educator's assistance in supporting the bill, because the educator informed Vernon, "I am glad that you feel that I had some part in helping you secure this aid."[16]

At this time, in addition to assisting Western University, Tanner wrote two important pieces, *The Descent of the Negro* (1898) and *The Dispensations in the History of the Church and the Interregnum* (in two volumes, 1899). *Descent* was a reply to the Rev. Drs. S. H. Vincent, J. M. Freeman, and J. L. Hurlbut, editors of the *Sunday School Journal for Teachers and Young People* of the M.E. Church, who said that blacks were probably not descended from Ham. Tanner, who still did not care for the term "Negro," responded to the trio with the comment that "Ham is the father of all Africa and the negro being of Africa is necessarily of Ham." He accused the Methodist clergymen of believing that the Negro was Adamic but not Noahic. If the Bible is truthful, he declared, then only eight persons survived the flood. Did they believe that the Negro escaped the flood? he asked. Emphatically Tanner declared, "The negro is a man. He is of Adam. He is of Noah. The negro is a brother, and will be until science can demonstrate the Bible to be no more than a fable. That Moses made mistakes, and the divine Son of God . . . endorsed them."[17]

Some of the themes covered included the flood, the origin of man, ordination of women, and baptism. In the preface Tanner noted, "The demand of the hour is for negro [s]cholarship; especially in the line of Biblical ethnology. . . . [N]o other book does the white man swear by, if, indeed he swears by this." Tanner's concern was that if the M.E. Church cried "the negro is not of Ham," soon other white Protestants would claim "the negro is not of Adam." "Our duty," he declared, "is to rally around . . . Genesis, tenth chapter. Make it the citadel of our contention for a share in the common heritage." He called upon other Christian scholars to preserve the words of the Bible writers. "When they say Mitzrahim [or Mizraim] . . . and not Egypt, let it be. When they say Cush . . . and not Ethiopia, let it be. Moses knew nothing about Egypt; as did Jeremiah know of Ethiopia. Our scholars . . . the few that are, the host that will be must listen to Longfellow: 'Let us then be up and doing / With a heart for any fate.'"[18]

Dispensations was richly praised by the nation's African American reviewers. William Derrick in his introduction to the work described it "as the crowning act of [Tanner's] literary life." Other reviewers concurred. The Rev. L. H. Reynolds stated, "It was Ham that educated and trained Moses. It was Ham that sheltered . . . Jesus . . . in infancy and helped Him to bear the cross." In 1900 Tanner expanded his theme in *The Negro in Holy Writ*. He used "Negro" in the title to mean ancient people who were black in complexion even though the term was not in the Bible. Still, Tanner believed that blacks were in the Bible in fact if not name, and he cited the Greek word "Ethiopia," mentioned forty times and meaning "burnt face," to prove his point. He said that the prophet Jeremiah described Ethiopians as black. Two years later Tanner accused the *Daily Times*, the American Old Testament Revision Company, and others of seeking to remove Ethiopia from the Bible because they feared that blacks and Africa were too related to the location of the Garden of Eden. He added, "Aryan scholarship has its theory . . . and if any fact stands in the way it is to be removed." Tanner's solution to false scholarship was "If the head is too big for the hat it must be shaved down."[19]

In his personal life Bishop Tanner was as devoted to his family as he was to ministering to the members of the Fifth Episcopal District. He encouraged his wife and daughter Bertha to be active in the Kansas City community, and he supported their membership in the Pierian Club, a women's study group that examined subjects from art and music to science. Henry spent the summer of 1897 in Kansas City painting in a supportive family atmosphere. In the fall Henry returned to France. Proud of his son. the bishop arranged during the winter of 1898 to sell from his residence 8$^1/2$" x 10$^1/2$" photographs of Henry's *Raising of Lazarus*, which had won a gold medal in France and was purchased by that country's government to hang in a Luxembourg gallery. Bertha Tanner was responsible for collecting fifty cents for walk-in orders and sixty cents for mail orders, thus learning simple accounting, service, and public relations.[20] A somber note struck the family in April when the Rev. Richard Tanner, the bishop's brother, died at age fifty-three in Pittsburgh. A happier occasion was when the Tanners celebrated their fortieth wedding anniversary on August 19, 1898, at their Kansas City home with musical selections, poetry, addresses from the city's leading citizens, and congratulatory telegrams from other bishops.[21] On February 11, 1899, the Tanners received a pressed flower specimen from Henry, who was in Jerusalem obtaining archaeological information for his future religious paintings.[22] For his accomplishments the bishop was elected to *Who's Who in America* in 1899–1900; Henry followed in 1901–2.[23]

Tanner's pleasure in his family was supplemented by the satisfaction he took in presiding over the Colorado Annual Conference that met September 4, 1899, at Pike's Peak, the first time a conference met at that famous spot. J. T. Smith proudly reported that the Colorado Conference set new standards by raising $1221.36 in dollar money from among its eight hundred members. He noted that the $1.52 raised from each member was a challenge to other conferences "to come up higher." The happy members presented Tanner with a cash gift of thirty dollars as well as ten dollars each for Sadie and Bertha.[24]

Tanner's devotion to the church and his scholarship did not blind him to the problems of the nation, and although he wrote predominantly on religious subjects during this period, he was not completely silent on issues of secular importance. The breakout of war with Spain in 1898 brought acute attention to the issue of color, both among the men of the 9th and 10th Cavalries and the 24th and 25th Infantries, who became known as the Colored Regulars, and among the darker-complexioned populations of Cuba, Puerto Rico, and the Philippines, areas liberated by American military prowess. The men of the Colored Regulars saw it as their duty to fight for the country's flag, but other African Americans, including Tanner, were not blind patriots. "The splendid little war" left many in the race ambivalent. While some believed it was their duty, irrespective of their second-class citizenship, to support the government, others were unwilling to back a war that they viewed as imperialistic, an extension of American racism to the Caribbean and Asia, or both. Lewis Douglass, a Civil War veteran and son of Frederick Douglass, believed it hypocritical for black men to fight for a government that did not protect their basic human rights. Tanner bluntly declared that President William McKinley would not recognize a free Cuba because of that island's large African-descended population.[25] It was ironic that Tanner, who had supported anti-slavery activity decades earlier in the Spanish American territories because it represented an opportunity for Protestant missionary work, was now silent when the possibility of American military victory meant probable evangelization in Cuba and Puerto Rico.

Easter coincided with the declaration of war. Fittingly, Tanner wrote a poem that praised Christ's resurrection as a sign of peace.

Easter

As come and go these Easter days
So full of hope, so full of praise
Hope for the coming life,
Praise for the end of strife
We hear from the earth in thought arise
The earth so full of pain and death,
Of days malarious, poisonous breath,
And towards the ever shim'ring skies
Lift up the thoughts, lift up our voice,
And with the church of Christ rejoice.[26]

Tanner's sentiment was editorially shared by the *A.M.E. Church Review*, which stated that it was the duty of the preacher to abhor war and not to use the pulpit to "spur young men on to enlistment with the thought of winning glory by shedding human blood."[27] In 1900, two years after the Spanish-American War ended but before American pacification was complete in the Philippines, Tanner noted that most African Americans sympathized with the Filipinos in their struggle against the United States. Tanner offered the novel observation that it was God's will for Americans to control the Philippines because the United States needed another dose of the "Race Question." Years earlier, when Tanner experienced seasickness, an Englishman informed him that only if he first got fully sick would he have a complete recovery. The nation needed a larger dose of prejudice before it would be cured of racism, insisted Tanner. The six to eight million blacks in the United States represented a teaspoon of medicine, whereas the addition of eighteen to twenty million Filipinos, Cubans, and Puerto Ricans would provide the United States with the tablespoon of medicine necessary.[28] Tanner's cynicism was matched by the editor of the *A.M.E. Church Review*, who expressed happiness in learning that whites were lynching other whites. "We have for a long time waited for it," he wrote, because "there is no reason . . . why the best citizens . . . should not command the best victims in the market." He added tongue-in-cheek that it was better to lynch an honorable white than five hundred "ignorant trembling Negro[es] of no social standing."[29]

Tanner, who wanted the nation to recognize the equality of all persons, was pleased when the *Kansas City Star* editorialized in 1898 that both races had good and bad representatives, a fact that whites often ignored when evaluating people of color. Tanner was disturbed that white ruffians disrespected the wives and daughters of respectable black gentlemen. It incensed him when his unidentified daughter, a student at Drexel Institute, and her friends had to hear "by gone" language from white toughs in the soda fountain.[30] Similar views were expressed by two Alabama newspapers, the *Wide-Awake* in Birmingham and the *Montgomery Enterprise*, when they declared that it was wrong for whites to lump refined blacks with the low-down class of blacks, who were just as repugnant to the black elite as to whites.[31]

Tanner's last year in the Fifth Episcopal District was an eventful one. Back home in Philadelphia for vacation awaiting the summer and fall conferences, Tanner preached in early June 1899 at Bethel A.M.E. Church on John 21:15–16, "Jesus said unto Simon Peter three times, lovest thou me more than [others]? He saith unto him, yea, Lord, thou knowest that I love thee. He saith unto him, feed my lambs." The *Recorder* indicated that following the powerful sermon "there were but few dry eyes in the house. All felt the force of the discourse and at the same time realized that they had been instructed. [His] great learning coupled with his large experience, fits him to be the instructor of the people. Truly, in the message of Jesus, Tanner fed the sheep and the lambs."[32] At year's end, Tanner expressed his personal faith.

Saved by Grace
Let it live in thy thought
Saved by grace
Let it live in thy word
Saved by grace
Let it live in thy death
Saved by grace.[33]

Tanner began his final conference in St. Louis in early October. After packing up their belongings in Kansas City and saying their farewells, Benjamin, Sadie, and Bertha passed through St. Louis on January 9, 1900, en route to Philadelphia. Dr. C. W. Preston of St. Louis informed the *Recorder*, "They leave behind them an affectionate and grateful people who know his worth to the race and the dignity that his administration in church and race affairs has brought to a great connection." The Tanners arrived home soon afterward in "prime condition," and the bishop preached at Union A.M.E. Church on January 14, 1900.[34]

Before going to Columbus, Ohio, for the May General Conference meeting, Tanner suggested in late March 1900 that members of the Fifth Episcopal District give offerings for Easter and for the twentieth century because (1) God had done much for the race in the nineteenth century since both the slave trade and slavery were abolished; (2) since 1800 African people had gone from enslavement, barbarism, and heathenism to an acceptance of Christianity; (3) in 1800 there were no churches, deacons, elders, nor bishops who professed an allegiance to African Methodism, but now, in 1900, the connection had 5200 churches, 663,000 members, nine bishops, sixty-five annual conferences, and 5439 ministers.[35] Tanner went to Columbus knowing that he had done his best for the Fifth Episcopal District. The *Christian Recorder* considered him to be a Christian hero, for "he has made the humblest pastor feel that he is his brother and a coworker in the vineyard of the Lord." While Tanner served the district well, he never pretended to know everything, and he submitted the gravest questions for council. Perhaps his greatest achievement during the past four years was helping to convince the Kansas legislature to provide ten thousand dollars for the establishment of an industrial department at Western University. According to O. J. W. Scott of Denver, Tanner "put himself earnestly in touch with the many problems before [the people]. All the brethren love and honor [him]."[36]

Tanner's new assignment had him in the Ninth Episcopal District, comprising Tennessee and Kentucky and divided into four conferences. New bishops elected were Cornelius T. Shaffer, Evans Tyree, Charles C. Smith, Levi J. Coppin, and Morris M. Moore (who died November 23, 1900, before entering active service). Coppin, who was assigned to the Fourteenth Episcopal District with conferences in South Africa and Transvaal, was the first A.M.E. resident bishop to work permanently in southern Africa. Although Bishop Turner had traveled to South Africa, it was not until Coppin's arrival on February 19, 1901, that an African Methodist bishop officially visited that land. During the summer of 1900 Bishops Tanner, Coppin, and Handy contributed twenty-five dollars each toward the goal of five hundred dollars to establish an A.M.E. college in South Africa.[37]

Tanner had departed the rocky wilderness and rugged beauty of the Southwest and the full-fruited plains of Kansas and Missouri to labor in the bluegrass country of Kentucky and the splendor of Tennessee's Smoky Mountains. He welcomed the challenge.

Chapter 10

Bishop of the Ninth Episcopal District, 1900–1904

Forming an Educated Ministry amid Family Tragedies

The beginning of Tanner's assignment was underscored by a minor controversy involving him and Henry T. Johnson, the editor of the *Christian Recorder*. After Johnson was elected to a third term in May, he called upon the bishops to recruit more subscribers, and Tanner took extreme offense to the suggestion. As a former editor, Tanner believed that it was not the responsibility of a bishop to obtain subscribers; that was the jurisdiction of the publisher and editor. The lack of records clouds the controversy, but Tanner's assertions showed that he had no tolerance for those whom he did not personally like or those who lacked logical thought. Johnson said that his opponents were upset because he did not carry his brains "under other men's hats!" Tanner responded by noting that former editor Benjamin F. Lee carried his brains under his own hat and so did he, which did not prevent either from becoming bishop. Publisher R. H. W. Leak had the final word. "We must have 100,000 subscribers [to wipe out financial problems] . . . hat or no hat, or brains or no brains."[1]

The controversy aside, Tanner challenged the members of the Ninth Episcopal District to remove "can't" from their vocabulary and replace it with "must." Since the future of the race was in the strength of the young men, Tanner told the ministers to heed the words of Zechariah 2:4, "Run, speak to this young man."[2] In August he informed the men of the district that many needed to prove their manhood. His message "to the weak and trifling [was] GET OUT OF THE WAY, . . . we are so building that no breach shall be left in our wall." This succinct message was taken in the fall to conferences in Danville, Kentucky (September 26), Columbus, Kentucky (October 10), Chattanooga (October 24), and Memphis (November 14).[3]

In 1900 Tanner, who had briefly served as dean of Payne Theological Seminary in 1891 following the death of his predecessor, J. S. Mitchell, resumed those duties as well as writing a regular column for the *Christian Recorder*. Payne faced a deficit of fourteen thousand dollars and was in imminent danger of closing unless funds could be raised. A believer in self-reliance, Tanner deemed it important that African Methodists take the initiative in erasing the deficit. He offered for five dollars a Payne memorial watch, which had a portrait of the late bishop with the inscription "the father of an educated ministry." To spur on sales, Tanner declared in the October 4 issue of the *Recorder* that he was putting aside his watch of twenty years in favor of the honor of wearing the first Payne watch. He asked, "Who will be the second?" Favorable responses came from Hallie Q.

Brown, Mrs. Bishop Campbell, and a member of the Kentucky conference who sold his five display samples.[4] There were some, however, who saw something unchristian in the Payne watch campaign. S. D. Cutcher of London, England, thought it "a step against education to offer a watch as a prize." He added that it was a sinful gesture and not a biblical solution. Cutcher instead recommended that churches pray for the means as well as solicit freewill offerings. He further noted that instead of buying a watch, people should sell their gold watches and donate the proceeds to Payne Theological Seminary. Cutcher enclosed five dollars to show his support but requested that a watch not be sent to him.[5]

In addition to his own district responsibilities and the deanship, Tanner assumed responsibility for the Eighth Episcopal District after Bishop Morris M. Moore died November 23, 1900. Three days after Moore's death, Tanner, who was en route to conference in Port Gibson, Mississippi, wrote from Helena, Arkansas, that 848 subscribers had requested Payne watches. In December he proudly proclaimed that between them the Demopolis and Florence conferences in Alabama had pledged one hundred watch subscriptions. Tanner was pleased that the people in those conferences and elsewhere were eschewing tobacco and liquor to purchase the Payne watch. Dismissing his critics, he added that the watch was the prize for raising money just as heaven was the prize for faith. Asking for God's help without using effort to obtain it was not the answer, he asserted.[6]

Bishop Tanner was extremely happy to report on December 28 that there was tremendous support in the South for Payne Theological Seminary. He cited the example of N. A. Mott, a white merchant in Yazoo, Mississippi, who raised $206 for the cause. Mott attended a conference and suggested they sing "All Hail the Power of Jesus' Name." Tanner was moved by Mott's display of brotherhood. "I rubbed my eyes and asked myself: is this an actual happening, and that in Mississippi?" Support came from all over the land. By January 25, 1901, Tanner reported that 1270 subscription books had been distributed. Send the money, he implored.[7]

Tanner arrived at Payne sometime in February 1901, ready to assume the duties of dean. The *Recorder* viewed him as a zealous advocate of the seminary. "Should he succeed . . . he will have crowned an unusually long and useful career with its chief glory and will leave that which above all things else will give hope of the perpetuity and continued growth of our church," commented the editor.[8]

Tanner's concern for the growth of ministers took two forms at this time. First, he understood that the power of speech was key in attracting people to God's message. Therefore, he invited Hallie Q. Brown, an elocutionist, to give instructions at conferences. Taylor S. Johnson, who attended the West Tennessee Conference, commented that Brown's presentation "represents what a woman can do if permitted. Conference sentiment says 'Miss Hallie is a Godsend.'"[9]

Second, in 1900 Tanner wrote a ninety-six-page pamphlet, *Hints to Ministers*, out of his conviction that the race needed scholarship and his desire to share the wisdom of his experiences. The avoidance of fornication was among his hints, because the body was a temple to the glorification of God. He strongly recommended that knowledge of grammar and punctuation be acquired by ministers who represented hope for leadership to the race. Tanner told ministers to be tenacious, as his son Henry was in pursuing an art career.

In 1901 Tanner again suggested that ministers "study science. . . . [W]aste no time on books written by small men, when large men have written upon the same." He further advised them to study the history of all races but to "study . . . in the light of original data, . . . and not in the light of the white man's conclusion." Operating in the center of black-oriented historiography, Tanner added that ministers should "push aside the mist which white scholarship has thrown over every race, save its own—push it aside, and aim to give [your race] correct views of the past; especially of Mizraim and . . . Cush, whence we on our African side sprang." Tanner's evaluation of biblical history did not mean that he supported black supremacy or even agreed with Bishop Henry M. Turner's contention that "God is a Negro" but rather that Europeans were not the only qualified interpreters of world history.[10]

During the waning days of the nineteenth century, Tanner instructed the elders and ministers in the Ninth Episcopal District to meet at 12:15 A.M. in churches on January 1, 1901, to "offer thanksgiving and praise to El Shaddai whom the patriarch and prophet, the apostles and disciples . . . have adorned." They were instructed to preach at 10:00 A.M. from Hebrews 18:8, "Jesus Christ is the same yesterday and today, yea and forever." At the conclusion of the service, the ministers were to collect offerings in the name of debts resting upon the church. He ordered the two Kentucky conferences to select a Sunday in January to collect for Wayman Seminary and the three conferences in Tennessee to take an offering for the Mitchell Bible Training School in Shelbyville.[11]

In February Tanner informed the ministers in the Ninth Episcopal District that their first priority was to save souls; therefore they had to back up their preaching by living exemplary lives. He implored them to reach out to the young men because it was "from their ranks [that] came the fuel that feeds the . . . fires of the lynchers." "Aim," he added, "to bring them under the saving influence of the church." Tanner cautioned them that disease, pestilence, dirt, and poverty were direct results of sin. While his advice was sound, it was directed toward the wrong group. Instead of placing blame squarely on lynchers, he, not unlike Booker T. Washington, suggested that black men could avoid lynching by behaving themselves.[12]

While it was clear that Tanner wanted young men in the church to replenish it with new vigor, it was not clear to some whether or not the church really wanted young men to succeed in the ministerial ranks. James G. Martin informed the *Recorder* in March 1901 that the Baltimore Annual Conference had sent twenty young ministers, many of whom were former schoolteachers with college credits, to languish in rural districts with no prospect of being brought to the front until they were too old to do the work. He questioned the wisdom of making them wait for years before giving them work to justify their sacrifice in attaining an education. Martin concluded that it was bad policy for bishops or presiding elders to say that they wanted "big men" for the "big churches." Give the young men an opportunity or the church suffers, Martin warned.[13]

Fortunately, Tanner was different, and for this reason young men respected him. In March the bishop was in Frankfort, Kentucky, where on the fifteenth a banquet was given in his honor. Two days later Tanner preached two sermons "full of wisdom and replete with practical instruction which met with a hearty response." That afternoon he told 150 young men to get on the right track "and [make] the port of success on schedule time." His words moved many to vow to change their sinful ways.[14]

Tanner's devotion to the young men did not cause him to overlook the women in the church. He informed the presiding elders and ministers of conferences that a three-day convention for women interested in missionary work would be held in Nashville on May 30, followed by one in Louisville on July 2. His objective in having the convention was twofold: it would permit women to work unitedly and effectively for a good cause, and it would lead to better coordination of the missionary work, which extended from Canada to South Africa. In a turnabout, women at the convention voted, whereas men could become honorary members by paying twenty-five cents but were ineligible to vote. Sadie Tanner was active in assisting her husband.[15]

Tanner's joy at speaking with young men and organizing the women's convention was overshadowed by the unexpected death of his daughter Halle, a mother of four who died in late April due to childbirth complications. Crushed but believing that her soul would have everlasting life, the bishop accepted the loss of his talented daughter. Again, he found comfort in writing a poem.

In Memoriam
Halle is dead
The wires sadly say
Not so, my love,
She is not dead,
As thou hast said
Only the eve has come,
When weary feet turn home,
At close of labor done,
At close of setting sun
For largely sad has been her day
And joyless, too her stay
Upon the earth—

A strength to all mirth
But now to her the eve has come
And Halle is at home
The joy and rest denied her here
Are hers forever there

. . .

But do the birds not live?
Sweet music not still give?
And trees and fields, and flowers;
Will they not smile to April showers?
So, too, our Halle lives
And ceaseless praises gives.

Drawing upon his faith, Tanner took comfort in the message of I Corinthians 15:55, "O death, where is thy sting? O grave, where is thy victory?"[16] To add to the bishop's pain, on July 13 his son the Rev. Carlton Tanner was brutally assaulted in Philadelphia by the Rev. H. C. C. Astwood, who had recently been expelled from the Philadelphia Annual Conference. Astwood was angry that Carlton declined his request to get the bishop to reinstate him into the ministry.[17]

The loss of Halle was somewhat eased when the A.M.E. Church invited Tanner and H. T. Keating, editor of the *Review*, to read papers at the Methodist Ecumenical Conference in London, September 4–17, 1901. Commenting on Tanner's selection as one of the twenty-one representing African Methodism in London, William D. Chappelle described the bishop as a ship with "streams of sunshine . . . [radiating] from her brow while she plows the intellectual waters with ease. Her mighty structure . . . [is] anchored away out of full blast of the mighty winds of the nineteenth century. She is now cruising in the poetic waters, leaving streaks of her love behind her, that coming generations may know of her path and learn to walk therein."[18] Less poetic but equally admiring was the view of another minister who declared that the bishop did not "pick his brethren, but [met] them on a common level. There is no material difference between the humble mission pastor and the pastor in the largest station."[19]

Before his departure, Tanner informed the members of the Ninth Episcopal District that during his three months' absence he wanted them to pay off their church debts, organize mite missionary societies, study the church discipline, and raise at least five dollars in each church for the A.M.E. schools in Harrodsburg and Shelbyville. He added that the people should turn a deaf ear to malcontents and traitors and not be lured away from the church that brought them the gospel.[20]

Even before the twenty-one delegates departed for London questions were raised about the selection process and the value of the conference. Criticism was directed toward the church's financial board for voting to spend four hundred dollars for each delegate in light of limited funds for numerous projects. Some questioned the wisdom of sending ten bishops when more ministers should have had the opportunity. Contrary arguments were presented by the Rev. R. C. Ransom, who believed that the outlay of funds was insignificant in light of the wisdom and organizational skills the delegates would bring home. After the conference ended, P. A. Hubbard, financial secretary, noted that one could not measure by dollars the eloquence black men showed the world.[21]

Tanner departed for England on August 10 aboard the Cunard Line's *Campania* with a hundred dollars from members of the Ninth Episcopal District, in addition to four hundred dollars allocated from the church's financial board—contrasted to his first voyage to England in 1881, when he arrived with only $150, slept in second- and third-rate boarding houses and had to borrow money to return home, arriving without a cent.[22]

Although the Ecumenical Conference attracted Methodists from Asia, Africa, Europe, and North America, only fifty of the five hundred delegates were "colored" persons, all of them African American, and the representatives from non-European areas were not indigenous people but European missionaries. Despite their low status in America, black delegates were in high demand to preach in churches throughout Great Britain. Prejudice against them was absent, although some Americans walked out when A.M.E.Z. Bishop Alexander Walters stated that white Americans sought to destroy the good opinion the English had in regard to American blacks.[23] The cordial atmosphere led Bishop William B. Derrick to exclaim, "I am quite sure that America will never be just the same to many of us who have enjoyed the larger freedom here, because we shall not be just the same but other than what we were." Bishop Charles S. Smith added, "The dreaded ghost of American assemblages, sectionalism and colorphobia, was far removed."[24] Tanner and the other black delegates who spoke were praised by the London *Methodist Recorder* for their scholarship, a marked improvement since the 1881 meeting when only one, John C. Priel, received such acknowledgment. Tanner spoke on September 16 about "The Elements of Pulpit Effectiveness," emphasizing that a minister who had the divine call must display a solid knowledge of the gospel. He noted that ministers had to have healthy bodies because sickly preachers cannot be missionaries to the world. This was an important consideration for him because he believed it the duty of Christians to bring all the races to Christ, including the orthodox Jews, who should "forget their Abramic blood, their history, their supposed destiny."[25]

During conference proceedings, delegates were shocked to learn that President William McKinley, wounded by an assassin's bullet on September 6, died eight days later. The African Methodist delegates offered the first words of sympathy after hearing about his demise.[26]

Tanner departed Liverpool September 28 aboard the *Umbria,* arriving in New York October 6. Soon after, he departed for conferences in Kentucky and Tennessee.[27] A family tragedy struck while he was presiding over the East Tennessee Conference on October 30 with the news that his daughter Sarah Tanner Moore, wife of Professor Lewis B. Moore of Howard University, had died. Tanner returned to Philadelphia to bury his daughter, who was not yet thirty. Saddened but believing that she was in heaven, he returned to complete conference assignments.[28]

Leaving behind 1901 with its bittersweet memories, Tanner embraced the new year. On January 20 he attended the Bishops' Council meeting in Philadelphia. The *Recorder* described him as holding his own physically and as "quite above" the other bishops in "spirits, intellect and nervous condition[;] he is the most voluminous author of the bench and never allows the work of his district to flag."[29] On February 3 he reminded the president of the conference Mite Missionary Society branches and the women in the Ninth District that they needed to raise funds to support the mission work in Africa. South Africa represented a fertile field for African Methodism, and twenty churches would be dedicated there in 1902. Not all converts were black. Bishop Levi J. Coppin wrote in the *Independent* that when he dedicated an A.M.E. church at Arensdale on March 31, 1901, a Boer worshiper said, "I observe no difference in the spirit of pure Christianity by belonging to a Negro church. In my wickedness, I associated with [blacks]. They were good enough for me then. In my endeavor to lead a better Christian life now I find them equally good." Theophilus G. Steward, chaplain of the 25th United States Colored Infantry, also called upon the A.M.E. Church to fulfill its obligation to spread the gospel. He saw opportunities not only in South Africa but in Puerto Rico, Cuba, and the Philippines, where he served for several years. But this missionary outreach called for a better-trained ministry, more discipline, and less criticism of the bishops, suggested Steward.[30]

Tanner, of course, supported foreign mission endeavors, but securing financial aid for the church schools in his district was his immediate concern. In April 1902 he informed the pastors in Tennessee that the Shelbyville school faced a dire financial future. Tanner instructed the presiding elders in the state to read John 2:15, "Whatever he saith unto you, do it." J. H. Turner informed the ministers and laity in the Chattanooga District to send in money at once to support Shelbyville in response to Tanner's challenge, "We must push or be pushed."[31] In June Tanner called for special collections to support the schools. "Leave nothing undone" was his message to the district.[32] A few weeks later, Tanner demanded that the Kentucky conferences make a strong effort to procure funds for education. He stated, "Let nothing intervene between you and the lifting of this collection. Let it be 'a long pull, a strong pull, and a pull altogether.'"[33]

Like the other bishops, Tanner had to make strong appeals for fundraising. Although the A.M.E. Church boasted nearly seven hundred thousand members in 1902, they supported 5715 churches, 2075 parsonages, forty-one schools and universities, thirteen bishops, twelve general officers, 6343 traveling preachers, and 16,226 local preachers. Fiscal inefficiency was their bane.[34] Some of the ministers were poor organizers or had difficulty in requesting money from others even though church discipline compelled them to collect dollar money from every worshiper. Others openly refused to collect funds because they resented the itinerary system that shifted them from church to church, often hundreds of miles away. One minister, for instance, was upset that he was transferred from New York City to Atlantic City, New Jersey, which meant to him a "fall . . . a letting down."[35]

What the church lacked was more bishops like Tanner, whose leadership and application of his motto "Push or be pushed" inspired the Ninth Episcopal District to live up to his expectations. The East Tennessee Conference that met in Fayetteville in October collected seventy-five dollars more in dollar money than in the previous year.[36]

The West Tennessee Annual Conference's November meeting witnessed a minor confrontation between Tanner and H. B. Parks, secretary of the missionary board, after the latter failed to print the conference matters and convention meetings of the Ninth Episcopal District in the minutes. Tanner attributed the omission, which Parks said was unintentional, to the district's meager Easter Day collection earmarked for foreign missions. Parks "exhibited a turbid appearance even after [Tanner's] conciliatory and apologetic explanation." The meeting continued with "ordinary and rigid politeness," reported the *Recorder*. Perhaps the confrontation with Parks taxed Tanner's health; the bishop was feeble for part of the session but improved as the singing uplifted him.[37] The respite was only temporary, as Bishop Tanner returned to Philadelphia indisposed and was confined to his bed with his physician's orders to "take a good rest." By Christmas he was much improved in health.[38]

Clearly Tanner had worked himself to exhaustion, but he was not inclined to rest for long. He did not believe in either idle minds or idle hands. Commencing February 13, 1902, he contributed to the *Recorder* an irregular column, "Stray Thoughts," which ran until July 16, 1908, and as its name implied covered diverse topics. His poetry, inspired by the Holy Scriptures, provided him with peace during periods of depression, illness, and family tragedy. "The Sun of Righteousness," written on February 4, was from Malachi 4:2.

> Thou Sun of Righteousness
> No need that we confess
> How deep the darkness of our day—
> The darkness of our way
>
> No need that we confess,
> Oh, Sun of Righteousness
> How bleak the sweeping winds and cold—
> Lambskin without the fold

And lifeless, we confess Thou Sun of Righteousness,
These deadened souls of ours to be—
Lifeless toward thine and thee

Arise, oh, glorious Sun
And let thy work be done
Give us to light and heat and life
Lord, and end the strife.[39]

In the same pensive mood, five days later he wrote "Thy Presence," based on Exodus 33:14.

We only Lord, thy presence pray—
Only thy presence all the day;
And when the shades of night come on
Be with us, Lord, till night be gone

When through earth's desert wild we go
We ask not that the stream should flow
To quench our thirst, while on the way
Only thy presence, Lord, we pray
And when on life's great sea we roam,
We ask not that no bilious foam,
No blowing winds, no dashing spray—

Only thy presence, Lord, we pray
If with us, Lord, then all is well,
As joyfully thy people tell—
Thy people who are wont to say
We only, Lord, thy presence pray.[40]

Tanner continued in this vein with his interpretation of Psalms 2:8, "Ask of me, I shall give thee the heathen for thine inheritance, and the uttermost parts of the earth for thy possession."

Ask of Me
We ask possession of the land
Much yet remains
From mountain peak to ocean stand
We ask possession of the land

We ask its cities to possess
Their gates and towers

> That . . . master shall confess
> We ask its people to control
> The weak, the strong,
> In every part in very whole
> We ask its people to control
> As Christ's viceregents here we stand
> The promise claim,
> And in His name make the demand
> For people, cities and the land.[41]

When the demons in Tanner's mind robbed him of intellectual energy, he turned to God for deliverance. Tested again and again, this intense faith shone through the fog of depression. It was in these moments of revelation that he rejoiced. In July he wrote "A Song of Love" from Psalms 45:1–17, which expressed his exhilaration in the power of Christ's spirit to bring salvation.

> Thou spirit of the living Christ
> Who hast the ages brought
> From death and darkness to the light,
> Bring me to light long sought
>
> Who hast the men of every race
> So long estranged and wild
> Subdued and brought within thy love
> Subdued and make me mild
>
> And all the gods of men's devise
> Them didst thou, Lord, uncrown
> And dash into the moles and bats
> Last thou my gods all down
>
> Thou conquering spirit of the world
> Orient, Occident
> Pale northern, bronzed men of the south
> My nature circumvent.[42]

A letter inspired one of Tanner's "Stray Thoughts" topics. After receiving a letter from Chaplain Theophilus G. Steward, who observed that in the Philippines Catholic priests reached the people better than did Protestants by utilizing the great festivals as religious days, Tanner wrote in the March 13, 1902, *Recorder* that African Methodists should emulate their religious rival by preaching on the great festival days of Advent, Ash Wednesday, Palm Sunday, Maundy Thursday, Good Friday, Whit Sunday, and Trinity Sunday besides Easter.[43]

Tanner's thoughts were generally appreciated, but his column on March 27, "Episcopal Arrogance," caused a stir with his assertion that bishops, who were expected to enforce church law, should at no time give the impression that they would use their position for personal gain. The *Recorder* noted in an editorial that some bishops had been criticized because they "believed more in form and letter than in substance and spirit of true worth and good works." The editor added that one bishop presiding over a meeting broke his gavel and passionately threw its handle "with furious recklessness," while another bishop threatened to knock down a speaker who was slow in responding to a request to take his seat. As a reader observed, criticism of the bishops was justified because too many were selected for political reasons and condemned for the same.[44]

Since his 1903 episcopal duties engaged him only from September 23 through November, Tanner had ample time to devote to his column. In March he urged ministers to emulate the prophets and disciples who spoke against adultery, and he demanded that they stop being polite and speak out forcefully against lynching and caste discrimination and display the courage to reprimand the powerful in government or corporations.[45] Clearly, while he supported Booker T. Washington's industrial education program, he was beginning to distance himself from the Wizard's accommodation policy.

Tanner understood that a cowardly church would never draw members from a community that insisted on having their constitutional rights, which partly explains his renewed interest in militancy. He also recognized the folly of bringing people into the church and then attempting to alter their previous denominational beliefs. Trying to encourage Baptists to embrace Methodism was a mistake because it led to alienation and ultimate withdrawal from all organized religion, he argued.[46] Yet he noted that when a true conversion had taken place, the converted had an obligation to bear witness for Christ. "The converted Jew," he declared, "must go and tell the Samaritan of the surprising love of Jesus [for] the principle involved is that a religion that will not bear telling to our enemies comes short of that that is essential to its completeness."[47]

Tanner's "Stray Thoughts" provided him with a solace that was reassuring. In July both he and Sadie were indisposed. As they spent several weeks recuperating at a seaside resort in Pleasantville, New Jersey, his thoughts dealt with the strength that faith in God provided. "He slumbers not, nor sleeps. And He [watched] o'er all creatures whether in the heights or deep," he wrote.[48]

Because Tanner wanted to educate clergy and laity alike, his thoughts often dealt with religious interpretations. He explained that when worshipers said "I believe in the holy catholic church," they were not honoring the pope but stating that the Christian church was universal, the meaning of the Greek *katholikos*, from which "catholic" was derived. When Charles S. Long, a reader, sent a copy of this essay to Dr. R. F. Clark of the Episcopal Church, the latter replied, "I never dreamed that there lived such an advocate of the principles of the Protestant idea of the church universal wrapped in black skin as Mr. Tanner. My respect for your race, and especially your church, has been deepened and I am sure such contributions will tend to the advancement of humanity."[49] The complimentary words underlined the ignorance that white America had about her darker citizens and justified Tanner's insistence that whites needed to understand that no race had a monopoly on intelligence or scholarship.

Despite his attacks on the Catholic Church thirty years earlier, now Tanner found much to admire in its policies. For instance, he stated that African Methodists needed to imitate Catholics and those Protestant sects that confirmed at age thirteen, arguing that the A.M.E. Church's ban on confirmation at that age was based on custom and not church law.[50] This essay was written in early September 1903, a few days before Tanner departed for conference in Kentucky. It would be his last "Stray Thought" for six months because conference time was not the right time to write. He missed "the deep satisfaction" the writing afforded, he wrote in the March 3, 1904, *Recorder*. While in the South Tanner thought about addressing the subjects of Jim Crowism or race relations, but back in Philadelphia he faced this question: "Where [was] the good in sending out a Stray Thought upon any of [those] themes . . . ; or any indeed akin to them? . . . Is not the general status of the race better today than it was yesterday? And does not tomorrow give promise of being better than today?" Reverting back to an earlier conservatism, Tanner mused that whites who controlled the legislatures and courts in the South would change once blacks changed their condition from poverty to richness, ignorance to education, and folly to wisdom. "Change our immorality to morality . . . and Jim Crowism . . . will have to go," Tanner concluded. This view, while popular with Washington's supporters, was not acceptable to militant civil rights advocates who rallied around W. E. B. Du Bois's courageous essay "Of Mr. Booker T. Washington and Others," in his seminal *Souls of Black Folk*, published in 1903. It was remarkable that Tanner had such faith in a changing America since men and women of his race were victims of lynching, disenfranchisement, the convict lease system, and Jim Crow schools and public facilities, which combined to hammer home an ideology of white supremacy. As noted by Alexander Crummell in 1898, the American creed told black people "This far and no farther."[51] Clearly Tanner was seeing what he wanted to see, which was the possibility that Americans of all races and colors would live in harmony. Unfortunately, reality suggested otherwise.

Tanner's last "Stray Thought" before the General Conference met in May was devoted to his insistence that the A.M.E. Church, unlike other Protestants save Unitarians, use the phrase "Holy Ghost" in their rituals. The concerned bishop suggested that the delegates to the forthcoming meeting add "Holy Ghost" to their motto "God Our Father; Christ Our Redeemer; Man Our Brother" because "the Holy Ghost, proceeding from the Father and the Son, is of one substance, majesty and glory with the Father and the Son, very and eternal

God." More particularly, he stressed that "we are living in the dispensation of this same spirit whose very existence we do not recognize." Bishop Tanner further believed that African Methodists' motto should be "God Our Father; Christ Our Redeemer; the Holy Ghost Our Comforter." He left out man because he deemed that all in the world were of common parentage and thus brothers.[52]

The absence of replies to Tanner's thought suggested that readers of the *Recorder* were concerned instead with the quadrennial question of electing bishops. The Rev. S. Timothy Tice requested more bishops since too many pastors and congregations never saw any. Tice particularly wanted a bishop for West Africa and two more for South Africa. The concerned minister contended that although several bishops had made contributions in the past, they were now old and feeble and no longer able "to endure the strenuous demands of the growing church and cope with the rapid changes of the age." Without citing names, Tice called for their retirement; otherwise, "the church should not tolerate their dotage and detrimental [behavior]."[53]

Should bishops be superannuated because of physical disabilities regardless of their wishes? asked the Rev. James Dean. Although Bishop Turner had temporary paralysis in 1900, he rallied and attended the General Conference meeting in Columbus, Ohio. Even though Turner missed a conference in Georgia due to illness, Dean did not think that he was a candidate for either forced relocation or superannuation. His sentiment may have been attributed more to fear of Turner than sound reasoning, because the bishop was seriously ill during the winter of 1903. Bishop James A. Handy, who also suffered from poor health, was not spared such sympathy.[54] Rumors circulated that Tanner could no longer handle his responsibilities, but supporters came to his defense. James M. Turner, who visited the Kentucky Conference at Lexington in September 1903, considered Tanner to be "at his best." The Rev. John H. Grant reported that Tanner spent five months traveling and often preached three times on Sunday as well as during the week. Grant claimed that Tanner's detractors or those who wanted their friends elected to the bishopric were behind the rumors of his poor health. He added that Tanner was too busy or too indignant to deny the published accounts of his declining health. Ironically, Tanner's "Stray Thought"—"Believed Herself Crazy," which appeared in the March 17 issue as did Grant's defense, described a woman who believed that she was simple, if not crazy, because her parents told her that she was. Tanner's cryptic message could be interpreted to mean that people wanted for personal reasons to believe that he was ill when he was not.[55]

As the General Conference approached, letters to the editor called for the retirement of Tanner, Turner, and B. W. Arnett. Others felt that Arnett should be retained but that Handy was incompetent and that Turner, who had given so much to the church, should die in office. The Bishops' Council made all the speculation moot by opposing the election of new bishops. Their counsel was heeded, nor were any bishops retired, located, or superannuated at the Chicago meeting.[56]

Perhaps the bishops shied away from superannuating some likely candidates because, as noted by Henry T. Johnson, editor of the *Recorder,* the church had no provision for superannuating ministers, widows, or orphans. "We sincerely hope we shall hear no more about retiring any of our bishops on account of age," Johnson added. Still, Johnson believed that arrangements should be made to provide financial security for those too feeble to continue their duties, and in turn they would "gladly superannuate and provide their church with their wisdom in [writing] books." Perhaps Johnson had in mind Bishop Handy, who missed the General Conference due to age and affliction. But the mood was set for 1908, when Handy and Tanner were involuntarily retired.[57]

Meanwhile, the Chicago meeting was a raucous one that had charges of bishops openly carrying whiskey bottles while cavorting with prostitutes. Bishop Henry M. Turner created conflict at the gathering when he objected to the playing of the National Anthem at the opening of the conference. "How can my people sing 'Sweet Land of Liberty' in a country where they are burned and hanged and shot down without even semblance of trial or form of justice?" he exclaimed. It is "no song for us," he defiantly concluded. At the end of the conference, Tanner poked criticism at Turner when he wrote that loose tongues full of curses and evil sayings were worse than a loose hungry lion. Without mentioning names, his message took in presiding elders, ministers, and certainly bishops who bickered too much in Chicago. Tanner advised all to have nothing to do with tattlers regardless of their status.[58]

Again, the episcopal system assigned Tanner to the Eleventh District, now realigned to include conferences throughout Florida. Unbeknown to Tanner, this would be his last assignment as bishop.[59]

Chapter 11

Bishop of the Eleventh Episcopal District, 1904–1908

Florida and the Move to Oust Tanner

Florida's mild winter climate provided Tanner with a respite from the snow and cold of Philadelphia and restored him mentally and physically. Since conferences met in the winter to avoid the high humidity of summer, Tanner had time to write his column and to rejoice in the accomplishments of his children. In early 1904 Henry was living in Mt. Kisco, New York. The artist informed Booker T. Washington by letter dated February 4, 1904, that his wife, Jessie, had been ill for several months after giving birth to their son Jesse on September 25, 1903. Henry wrote to the Tuskegee Wizard on March 3 soliciting assistance in selling his latest work, *Daniel in the Lion's Den*, which he hoped to sell for three thousand dollars to one of Washington's associates after exhibiting it in the National Art Club in the District of Columbia.[1] Washington viewed Henry as a man who was "proud of his race. He feels deeply that as a representation of his people he is on trial to establish their right to be taken seriously in the world of art." The bishop was happy for his son, who, while unwilling to follow his father into the ministry, painted religious subjects. A friend of the artist declared, "He has not selected religious subjects because they are nice to paint, but because he considers them the most vital and interesting in all human history." In 1906 Henry would win the five-hundred-dollar Harris Prize for *Two Disciples at the Tomb*, which was the best painting shown in the Nineteenth Annual Exhibition of American Paintings at the Chicago Art Institute. Henry T. Johnson, editor of the *Recorder*, noted that Henry was the best "not by egotism, bombast or chicanery, but by steady, patient working and ability. . . . [M]ay his example inspire our younger men . . . regardless of the profession they follow."[2]

In April 1904 Bertha gave her parents a severe scare when a tooth extraction caused a hemorrhage. After her recovery, she was married by her father on June 29 in the family's residence to Dr. Samuel P. Stafford, a physician from St. Louis.[3]

While anticipating Bertha's nuptials, the bishop was active in motivating his new members. "Roll Up Your Sleeves" was his June 16 challenge to the district's ministers and elders. He counseled them to prepare to war against sin the way boxers train to fight opponents—with their sleeves rolled up. He asked them to use all their moral powers to combat personal jealousies and petty hates while building churches and schools, paying off debts, and saving souls. Charles S. Long of Orlando responded a month later that Floridians were used to hard work and that figures from the last quadrennial showed that per capita that they had "raised more money, got more converts than any state in African Methodism." Speaking for many, he added, "We hail Tanner's arrival with great delight."[4]

In preparation for conferences, Tanner instructed the presiding elders and ministers to put ministerial education first in their priorities. He requested that presiding elders take up offerings to assist the church in educating the clergy. "Let there be no drawback in regard to this; especially let there be no excuse," he warned.[5] Bishop Tanner arrived in Jacksonville in early October, where he met with the Presiding Elders' Council and the trustees of Edward Waters College, eager to reopen the school after its devastation by a fire and hurricane. A banquet was held in Tanner's honor where he was praised for his intellect, character, and interest in education. Dr. A. W. Watson declared that no bishop in the church possessed more "power to command the attention and interest, the feeling of an audience" than Tanner. Tanner was the first bishop to visit many of Florida's smaller churches, an act that both amazed and pleased clergy and laity alike. The ministers loved him because he disdained political tricks. Many believed that he would accomplish for African Methodism in Florida what Bishop Henry M. Turner had achieved for Georgia.[6]

Tanner spent eight months in Florida visiting missions and stations from Pensacola to Miami and preached, lectured, and attended receptions until late in the evening without ill effects to his health. He arrived in Philadelphia on May 5, 1905, "looking the picture of improved health and spirit," reported the *Recorder*.[7] The Florida trip was spiritually rewarding for the bishop, as he was a witness to the church's growth, but on an ominous note, Tanner was inundated with imagery of white supremacy, most visibly in the form of the odious Jim Crow railroad car. Throughout 1904 southern blacks in Augusta and Atlanta, Georgia, Columbia, South Carolina, New Orleans, Mobile, and Houston boycotted streetcars to protest Jim Crow laws. Mississippi and Maryland also instituted Jim Crow streetcars, and South Carolina segregated its ferries. These and other denials of basic rights to African Americans inspired Tanner to make his first "Stray Thought" topic after being absent from his desk for eight months the humiliation of the segregated car. It disturbed Tanner that refined black girls and women (his daughter Halle was such a victim in 1891) were subjected to the vulgar behavior of white ruffians who came to the colored cars for shoe shines, liquor, or tobacco. In the colored cars, he wrote, were "disorder, loud talk, peanut shells, orange peelings, chicken bones." When he complained to a conductor about the misbehavior of a black ruffian, the conductor refused to put the incident on record. Tanner's objection was not to racial separation but to the absence of equal facilities. "Let us alone," he declared, "and we will naturally gravitate toward each other, as the nation will see even to its hurt, before this century passes away." Tanner's concern, which was shared by other black elite, was that ruffians of both races should stay in their own cars and not invade the privacy of decent white or black persons. He found it offensive that the purchase of a first-class ticket did not warrant first-class accommodations.[8]

Florida adopted a law on July 1, 1905, that separated the races on the street-cars. Black citizens boycotted the cars for three weeks. The situation brightened in August when a Florida judge declared that Jacksonville's segregated streetcar law was in violation of both the Florida Constitution and the Fourteenth Amend-ment to the United States Constitution. In the flush of an apparent victory, Tan-ner exclaimed, "We feel like singing all hail the pow'r of Jesus name, let angels prostrate fall; bring forth the royal diadem and crown Him lord of all." Tanner cautioned the black residents of the city to not seek revenge but to show that they understood the difference between "anarchy and liberty" and that they were ca-pable of making liberty manifest. The decision was appealed to the Florida Su-preme Court, which overturned the ruling and resegregated the cars. (It was not until 1961 that black Americans received equal accommodations on interstate public carriers throughout the land.)[9]

While Tanner supported equal accommodations, his moderate views were based on the belief that African Americans did not have the hardest lot in the world, a view that he held even prior to his 1881 visit to Ireland. There he saw Irish living with pigs and cows in huts that were inferior to black southern shacks. "Let us save a large percent of the breath we are wasting in our abuse of the white, and let us 'whip up the left horse,'" he advised. "Don't blame whites if we stand on corners moneyless and workless. Let whites 'sow to the wind' . . . and 'reap the whirlwind,'" he added "but let us be of those of whom it is said 'blessed are ye that sow beside all waters.'" Tanner's perception was that "there is an awful enforced inequality be-tween the 'good' Negro and the 'good' white man"; regardless of the former's intel-ligence or advancements, whites dismissed them with "oh, well, he is a Negro." "I want a new standard of recognition for the American Negro," he insisted, which was "first class accommodations for first class Negroes."[10]

A similar optimistic view of black self-reliance was offered by Stephen S. Steward, who worked in the publication department during Tanner's editorial tenure at the *Recorder* in the late seventies. Now, in 1906, he argued that Jim Crowism, lynching, and rights violations would not deter the race and that, though they had not had enough time to produce a John D. Rockefeller, Theodore Roosevelt, Andrew Carnegie, or J. P. Morgan, they would if they moved forward despite the efforts of bigots. "Hurrah for the American Negro," he declared. His brother, Chaplain Theophilus G. Steward, was glad to see the people agitating, but he, too, cautioned them not to focus only on the Negro problem, because there was a big world beyond it. Bishop Henry M. Turner ex-perienced nothing to remind him of his race or color while traveling in Mexico, but in Texas two conductors and a ticket agent deferred to his ecclesiastical posi-tion and declined to send him to the Jim Crow car. Turner noted that "the recognition that is to ultimately win respect and abrogate all discriminating laws . . . must be achieved by merit, and merit alone."[11]

Others were not so sanguine. The Niagara Movement, meeting at Harpers Ferry, the site of John Brown's raid in 1859 against slavery, endorsed Du Bois's manifesto, which declared that white Americans "fear to let black men even try to rise lest they become equals of the white. And this in the land that professes to follow Jesus Christ."[12] Following the example of militants, in February 1908 twenty-five bishops representing the A.M.E., A.M.E.Z., and C.M.E. churches met in Washington to present "an address to the American people" in which they requested "justice, . . . equality, . . . freedom of action and opportunity before the law and in the industrial life of the land, North and South alike." They also expressed opposition to the "color line," mob violence, peonage, the convict lease system, and Jim Crow cars. Tanner successfully offered at the conference a resolution that "the Bishops . . . pledge . . . of all we have recommended, nothing individually or collectively shall be left undone to consummate the work to the end."[13]

While Tanner was one of the signers, he, like Booker T. Washington, insisted that the African American needed to emulate Jews and Irish, who also faced discrimination but who by perseverance and character were molding themselves into a people to be respected by the Anglo-Saxon. He called upon blacks to imitate Jews in business acumen, sobriety, industry, and economy, which led to success despite persecution. Tanner noted in 1905 that blacks then were where the Irish were in the seventeenth century—a barely civilized people—but the Irish had overcome. He asserted that people of his race would never achieve respect from others until they respected themselves. To accomplish this, he urged them to display pride in their skin color, their kinky hair, and the history they had made. "Are we black or mixed?" he asked, and answered, "We prefer to say with Jeremiah 'our skin is black like an oven because of the burning heat of famine' than to say with Solomon: 'I am black but comely.'" Tanner added that the race would achieve once it established priorities and recognized the need for moderation in "food, drink and all that they do to the glory of God." Specifically, he believed that black people were extremist in matters of hospitality; instead of one meat or dessert, they wanted two or three, which depleted their meager resources. By comparing Irish and Jews to blacks, Tanner overlooked the repugnance many whites felt for African Americans. It was not simply a case of cleaning up one's person and dress in order to achieve respectability and acceptance. White aversion and indifference to African people was deeply rooted in slavery, and forty years of emancipation had done little to lessen this animosity. While it was true that the race needed to show more self-respect, it was incorrect for Tanner to assume that either self-respect or business acumen would make blacks more acceptable to whites. All he had to do was to remember how the *Memphis Scimitar* savaged President Theodore Roosevelt and Booker T. Washington in 1901 when the two dined at the White House. "The President of the United States has committed a crime against civilization, and his nigger guest has done his race a harm which cannot soon be erased," the paper declared to the approval of much of the nation and to the chagrin of liberal-minded Americans.[14]

Tanner wanted America to change; he desired that it would develop the continental race that he advocated in 1884, but unlike militants, he believed that prejudice was surmountable. Yet black people could not simply become equal citizens merely by respecting property, accumulating wealth, and acquiring knowledge. Unfortunately, too many whites in the media, clergy, and politics, as well as the illiterate and ignorant, harbored feelings that African Americans were incapable of acquiring "civilized" behavior unless they had a large infusion of white blood, and the fear that more would acquire white blood through miscegenation frightened them. It was easier to exclude all of them than to make any genuine effort to admit a few into the circle of equality. Thus it was futile for Tanner to entertain thoughts that his people would receive civil and political rights by being thrifty, lawabiding, and accommodating. For instance, Tanner believed that black people would advance more quickly if they stopped dancing in the evening, for such persons not only wasted valuable time but risked losing their souls.[15]

While Tanner's viewpoint was muddled at times, he clearly had race pride, and this motivated him to insist that people of African descent call themselves by their correct name. He still used the appellation "Negro" only reluctantly and rarely capitalized it. He believed that it was a name imposed by others. "Whenever we as a people have spoken the appellation has been discarded," he thundered, and he thought the appellation would have disappeared except that the "imperial" Alexander Crummell had used it in 1897 when he organized the American Negro Academy. By now, Tanner had started to use "Afro-American," a term that E. J. Waring claimed that he coined in 1878 and that was favored by *New York Age* editor Timothy Thomas Fortune.[16]

Tanner, despite bouts of depression and poor health, was a tireless worker. He was given responsibility for the New York conference (Bishop Benjamin W. Arnett was ill and would die a year later on October 7, 1906), where he devoted five weeks in the fall of 1905 to observing African Methodists who attended the state convention of missionary workers. For three weeks he attended church services nightly, and he spoke two or three times every Sunday in churches that had not seen a bishop in up to twelve years. Members of both races heard him lecture or attended receptions in his honor. "He did not play to the gallery; God seemed to have given him a special message from every place and occasion," S. Timothy Tice reported to the *Recorder*. In 1906 Tanner presided over New York conferences with assistance from Bishop W. J. Gaines in addition to handling his duties in Florida.[17] Despite his busy schedule in two states, in 1905 Tanner wrote a 141-page book, *Joel, the Son of Pethuel*, dedicated to the students at Edward Waters College, which reopened in temporary quarters on October 3, 1905, with one hundred students.[18] Four acres of land were secured for a permanent campus, and buildings were scheduled for erection during the spring and summer of 1906, a testament to Tanner's leadership.[19]

In June 1906 Tanner attended the fiftieth anniversary of Wilberforce University's founding. Booker T. Washington delivered the main address, and Tanner gave the Golden Jubilee Sermon, which emphasized "the mission or work of a university." He requested the faculty to teach science because students needed to know the world they had to subdue and because science provided them with intellectual, moral, and religious discipline. He admitted that while theology must be a large part of the curriculum, it should be "not the theology given in science . . . nor the theology of providence as seen in government, but the theology that is revealed." He challenged students to push aside opposition "of poverty, of weakness, of contempt and derision" and go forward and see in themselves a Thomas Edison, Benjamin Banneker, Daniel A. Payne, or Lucretia Mott (who was a preacher and an anti-slavery and women's rights advocate). At this time, Tanner also reiterated his call for unity among all the branches of Methodism because the bishop understood that color and race, not doctrinal differences, separate white and black Methodists. Additionally, Tanner believed that a union of all branches of African Methodism would lead to a consolidation of publication departments, educational institutions, Bishop's Councils, and other duplicated areas, thus leading to savings and better services for the church community.[20]

From November 27, 1906, to mid-February 1907, Tanner presided over conferences in Florida. In Monticello, the town's white population asked him to preach at the opera house. The Rev. C. A. Whitfield described the occasion as a masterpiece, as the bishop "covered himself, the connection and the race with glory."[21] The Rev. Carlton M. Tanner returned from his assignment in South Africa in August to take up duties in Pittsburgh as editor of the *Witness*. Carlton suffered from a severe illness in the spring of 1907 that convinced his doctors, nurse, and family that he was near death. During Carlton's seven-month recovery period, the bishop tended to his duties with a heavy heart.[22] In September 1907 S. Timothy Tice reported that church and educational work in Florida had advanced under Tanner's tutelage; in particular, he accomplished much in moving Edward Waters College toward parity with the connection's fourteen other educational holdings.[23]

Again, as General Conference approached, the question of more bishops came up for debate. Carlton M. Tanner suggested that up to six bishops be elected, three or four for the United States and two for Africa. He called for an episcopal rotation that would permit bishops to represent the entire church instead of a district. It would, he stressed, be a way to avoid sycophants "who get and hold their place by slandering, tattling and ecclesiastically assassinating every man who is in their way to continue their nefarious work."[24] It is not known if Carlton wrote this to gain an edge for his father, who despite his impressive credentials had his detractors. The Rev. J. M. Holt opposed retiring older bishops, because they made the connection what it was. Nevertheless, he believed that there should be five or six new bishops to assist the older ones. The Rev. John Q. Johnson viewed it revolutionary to retire bishops, but he recommended that African Methodists follow the examples of the government, the military, and the M.E. Church and superannuate those who have "to be nursed and coddled." He was referring to Bishops Handy and Turner, who were both weak in health.[25]

Many, however, opposed superannuating bishops. Some saw it as a political maneuver to make room for the ambition of others. The Reverend S. H. Betts, a voice from West Florida, argued that age had nothing to do with performance: the seventy-two-year-old Tanner visited more churches in western Florida than any of his predecessors.[26]

Tanner, who was the subject of several superannuation articles, had given his own view on the subject in his July 1905 essay "If You Dance, Pay the Fiddler." He commented that each year the bishops lost mental and physical vigor and that perhaps the church should retire some who were unfit because of age.[27] In the event that more bishops were elected, Tanner recommended that they be deserving. Take only those "who are sober, faithful, temperate, orderly, responsible, gentle, not contentious, not a lover of money," he emphasized.[28]

The Twentieth Quadrennial Session of the General Conference met from May 4 to 21 in Norfolk, Virginia. Those who supported superannuating some bishops were heartened by the absence of a sickly Bishop James A. Handy. Bishop Turner was also ill but came to the meeting on the seventh day.[29] Tanner did not aid his own cause when he informed the Episcopal Committee that he could not take charge of a large district but desired to handle a small one. The delegates, however, were determined to retire bishops. Handy and Tanner were retired with half pay, or $1250 per annum. Bishop Turner, whom the *Recorder* described as having "national popularity," was retired with full pay, permitted to keep his title of senior bishop, and made church historian. The latter position was established after Theophilus G. Steward, retired chaplain, suggested in 1907 that a bishop be given full pay to write the history of African Methodism, to be available in time for the 1916 centennial of the A.M.E.'s quadrennial conferences. Turner coveted the position, but it proved to be unsuitable for him. The *A.M.E. Church Review* referred to the retirements as an act of love. Tanner accepted the decision as a "dutiful son of the Church," but the absence of a diary or correspondence makes it impossible to ascertain if this represented his true sentiment.[30] The newly elected bishops were Henry B. Parks, former missionary board secretary and editor of *Voice of Missions*, Edward W. Lampton, former financial secretary of the connection, John A. Johnson, J. S. Flipper, and William H. Heard.[31]

The decision to retire Tanner meant that there would be no more long separations from his beloved Sadie or his grandchildren. Especially it meant ample time to write his "Stray Thoughts" series, which delighted readers, who inquired, "When will be the next?"[32] As one who had witnessed hundreds of church gatherings and had seen ministers, elders, and bishops answer questions with "cut and dried" replies, it was appropriate that Tanner in his first essay after retirement dealt with the issue of appropriate responses. He informed readers to answer with spirit and from the heart even if the reply was ungrammatical. This was a profound statement from one who had so long called for an educated ministry. He, who questioned the lack of fire in his heart forty-two years earlier, finally realized that God hears the believer regardless of his station.[33] While some may have thought that his forced retirement was unceremonious or humiliating, Tanner willingly undertook his new mission: to teach young and untutored ministers to be better pulpit preachers and ultimately better shepherds to the straying flock.

Chapter 12

Retirement and Final Years

Although Tanner downplayed his retirement, he often capitalized the word when he referred to it in the *Recorder*, a signal that it weighed heavily on him. Still, Tanner's retirement provided him with time to be with Sadie, who was his closest confidante. On August 19, 1908, the couple celebrated their fiftieth wedding anniversary in their home with all five of their living children in attendance. The home was festive with good food and joyous congratulations from Henry, Jessie, and little Jesse. The other children traveled to be with their parents on their honored day: Mary Tanner Mossell from Washington, D.C., Isabelle Tanner Temple from Scranton and Carlton from Allegheny, Pennsylvania, and Bertha Tanner Stafford, now prominent in church missionary work, from St. Louis. Altogether seven grandchildren added to the couple's joy.[1]

Though the bishop also had ample time to write his "Stray Thought" essays, for unknown reasons he only wrote a few more before retiring that title with the July 16, 1908, *Recorder*. In the June 18 issue he complained about senseless noise and confusion in worship. Once, in Delaware, he attempted to gently stop a frenzy of worship and was met with the reply, "Do not be surprised at what you see [for] the majority of our great city churches is no more decent or in order [nor] no more uplifting." Unfortunately, as Tanner noted, too many ministers and some bishops considered themselves failures as pulpit preachers unless they "stirred up a dust" during worship.[2]

Tanner's last essay in the "Stray Thought" series was a description of a penniless young woman who had a young child and was ill with a high temperature and consumption. Her husband refused to assist her, was often absent from home, and spent his money on cigars and other frivolities. The woman who believed that "the lord will provide" made no effort to improve her lot. Tanner urged ministers to look after their own souls before attempting to save the souls of their flock. His lesson: "Despise nothing that God in providence of our life lays upon us to do whether seeming for ourselves or for another. Comfort ourselves and God will see to it that by so doing we comfort somebody else." He added that many believe that they should love their neighbor more than themselves. "No," he declared, "we do well if we love them, as well as we love ourselves." This homily would be representative of Tanner's relationship to African Methodists as he faced his twilight years. While he would continue sporadically to comment on major current events, over the next two years Tanner would more frequently attempt to elevate laity and ministers alike with similar comments. He believed that by concentrating on uplifting the oppressed, he would assist them to share in civilization's advances and advantages. This was a trying period for African Methodists who "failed to see that emerging social divisions in the black community would deprive them of both rich and poor." The nineteenth-century black church leaders often accommodated themselves to the nation's political system. Some, like Benjamin W. Arnett, served in state legislatures or sought favors from elected officials even as they fought for school integration, anti-lynching legislation, elimination of Jim Crow enactments, and an end to southern political disenfranchisement. But as turn-of-the-century migration from the South—both rural and urban—led to the development or expansion of black ghettoes, African Methodists found themselves unable to broker the needs of the masses who were expected to espouse capitalistic principles while eschewing revolutionary change. The black Methodists were less able to offer viable solutions to the ever-increasing problems of northern African American communities. Many of the migrants were not formerly exposed to African Methodism; thus they shunned that denomination for the National Baptist Convention and the Pentecostal Church of God in Christ, which dwarfed the A.M.E. connection. In 1915, Robert H. Pierce, pastor of the First African Baptist Church of Germantown, Pennsylvania, and editor of the *Philadelphia Tribune*'s "In Our Pulpit and Pew" section, argued that "the spirit of the church of today is so much different from the church of former days that the reverence for it is not the same at all." It became more difficult for the African Methodists who were unable to deviate from their political accommodation strategy to speak for the larger black community with any degree of confidence or success. The early decades of the twentieth century witnessed also a decline in the influence of the white churches as their revising and editing of the Bible rendered religious worship ineffectual.[3]

The bishop's love and respect for the people extended to the *Christian Recorder*. After editing it for sixteen years, he had contributed essays every year since his departure in 1884. Several times throughout its existence, when the newspaper had struggled to pay its bills, a benefactor (usually a bishop or two) had stepped forward with a timely loan or paid the debt. In the fall of 1908 the *Recorder* faced the possibility of suspending printing until Bishops Abram Grant, Cornelius T. Shaffer, Henry M. Turner, and Tanner supplied it with necessary funds. Within months, however, their munificence was nearly undone as problems plagued the newspaper. The editor's prolonged illness kept it on the threshold of death for weeks. When it irregularly appeared it was but a shadow of itself. Thousands of dollars were owed to the Book Concern by readers who neglected to pay for their subscriptions, and the church did not hound them because it did not want the disgrace of removing them from the subscription roll. In April 1909 the *Recorder* had liabilities of $17,140.71 with assets of $10,000. Credit was no longer extended to the *Recorder* in the Philadelphia market. To stabilize its operation, the Bishops' Council in conjunction with the Publication Board of the A.M.E. Church decided to run the Book Concern on a purely business basis. The manager was now expected to earn his income out of the business and would for the first time pay a percentage to the church.[4] To improve circulation, the June 3, 1909, issue was a special education issue with 14,500 copies instead of the normal 5600. This proved so successful that the October 28 issue of the *Recorder* was a special woman's issue with articles on women in business, the home, and mission work, to name a few. Women performed some of the mechanical work to put out the paper; Ella Whitaker printed the issue, while other women folded copies on a folding machine and mailed the 20,162 copies.[5]

The June 3 and 10 issues printed the views of some bishops who chose to write about education as a vehicle leading to success. Tanner wrote in the June 10 issue on "The Successful Life," which he attributed to a healthy body derived from good eating, drinking, sleeping, bathing, and exercising habits. He suggested that people needed to decide as a child the kind of person they wanted to be and should not swerve from their goals. Ever the Spartan, he added that goal seekers should "allow nothing to cross [their] path [but] keep a clear track before you." He noted that they should depend upon God for help and guidance and that nothing should stand between them and God, "nothing save His son."[6]

Tanner was favorably disposed toward educating ministers because he realized that there were some, not unlike himself in his youth, who were not ready for the moral and spiritual responsibilities of the ministry. He understood that few were actually called to minister, but once the decision to preach was reached, they must heed Jesus' admonition to drop everything. Tanner urged them to preach "not the legalism of Moses or the Jews; not the poetry of Greece; not the oratory of Rome but the gospel of Jesus Christ."[7]

More typical of Tanner's pronouncements were his comments on April 25, 1909, after preaching the ordination sermon at Jersey City, where he told the congregation to bow to the Bible as the final arbiter. "Study, study, study" should be the motto for ordained ministers, he proclaimed. He suggested that they read the Bible with diligence, as well as approved Christian authors, but avoid the inflammatory yellow press (so named for the yellow paper the comic strips they featured were printed on) and read magazines only "in general." June was Tanner's busiest month since retiring a year earlier. He attended the Bishops' Council meeting in Atlantic City on the 13th, arrived at Wilberforce two days later, traveled on June 20 to Washington, Pennsylvania, and dedicated a church a week later in Port Jefferson, New York.[8]

Tanner was a scholar who appreciated the value of knowledge but he had disdain for those who cheapened the acquisition of knowledge by the indiscriminate distribution of honorary degrees, which was a common practice in 1909. Although Tanner was the recipient of three such degrees, he knew that he was deserving which the bishop could not say the same for all the recipients of honorary doctorates in philosophy, law, divinity, and civil law. Opponents of honorary degrees challenged this practice because they understood that every semi-literate minister wanted a D.D. or Ph.D. attached to his name. This provoked Tanner to call for an abatement of honorary degrees, for he believed that it was better to "be rather than to seem, or, be what you seem to be." His conclusion was that recipients of honorary degrees must be able to teach the subject of the degree or decline the honor.[9]

The awarding of honorary degrees by Wilberforce University, Payne Theological Seminary, and other A.M.E. institutions was symptomatic of the church's growing separation from progressive people. Many no longer saw the church as a viable nor relevant institution, and Theophilus G. Steward's evaluation aptly described the decline of African Methodism. Steward did not believe that it represented "the highest possible form of human organization," nor was it "the perfect incarnation of either the Christ teaching or the Christ spirit." Tanner did not join this chorus in attacking the church that he had labored nearly six decades for, but he clearly understood that hundreds of ministers who lacked formal collegiate or even secondary training were in need of informal education. Therefore, in early January 1910 Tanner commenced a new weekly column in the Recorder, "Papers on the Ministry." He was now seventy-four and could not say how much longer he would be able to write, but he was determined to write for the ministers, deacons, elders, and even bishops. Wanting his remaining time on earth to be profitable, Tanner quoted Martin Luther, "Death is the wages of sin, but the fever of God is the beginning of wisdom." He wanted to serve both the Cross and Jesus by writing this column because he was "the bond servant of the crucified, and as such [was] ready to do His bidding."[10]

Up to March 16, 1911, Tanner would contribute to the Recorder forty-eight "Papers" essays. Many were simply introductions to biblical passages, while others explained the complexity of nature in Christian terms. A few were profound in their insightful analysis, but biblical history was the theme of the majority of the essays. Clearly they reflected his scholarship; even more, they showed his great love for the church and his continued willingness to help develop an educated ministry. In his fifth essay, "Ministry of the Prophets," Tanner stated that God chose to speak through man, but that was a generic term, since women are also found in His service. He indicated that not all the prophets were Jews, because some antedated Jewish faith, nor were all men, "for women largely shared in the work." Again, he reiterated his earlier view that women could deliver a providential message from God, but not in the regular ministry.[11]

Tanner's thirteenth essay, "The Character of It: Devotion," described his reason for writing the essays: he wanted to develop the character of preachers, who had to understand that without Jesus' assistance they could not properly teach and guide their congregations. Subsequent essays called upon ministers to have humility, courage, honesty, and hospitality.[12] Additionally, Tanner informed ministers that they needed to be industrious. He described the reactions of relatives when he received his calling. They said half in jest, "He is too lazy to work." The bishop reminded readers that they were the example makers and that God helps those who help themselves.[13]

Bishop Tanner reminded readers that God gave Adam, and by extension all men, the work of subduing the earth, the sea, and the air. He said that men should conquer the air with flying machines; they had already constructed wireless telegraphs and were capable of constructing tunnels beneath oceans or through mountains. His view was an example of his own personal growth, for fifty years earlier Tanner himself had stated that man should not abuse the earth: nature belonged to God, as did man, and neither had an unholy part to play. His new reasoning represented his better understanding of the Bible, as he now believed that, as God's highest creation, man reflected His glory and it was the duty of man to use his technological and inventive genius in carrying out the will of God.[14]

While the series did not represent his finest literary work, he derived immense pleasure from writing the essays, and they struck a positive chord in his readers. James T. Gilmore considered them an inspiration to the church and especially to ministers. He also believed that they would attract new subscribers. May the church and race "be elevated to a high standard of nobility, excellency and usefulness by this worthy educator," Gilmore concluded.[15]

At the same time, important events occurred that Tanner completely ignored. His mighty pen and insightful logic were missing when the National Association for the Advancement of Colored People was organized in 1909 and began publishing the *Crisis* in 1910. He had nothing to say about the rising tide of racism reflected by an increase in lynching and the national debate over the showing of D. W. Griffith's *The Birth of a Nation,* which falsely depicted emancipation, enfranchisement, and black participation in Reconstruction. Surprisingly, considering Tanner's support for an amalgamated society, he had no comment when Ohio sought in 1913 to outlaw racial intermarriage after the boxer Jack Johnson married a white woman. The bill passed the lower house by a vote of 63 to 33, but its failure to pass in the senate spared Tanner's friends William and Sarah Scarborough and approximately fifty other couples the indignity of breaking up their marriages or leaving the state. He was equally silent on the outbreak of war in Europe in 1914 as well as the passing of his friend Booker T. Washington the following year.

Unfortunately, his silence on these and other major issues, as well as advanced age, poor health, periodic depression, and greater dependency upon religious doctrine (he believed that a wider Christian ethic in the nation would lead to an end of discrimination against blacks in business, social, and religious spheres) as a solution to racial problems, led to the rise of younger, more militant and confrontational leaders who eschewed accommodation—notably W. E. B. Du Bois, Ida Wells-

Barnett, and Francis J. Grimké, pastor of Washington's Fifteenth Street Presbyterian Church—who picked up the leadership baton courageously carried by Tanner in past years. Although Tanner provided much leadership during the nineteenth century as the race struggled to obtain the franchise and citizenship rights, he never considered himself a leader. Oddly, he reasoned that leaders were discordant voices. "To be a leader," he insisted in 1909, "would entail silence . . . for is not leadership largely of the nature of bribe? Would you be a leader says the ages, then you must be quiet." Tanner, of course, was not suggesting that oppressed people surrender but rather that they eschew loud voices and rhetoric, which he considered signs of egotism and not reflective of a leader who would quietly assess the situation before taking action. Similarly, Alexander Crummell declared in 1875 that he opposed agitation because it was "the expenditure of force." A better solution, he suggested, was for the race to attain to "such general superiority that prejudice must decline."[16]

Ironically, Tanner, who earlier was obsessed with his study, was now equally obsessed with religion. This denied him the balance needed to carefully view all the problems that faced the African American. Instead, his concentration on a narrow religious perspective alienated him from those outside of the church who desired solutions to their myriad problems. And his disinterest in current events obscured his growing depression, which was not aided by the passing of close associates and accelerated later by the loss of his beloved Sadie. Bishop Edward W. Lampton, whom Tanner had appointed to a church in Greenville, Mississippi, twenty years earlier, died July 16, 1910, in Petosky, Michigan; Tanner wanted to speak at his funeral in Mississippi but decided that his health could not take the trip to the humid South. Bishop Abram Grant passed away January 22, 1911, which Tanner considered a blow to the church comparable to the deaths of Richard Allen and Daniel A. Payne. Tanner was scheduled to speak at the funeral, but then decided that it would only be possible for him to be present in spirit. On October 5, 1911, Bishop James A. Handy succumbed to a long illness, and Tanner felt well enough to attend his funeral in Baltimore. The deaths of three bishops prompted the *Recorder*'s editor to declare that "there is no man living, except . . . Bishop Turner, whose life means so much to the Church as Bishop Tanner," who should write his autobiography, a suggestion that, unfortunately, Tanner ignored. The subsequent deaths of Bishops W. J. Gaines (January 12, 1912), Moses B. Salter (March 24, 1913), and William B. Derrick (April 15, 1913) left Tanner pondering his own mortality. He did not attend any of these funerals, but he did attend and preach at the funeral services of Fanny Jackson Coppin, wife of Bishop Levi J. Coppin, who died on January 27, 1913. He selected his sermon from Proverbs 31:14, "She is like the merchants' ships; she bringeth her food from afar." He advised the women in the audience to read the Bible because in the sacred book "her womanhood is well guarded . . . [and] the woman's hand should point out the way we should go." He praised Coppin, who had been the principal of Philadelphia's Institute for Colored Youth when his children were students there, for her Christian grace, which led her "to carry on her idea of her faith in God." He saluted her as a good friend of the *Recorder* and as a warm and close family friend.[17]

These frequent deaths of colleagues and friends undoubtedly made him more appreciative of his precious Sadie, who was still active in the Women's Parent Mite Missionary Society. However, largely because of her declining health, she resigned as treasurer on January 25, 1912. She informed the delegates at the society's Fifth Quadrennial Convention that met in Chicago from November 9 to 13 that "circumstances over which I had no control compelled me to resign."[18] It was a sad occasion for her. She had been one of the organization's six founders in 1874, had served as its president, and had seen its membership grow to twenty thousand.

The *Recorder* reported in the June 4, 1914, issue that Sadie was seriously ill with her children Carlton, Mary, and Bertha at her bedside. After lingering for two months, Sadie died on August 2, at age seventy-four. The *Recorder*'s news item of her passing described her as one who influenced the church and the community, a charter member of the Women's Parent Mite Missionary Society and the Frederick Douglass Memorial Hospital in Philadelphia. "Distinguished for her great patience and devotion to her husband and her children," she was "an indulgent, loving, wise and Christian mother," the *Recorder* mentioned. "Christian mother" was also the theme used by the paper's editor, Richard R. Wright Jr., in his August 13 editorial. He praised Sadie's contribution to the church's missionary endeavor and suggested that her "active outside life proved that the arduous duties of a mother do not necessarily mean the neglect of other things needful." This was a remarkable assessment in light of society's preoccupation at the time with the "true cult of womanhood" that relegated women, regardless of their education or talent, to the dual roles of nurturer and helpmate. Still, it was as a mother that Wright chose to eulogize her. He believed that her children were her greatest gift to the world, for "no woman can achieve anything to equal motherhood," he declared. The bereaved family, unable to respond to the numerous cards of condolence, sent a note to the *Recorder* to inform all of their thanks.[19]

Sadie was loved and respected by her colleagues, who in 1915 established in her memory the Sarah E. Tanner Memorial Fund to support widows and orphans of African Methodist missionaries.[20] Tanner deeply missed his companion of fifty-six years, and she was constantly in his thoughts. In an undated letter to Rosa, his housekeeper since 1894, Tanner wrote, "I arrived at home yesterday. At least what remains of home with the dear mama in heaven and you absent with the grandchildren makes what I found to be a real change. Mary [his daughter lived with him after her husband deserted her] is holding the reigns of management but the dear mama is greatly missed."[21]

Little is known about the bishop's life after Sadie died. Perhaps the enormity of life without her was overwhelming. He no longer wrote essays for the *Recorder*, but he did regularly attend weekly preachers' meetings in Philadelphia, a forum for intellectual discourse, and went to the Bishops' Council meeting in New Orleans in February 1915. On September 2, 1915, the *Recorder* printed his photo with the caption "He is loved and revered by his brethren."[22]

The passing of Henry M. Turner on May 8, 1915, probably saddened him, as one of the giants in the church was no longer. Tanner did not attend the funeral in Atlanta, but he gave remarks at a May 17 memorial meeting at the Philadelphia preachers' meeting.[23] At the General Conference that met in Philadelphia in May 1916, he limited his participation to the announcement of two hymns and recitation of a verse of scripture. In the fall the Fifteenth Street Presbyterian Church in Washington, the church he had pastored from October 1860 to April 1862, invited the bishop to deliver an address at its seventy-fifth anniversary celebration.[24]

Tanner, now in the twilight of his life, was an elder statesman in the A.M.E. Church, respected but not needed. In 1921 the *Recorder* printed a photograph of Tanner wearing his reading glasses and favorite cap while engaging in his pastime of reading. The paper's management and employees wished him a happy eighty-sixth birthday in the December 29 issue.[25] He had now completely removed himself from public life, "simply waiting" until his time to die. Years earlier, in 1860, he had mused that "as the body becomes weak and feeble the soul becomes more prepared for eternity. As the outward man decays, the inward man is renewed . . . [and] the man becomes the saint; and earth is merged into heaven."[26] His health had been poor for a decade, and he fully trusted that God would take him when He was ready. There was no fear, as he knew that someday he would join the multitudes in Jesus' bosom.

> Breathe on me when the pulse is low
> When the spirit's tired and the heart
> Is sad and weary, and all the glow
> Of hope and feeling (dwells apart)
>
> Breathe on me with the eve's mild breath
> The calm of quietness and peace
> The breath of heaven, the breath of earth
> Soothing the fretting cares of life.[27]

Tanner turned eighty-seven on Christmas Day 1922. He was now living a contradiction of his earlier life. Once, he questioned his holiness as well as the lack of fire in his heart for God's message; now, he was secure in his acceptance of God, for his faith was strong. His voice and pen that had defended the church and the race with the power of his eloquence were virtually silent as he became more reclusive. He resolved to let younger minds meet the challenge that still confronted the race. The only constant in his life was his poor health. At times he suffered from depression, and in the end he was victimized by dementia, not knowing his whereabouts and often forgetful of personal hygiene. At 4:30 P.M. on January 14, 1923, the spirit departed Tanner's body.

Death

You simply go to sleep; that's all you know
How sweet this is—this soft slipping away
From pain and worry—from the cares that grow

. . .

The spirit home with God—and all is well

. . .

Death is misjudged, misnamed with terrors, strife
It gives the tired body rest—the spirit life.[28]

In retrospect, Tanner was a man of many seasons. While he made no pretense to scholarship, he "was really a scholar of no mean ability. He was one of [the] great intellectual lights in the church."[29] He was a gifted and at times a poetic writer who used his skills "not only to defend but to dignify the church and give it a place among the forces making for the betterment and salvation of humanity," declared the *Recorder* after his death.[30]

At his best, Tanner was the powerful voice agitating for an end of slavery, condemning bias against Chinese immigrants, and denouncing human rights violations against Jews in eastern Europe. He influenced hundreds and perhaps thousands who read his editorials, essays, and books. A representative voice from that group was Richard Wright Jr., who met Tanner in 1888 when he was ten years old. Tanner gave the boy his autograph with these words: "Dear Richard: Always choose for your associates those who you have reason to believe are better and wiser than yourself." The sage advice and Tanner's example inspired Wright, who became editor of the *Recorder* and eventually a bishop in the A.M.E. Church.[31]

Notes

Abbreviations
CR = *Christian Recorder*
A.M.E. C.Rev. = *A.M.E. Church Review*
Tanner = Benjamin Tucker Tanner

Preface
1. David W. Blight, "In Search of Learning, Liberty, and Self-Determination: James McCune Smith and the Ordeal of the Antebellum Black Intellectual," *Afro-Americans in New York Life and History* 9 (July 1985): 7–25.
2. "The Coming Race—What Is It to Be?" *CR*, May 15, 1884, 1.
3. "Learn to Endure," *CR*, June 8, 1882, 2.
4. "Our Bishops in the Nineteenth Century," *CR*, Aug. 29, 1907, 2.
5. Richard R. Wright, *The Encyclopedia of the African Methodist Episcopal Church*, 2d ed. (Philadelphia: Book Concern of the A.M.E. Church, 1947), 5.

Chapter 1
1. Edward R. Turner, *The Negro in Pennsylvania, Slavery—Servitude— Freedom, 1639–1861*. (Washington: American Historical Association, 1911), 134, 163. Ann G. Wilmoth, "Pittsburgh and the Blacks: A Short History," (Ph.D. diss., Pennsylvania State Univ., 1975), 1, 7, 17, 23, 154.
2. B. W. Arnett, *The Budget for 1884* (Dayton: Christian Publishing House, 1885), 8–11. William J. Simmons, *Men of Mark: Eminent, Progressive, and Rising* (Cleveland: George M. Rewell, 1887), 985. "The Tanner Family," *Negro History Bulletin* 10 (Apr. 1947): 147. Diary of Benjamin Tucker Tanner for Dec. 22, Jan. 28, Feb. 3, 1851, Dec. 23, 1852, Dec. 23, 1860, in Benjamin Tucker Tanner Papers (hereafter cited as BTT Diary). *CR*, Oct. 31, 1868, 2. Tanner, "My Mother," *CR*, June 4, 1891, 2.
3. BTT Diary, Feb. 9, Mar. 9, 17, 1851.
4. BTT Diary, Mar. 21, 25, 31, Apr. 9, 17, 1851.
5. BTT Diary, Mar. 24, Apr. 12, 1851. Herbert Aptheker, ed., *A Documentary History of the Negro People in the United States* 1 (New York: Citadel Press, 1951), 299–326.
6. "The Emigration Movement," *CR*, Apr. 18, 1878, 2. Tanner to brother [Andrew], June 14, 1858, in Sadie Tanner Mossell Alexander Papers, box 76, folder 78. Robin W. Winks, *The Blacks in Canada* (New Haven: Yale Univ. Press, 1971), 155–62.
7. BTT Diary, Apr. 29, Sept. 8, 1851. Simmons, *Men of Mark*, 985–86. Benjamin W. Arnett, ed., *The Budget: Containing Biographical Sketches, Quadrennial and Annual Reports of the General Officers of the African Methodist Episcopal Church of the United States of America* (Dayton: Christian Publish-

ing House, 1884), 8. *General Biographical Catalogue: The Western Theological Seminary of the Presbyterian Church* (Pittsburgh, 1827–1927), 98.

8. BTT Diary, June 9, 12, 13, 29, July 1, 16, Aug. 16, 1851.

9. BTT Diary, Aug. 20, Sept. 6, 20, 1851.

10. BTT Diary, Oct. 22, Nov. 5, 8, 12, 15, 19, 22, 29, 1851.

11. BTT Diary, Dec. 25, 1851.

12. BTT Diary, Feb. 2, 3, May 8, 17, 28, Sept. 7, 13, Oct. 29, 1852.

13. BTT Diary, July 27, Aug. 1, 3, Oct. 9, Nov. 2, 3, 23, 1852.

14. BTT Diary, Aug. 25, Nov. 29, Dec. 7, 10, 17, 1852; Feb. 10, 18, Mar. 16, 17, 20–24, 28, 1853. *CR,* Dec. 31, 1896, 7.

15. BTT Diary, Mar. 29, Apr. 3–8, 11, 1853. Tanner, "My Mother," *CR,* June 4, 1891, 2.

16. BTT Diary, Apr. 13, 1853.

17. BTT Diary, Apr. 9, June 15, 1843. Herbert Aptheker, *American Negro Slave Revolts* (New York: International Publishers, 1943), 343–44.

18. BTT Diary, June 4, 11, 14, 25, 26, 30, July 4, 5, 13, Aug. 4, 10, 13, 14, 18, 19, 1853.

19. "Mrs. Sarah E. Tanner Dead," *CR,* Aug. 6, 1914. Rae Alexander-Minter, "The Tanner Family: A Grandniece's Chronicle," in Dewey F. Moseby, ed., *Henry Ossawa Tanner.* (Philadelphia: Philadelphia Museum of Art, 1991), 23–24, 147–52, 167. "Bishop B. T. Tanner," *A.M.E. C.Rev.* 1 (July 1888): 1–6. Robert I. Vexler, comp. and ed., *Pittsburgh: A Chronological and Documentary History, 1682–1976* (Dobbs Ferry, N.Y.: Oceana Publications, 1977), 32, 111–12.

20. BTT Diary, July [18], 1856.

21. BTT Diary, "The Fugitive Slave Law," n.d.

22. BTT Diary, n.d. 1858.

23. *Pittsburgh Gazette,* Mar. 18, 1859, as quoted in Alexander-Minter, "The Tanner Family," 23. *Douglass Monthly,* Apr. 1859, 64.

24. Deeds and Certificates, 1858–72, in Benjamin Tucker Tanner Papers. Rudolph M. Lapp, *Blacks in Gold Rush California* (New Haven: Yale Univ. Press, 1977), 7–9, 49, 158, 160–62, 238–39, 268–69. Delilah L. Beasley, *The Negro Trailblazers of California* (Los Angeles: Delilah L. Beasley, 1919), 158.

25. *Pittsburgh Dispatch,* [1860,] as cited in *Weekly Anglo African,* June 9, 1860, 2. BTT Diary, May 29–30, 1860.

26. BTT Diary, June 15, 1860.

27. BTT Diary, June 17–18, 1860.

28. BTT Diary, June 19, 1860.

29. BTT Diary, June 17–20, 23–26, July 8–9, 11–14, 16–17, 23, 1860.

30. BTT Diary, July 22, 29, 1860.

31. "Leper from Fair Haven," *Weekly Anglo African,* Nov. 24, 1860, 1. "Our Washington Letter," ibid., 2; Simmons, *Men of Mark,* 986. Tanner to Sadie, Sept. 2, 1860, in Sadie Tanner Mossell Alexander Papers, box 76, folder 78. "Anniversary Address Delivered on the Seventy-fifth Anniversary of the Fifteenth Street Presbyterian Church, Washington, D. C., Nov. 19, 1916," in Carter G. Woodson, ed., *The Works of Francis J. Grimké,* 4 vols. (Washington: Associated Publishers, 1942), 1:532. Willard B.

Gatewood, *Aristocrats of Color: The Black Elite, 1880–1920* (Bloomington: Indiana Univ. Press, 1990), 40–41.

32. BTT Diary, June 21, Nov. 3, 1860. Alexander-Minter, "The Tanner Family," 25. "Our Washington Letter," *Weekly Anglo African,* Nov. 24, 1860, 2.

33. BTT Diary, Nov. 6–8, 1860.

34. BTT Diary, Nov. 12–16, 19–20, 23, 28–29, 1860.

35. BTT Diary, Dec. 13–14, 21, 1860.

36. BTT Diary, 7 June 25, July 19, Nov. 18, 20, 24, 1860; Jan. 9, 1861.

37. BTT Diary, Nov. 23, Dec. 4–6, 9, 11 13, 15, 16, 29–30, 1860. Alexander-Minter, "The Tanner Family," 25–26.

38. BTT Diary, July 30, 1860.

39. BTT Diary, Feb. 6, 1861. "Our Washington Letter," *Weekly Anglo African,* Nov. 24, 1860, 2–3; Dec. 29, 1860, 2; Jan. 5, 1861, 2.

40. BTT Diary, Dec. 19, 21, 24, 28, 1860; Jan. 3, 5, 10, 1861.

41. BTT Diary, Dec. 31, 1860; Jan. 1–3, 6, 1861.

42. BTT Diary, Dec. 11, 1860. Alexander-Minter, "The Tanner Family," 27.

43. BTT Diary, Dec. 22, 1860; Jan. 16, 1866.

44. BTT Diary, June 22, 1860.

45. BTT Diary, Feb. 27, 1861.

46. Tanner to brother, Oct. 11, 1861, in Sadie Tanner Mossell Alexander Papers, box 76, folder 78.

47. Tanner to editor, *CR,* Mar. 29, 1865, 1. Arnett, *The Budget for 1884,* 8–11.

48. *CR,* Nov. 25, 1865, 2.

49. BTT Diary, Mar. 12, 1866.

50. BTT Diary, Jan. 16, 26, 1866.

51. BTT Diary, Jan. 30, 1866.

52. BTT Diary, Feb. 10, Mar. 9, 12, 1866.

53. BTT Diary, May 8, 1866.

54. T.W.C., "Impressions of Baltimore, no. 2," *CR.* Oct. 20, 1866, 2. Simmons, *Men of Mark,* 986. "Echoes from Behind and Before. Memories of Eden," in Benjamin Tucker Tanner Papers.

55. BTT Diary, Jan. 1, 10, 15, 26, 1867.

56. BTT Diary, Feb. 1, 9, 1867.

57. BTT Diary, Jan. 23, 30, 1867.

58. BTT Diary, Feb. 20, 1867.

59. BTT Diary, Aug. 13, Nov. 29, Dec. 4, 1867. Tanner, "Our Latest Works," *A.M.E. C.Rev.* 7 (Oct. 1890): 129.

60. BTT Diary, Feb. 21, 1868.

61. Alexander-Minter, "The Tanner Family," 26.

62. James Lynch, "Our Western Trip," *CR,* Feb. 2, 1867, 2.

63. "Apology for African Methodism," *CR,* Feb. 23, 1867, 2. "Baltimore A.M.E. Conference," *CR,* May 4, 1867, 1. John W. Stevenson, "Colored Authors," *CR,* July 13, 1867, 1. Abel Stevens to Tanner, *CR,* June 22, 1867, 2. Daniel Elliot to Tanner, *CR,* July 13, 1867, 2. *CR,* Aug. 31, 1867, 2.

64. Tanner, *Apology for African Methodism* (Baltimore: B. T. Tanner, 1867), v–vii, 16, 115–17. Edward W. Lampton, *Digest of Rulings and Decisions of the Bishops of the African Methodist Episcopal Church from 1847 to 1907* (Washington: Record Publishing, 1907), 45–50.

65. "Books of the Week," *New York Tribune,* Nov. 11, 1867, 6.
66. Simmons, *Men of Mark,* 986.
67. *CR,* Nov. 30, 1867, 2.
68. See Tanner on "The African Methodist Church" in Daniel A. Payne, *The Semi-Centenary and the Retrospection of the African Methodist Episcopal Church in the USA* (Baltimore: Sherwood, 1866), 143.
69. W. E. B. Du Bois, *Against Racism: Unpublished Essays, Papers, Addresses, 1887–1961,* Herbert Aptheker, ed. (Amherst: Univ. of Massachusetts Press, 1985), xi.
70. *CR,* Nov. 16, 1867, 2.

Chapter 2

1. Charles S. Smith, *A History of the African Methodist Episcopal Church, Being a Volume Supplemental to a History of the African Methodist Church, by Daniel Alexander Payne* (Philadelphia: Book Concern of the A.M.E. Church, 1922), 78.
2. T. G. Steward, *From 1864 to 1914: Fifty Years in the Gospel Ministry* (Philadelphia: A.M.E. Book Concern, 1921), 80, 106. 108. For a discussion of missionary activity in the South following Emancipation, see William Seraile, *Voice of Dissent: Theophilus Gould Steward (1843–1924) and Black America.* (Brooklyn: Carlson Publishing, 1991), chapters 2 and 3.
3. Richard R. Wright, comp., *Who's Who in the General Conference, 1924* (Philadelphia: A.M.E. Book Concern, 1924), 352. James A. Handy, *Scraps of African Methodist Episcopal History* (Philadelphia: A.M.E. Book Concern, 1901?), 269–71. Charles Killiam, "Bishop Daniel A. Payne: Black Spokesman for Reforms" (Ph.D. diss., Indiana Univ., 1971), 157.
4. *CR,* June 8, 1867, 1. "Valedictory First—Valedictory Last," *CR,* June 29, 1867, 2. "An Editor's Farewell," *CR,* June 20, 1868, 2.
5. "The New Editor," *CR,* June 20, 1868, 2.
6. "True Recreation," *CR,* July 4, 1868, 2. Roger Lane, *William Dorsey's Philadelphia and Ours: On the Past and Future of the Black City in America* (New York: Oxford Univ. Press, 1991), 67.
7. "Southern Negro Democrats," *CR,* July 18, 1868, 2. "Negro Democrats," *CR,* Sept. 5, 1868, 2.
8. "A Wonder," *CR,* Aug. 8, 1868, 2. "A Jewish Plea," *CR,* Apr. 16, 1874, 4. "The Exiles," *CR,* June 1, 1882, 2. "Bishop B. T. Tanner on the Siberian Question," *CR,* May 15, 1890, 1. Bertram Wallace Korn, "Jews and Negro Slavery in the Old South, 1789–1865," in *Jews in the South,* ed. Leonard Dinnerstein and Mary Dale Palsson (Baton Rouge: Louisiana State Univ. Press, 1973), 89–134. "The Persecuted Jews," *CR,* Feb. 9, 1882, 2. "The Jew the Master of Europe," *CR,* Nov. 8, 1883, 2. "Jews versus Prayers," *CR,* Apr. 23, 1874, 4. *CR,* June 2, 1881, 2.
9. Samuel F. B. Morse, *Imminent Dangers to the Free Institutions of the United States through Foreign Immigration and the Present State of Naturalization Laws* (New York: Arno Press and the *New York Times,* 1969), ix, 13, 15.
10. Tanner, "Paul and John vs. Pius IX: A Sermon Preached in Bethel Church

Baltimore on November 29th, 1866, Thanksgiving Day," copy in the Library Company of Pennsylvania, Philadelphia. Harold A. Beutow, *Of Singular Benefit: The Story of Catholic Education in the United States* (London: Macmillan, 1970), 120. "A Demoralized Church," *CR,* Aug. 15, 1868, 2.

11. Cyprian Davis, *The History of Black Catholics in the United States* (New York: Crossroads Publishing, 1990), 125, 132. *The Sixteenth Session and the Fifteenth Quadrennial Session of the General Conference of the African Methodist Episcopal Church, Atlanta, May 1–18, 1876,* 121–25. "One Hundred vs. One Hundred," *CR,* Oct. 30, 1869, 2–3. "Catholic Aggressions," *CR,* Apr. 2, 1870, 2. "The Immorality of Romanism," *CR,* July 8, 1871, 2. "New York Romanism," *CR,* July 22, 1871, 2. *CR,* July 29, 1871, 2. *CR,* Mar. 9, 1872, 2. *CR,* Mar. 23, 1872, 2. *CR,* Dec. 4, 1873. "The Priests and the Freedmen," *CR,* Feb. 5, 1874, 4. "Romanism in Mexico," *CR,* Apr. 21, 1874, 4. *New York Times,* Mar. 17, 1874, 1. Tanner, "The Fruits of Caste in the Church," *Independent* 27 (Mar. 25, 1875), 2. Tanner, "A Remedy Worse Than the Disease," *Independent* 27 (Sept. 30, 1875): 4, 5.

12. "Catholics Laboring with the Negroes," *New York Times,* Jan. 3, 1879, 3. Stephen J. Ochs, *Desegregating the Altar: The Josephites and the Struggle for Black Priests, 1871–1960* (Baton Rouge: Louisiana State Univ. Press, 1990), 3, 9, 10. John T. Gillard, *The Catholic Church and the American Negro* (Baltimore: St. Joseph's Society Press, 1929), 1, 42, 85. Davis, *The History of Black Catholics,* 133, 136. David Spalding, "The Negro Catholic Congresses, 1889–1894," *Catholic Historical Review* 55 (Oct. 1969): 337–57. *Congress of Colored Catholics of the United States: Three Catholic Afro-American Congresses* (Cincinnati: American Catholic Tribune, 1893), 10–13, 74, 76, 98, 146. *CR.* July 14, 1904, 1. James T. Haley, comp., "Colored Catholics," *Afro-American Encyclopedia; or, The Thoughts, Doings and Sayings of the Race* (Nashville: Halley & Florida, 1895), 415–16. Albert J. Raboteau, *A Fire in the Bones: Reflections on African American Religious History* (Boston: Beacon Press, 1995), 122–25.

13. T. G. Steward, "Romanism Preferred," *CR,* Mar. 15, 1877, 1. Tanner, "Catholic Confession and the Basis It Has in Scripture," *A.M.E. C.Rev.* 14 (Oct. 1896): 179–91.

14. William Seraile, "The Struggle to Raise Black Regiments in New York State during the Civil War," *New-York Historical Society Quarterly* 8 (July 1974): 215–33.

15. "The Issue before the People," *CR,* Sept. 19, 1868, 2.

16. *CR,* Oct. 31, 1868, 2. For Randolph's death, see *Harper's Weekly,* Nov. 21, 1868. William Seraile, "New York's Black Regiments during the Civil War" (Ph.D. diss., City Univ. of New York, 1977), 104–5.

17. "Victory," *CR,* Nov. 7, 1868, 2.

18. "The Religious Bearing of the XV Amendment," *CR,* Jan. 8, 1870, 2. "The XV Amendment," *CR,* Apr. 9, 1870, 2. "Letter from Bishop T. M. D. Ward," *CR,* May 21, 1870, 3.

19. "The African Methodist," *Christian Advocate,* May 16, 1867, 4. *CR,* Apr. 20, 1867, 2.

20. "Is the M.E. Church Our Mother?" *CR,* June 12, 1869, 2. T. G Steward, "The M.E. Church: Keep It before the People," *CR,* July 3, 1869, 3. "Methodist Unity," *CR,* July 31, 1869, 2. *CR,* Mar. 19, 1870, 2. B. T. Tanner, "Methodist Union," *Methodist,* Apr. 16, 1870, 1.

21. Tanner, "The Methodist Union," and editor's response, *Zion's Herald* 48 (Sept. 28, 1871): 463. For efforts to provide a black bishop in the M.E. Church, see *CR,* May 12, 1904, 2, and June 4, 1908, 2; Tanner, "A Methodist Confederation," *Independent* 45 (Apr. 13, 1893): 489–90; John Wesley Edward Bowen, *An Appeal for Negro Bishops but No Separation* (New York: Eaton & Mains, 1912), 8, 36–37, 55–56, 82–88; "Two Negro Bishops in the M. E. Church," *Competitor* 1 (June 1920): 5; *The History of American Methodism,* 3 vols. (New York: Abingdon Press, 1964), 1:15–17.

21. *New National Era,* June 1, 1871, 1. *People's Advocate,* May 29, 1880, 4; Sept. 6, 1876, 1; Oct., 11, 1879, 2. John C. Dancy, "Union of Methodist Bodies," *Independent* 45 (Apr. 13, 1893): 490. Sylvia M. Jacobs, "Francis Burns, First Missionary Bishop of the Methodist Episcopal Church, North," in *Black Apostles at Home and Abroad: Afro-Americans and the Christian Mission from the Revolution to Reconstruction,* ed. Richard Newman and David W. Wills (Boston: G. K. Hall, 1982), 255–63.

22. *Historical Statistics of the United States: Colonial Times to 1970, Part 1* (Washington: Government Printing Office, 1975), 364–65, 370, 382.

23. *CR,* Apr. 4, 1868, 2; July 25, 1868, 2; Aug. 8, 1868, 2; Aug. 15, 1868, 2; Nov. 14, 1868, 2; Feb. 13, 1869, 2.

24. *CR,* Jan. 16, 1869, 2; Jan. 30, 1869, 2.

25. *CR,* June 12, 1869, 1; June 26, 1869, 3; July 3, 1869, 1.

26. T. G. Steward to editor, *CR,* Aug. 14, 1869, 3.

27. "Editorial Wants," *CR,* Oct. 16, 1869, 2. "Help! Help!" *CR,* Oct. 16, 1893, 2–3.

28. "Publisher's Appeal," *CR,* Oct. 23, 1869, 1; Dec. 18, 1869, 1.

29. "A Press at Last," *CR,* Dec. 18, 1869, 2.

30. *CR,* Apr. 16, 1870, 2. "Personal," *CR,* May 21, 1870, 1–2.

31. *CR,* Oct. 8, 1870, 1–2; Dec. 3, 1870, 2; Dec. 31, 1870, 2; Jan. 28, 1871, 2; July 29, 1871, 2.

32. *CR,* Sept. 30, 1871, 2.

33. *CR,* Nov. 25, 1871, 1; Jan. 27, 1872, 3; Mar. 16, 1872, 1; Sept. 28, 1872, 4. *The Fifteenth Quadrennial Session of the General Conference of the African Methodist Episcopal Church, Nashville, Tennessee, May 6–24, 1872,* 64–67.

34. L. L. Berry, *A Century of Missions of the African Methodist Episcopal Church, 1840–1940* (New York: Gutenberg Printing, 1942), vi–vii, 47.

35. Payne, *The Semi-Centenary and the Retrospection of the African Methodist Episcopal Church,* 143–46. "Our Colored People," *Methodist,* Nov. 3, 1860, 132. Rev. B. P. Raymond, "A Belated Race," *Twentieth Annual Report of the Freedmen's Aid Society of the Methodist Episcopal Church for 1887* (Cincinnati: Western Methodist Book Concern Press, 1887), 41–48.

36. Steward, *From 1864 to 1914,* 26. Clarence E. Walker, *A Rock in a Weary Land: The African Methodist Episcopal Church during the Civil War and Reconstruction* (Baton Rouge: Louisiana State Univ. Press, 1982), 50. Daniel A. Payne, *History of the African Methodist Episcopal Church* (Phila-

delphia: A.M.E. Sunday School Union, 1891), 469. Clara De Boer, "The Role of Afro-Americans in the Origin and Work of the American Missionary Association, 1839–1877" (Ph.D. diss., Rutgers Univ., 1973), 3. Daniel A. Payne to Executive Committee, AMA, May 8, 1865, #0874, reel 15, Black Abolitionist Papers.

37. *CR*, May 16, 1868, 2. "The Unitarians," *CR*, Oct. 24, 1868, 2; Nov. 14, 1868, 2. "Unitarian Liberality," *CR*, Jan. 16, 1869, 2. "The Christian Register," *CR*, Mar. 19, 1870, 2. De Boer, "The Role of Afro-Americans in the Origin and Work of the American Missionary Association," 3. *New York Times*, Oct. 8, 1868, 8; Oct. 9, 1868, 2.

38. *CR*, Sept. 12, 26, 1868, 2.

39. "The American Negro," *CR*, Nov. 21, 1868, 2. A. F. Beard, "The Providence of God in the Historical Development of the Negro," in Haley, *Afro-American Encyclopedia*, 25.

40. Editorial, "Where Is Africa's Hope?" *CR*, Dec. 26, 1868, 2; June 12, 1869, 2.

41. Joseph J. Roberts, "African Colonization," address delivered at the fifty-second annual meeting of the American Colonization Society, Washington, D.C., Jan. 19, 1869, 1–16. Alexander Crummell to William Whipper, May 19, 1869, *CR*, Aug. 28, 1869, 1.

42. *CR*, June 26, 1869, 2. "Dr. Livingstone," *CR*, Oct. 23, 186Y, 2. "The M.E. Church and Africa," *CR*, Sept. 28, 1872, 4.

43. "Annexation of Liberia," *CR*, Mar. 19, 1870, 2. Letter to the editor, *CR*, May 17, 1870, 2; July 31, 1870, 2. For Tanner's anti-colonization view, see "Colored Conferences," *CR*, Oct. 17, 1868, 2.

44. "The Revolution in Spain," *CR*, Oct. 17, 1868, 2, Nov. 7, 1868, 2. "Cuba," *CR*, Nov. 14, 1868, 2. "After Emancipation and Enfranchisement, What?" *CR*, Dec. 5, 1868, 2.

45. *CR*, Feb. 13, 1869, 2. *New York Times*, Apr. 6, 1869, 1. "The American Mania—Cuba and San Domingo," ibid., Apr. 8, 1869, 4. "The Mania for Expansion—The St. Domingo Negotiations," ibid, Feb. 8, 1869, 4. "The St. Domingo Job," ibid., Feb. 10, 1869, 4. "San Domingo and Sarnana-Samana and Guano," ibid., Feb. 11, 1869, 4.

46. "Religion in Cuba and Porto Rico," *CR*, Nov. 6, 1869, 2. "Annexation of Dominica," *CR*, Apr. 2, 1870, 2; June 2, 1870, 4. *New York Times*, July 1, 1870, 5. "Blow the Trump," *CR*, Jan. 7, 1871, 2.

47. *CR*, Nov. 25, 1871, 2.

48. Letter to the editor, *CR*, Feb. 22, 1872, 2. "Dominica," *CR*, Jan. 23, 1873, 4. "What Hinders," *CR*, Jan. 30, 1873, 4. "Spain's for Cuba," *CR*, Feb. 29, 1873, 4.

49. *CR*, Nov. 14, 1868, 2; Nov. 21, 1868, 1. "Christian Convention," *New York Times*, Nov. 18, 1868, 8.

50. "Wilberforce Univ.," *CR*, Dec. 12, 1868, 2; June 18, 1870. "Extravagance," *CR*, Apr. 9, 1870, 2.

51. "Our Local Ministry," *CR*, Oct. 24, 1868, 2; "Pulpit Eloquence," *CR*, Oct. 31, 1868, 2; "Editorial Correspondence," *CR*, June 18, 1870, 1.

52. "The Young Men's Christian Association," *CR*, Nov. 21, 1868, 2. "The Young Women's Christian Association," *CR*, Dec. 12, 1868, 2; May 26, 1881, 2.

53. "Theater Going," *CR*, May 21, 1870, 2.

54. "Intemperance," *CR*, Apr. 22, 1871, 2; July 29, 1871, 2; Oct. 28, 1871, 2; Aug. 3, 1872, 4. "Bishop Payne's Letter to National Convention," Feb. 13, 1869, in *Proceedings of the National Convention of the Colored Men of America, Held in Washington, D.C., January 13–16, 1869.* (Washington, D.C., 1869), 13–15.

55. *CR*, "Our Friends and Our Foes," *CR*, Nov. 7, 1868, 2; "The Home of Civilization," *CR*, Oct. 29, 1870, 2. *Proceedings of the National Convention of Colored Men . . . 1869*, 13–15.

56. Ariel, *The Negro: What Is His Ethnological Status?* (Cincinnati: n.p., 1867), 1–48. Robert A. Young, *The Negro: A Reply to Ariel* (Nashville: J. Ferren, 1867), 1–48. B. T. Tanner, *The Negro's Origin and Is the Negro Cursed?* (Philadelphia: A.M.E. Book Depository, 1869), 8, 9, 20–22, 25, 31, 34, 38. Rufus L. Perry, *The Cushite or the Descendants of Ham* (Springfield, Mass.: Willes, 1893), iii, iv, v, x, 41, 155–56, 158, 161. *CR*, Feb. 6, 1869, 2. George M. Fredrickson, *The Black Image in the White Mind: The Debate on Afro-American Character and Destiny, 1817–1914.* (New York: Harper & Row, 1971), 188–89.

57. "Our Weakness," *CR*, Nov. 26, 1870, 2; Aug. 3, 1872, 4. "Our Weakness," *New National Era*, Dec. l, 1870, 2; Dec. 15, 1870, 2.

58. *The Fifteenth Quadrennial Session*, 40. "Our Missionary Work," *CR*, May 11, 1872, 1–2. T. G. Steward, "The Mission of San Domingo," *CR*, May 19, 1872. Tanner, *An Apology for African Methodism*, 374.

59. *The Fifteenth Quadrennial Session*, 14, 112.

60. *CR*, June 8, 1871, 2–3. "Our Second Bow," *CR*, June 8, 1872, 4. I. Garland Penn, *The Afro-American Press and Its Editors* (Springfield, Mass.: Wiley, 1891), 80. Deeds and Certificates, 1858–72, Benjamin Tucker Tanner Papers.

Chapter 3

1. "Ministerial Comfort," *CR*, June 8, 1872, 4. "Which Manhood—A Word to Young Men," *CR*, July 6, 1872, 4. T. H. Jackson, "To The Young Men," *CR*, Mar. 22, 1877, 1.

2. *CR*, Nov. 9, 1872, 4. "The Christian Recorder," *New National Era*, Nov. 14, 1872, 2. *CR*, Nov. 28, 1872, 2.

3. John T. Grayson, "Frederick Douglass' Intellectual Development: His Concept of God, Man, and Nature in Light of American and European Influences" (Ph.D. diss., Columbia Univ., 1981), 108, 179. "Blind but Powerless," *CR*, Apr. 22, 1875, 4.

4. "Hillsdale Speech no. 1," *CR*, July 15, 1875, 4. "Hillsdale Speech no. 2," *CR*, July 22, 1875, 4. Tanner, "Frederick Douglass' Speech," *Independent* 27 (July 29, 1875): 5. John Blassingame and John R. McKivigan, eds., *The Frederick Douglass Papers*, 5 vols. (New Haven: Yale Univ. Press, 1979–92), 4:414–22. "Frederick Douglass," *Louisianian*, Aug. 21, 1875, 2. William H. Ward, "Sixty Years of the *Independent*," *Independent* 65 (Dec. 10, 1908): 1345–51.

5. Frederick Douglass to the Rev. Russell Lane Carpenter, Apr. 30, 1881, Frederick Douglass Papers, reel 3, container 4–5. Douglass to Tanner, Jan.

18, 1883, *CR*, Apr. 5, 1883, 2; Jan. 11, 1883, 2. "The Douglass Banquet," *CR*, Jan. 11, 1883, 3. "Greener and Douglass," *CR*, May 31, 1883, 2; Apr. 3, 1884, 2. *Washington Bee*, Feb. 23, 1895, 2.

6. Waldo E. Martin Jr., *The Mind of Frederick Douglass* (Chapel Hill: Univ. of North Carolina Press, 1984), 98. For views on Douglass's marriage, see *Washington Grit*, Jan. 26, 1884, 4; *People's Advocate*, Feb. 9, 1884, 2; *CR*, Feb. 7, 1884, 3; *CR*, June 18, 1870, 1; "Fred Douglass Married to a White Woman," *State Journal*, Jan. 26, 1884, 1.

7. Tanner, "Douglass," *A.M.E. C.Rev.* 18 (July 1900): 35–44; Tanner to John E. Bruce, Aug. 189?, John Edward Bruce Papers, reel l. Frederick Douglass to T. G. Steward, July 27, 1886, Frederick Douglass Papers, reel 9, container 12 (this letter is incomplete; for complete letter, see Steward, *From 1864 to 1914*, 232–36).

8. Wilson J. Moses, *Alexander Crummell: A Study of Civilization and Discontent* (Amherst: Univ. of Massachusetts Press, 1992), 197–98. "Washington Episcopalians," *CR*, Jan. 20, 1876, 4. Crummell to Tanner, Jan. 23, 1876, in *CR*, Feb. 3, 1876, 4. "Crude and Tumultuous," *CR*, Feb. 17, 1876, 4.

9. Hollis R. Lynch, *Edward Wilmot Blyden, Pan Negro Patriot* (London: Oxford Univ. Press, 1967), 105. "Prof. Blyden at Hampton," *CR*, Aug. 13, 1874, 4.

10. "African Emigration," *CR*, Oct. 21, 1875, 4. "African Destiny," *CR*, Nov. 16, 1876, 4. Edward Blyden, "Visit to Bospora," letter to William Coppinger, Mar. 1877, *CR*, June 14, 1877, 1. "Brevities," *CR*, June 14, 1877, 2.

11. "Rev. Alexander Crummell, A.M.," *CR*, Sept. 21, 1872, 4. "Who Shall Rule?" *CR*, Mar. 19, 1870, 2; May 13, 1871, 2. "Religion in Japan," *CR*, Sept. 4, 1873, 4; June 3, 1871, 2.

12. "The Ashantee War," *CR*, Nov. 6, 1873, 4; Jan. 8, 1874, 6.

13. "The Bishops' Message," *CR*, Dec. 18, 1873, 4.

14. "Our Letter," *CR*, Feb. 26, 1874, 4; Bishop Brown's letter is not available, as the Feb. 19 and 26 front pages are missing.

15. R. G. Mortimor, "That Letter," *CR*, Mar. 12, 1874, 1. Mattie V. Holmes, "A Woman's Letter," *CR*, Apr. 9, 1874, 2. "An Open Letter," *CR*, May 14, 1874, 1, signed by seven bishops' wives: Mary Quinn, Eliza Payne, Harriet Wayman, Mary A. Campbell, Maria Shorter, Mary L. Brown, and Mrs. Bishop Ward. Hattie Wayman, "The Work of Women," *CR*, May 21, 1874, 2. "How to Organize," *CR*, May 21, 1874, 4.

16. Bishop J. M. Brown, "That Meeting—The Ball in Motion," *CR*, June 4, 1874, 1; "Mohammedanism in Africa," *CR*, July 23, 1874, 4.

17. *CR*, June 25, 1874, 1.

18. *CR*, Aug. 20, 1874, 2.

19. "The Mite Society," *CR*, Mar. 4, 1875, 4; Apr. 1, 1875, 2. John T. Jenifer, *Centennial Retrospect History of the African Methodist Episcopal Church* (Nashville: Sunday School Union, 1915), 319–20.

20. William Seraile, "Afro-American Emigration to Haiti during the American Civil War," *Americas* 35 (Oct. 1878): 185–200.

21. James Redpath to Daniel A. Payne, Mar. 12, 1862, in *Correspondence of James Redpath, Commercial Agent of Hayti for Philadelphia, Joint Plenipo-*

tentiary of Hayti to the Government of the U.S. and General Agent of Emigration to Hayti for the U.S. and Canada, December 31, 1861, to May 12, 1862, James Redpath Papers. T. G. Steward, "The Santo Domingo Mission," *CR,* May 18, 1872, 2. Tanner, *An Apology for African Methodism,* 374.

22. Seraile, *Voice of Dissent,* 49–55. James A. Handy, "Our Haytian Mission," *CR,* May 14, 1874, 1.

23. "The New Year," *CR,* Jan. 7, 1875, 4. *CR,* Feb. 18, 1875, 8; Apr. 1, 1875, 2. Bishop J. M. Brown to Bishop Campbell, *CR,* Mar. 29, 1875, 1; Apr. 29, 1875, 1.

24. Rev. Alex Jackson to Bishop Brown, *CR,* Feb. 18, 1875, 1; May 27, 1875, 1.

25. "The Call Renewed," *CR,* May 27, 1875, 4. "Our Missionary," *CR,* June 24, 1875, 4. "Who Will Bear It?" *CR,* Sept. 9, 1875, 4.

26. "Bishop Brown for Hayti," *CR,* Nov. 9, 1876, 4. "Our Mission Work," *CR,* Nov. 30, 1876, 4; Dec. 28, 1876, 1. "Our Missionary Off," *CR,* Apr. 19, 1877, 2. "A Bishop For Hayti," *CR,* May 17, 1877, 2.

27. "The Cabinet Question," *CR,* Dec. 7, 1872, 4; see *CR,* Nov. 30, 1872, for pros and cons on this issue.

28. "The Jersey Convention," *CR,* May 15, 1873, 4; Feb. 18, 1875, 4.

29. "Kansas," *CR,* July 9, 1870, 2. "Important Notice," *CR,* Apr. 22, 1871, 2; May 13, 1871, 2; July 29, 1871, 2. "Our Necessity," Feb. 6, 1873, 4. "Brevities," *CR,* Mar. 1, 1877, 4. "Philadelphia Matters," *CR,* Aug. 29, 1878, 3. *CR,* Sept. 5, 12, 1878, 3. "The Colored School," *CR,* Sept. 19, 1878, 2.

30. Clara Bell Anderson, "Female Education," *CR,* Feb. 20, 1873, 4. "Important Notice," *CR,* Apr. 22, 1871, 2; May 13, 1871, 2. Emily Faithful, "Women and Work," *CR,* Apr. 17, 1873, 7.

31. "Editorial Correspondence," *CR,* Apr. 9, 1870, 2.

32. *Christian Advocate,* n.d., in *CR,* Apr. 13, 1872, 4. "Dr. Fuller on Civil Rights," *CR,* Aug. 27, 1874, 4.

33. Aptheker, *A Documentary History of the Negro People in the United States* 2:636–41. *Memorial of the National Convention of Colored Persons, December 19, 1873,* U.S. Senate, 43rd Congress, 1st session, Miscellaneous Document no. 21 (Washington: Government Printing Office, 1873), 1–5.

34. "Address to the Colored Men," *New York Times,* July 25, 1873, 2.

35. "Civil Rights," *CR,* Feb. 26, 1874, 4.

36. "The Civil Rights Bill," *CR,* May 21, 1874, 4. "Civil Rights Bill," *CR,* June 11, 1874, 4. "President Grant and the Civil Rights Bill," *CR,* June 25, 1874, 4.

37. "Exit Civil Rights," *CR,* July 2, 1874, 4. "The Civil Rights Bill," *CR,* Mar. 11, 1875, 4; Dec. 16, 1875, 5. Tanner, "The Nation's Ultimatum," *Independent* 27 (Dec. 30, 1875): 7.

38. "California and the Chinese," *CR,* June 19, 1873, 4. "California Christian Churches and the Chinese," *CR,* Aug. 21, 1873, 4. "The New Outrage," *CR,* Mar. 28, 1882, 2. "Two Quotations," *CR,* Aug. 10, 1882, 2. *A.M.E. C.Rev.* 1 (July 1884): 70–71.

39. For Greener's view, see *New York Times,* Mar. 31, 1882, 8. "Princeton: A Difference," *CR,* July 23, 1874, 4. Editorial, "No Room for the Chinese," *The Colored American,* Dec. 28, 1901, 8; Feb. 1, 1902, 7.

40. Tanner, "Three Suppositions," *Independent* 26 (Nov. 12, 1874): 1–2. "Employment for Women," *CR*, July 22, 1871, 2. "Employment of Women," *CR*, Mar. 25, 1871, 4.

41. Tanner, "Social Equality," *Independent* 27 (Feb. 25, 1875): 3.

42. R.G.M. to [Tanner], *CR*, Jan. 15, 1870, 2. Frances E. W. Harper, "Sowing and Reaping," *CR*, Jan. 4, Jan. 11, 1877, 1. "'Grass' Widow Two Wives," *CR*, Aug. 12, 1880, 2. Eleanor Kirk Ames [Eleanor Maria Estabrook], *Up Broadway, and Its Sequel: A Life Story* (New York: Carleton, 1870). For Tanner's review of *Ecce Femina*, see *CR*, Jan. 15, 1870, 1; for a review of *Up Broadway*, see *CR*, Feb. 19, 1870, 2.

43. T. G. Steward, "Two Alterations in Our Discipline Suggested," *CR*, Mar. 19, 1870, 1; Dec. 23, 1875, 4; Nov. 17, 1881, 2. "Reform Needed," *CR*, Dec. 29, 1881, 2. "Editorial Correspondence," *CR*, Sept. 21, 1882, 2.

44. "Kansas," *CR*, July 9, 1870, 2. "Letter from Lincoln, Nebraska," *CR*, June 18, 1874, 2. "Turner's Manifesto," *CR*, Dec. 17, 1874, 4.

45. *CR*, Aug. 13, 1870, 2. "Extravagance," *CR*, May 22, 1873, 4. "The Panic and How It Came," *CR*, Oct. 2, 1873, 4. "Hard Times," *CR*, Dec. 3, 1874, 4.

46. "White People Do So," *CR*, Mar. 4, 1871, 2. "Philadelphia Society," *CR*, Mar. 14, 1878, 2.

47. "Who? Who?" *CR*, Jan. 16, 1873, 4; June 19, 1873, 1; July 17, 1873, 4. "Wilberforce University," *CR*, July 24, 1873, 5.

48. W. S. Lankford to Tanner, *CR*, Oct. 14, 1873, 1. Granville, "A Young Men's Hall," *CR*, Jan. 5, 1874, 2. B. F. Lee, "A Young Men's Hall," *CR*, Dec. 11, 1873, 5.

49. "Our Swivel," *CR*, Sept. 25, 1873, 4. "To the Friends of Education, Appeal of Bishop D. A. Payne and John A. Clark," *CR*, Sept. 21, 1875, 7; Sept. 23, 1875, 5; Oct. 7, 1875, 2; Sept. 30, 1875, 4.

50. "Ministerial Gravity," *CR*, Sept. 3, 1870, 2; Sept. 18, 1873, 4.

51. *CR*, July 17, 1873, 4.

52. "Why Can't We Do It?" *CR*, Mar. 5, 1874, 4. "Self Respect," *CR*, May 14, 1874, 4.

53. "That Statue to Allen," *CR*, July 30, 1874, 4; Aug. 13, 1874, 4; Sept. 3, 1874, 2. James A. Handy, "That Statue," *CR*, Sept. 10, 1874, 7.

54. Bishop J. M. Brown, "Allen Monument," *CR*, Nov. 5, 1874, 1. "The Centennial Exhibition," *CR*, Mar. 11, 1875, 4. "A Call to Wilberforce," *CR*, July 29, 1 87, 4.

55. Amos A. Williams, "Allen Statue," *CR*, Jan. 11, 1876, 8; Jan. 27, 1876, 1. Amos A. Williams, "We Are Coming," *CR*, Feb. 3, 1876, 8. "The Allen Monument," *CR*, Apr. 13, 1876, 4. "Brevities," *CR*, May 11, 1876, 4; June 15, 1876, 4. "The Allen Monument a Success," *CR*, Sept. 7, 1876, 1; Oct. 12, 1876, 5; Oct. 26, 1876, 5; Nov. 9, 1876, 4.

56. "Bishop Allen Monument," *CR*, Nov. 9, 1876, 4–5.

57. *CR*, Sept. 18, 1873, 1; Jan. 8, 1874, 4; May 1, 1873, 4.

58. Joseph E. Hayne, "Why The "Recorder" Don't Pay," *CR*, Aug. 6, 1874, 1. C. W. Foster, "Rum and Tobacco," *CR*, June 17, 1875, 2. "The War of the Women," *CR*, Feb. 2, 1874, 4; July 15, 1875, 4. BTT Diary, July 4, 1860.

59. W. H. Hunter, "The Church Paper," *CR*, Sept. 11, 1873, 7.

60. *CR*, Sept. 4, 1873, 2; Nov. 27, 1873, 2; Apr. 2, 1874, 2; May 7, 1874, 6.

61. "The Integrity of the 'Dollar System,'" *CR*, June 4, 1874, 4. Bishop J. P. Campbell to Tanner, *CR*, Jan. 20, 1876, 5, 8. "A.M.E. Church Statistics for 1875," *CR*, Mar. 9, 1876, 4.

62. *CR*, Mar. 4, 1871, 2; May 27, 1871, 2; Apr. 3, 1873, 4.

63. "General Conference Papers VI Publishing Department (C)," *CR*, Feb. 10, 1876, 4. "The Recorder's Opportunity," Mar. 23, 1876, 4.

64. "Our Swivel," *CR*, Aug. 20, 1874, 4. "Colored Papers and the Necessity of Supporting Them," *CR*, Aug. 27, 1874, 4. *People's Advocate*, May 13, 1876, 2.

65. *CR*, June 25, 1874, 5.

66. *The Sixteenth Session and the Fifteenth Quadrennial Session of the General Conference of the African Methodist Episcopal Church, Atlanta, May 1–18, 1876*, 74–75.

67. Ibid., 56. *CR*, May 25, 1876, 4. "Salutatory Third," *CR*, June 1, 1876, 4. For Carr's remarks, see *CR*, May 14, 1874, 4. For Jenifer's remarks, see *CR*, June 3, 1875, 1.

68. Stephen W. Angell, *Bishop Henry McNeal Turner and African American Religion in the South* (Knoxville: Univ. of Tennessee Press, 1992), 123–24.

Chapter 4

1. "Personal Items," *CR*, Jan. 20, 1876, 5. "Letter from Dr. Turner," *CR*, Mar. 9, 1876, 1. "A Word about Exchanges," *CR*, Mar. 9, 1876, 4; Nov. 15, 1877, 2. For Dr. Hamilton, see *CR*, Jan. 17, 1878, 4.

2. W. H. Prince, *The Stars of the Century of African Methodism* (Portland, Ore.: n.p., 1916), 13–14.

3. H. M. Turner, "Brief History of the Christian Recorder," *CR*, July 20, 1911, 1. *CR*, Jan. 14, 1875, 4.

4. Angell, *Bishop Henry McNeal Turner*, 8.

5. *CR*, July 20, 1911, 1.

6. "The New Manager's Inaugural," *CR*, June 29, 1876, 1.

7. "Another Appeal from the Manager," *CR*, July 13, 1876, 1, 4. T. G. Steward, "Our View," *CR*, Aug. 10, 1876, 2; Aug. 17, 1876, 4. "Another Word from the Manager," *CR*, Aug. 10, 1876, 5.

8. Tanner, "The Sioux Revenge," *CR*, July 20, 1876, as quoted in Philip S. Foner, ed., *The Voice of Black America: Major Speeches of Negroes in the United States, 1791–1971* (New York: Simon and Schuster, 1972). 443–44.

9. "The Nominee," *CR*, June 22, 1876, 4. "Tilden's Election," *CR*, Nov. 9, 1876, 4; Nov. 16, 1876, 4. "Never Fear," *CR*, Dec. 7, 1876, 4. "The Compromise," *CR*, Jan. 25, 1877, 4. "Brevities," *CR*, Mar. 8, 1877, 4.

10. "General Mention," *CR*, July 12, 1876, 2. "A Lesson," *CR*, Mar. 15, 1877, 4, 8; Mar. 22, 1877, 4. "Our Future," *CR*, Aug. 9, 1877, 2. "Disadvantages," *CR*, Aug. 30, 1877, 2. "Brevities," *CR*, Sept. 1, 1877, 2. "The President's Message," *CR*, Dec. 15, 1881, 2. George W. Julian, "The Death Struggle of the Republican Party," *North American Review* 126 (Mar.-Apr. 1878): 262–92.

11. *CR*, Oct. 19, 1876, 4. H. M. Turner, "Presidency of Howard University," *CR*, Dec. 28, 1876, 2.

12. "A President for Howard University," *CR*, May 3, 1877, 2.

13. "A Reason," *CR*, Aug. 4, 1876, 4.

14. *CR*, Aug. 17, 1876, 5. "Brevities," *CR*, Oct. 19, 1876, 4. "It Will Be Necessary," *CR*, Nov. 2, 1876, 4. "An Interrogative with an Answer," *CR*, Aug. 4, 1876, 4. "Where Responsibility Comes In," *CR*, Oct. 12, 1876, 4 (the title page should have been labeled October 5); Dec. 15, 1881, 2.

15. *CR*, Aug. 31, 1876, 7. H. M. Turner, "Read This without Fail," *CR*, Sept. 21, 1876, 1. H. M. Turner, "To Our Subscribers," *CR*, Oct. 12, 1876, 4. "Personalities," *CR*, Nov. 9, 1876, 4.

16. T.G.S. [Theophilus Gould Steward], "It Is Time to Stop," *CR*, Nov. 16, 1876, 7. "Charge and Counter Charge," *CR*, Nov. 30, 1876, 1.

17. *CR*, Nov. 30, 1876, 2; Dec. 14, 1876, 4.

18. "Local Item," *CR*, Dec. 21, 1876, 4. "Brevities," *CR*, Sept. 13, 1877, 2.

19. H. M. Turner, "Notice," *CR*, Jan. 11, 1877, 4. "Brevities," *CR*, Feb. 2, 1877, 4.

20. "Editorial Personal," *CR*, Apr. 5, 1877, 4; Apr. 12, 1877, 1, 2. For responses to the *Christian Recorder*'s new appearance, see the issue of May 10, 1877, 2.

21. J. T. Jenifer, "Doings at Little Rock," *CR*, June 21, 1877, 1. "Our Church News," *CR*, Feb. 14, 1878, 4. Joseph S. Shaw, "How Shall the Confidence of the People be Restored," *CR*, Feb. 14, 1878, 1. "Statement of Bishops in Regards to Their Work," *CR*, June 13, 1878, 1.

22. H. M. Turner, "The Manager Speaks," *CR*, June 21, 1877, 2. "Brevities," *CR*, June 28, 1877, 2. "The Manager Speaks Again," *CR*, June 28, 1877, 2. "Brevities," *CR*, July 5, 1877, 2. "Still the Manger Speaks," *CR*, July 5, 1877, 2. Rev. A. H. Newton, "An Echo to the Manager's Call," *CR*, July 12, 1877, 1. "Brevities," *CR*, July 12, 1877, 2. H. M. Turner, "Words of Warning to Our Subscribers," *CR*, July 26, 1877, 2.

23. "Don't Read the Recorder," *CR*, Aug. 2, 1877, 2. "Kari-Kari," *CR*, Aug. 2, 1877, 2. "Brevities," *CR*, Aug. 2, 1877, 2.

24. "Brevities," *CR*, Aug. 2, 1877, 2.

25. "Brevities," *CR*, Aug. 23, 1877, 2.

26. *CR*, Aug. 30, 1877, 1. "Dr. Johnson's Moves," *CR*, Sept. 20, 1877, 2. "The Official Board of Offering," *CR*, Sept. 24, 1877, 2.

27. "Shall It Be," *CR*, Jan. 31, 1878, 2. "Word from Ex-Manager Hunter," *CR*, Feb. 7, 1878, 2. "The Facts in This Case," *CR*, Feb. 14, 1878, 2.

28. "Our Ministry," *CR*, Feb. 21, 1878, 2. "Manager Turner's Appeal," *CR*, Feb. 28, 1878, 2. H. M. Turner, "The Last Recorder," *CR*, Mar. 7, 1878, 2. H. M. Turner, "Bump! Bang!! Here We Go Again," *CR*, Mar. 14, 1878, 2.

29. "Our Work," *CR*, Apr. 11, 1878, 2. "Brevities," *CR*, Apr. 18, 1878, 2. J. H. Madison to Turner, n.d., *CR*, May 2, 1878, 2. "Journalistic Magnanimity," *CR*, May 16, 1878, 2.

30. Robert J. Holland, "National Union Masonic Conventions," *CR*, May 16, 1878, 2. "The Masonic Unions," *CR*, May 23, 1878, 2; ibid. for *Report of the Proceedings of the Convention of Colored Masons (National and Independent) Held in the City of Wilmington, Del., May 8th, 9th, and 10th, 1878.*

31. *CR*, June 6, 1878, 2; July 4, 1878, 3. Angell, *Bishop Henry McNeal Turner*, 126.

32. Theodore Gould, "To Our Friends and Subscribers," *CR*, Aug. 29, 1878, 1; Oct. 31, 1878, 2.

33. Gould, "To Our Friends and Subscribers," *CR*, Nov. 7, 1878, 3.

34. "That Bazaar," *CR*, Nov. 14, 1878, 3; Dec. 12, 1878, 3.

35. H. M. Turner, "Shall Our Paper Suspend," *CR*, Dec. 26, 1878, 2. "Resignation of Manager Turner—Bishop Brown's Reply," *CR*, Dec. 26, 1878, 3.

36. "The Bazaar," *CR*, Jan. 1, 1880, 3. Theodore Gould, "On Behalf of the Recorder," *CR*, Jan. 8, 1880, 3; Jan. 22, 1880, 2.

37. "The Black Elephant," *New York Times*, Apr. 20, 1875, 6. *People's Advocate*, June 10, 1876, 2. Edward W. Blyden, "Negro Emigration," *CR*, Nov. 8, 1877, 2.

38. *CR*, Jan. 10, 1878, 2. D. A. Wilson, "Africa Waiting to Be Redeemed by Her Own Sons," *African Repository* 54 (Jan. 1878): 1–2. J. A. Newby, "African Emigration," *CR*, Jan. 3, 1878, 1. "The Emigration Movement," *CR*, Apr. 18, 1878, 2. "Brevities," *CR*, Apr. 18, 1878, 2; May 16, 1878, 3.

39. "Brevities," *CR*, May 23, 1878, 3. "A Lively Discussion," *CR*, May 23, 1878, 3. Mary Ella Mossell, "Father Forgive Them, They Know Not What They Do," *CR*, May 16, 1878, 1. "Ex Minister Turner on Liberia," *CR*, July 11, 1878, 2.

40. Daniel A. Payne to Rev. Charles H. Pearce, June 27, 1878, *CR*, July 25, 1878, 2. For Payne's second letter, see *CR*, Aug. 8, 1878, 2. For Turner's letter dated July 31, see *CR*, Aug. 22, 1878, 1.

41. "White Men in Africa," *CR*, Oct. 10, 1878, 2. "African Cruise," *CR*, Oct. 24, 1878, 2.

42. "Dr. Blyden's Opinion," *CR*, June 24, 1880, 2. William E. Montgomery, *Under Their Own Vine and Fig Tree: The African Methodist Church in the South, 1865–1890* (Baton Rouge: Louisiana State Univ. Press, 1993), 206. Lynch, *Edward Wilmot Blyden*, 111.

43. James Lynch, "The Word 'African' in the Discipline of the A.M.E. Church," *CR*, Apr. 9, 1864, 1. James Lynch, "Let the Word 'African' be Stricken From the Discipline," *CR*, Mar. 25, 1865, 1. For another opposing view, see *CR*, Apr. 8, 1865, 1–2. A. L. Stanford, "The Word 'African' in Our Denominational Title," *CR*, July 23, 1870, 1. Rev. A. Johnson, "The Word 'African' in Our Denominational Title," *CR*, Aug. 27, 1870, 2. *The Sixteenth Session and the Fifteenth Quadrennial Session*, 226–28. *Journal of the Seventeenth Session and Sixteenth Quadrennial*, 26. Tanner, "A Prophecy in a Prefix," *Independent* 27 (July 1, 1875): 4–5.

44. "Editorial Notes," *A.M.E. C.Rev.* 1 (Oct. 1884): 173.

45. Lynch, *Edward Wilmot Blyden*, 93–94. "Prospectus, The Negro," *CR*, Apr. 17, 1872, 7. Edward W. Blyden, "Negro Emigration," *CR*, Nov. 8, 1877, 2.

46. "Leading Thinkers' Course of Lectures," *CR*, Jan. 31, 1878, 1–2. "Americans: Not Negroes," *CR*, Mar. 14, 1878, 2. Greener letter to Tanner and "Answer to Prof. R. T. Greener," *CR*, Mar. 21, 1878, 2.

47. "American and Negroes: Both," *CR*, Mar. 28, 1878, 2.

48. *CR*, Jan. 22, 1880, 2.

49. Editorial, "Penny Wise," *CR*, Oct. 21, 1880, 2. John D. Bagwell, "Who We Are," *CR*, Dec. 23, 1880, 1. J. H. Scott, "Who Are We?" *CR*, Dec. 30, 1880, 1. J. M. Proctor, "Who Are We?" *CR*, Jan. 13, 1881, 1. "Who Are We?" *CR*, Jan. 13, 1881, 2. William E. Walker, "Who We Are," *CR*, Jan. 20, 1881, 1. A. J. Kershaw, "Who Are We?" *CR*, Jan. 27, 1881, 3. J. H. Scott,

"Who Are We?" *CR*, Feb. 3, 1881, 3. Martin R. Delany, "An Indisputable Moral Problem," ibid., Apr. 29, 1880, 2.

50. Gatewood, *Aristocrats of Color*, 219. Alfred A. Moss Jr., *The American Negro Academy: Voice of the Talented Tenth* (Baton Rouge: Louisiana State Univ. Press, 1981), 38.

51. "Pure Negroes," *CR*, Nov. 28, 1878, 2.

52. "Colored People's Day," *CR*, Nov. 8, 1877, 2. *CR*, Apr. 4, 1878, 4. "That Literary Congress," *CR*, Apr. 11, 1878, 2. M. Edward Bryant, "Literary Congress of the A.M.E. Church," *CR*, Apr. 25, 1878, 1. H. M. Turner, "The Literary Congress," *CR*, May 9, 1878, 2. "Local Column," *CR*, May 23, 1878, 3; Rev. H. A. Knight won the $10 first prize. H. M. Turner, "Literary Congress," *CR*, June 6, 1878, 2.

53. *People's Advocate*, Oct. 18, 1879, 2.

54. Angell, *Bishop Henry McNeal Turner*, 124–25. *Journal of the Seventeenth Session and the Sixteenth Quadrennial*, 93, 108. *Daily Christian Recorder*, May 5, 1880, 11, 29, 31, 33, 35.

55. *CR*, Mar. 23, 1876, 4; Mar. 30, 1876, 4. "Bishops in the South," *CR*, July 5, 1877. Two bishops lived in Wilberforce, Ohio, two lived in Washington, D.C., and one each in Philadelphia and Baltimore. R. H. Cain, "The General Conference," *CR*, Jan. 29, 1880, 1.

56. J. M. Cromwell, "Lee, Turner and Tanner," *CR*, Apr. 29, 1880, 2.

57. *Journal of the Seventeenth Session and Sixteenth Quadrennial*, 49–50; "The New Bishops," *People's Advocate*, May 22, 1880, 2.

58. H. M. Turner, "Bit of History of the Christian Recorder," *CR*, July 20, 1911, l. *Journal of the Seventeenth Session and Sixteenth Quadrennial*, 35.

59. "Philadelphia's Matter," *CR*, Mar. 4, 1880, 3. "Bishop B. T. Tanner," *A.M.E. C.Rev.* 5 (July 1888): 4.

Chapter 5

1. *CR*, June 24, 1880, 2. Henry M. Turner, "Manager Gould," *CR*, Aug. 25, 1880, 1.

2. *CR*, July 8, 1880, 3; Sept. 2, 1880, 1; Nov. 16, 1880, 3.

3. Theo Gould, "Read! Read! Read!" *CR*, Aug. 15, 1880, 3. "Local News," *CR*, May 19, 1881, 3.

4. "We the People," *CR*, Feb. 24, 1881, 2. "Aim High," *CR*, Mar. 31, 1881, 2. B. W. Arnett, ed., *The Budget For 1881* (Xenia, Ohio: Torchlight Printing, 1881), 122.

5. "Brevities," *CR*, Oct. 18, 1877, 2. "White Religionists and the Color Line," *CR*, Oct. 11, 1883, 2.

6. "Caste Church," *CR*, June 17, 1875, 4. "Editorial Correspondence," *CR*, Sept. 21, 1882, 2. "The Connectional Literary Association," *CR*, Oct. 12, 1882, 2.

7. *CR*, Oct. 14, 1875, 4. "Editorial Briefs," *CR*, Oct. 14, 1875, 4. "Union of Methodists," *CR*, Dec. 2, 1875, 5.

8. "Methodist Union," *CR*, Aug. 1, 1878, 2.

9. *Proceedings of the National Conference of Colored Men of the United States Held in State Capital at Nashville, Tennessee, May 6, 7, 8, and 9, 1879* (Washington: Rufus H. Darby, 1879), Appendix G, "The Theory and Practice of American Christianity," 78–79.

10. "African Methodist Union," *CR*, Aug. 15, 1880, 2. "African Methodist Union," *CR*, Sept. 9, 16, 23, 1880, 2; Apr. 14, 1881, 2; Apr. 28, 1881, 2. For Holly's letter to Payne, see *CR*, Feb. 4, 1881, 2. *Journal of the Seventeenth Session and the Sixteenth Quadrennial*, 205–6.

11. *Journal of the Seventeenth Session and the Sixteenth Quadrennial*, 222–23, 237. *CR*, Sept. 9, 1880, 2. Daniel A. Payne, "Thoughts about the Past, the Present and the Future of the African M.E. Church," *A.M.E. C.Rev.* 1 (Apr. 1885): 314–20.

12. "The Forthcoming Conference," *CR*, Apr. 13, 1882, 2. May 3 [should be May 4], 1883, 2; *Journal of the Eighteenth Session and Seventeenth Quadrennial Session of the General Conference of the African Methodist Episcopal Church in the World, Held in Bethel Church, Baltimore, Md., May 5th to 26th, 1884* (Philadelphia: A.M.E. Book Concern, 1884), 80, 82, 197. "Editorial Notes," *A.M.E. C.Rev.* 1 (Oct. 1884): 176.

13. *CR*, May 26, 1881, 2.

14. "A Word to Our Exchanges," *CR*, June 9, 1881, 2.

15. "Local News," *CR*, June 9, 1881, 3. "Editorial Correspondence," *CR*, June 23, 1881, 2; June 30, 1881, 2.

16. "Editorial Correspondence," *CR*, July 7, 1881, 2. "Editorial Log," *CR*, July 28, 1881, 2. "Editorial Log—4th Day," *CR*, Aug. 4, 1881, 2. "Editorial Log," *CR*, Aug. 11, 1881, 2.

17. "The Editor Abroad," *CR*, Sept. 1, 1881, 2. "Our Return," *CR*, Oct. 13, 1881, 2. "Letter from England," *CR*, Oct. 20, 1881, 1.

18. "Letter from England," *CR*, Oct. 6, 1881, 2; Oct. 20, 1881, 2. "Our Log," *CR*, Nov. 3, 1881, 2; Dec. 1, 1881, 2; Dec. 22, 1881, 1; Jan. 5, 1882, 2; Jan. 12, 1882, 2; Feb. 2, 1882, 2.

19. "Local News," *CR*, Oct. 20, 1881, 3; Nov. 3, 1881, 2; Nov. 10, 1881, 3; Feb. 2, 1882, 3.

20. "Our Return," *CR*, Oct. 13, 1881, 2; Oct. 27, 1881, 2. "A Word Personal," *CR*, Dec. 22, 1881, 2; Oct. 12, 1882, 2.

21. "A Word Personal," *CR*, Oct. 13, 1881, 2. "Our Heroes," *CR*, Oct. 20, 1881, 2. "Strong Characters," *CR*, Nov. 10, 1881, 2.

22. "Profanity Forbidden by God," *CR*, Apr. 12, 1877, 2. "White People Do It," *CR*, Nov. 24, 1881, 2.

23. "A Questionable Project," *CR*, Nov. 17, 1881, 2.

24. "A Step Backwards," *CR*, Nov. 3, 1881, 2; Jan. 19, 1882, 2. "Is it So?" *CR*, Feb. 2, 1882, 2.

25. *CR*, Nov. 24, 1881, 2. L. J. Campbell to Rev. S. F. Flegler, July 14, 1881, *CR*, Oct. 27, 1881, 2. "Bishop Turner's Review," *CR*, Dec. 8, 1881, 2. Otis H. Tiffany. *Africa for Africans: Being the Annual Discourse Delivered at the Sixty-seventh Anniversary of the Colonization Society Held in Foundry Methodist Church, Washington, D.C., Sunday, January 13, 1884* (Washington: American Colonization Society, 1884), 1–14. Anthony W. Gardner to William Coppinger, Dec. 1, 1881, *CR*, Mar. 2, 1882, 2.

26. Thomas H. Jackson, "Help! Help! Help!" *CR*, Jan. 19, 1882, 1.

27. *Journal of the Seventeenth Session and the Sixteenth Quadrennial*, 306–9; Charles Mossell's letter, n.d., *CR*, Mar. 16, 1882, 2. Flegler's letter, *CR*, Oct. 27, 1881, 2. "Brother Flegler," *CR*, Apr. 27, 1882, 2. "The Colored

Methodists," *State Journal*, May 17, 1884, 1. *Journal of the Eighteenth Session and the Seventeenth Quadrennial*, 205–6.

28. Edward W. Blyden to Tanner, *CR*, Mar. 9, 1882, 2. "Dr. Blyden's Letter," *CR*, Mar. 9, 1882, 2. George R. Statson to Tanner, Oct. 26, 1882, in "That Letter from Germany," *CR*, Nov. 30, 1882, 2. "Our Editorial," *A.M.E. C.Rev.* 2 (July 1885): 92.

29. "The Blood That is in Us," *CR*, Aug. 17, 1882, 2. "Fraternity: Dr. Ridgeway," *CR*, June 8, 1882, 2. "The Negro Controversy," *CR*, Aug. 3, 1882, 1. "That Big *N*," *CR*, July 26, 1883, 2.

30. Blyden to Tanner, Aug. 24, 1882, in "Dr. Blyden's Letter," *CR*, Sept. 7, 1882, 2. "Hon. John Smyth's Address," *CR*, June 29, 1882, 2, 3.

31. Blyden to Tanner, Sept. 12, 1882, in "Dr. Blyden's Letter," *CR*, Sept. 28, 1882, 2.

32. "Dr. Blyden's Scholarship," *CR*, Sept. 21, 1882, 2. "Arabi's Black Troops: The War in Egypt's War," *CR*, Sept. 14, 1882, 2. "William's History of the Negro," *CR*, Jan. 25, 1883, 2. For the current criticism of the African origin of Western civilization, see Mary Lefkowitz, "Combating False Theories in the Classroom," *Chronicle of Higher Education* 40 (Jan. 19, 1994): B1–2.

33. "Dr. Blyden's Influence," *CR*, Nov. 9, 1882, 2. "Belles Lettres, History, Law," *CR*, Nov. 9, 1882, 2; Dec. 14, 1882, 2. "Blydenism " *CR*, Jan. 18, 1883, 2.

34. T. McCants Stewart, "Our Fathers' Church," *CR*, Dec. 21, 1882, 1. Editorial, "Blydenism," *CR*, Dec. 21, 1882, 2.

35. "America in Africa," *CR*, Nov. 16, 1882, 2.

36. Matthew Anderson, "Advisory Committee on African Colonization," *CR*, Dec. 7, 1882, 3. "Advisory Committee on African Colonization," letter to Tanner from Meridian, Mississippi, Dec. 15, 1882, *CR*, Jan. 4, 1883, 3. "Bishop Turner on the Advisory Committee," *CR*, Jan. 4, 1883, 2. Tanner to Frelinghuysen, July 6, 1882, and Frelinghuysen to Tanner, July 15, 1882, *CR*, July 20, 1882, 1. Peyton M. Lewis, "Bishop Turner's Letter," *CR*, Jan. 25, 1883, 1. J. H. Scott, "Shall We Colonize Africa with American Negroes?" *CR*, Jan. 25, 1883, 1. "Bishop Turner's Reply," *CR*, Jan. 25, 1883, 2. T. H. Jackson, "The Future of the African in America," *CR*, Feb. 15, 1883, 1. See also *CR*, Mar. 1, 22, 1883, 1.

37. Edward W. Blyden to Tanner, Feb. 6, 1883, in "Letter from Dr. Blyden," *CR*, Feb. 15, 1883, 2.

38. H. M. Turner, "The African Question," *CR*, Feb. 22, 1883, 2–3. "Bishop Turner's Reply," *CR*, Feb. 2, 1883, 2. *Washington Bee*, Mar. 17, 1883, 2.

39. "Dinner to Dr. Blyden," *CR*, Mar. 29, 1883, 3. *Washington Bee*, Mar. 17, 1883, 3.

40. "Local News," *CR*, Apr. 5, 1883, 3. "What Shall Be the Policy of the Colored American toward Africa," *A.M.E. C.Rev.* 2 (July 1885): 68–75.

41. "The Future American," *CR*, Sept. 2, 1880, 2. "A New Acquaintance," *CR*, Dec. 7, 1882, 2. "A Continental Race," *CR*, Apr. 5, 1883, 2. "The German Element in the United States," *CR*, Apr. 12, 1883, 2. "Divide the Spoils," *CR*, Apr. 26, 1883, 2. "The Coming Race—What Is It to Be?" *CR*, May 15, 1884, 1. Abel Stevens, "The Problem of Our African Population," *Method-*

ist Quarterly Review 66 (Jan. 1884): 108–26. E. V. Smalley, "The German Element in the United States," *Lippincott's Magazine* 5 (Apr. 1883): 355–63. Moseby, "Reflections on Race Public Reception and Critical Response in [Henry] Tanner's Career," in Moseby, *Henry Ossawa Tanner,* 13.

42. T. G. Steward, "The Modification in the Race Idea Suggested by the Necessity of Modern Politics," *CR,* Apr. 26, 1883, 1; the *Competitor* 1 (first published in Jan. 1920) was organized by T. G. Steward and others who emphasized Americanism over color or race. For a current viewpoint, see Lawrence Wright, "One Drop of Blood," *New Yorker,* July 25, 1994, 50, 146–55.

43. Thomas F. Gossett, *Race: The History of an Idea in America* (New York: Schocken Books, 1965), 144–75.

44. Alexander Crummell, "The Social Principle among a People; and Its Bearing on the Progress and Development," in *The Greatness of Christ and Other Sermons* (New York: Thomas Whittaker, 1882), 294–311. W. E. B. Du Bois, "The Conservation of the Races," in Julius Lester, ed., *The Seventh Son: The Thoughts and Writing of W. E. B. Du Bois,* 2 vols. (New York: Vintage Books, 1971), 1:176–87.

45. "Our Employment," *CR,* July 12, 1883, 2. "Colored Hotels," *CR,* Aug. 24, 1882, 2; Aug. 17, 1882, 2. "The Country Filling Up," *CR,* Apr. 20, 1882, 2. "Go West Young Man," *CR,* Mar. 9, 1882, 2. *State Journal,* Feb. 2, 16, 1884, 4.

46. "Personals," *CR,* Mar. 2, 1882, 2. "What Have We to Say?" *CR,* Mar. 23, 1882, 2. "What Our White Friends Can Do," *CR,* Aug. 3, 1882, 2. "Not Charity, but Work," *CR,* Oct. 25, 1883, 2.

47. "The Press Convention," *CR,* July 6, 1882, 2. "The Revolt of Labor," *CR,* June 29, 1882, 2. "Our Editorial—Strikes," *A.M.E. C.Rev.* 3 (July 1886). *CR,* Aug. 28, 1890, 4. David W. Wills, "Aspects of Social Thought in the African Methodist Episcopal Church, 1884–1910." (Ph.D. diss., Harvard Univ., 1975), 215–16.

48. Aptheker, *A Documentary History of the Negro People in the United States* 2:650–51. Bruce Grit (John E. Bruce), "Lessons of the Strike," *The Colored American,* May 25, 1901, 1, 4, 9; editorial, *The Colored American,* Jan. 4, 1902, 8; Aptheker, *A Documentary History of the Negro People in the United States* 3:630–36.

49. "Editorial Correspondence," *CR,* Apr. 14, 1881, 2. "Civil Rights Does Work in the North," *CR,* Apr. 27, 1882, 2. "The Outrage upon Our Bishops," *CR,* Apr. 6, 1882, 2; Apr. 27, 1882, 2; June 8, 1882, 2; Aug. 10, 1882, 2–3; Nov. 21, 1882, 2. "Colored Methodists Indignant," *New York Times,* Mar. 30, 1882, 8; Mar. 31, 1882, 8; Apr. 13, 1882, 1. For Bishop Campbell, see *Philadelphia Bulletin,* Mar. 25, 1883, as cited in *New York Globe,* Mar. 31, 1883, 2.

50. "The Recent Decisions," *CR,* Oct. 25, 1883, 2; the same page includes a survey of press opinions on the Supreme Court decision. "The Recent Supreme Court Decision," *CR,* Nov. 15, 1883, 2.

51. "Political Preaching," *CR,* Feb. 23, 1882, 2; July 27, 1882, 2; Sept. 28, 1882, 2. Blassingame and McKivigan, *The Frederick Douglass Papers* 4:562–81.

52. "Independence South and North," *CR,* Oct. 19, 1882, 2. "Why Are We Republican?" *CR,* Oct. 26, 1882, 2; Nov. 16, 1882, 2. For Bruce's viewpoint, see Aptheker, *A Documentary History of the Negro People in the United States* 2:115.

53. "The Ohio Defeat—Its Real Cause," *CR,* Oct. 26, 1882, 2. "Answer to Mr. Downing's Queries," *CR,* Nov. 23, 1882, 2. "The Election of Judge Hoadly," *CR,* Oct. 18, 1883, 2. "A Coming Danger," *CR,* Nov. 29, 1883, 2. "The 'Vote at All Hazards' Article," *CR,* Jan. 10, 1884, 2.

54. "The Chicago Nominee," *CR,* June 12, 1884, 2. "A Word to Colored Democrats," *CR,* June 26, 1884, 2. *A.M.E. C.Rev.* 1 (July 1884): 74.

55. *New York Globe,* Oct. 21, 1883, 1; May 2, 1883, 1. *State Journal,* Mar. 17, 1884, 1. Emma Lou Thornbrough, *T. Thomas Fortune, Militant Journalist* (Chicago: Univ. of Chicago Press, 1972), 58.

56. "Views of Prominent Philadelphians on Blaine's Apparent Defeat," *CR,* Nov. 13, 1884, 2. "Views on Cleveland's Probable Election," *State Journal,* Nov. 13, 1884, 1. Steward, *From 1864 to 1914,* 220. "The Democratic Return to Power—Its Effect?" *A.M.E. C.Rev.* 1: (July 1884): 213–50.

57. *State Journal,* June 14, 28, 1884, 1. Lawrence Grossman, *The Democratic Party and the Negro: Northern and National Politics, 1868–1892* (Urbana: Univ. of Illinois Press, 1976), 73–75.

58. "Valedictory," *CR,* June 5, 1884, 2. Rev. H. H. Halloway, "Our Membership," *CR,* Dec. 12, 1878, 1. L. J. Coppin, "Fortieth Anniversary of the A.M.E. Review," *A.M.E. C.Rev.* 40 (July 1923): 3–4. *Sentinel,* n.d., in *CR,* Sept. 14, 1882, 2. B. W. Arnett, *The Budget for 1884* (Dayton: Christian Publishing House, 1884), 11.

59. Gilbert A. Williams, "The A.M.E. *Christian Recorder:* A Forum for Social Ideas of Black Americans, 1854–1902" (Ph.D. diss., Univ. of Illinois, 1979), 150.

60. "The Coming General Conference," *CR,* Apr. 23, 1883, 2. See Bishop W. F. Dickerson's Quadrennial Address in *Journal of the Eighteenth General Session and the Seventeenth Quadrennial,* 113.

61. *CR,* Sept. 22, 1881, 2. "That Endorsement," *CR,* May 11, 1882, 2. "Valedictory," *CR* June 5, 1884, 2.

62. *Journal of the Eighteenth Session and Seventeenth Quadrennial,* 66, 70. "Bishop B. T. Tanner," *A.M.E. C.Rev.* 5 (July 1888): 4.

63. Bishop R. H. Cain, "Issues for General Conference," *CR,* Nov. 8, 1883, 1. Cain's reference to "old clothes" was to Wanamaker & Brown Clothiers in Philadelphia.

64. "Valedictory," *CR,* June 5, 1884, 2.

Chapter 6

1. B. F. Lee, "The Centenary of Daniel Alexander Payne, Fourth Bishop of the African Methodist Episcopal Church," *A.M.E. C.Rev.* 28 (July 1911): 423–29.

2. *The History of American Methodism* 2:548. *CR,* Feb. 10, 1876, 4. "Brevities," *CR,* Feb. 24, 1876, 4. A. C. Crippen, "The Magazine," *CR,* Jan. 4, 1877, 2.

3. *Proceedings of the National Conference of Colored Men of the United States, 1879* Appendix C, William Stewart (should be Steward), "The Necessity of a National Review Devoted to the Interests of Colored Men of the Negro America," 53–56. *CR,* Jan. 22, 1880, 2.

4. Dr. [Henry M.] Turner, "Forty Things the General Conference Ought to Do," *CR,* Mar. 25, 1880, 1.

5. *CR,* May 25, 1882, 2, 3. H. M. Turner, "Literary Magazine," *CR,* Nov. 16, 1882, 2.
6. "TAWAWA," *CR,* May 31, 1883, 2.
7. *CR,* June 14, 1883, 2.
8. "Our Forthcoming Magazine," *CR,* Dec. 20, 1883, 2; Jan. 3, 1884, 2.
9. "Our Magazine," *CR,* Jan. 17, 1884, 2; Feb. 14, 1884, 2. "The New Quarterly," *CR,* May 29, 1884, 2. Jenifer, *Centennial Retrospect History,* 427. Tanner, "How the *A.M.E. Church Review* Came into Being," *A.M.E. C.Rev.* 25 (Apr. 1909): 30–62. Levi J. Coppin, *Unwritten History* (Philadelphia: A.M.E. Book Concern, 1919), 252–53. "Are We to Have a Magazine?" *CR,* Mar. 25, 1880, 2.
10. "Literary Notes," *New York Globe,* July 5, 1884, 2. Bishop Turner to Tanner, n.d., *A.M.E. C.Rev.* 1 (July 1884): 46–48, 73, 75.
11. Tanner, "The Recent New York Conference," *CR,* July 10, 1884, 2. "Editorial Notes," *A.M.E. C.Rev.* 1 (Jan. 1885): 287.
12. Wills, "Aspects of Social Thought," 94–96. Tanner, Payne, and others subscribed to the "cult of true womanhood." See Shirley J. Carson, "Black Ideals of Womanhood in the Late Victoria Era," *Journal of Negro History* 77 (Spring 1992): 61–73; Lizzie Isabelle, "The Women of Our Race Worthy Imitation," *CR,* Oct. 3, 1889, 3; Beverly Guy Sheftall, *Daughters of Sorrow: Attitudes towards Black Women, 1880–1920* (Brooklyn: Carlson Publishing, 1990). Turner, "Forty Things the General Conference Ought to Do," *CR,* Mar. 25, 1880, 1. Jualynne Dodson, "Nineteenth-Century A.M.E. Preaching Women," in Darlene C. Hine, ed., *Black Women in United States History,* 16 vols. (Brooklyn: Carlson Publishing, 1990), 1:336–37, 342–43. James H. A. Johnson, "Female Preachers," *A.M.E. C.Rev.* 1 (Oct. 1884): 102–5. "The Ordination of Women: What Is the Authority for It?" *A.M.E. C.Rev.* 3 (July 1886): 453–60. Tanner, *The Dispensations in the History of the Church and the Interregnums* (Kansas City, Mo., 1899), 128–34. "Female Preaching," *CR,* Mar. 9, 1872, 2. "Women as Pastors," *CR,* Nov. 5, 1885, 2. James A. Handy, *Scraps of African Methodist Episcopal History* (Philadelphia: A.M.E. Book Concern, 1901?), 189–90. Evelyn Brooks Higginbotham, *Righteous Discontent: The Women's Movement in the Black Baptist Church, 1880–1920* (Cambridge: Harvard Univ. Press, 1993), 120–23. J. M. Buckley, "What Methodism Owes to Women," in *Proceedings, Sermons, Essays, and Addresses of the Centennial Methodist Conference, Held in Mt. Vernon Place Methodist Episcopal Church, Baltimore, Md., December 9–17, 1884,* ed. H. T. Carroll et al. (New York: Philips & Hunt, 1885), 303–17. Tanner, *An Apology for African Methodism,* 135–39. Dorothy A. Peck, ed., *Women on the Way: African Methodist Episcopal Women Maximizing Their Human and Spiritual Potential* (Washington: Women's Missionary Society A.M.E. Church, 1983), 50–52. Tanner, *The Dispensations in the History of the Church,* 243–47.
13. Wills, "Aspects of Social Thought," 135, 90–94, 112.
14. T. G. Steward, *Memoirs of Mrs. Rebecca Steward* (Philadelphia: A.M.E. Publication Dept., 1877), 14, 15, 16, 19.
15. For a fuller discussion of Steward's theological views, see Seraile, *Voice of Dissent,* 88–91; *CR,* Apr. 19, 1888, 5. For Tanner's review of *Genesis Re-*

Read, see *A.M.E. C.Rev.* 1 (Apr. 1886): 235–37; Tanner, "The Higher Criticism," *A.M.E. C.Rev.* 10 (July 1893): 113–18; James Theodore Holly, "The Higher Criticism," *A.M.E. C.Rev.* 11 (Jan. 1895): 329–35.

16. Wills, "Aspects of Social Thought," 2–3, 123.

17. *A.M.E. C.Rev.* 3 (Oct. 1886): 209–10.

18. James T. Bixby, "The Religious Genius of the Races," *Unitarian Review and Religious Magazine* 22 (July 1883): 70–78.

19. *A.M.E. C.Rev.* 4 (Apr. 1888): 456–57.

20. *A.M.E. C.Rev.* 3 (Apr. 1887): 437–38. Wills, "Aspects of Social Thought," 132.

21. Wills, "Aspect of Social Thought," 130, 135. Henry M. Turner, "God Is a Negro," *Voice of Missions,* Feb. 1, 1898, as rpt. in *Black Nationalism in America,* ed. John Bracey et al. (Indianapolis: Bobbs Merrill, 1970), 154–55.

22. Thornbrough, *T. Thomas Fortune,* 69–78.

23. Thornbrough, *T. Thomas Fortune,* 70.

24. Gregory U. Rigsby, *Alexander Crummell: Pioneer in Nineteenth-Century Pan African Thought.* (New York: Greenwood Press, 1987) 1–158. "Our Book Table," *A.M.E. C.Rev.* 1 (Oct. 1884: 181. T. McCants Stewart, "Black and White," *A.M.E. C.Rev.* 1 (Jan. 1885): 287.

25. Stewart, "Black and White," 292–93. "Seven Weeks in the South," *A.M.E. C.Rev.* 1 (Apr. 1885): 396.

26. "Our Editorials," *A.M.E. C.Rev.* 1 (Apr. 1885): 398–400.

27. *A.M.E. C.Rev.* 2 (July 1885): 92.

28. "Our Editorials—What Becomes of Our Graduates?" *A.M.E. C.Rev.* 3 (Jan. 1887): 312–16.

29. "Race Love," *A.M.E. C.Rev.* 4 (July 1887): 547. *Paul Quinn Weekly,* Jan. 27, 1900, 2. Lane, *William Dorsey's Philadelphia and Ours,* 289–90.

30. "Terra Incognito," *A.M.E. C.Rev.* 4 (July 1887): 548–49.

31. "Church Troubles," *CR,* Nov. 1, 1883, 2. Tanner, *An Outline of Our History and Government for African Methodist Churchmen, Ministerial and Lay. Introduction by B. F. Lee.* (Philadelphia: B. T. Tanner, 1884), preface, 5–6.

32. "The A.M.E. Quarterly Review," *CR,* Apr. 19, 1888, 4. W. G. Alexander, "Dr. Johnson's 'More Bishops' Endorsed," *CR,* Jan. 5, 1888, 2.

33. Wills, "Aspects of Social Thought," 135. "Bishop B. T. Tanner," *A.M.E. C.Rev.* 5 (July 1888): 4, 5. *CR,* May 24, 1888, 2.

34. "Bishop B. T. Tanner," 5.

35. "The Making of a Great Editor," *CR,* Jan. 13, 1916, 4. T. Thomas Fortune, "Some Journalists I Have Known," *CR,* June 9, 1910, 3. "Lives of the Editors of the Review," *A.M.E. C.Rev.* 25 (Apr. 1909): 376–79.

36. *CR,* Apr. 5, 1888, 2, 3.

37. T. G. Steward, "Questions for 1888," *CR,* May 19, 1887, 1. For further discussion, see *CR,* June 30, 1887, 1; July 14, 1887, 1; Aug. 25, 1887, 1; Oct. 13, 1887, 1; Oct. 27, 1887, 1.

38. "The New Bishops," *CR,* May 24, 1888, 4. Daniel A. Payne, *Recollections of Seventy Years* (New York: Arno Press, 1968), 329–30. Smith, *A History of the African Methodist Episcopal Church* 154–55. Charles Killian, "Bishop

Daniel A. Payne: Black Spokesman for Reform" (Ph.D. diss., Indiana Univ., 1971), 163, 169–70.

39. "The New Bishops," *CR,* June 21, 1888, 1. R. C. Ransom, "Our Educational Department—Review of the Review," *CR,* Apr. 9, 1896, 6.

40. *CR,* June 7, 1888, 2, 4, 5. P. E. Mills, "Bishop B. T. Tanner D.D. and the Eleventh Episcopal District," *CR,* June 28, 1888, 2. J. A. Johnson, "African Methodism in Bermuda," *A.M.E. C.Rev.* 5 (Jan. 1889): 262.

41. *CR.* June 7, 1888, 5; June 14, 1888, 1, 4.

Chapter 7

1. J. M. Carpenter, "Wilberforce Annual Meeting—Trustees—Commencement—Quarto-Centennial Anniversary," *CR,* July 5, 1888, 2. Tanner, "The Spirit of Sacrifice," *CR,* June 28, 1888, 5.

2. Tanner, "Missionary Notes," *CR,* July 5, 1888, 5; July 19, 1888, 5.

3. "Word from Bishop Tanner," *CR,* Aug. 2, 1888, 1.

4. "Personal," *CR,* Aug. 9, 1888, 5. "A Letter from Bishop Tanner," *CR,* Aug. 16, 1888, 1. "Notes from Bishop Tanner," *CR,* Aug. 23, 1888, 5.

5. Tanner, "Missionary Notes," *CR,* Aug. 30, 1888, 5. J. A. Johnson, "African Methodism in Bermuda," *A.M.E. C.Rev.* 5 (Jan. 1889): 256.

6. "An Urgent Appeal," *CR,* Sept. 13, 1888, 2.

7. *CR,* Oct. 4, 1888, 4.

8. Tanner, "Missionary Notes," *CR,* Oct. 11, 1888, 2. "Personals," *CR,* Oct. 11, 1888, 4.

9. Tanner, "Can It Be One Full Day?" *CR,* Oct. 18, 1888, 1.

10. Tanner, "Notes from Bermuda," *CR,* Oct. 25, 1888, 1. Tanner, "Word from Bermuda," *CR,* Nov. 15, 1888, 1. H. T. Jackson, "Address of Welcome to Bishop Tanner," *CR,* Dec. 6, 1888, 1. "Bishop Tanner's Bermuda Trip," *CR,* Dec. 6, 1888, 4. "The Bermudas," *New York Globe,* Apr. 28, 1883, 2.

11. Tanner, "Home Again," *CR,* Dec. 13, 1888, 1. "Bermuda and African Methodism," *A.M.E. C.Rev.* 6 (Apr. 1890): 497–500. Johnson, "African Methodism in Bermuda," 263.

12. "The Emancipation Celebration," *CR,* Jan. 10, 1889, 4.

13. *CR,* Jan. 31, 1889, 4. Tanner, "Our Trip South," *CR,* Feb. 28, 1889, 1.

14. Tanner, "Pray for Hayti," *CR,* Feb. 21, 1889, 1.

15. Tanner, "The Forthcoming Easter," *CR,* Mar. 14, 1889, 5.

16. *CR,* Mar. 28, 1889, 4.

17. "Personal," *CR,* Mar. 21, 1889, 4. "The Haytian Mission," *CR,* May 9, 1889, 4. Solomon P. Hood, "Letter from the Sea," *CR,* May 10, 1889, 3; May 23, 1889, 3. Payne, *History of the African Methodist Episcopal Church,* 477, 482–83.

18. Tanner, "Our Haytian Visitation," *CR,* June 6, 1889, 1; June 13, 1889, 5. "Hayti," *CR,* June 6, 1889, 4.

19. S. P. Hood, "Our Haytian Letter," *CR,* July 4, 1889, 4; Oct. 24, 1889, 1.

20. Hood, "Our Haytian Letter," Dec. 26, 1889, 4.

21. Tanner, "Our Haytian Visit," *CR,* Sept. 26, 1889, 4. S. P. Hood, "Our Haytian Letter," *CR,* Nov. 21, 1889, 1.

22. Hood, "Our Haytian Letter," *CR*, Apr. 11, 1889, 4. Tanner, "Off to Bermuda," *CR*, Apr. 18, 1889, 5.

23. J. M. Henderson, "Where Is Africa?" *CR*, May 16, 1889, 5. "Where Is Africa?" *CR*, May 16, 1889, 4. J. R. Frederick, "Our African Missionary Letter—Sierre Leone," *CR*, Apr. 25, 1889, 1.

24. Tanner, "Missionary Outlook of the Hour," *CR*, Aug. 15, 1889, 5. W. B. Derrick to editor, n.d., *CR*, Oct. 17, 1889, 2. Tanner, "A Plea for Unity," *CR*, Oct. 17, 1889, 6.

25. T. G. Steward, "To Our Bishops," *CR*, Sept. 5, 1889, 6. "The Cost Is Infinitely Greater than the Worth of the Goods," *CR*, Aug. 15, 1889, 4.

26. Tanner, "That Solo," *CR*, Apr. 4, 1889, 1. Tanner, "Our Ontario Visitation," *CR*, Aug. 1, 1889, 2.

27. Tanner, "Our Nova Scotia Visitation," *CR*, Aug. 29, 1889, 1.

28. Tanner, "Our Mission Fields, Their Wants," *CR*, Sept. 5, 1889, 2. "Personal," *CR*, Sept. 12, 1889, 5; Sept. 19, 1889, 2.

29. "Personal," *CR*, Sept. 26, 1889, 4.

30. "Personal," *CR*, Oct. 3, 1889, 4.

31. Private Journal of John Albert Johnson, Hamilton, Bermuda, Nov. 6, 1889–Apr. 14, 1892, John Albert Johnson Papers. See Nov. 6, 1889.

32. Johnson Journal, Nov. 8, 12, 1889. Tanner described his November 12 lecture as "The First of August, Its Fruits and the Hopes Which Inspire It." See Johnson Journal as quoted in "Bishop Tanner's Lecture in Bermuda," *CR*, Dec. 19, 1889, 3.

33. Johnson Journal, Nov. 14, 30, Dec. 3, 9, 25, 31, 1889; Jan. 17, Aug. 6, Oct. 23, 1890. *CR*, Nov. 21, 1889, 4; Dec. 12, 1889, 2.

34. Tanner, "A Crisis—Our Foreign Mission," *CR*, Dec. 5, 1889, 1. "The Case of Our Missionary Department," Dec. 5, 1889, 4.

35. T. G. Steward, "How to Save Our Foreign Missions," *CR*, Dec. 19, 1889, 2; for Lee's response, see p. 4.

36. Tanner, "Our Connectional Prospects," *CR*, Dec. 26, 1889, 5.

37. "Personal," *CR*, Jan. 9, 1890, 4. Johnson Journal, Jan. 8, 1890.

38. *CR*, Feb. 6, 1890, 6; Feb. 13, 1890, 5.

39. *CR*, May 15, 1890, 3.

40. "Personal," *CR*, May 29, 1890, 4; June 5, 1890, 4; May 14, 1891, 4.

41. William H. Giles, "Missionary Convention at Kittrell, N.C.," *CR*, June 5, 1890, 5. C. K. King, "Bishop Tanner at Newberne, N.C.," *CR*, June 12, 1890, 2. Tanner, "Notice to the Brethren of the Second Episcopal District," *CR*, June 26, 1890, 5. R. M. Leak, "North Carolina in Need— Bishop Tanner on the Go," *CR*, June 19, 1890, 1. "Editorial Correspondence," *CR*, June 12, 1890, 4.

42. *CR*, July 17, 1890, 6. Tanner, *An Outline of Our History and Government*, 110.

43. Tanner, "Word from Our Work in the Dominion," *CR*, July 24, 1890, 2. James W. Lavatt, "A.M.E. Conference, Canada," *CR*, July 31, 1890, 2. Tanner, "God Owning His Word" *CR*, Aug. 7, 1890, 1. "Episcopal Itinerary," *CR*, Aug. 1, 1890, 2.

44. *CR*, Aug. 7, 1890, 4; Sept. 4, 1890, 4.

45. *CR*, Oct. 2, 1890, 4.

46. Tanner, "The A.M.E. Church Abroad," *CR*, Oct. 2, 1890, 2. Tanner, "Another Call," *CR*, Oct. 16, 1890, 1. Tanner, "Bermuda: Our Log," *CR*, Nov. 13, 1890; Nov. 6, 1890, 4. Johnson Journal, Oct. 12, 1890 (Johnson spelled it as Sealey).

47. S. P. Hood, "The A.M.E. Church in the West Indies," *CR*, Nov. 20, 1890, 1–2. S. P. Hood, "From Our Missionaries," *CR*, Jan. 8, 1891, 1.

48. Tanner, "West Indies and South America," *CR*, Nov. 20, 1890, 2. "Personals," *CR*, Dec. 18, 1890, 4. For obituary of Belle B. Dorce, see *CR*, Feb. 26, 1891, 6; Apr. 16, 1891, 4.

49. "Personals," *CR*, Dec. 18, 1890, 4. Johnson Journal, Oct. 21, 1890.

50. *CR*, Nov. 20, 1890, 4. "A Voice for the West Indies," *CR*, Aug. 27, 1891, 2.

51. Johnson Journal, Feb. 1, 1891.

52. "Our Work in Bermuda," *CR*, Aug. 20, 1891, 4.

53. Tanner, "To All Who Believe in Saving and Sustaining Work Already Begun," *CR*, Aug. 27, 1891, 5; see Lee's editorial in same issue, p. 4. Johns to Tanner, Aug. 25, 1891, *CR*, Sept. 24, 1891, 2.

54. Johnson Journal, Oct. 8, 16, 1891.

55. J. M. Henderson, "Go to Africa Yourself," *CR*, May 8, 1890, 1.

56. J. R. Frederick to Tanner, July 22, 1890, *CR*, Sept. 11, 1890, 1.

57. S. Jefferson Campbell to Tanner, Oct. 15, 1890, *CR*, Jan. 8, 1891, 1. J. P. Lindsey to Tanner, Feb. 12, 1891, *CR*, Apr. 23, 1891, 2. J. A. Frederick to Tanner, Feb. 18, 1891, *CR*, Apr. 23, 1891, 2. Tanner, "Missionary Money," *CR*, Apr. 23, 1891, 4. Payne, *History of the African Methodist Episcopal Church,* 483, 491–92.

58. "Sister Sarah E. Gorman in Africa," *CR*, June 4, 1891, 6. Berry, *A Century of Missions of the A.M.E. Church,* 70.

59. *CR*, June 11, 1891, 4.

60. Bishop H. M. Turner, "Who Wishes to Help Africa?" *CR*, Aug. 6, 1891, 1; Sept. 3, 1891, 4. "The Liberian Missions," *CR*, Sept. 17, 1891, 4; Oct. 15, 1891, 4.

61. "African Colonization," *New York Age,* Oct. 3, 1891, 2.

62. *CR*, Oct. 15, 1891, 4.

63. "Important Notice," *CR*, Nov. 19, 1891, 1.

64. "A Letter from U.S. Consulate at Sierre Leone," Oct. 8, 1891, *CR*, Nov. 19, 1891, 1. Angell, *Bishop Henry McNeal Turner,* 221–23. Berry, *A Century of Missions,* 151–53. Bishop Henry M. Turner, *African Letters* (Nashville: A.M.E. Sunday School Union, 1893).

65. J. M. Henderson. "Will the Negro Share the Glory That Awaits Africa?" *CR*, Dec. 30, 1892, 1. Mrs. N. F. Mossell, "Will the Negro Share the Glory That Awaits Africa?" *CR*, Jan. 5, 1893, 3. J. M. Henderson, "Draw a Line between African Evangelization and African Colonization," *CR*, Feb. 2, 1893, 3.

66. Sandy D. Martin, *Black Baptists and Foreign Missions: The Origins of a Movement, 1880–1915* (Macon: Mercer Univ. Press, 1989), 76, 117–18, 169, 189–96; Sylvia M. Jacobs, ed., *Black Americans and the Missionary Movement in Africa* (Westport, Conn.: Greenwood Press, 1982), 10, 131–33.

67. "Personals," *CR*, Apr. 23, 1891, 4. J. M. Henderson, "Bishop Tanner's Reception," *CR*, May 21, 1891, 1.

68. Henderson, "Bishop Tanner's Reception," *CR*, May 14, 1891, 4; see also "Personals," p. 4. "Bishop Tanner to the Eighth Episcopal District," *CR*, July 9, 1891, 1.

69. Tanner, "My Mother," *CR*, June 14, 1891, 2.

70. "Personals," *CR*, June 18, 1891, 4; Sept. 24, 1891, 5. "A Colored Female Doctor," *New York Times*, Sept. 22, 1891, 1. Tanner to Booker T. Washington, Aug. 20, 1891, in Louis R. Harlan, ed., *The Booker T. Washington Papers*, 13 vols. (Urbana: Univ. of Illinois Press, 1972–84), 3:138, 165–66.

71. *State Capital*, June 25, 1892, 1. "Personals," *CR*, Oct. 29, 1892, 5; June 22, 1893, 4.

72. *CR*, Mar. 12, 1893, 4.

73. J. M. Pawner, "Bishop B. T. Tanner as Seen at the General Conference of 1892," *CR*, Feb. 9, 1893, 2; May 18, 1893, 5.

Chapter 8

1. "Our Own Book Concern," *CR*, Sept. 10, 1891, 1. J. M. Henderson, "Remove the Book Concern to Nashville," *CR*, Oct. 22, 1891, 1; Jan. 19, 1893, 4; Apr. 13, 1893, 4. H. Mixon, "Why Not?" *CR*, Sept. 6, 1894, 1. "The Old or Better Way," *CR*, Sept. 6, 1894, 2. For A.M.E. statistics, see *Freeman*, Jan. 2, 1892, 7.

2. "Style versus Emotion," *Brooklyn Daily Eagle*, July 13, 1892, 1. "Revolt Is Threatened Unless Bishop Tanner Comes to Terms," ibid., Sept. 11, 1892, 8. "The Threatened Revolt," ibid., Sept. 16, 1892, 14. "A Change of Ministers," ibid., June 1, 1893, 5.

3. "Trouble in Bridge Street Church," ibid., Jan. 24, 1893, 1. "A Very Inharmonious Choir," ibid., Feb. 27, 1893, 5. "Colored Brethren Riled," ibid., Mar. 2, 1893, 1. Steward, *From 1864 to 1914*, 208–9, 211.

4. Tanner, "Book Readings," *CR*, Sept. 10, 1891, 2.

5. Tanner, "Our Latest Works," *A.M.E. C.Rev.* 7 (Oct. 1890): 129–38. Tanner, "The Value of a Denominational Literature in Promoting Denominational Success," *A.M.E. C.Rev.* 8 (Jan. 1892): 318–25. Tanner's *The Pulpit Commentary* was described by the *Recorder* as "deep, comprehensive, far reaching and scholarly," *CR*, June 25, 1891, 4.

6. Tanner, "The Negro and the Flood: A Correspondence," *A.M.E. C.Rev.* 8 (Apr. 1892): 43–44.

7. Tanner, "Certainly Hard," *Independent* 44 (Feb. 25, 1892): 261.

8. Tanner, "A Prayer to Jesus," *A.M.E. C.Rev.* 7 (Apr. 1891): 392. T. G. Steward, "Cultured Society and the Negro," *Independent* (Apr. 16, 1896): 514.

9. *Washington Bee*, May 28, 1892, 2; June 4, 1892, 2. "God and Prayer as Factors in the Struggle," in Carter G. Woodson, ed. *The Works of Francis J. Grimké*, 4 vols. (Washington: Associated Pub., 1942),1:281.

10. Harlan, *The Booker T. Washington Papers* 3:34.

11. Tanner, "Columbus' Discovery and the Negro: What?" *Independent* 44 (June 2, 1892): 753.

12. Otto H. Olsen, *Carpetbagger's Crusade: The Life of Albion Winegar Tourgee* (Baltimore: John Hopkins Univ. Press, 1965), 307–9, 347. For Tourgee's remarks, see *Cleveland Gazette*, May 28, 1892, 1; June 4, 1892, 1. "Boston

Lynching," *Monthly Review*, n.d., in *CR*, Sept. 13, 1894, 2. "An Eye for an Eye," *Cleveland Gazette*, May 7, 1892, 2. Tanner to Booker T. Washington, Sept. 25, 1895, in Harlan, *Booker T. Washington Papers* 4:28–29. Tanner, "God's Estimate of Human Life," *A.M.E. C.Rev.* 13 (Apr. 1896): 481–86.

13. Tanner, "The President's Power Limited," *Independent* 44 (Sept. 8, 1892): 1246–47.

14. Tanner, "The Republican Defeat: A Negro's Explanation," *Independent*, 44 (Nov. 24, 1892): 1658–59. "The Republican Defeat," *Washington Bee*, Nov. 12, 1892, 2.

15. *CR*, Sept. 18, 1890, 4; Dec. 18, 1890, 5; Dec. 25, 1890, 4; Mar. 19, 1891, 1. Harlan, *The Booker T. Washington Papers*, 3:271. *CR*, Mar. 23, 1893, 1–2. "Personals," *CR*, Apr. 20, 1893, 4. "Publication Department," *CR*, July 13, 1893, 6. "A Tribute and a Trophy," *CR*, Sept. 7, 1893, 4. Tanner, *Theological Lectures* (Nashville: A.M.E. Church Sunday School Union, 1894). Tanner, "Stray Thoughts," *CR*, Feb. 27, 1902, 1.

16. "Personals," *CR*, June 29, 1893, 4; May 25, 1893, 2; Sept. 7, 1893, 6; Sept. 14, 1893, 2.

17. "First Episcopal District," *CR*, Nov. 16, 1893, 2.

18. "Bishop Payne Dead," *CR*, Dec. 7, 1893, 2. "Personals," *CR*, Dec. 7, 1893, 3. "Bishop Daniel A. Payne Symposium," *A.M.E. C.Rev.* 10 (Jan. 1894): 412–13. "A Bust of Bishop Payne," *CR*, Dec. 14, 1893, 2. "Personals," *CR*, Jan. 11, 1894, 2. "In Memoriam Bishop Daniel A. Payne," *CR*, Jan. 18, 1894, 4; Jan. 25, 1894, 1, 5, 6. "Memorial to Daniel Alexander Payne," undated fragment in Frederick Douglass Papers, microfilm reel 16, container 25. Lane, *William Dorsey's Philadelphia and Ours*, 121–22. "Personals," *CR*, Aug. 23, 1894, 2; Aug. 29, 1882, 2.

19. "Personals," *CR*, Jan. 11, 1894, 2; Feb. 8, 1894, 2; Mar. 8, 1894, 2; Sept. 6, 1894, 2.

20. "Personals," *CR*, Apr. 26, 1894, 2.

21. "The New York Conference," *CR*, May 3, 1894, 2. "Some Fruits of Criticism," *CR*, June 6, 1895, 2.

22. "Notes and Comments," *CR*, Nov. 15, 1894, 2; *CR*, Nov. 22, 1894, 4.

23. Tanner, "Our Plea" and "A Coincidence: What?" *CR*, Dec. 20, 1894, 1; Steward's letter was dated November 23, 1894. *New York Age*, Nov. 15, 1894, as cited in Lane, *William Dorsey's Philadelphia and Ours*, 315. Tanner, "Darkness," in Haley, *Afro-American Encyclopedia*, 551.

24. "Personals," *CR*, Dec. 20, 1894, 2. "The Bridgeton A.M.E. Church, New Jersey," *CR*, Dec. 20, 1894, 6.

25. "Personals," *CR*, Dec. 27, 1894, 2. "The Holidays," *CR*, Dec. 27, 1895, 2.

26. Tanner, "Who?" *CR*, Jan. 10, 1895, 1. "The Divine Presence," *CR*, Jan. 31, 1895, 1.

27. Tanner, "God's Anointed," *CR*, Feb. 21, 1895, 1; Mar. 7, 1895, 2.

28. Tanner, "An Appeal to Reason," *CR*, Apr. 4, 1895, 1.

29. "Personals," *CR*, Apr. 4, 1895, 2. Tanner, "Immortality," *A.M.E. C.Rev.* 12 (Apr. 1895): 521.

30. Tanner, *The Color of Solomon—What? "My Beloved Is White and Ruddy"* (Philadelphia: A.M.E. Book Concern, 1895), 14, 15, 17–18, 24, 36, 39. *CR*, July 26, 1888, 2.

31. "The Color of Solomon—What?" *CR*, May 23, 1895, 2. T. McCants Stewart, "The Color of Solomon—What?" *CR*, June 13, 1890, 2.

32. "Was Solomon a Negro?" *CR*, Aug. 2, 1877, 2.

33. Tanner, "O Galilaen, Thou Hast Conquered," *CR*, May 23, 1895, 1.

34. "Personal," *CR*, June 6, 1895, 2. Tanner, "Work the Measure of Success," *CR*, July 18, 1895, 1.

35. "Wilberforce Notes," *CR*, July 4, 1895, 2. "The Episcopal Address," *CR*, July 4, 1895, 3. For Ward's death, see *CR*, June 21, 1895, 2.

36. J. M. Henderson, "Drs. Shaffer, Coppin, and Derrick, Bishop Tanner's Strength," *CR*, Oct. 11, 1894, 6.

37. H. C. C. Ashwood, "Bishop Tanner at Harrisburg," *CR*, Nov. 7, 1895, 2. For a critique of all the bishops, see *CR*, Jan. 23, 1895, 3; Feb. 6, 1896. For comments made about Sadie, see "The Women's Wonderful Convention," *CR*, Nov. 14, 1895, 2.

38. Tanner, "Our Loss; What Is To Be Gain?" *CR*, Dec. 19, 1895, 2.

39. Theophilus G. Steward, "A Most Deserving Candidate," *CR*, Apr. 23, 1896, 3.

40. "General Conference Proceedings," *CR*, May 14, 1896, 1; May 21, 1896, 3; June 4, 1896, 2. B. W. Roberts, "A Trip to Wilmington, N.C., General Conference—Scenes and Happenings to and From," *CR*, July 23, 1896, 1. For Tanner's sermon, see *Journal of the Twentieth Quadrennial Session of the General Conference of the African Methodist Episcopal Church held in St. Stephen's A.M.E. Church, Wilmington, N.C., May 4th to 22nd, 1896* (Philadelphia: A.M.E. Pub. Houses, 1896), 187–202, or Smith, *A History of the African Methodist Episcopal Church*, 187–89.

Chapter 9

1. Sarah J. W. Early, *Life and Labors of Rev. Jordan W. Early: One of the Pioneers of African Methodism in the West and South* (Freeport, N.Y.: Books for Libraries Press, 1971), 18, 21, 155, 158. *CR*, Apr. 26, 1900, 7. Church history brochure from Tanner Chapel A.M.E. Church, Phoenix, Arizona.

2. Tanner, "To the Members of the Fifth Episcopal District," *CR*, June 11, 1896, 4.

3. J. G. Robinson, "America—The United States," *CR*, Oct. 15, 1896, 1.

4. Joseph Wheeler, "Emancipation Hymn," *Race and Standard*, Jan. 1, 1897.

5. J. D. Barksdale, "Is the Negro Cursed?" *CR*, July 23, 1896, 6. J. I. Lowe, "The Negro in America," *CR*, July 23, 1896, 1.

6. *CR*, May 11, 1899, 6; June 8, 1899, 2. H. T. Johnson, "The Blackman's Burden," *CR*, Feb. 23, 1899, 1. "The Negro Academy," *CR*, Jan. 4, 1900, 2. Moss, *The American Negro Academy*, 31, 33, 115.

7. Tanner, "To the Members of the Fifth Episcopal District," *CR*, June 11, 4. "Personals," *CR*, Sept. 10, 1896, 2.

8. "Personals," *CR*, Oct. 22, 1896, 2. Tanner, "The Fifth Episcopal District," *CR*, Nov. 5, 1896, 1.

9. C. R. Runyon, "Bishop Tanner," *CR*, Nov. 26, 1896, 2. James H. Hubbard, "Bishop Tanner at His Post," *CR*, Dec. 31, 1896, 7.

10. "Personal," *CR*, Jan. 21, 1897, 2. Tanner, "Thoughts Personal," *CR*, Feb. 4, 1897, 1; Oct. 27, 1898, 3. Tanner, "Up!" *CR*, Nov. 3, 1898, 1. *Western Christian Recorder,* Oct. 15, 1898, 1. Tanner, "Surrender," *Western Christian Recorder,* Nov. 5, 1898, 1.

11. Bishop J. C. Embry, "No More," *CR*, Aug. 12, 1897, 2. "Eulogies to Embry," *CR*, Sept. 9, 1897, l.

12. E. W. Lewis, "Fifth Episcopal District," *CR*, Mar. 4, 1897, 1. H. B. Parks, "The Fifth Episcopal District," *CR*, Oct. 21, 1897, 1. "Personals," *CR*, Oct. 21, 1897, 2.

13. "A Word from Bishop Tanner," *CR*, June 24, 1897, 1; June 9, 1898, 2. "Tanner to Fifth District," *Western Christian Recorder,* Oct. 29, 1898, 1.

14. Tanner, "Life's Day," *CR*, Nov. 18, 1897, 1.

15. M. B. Sheppard, "Our Heritage," *CR*, Feb. 24, 1898, 5.

16. Smith, *A History of the African Methodist Episcopal Church,* 137, 360, 361, 369. *Western Christian Recorder,* Mar. 5, 1898, 1; Oct. 22, 1898, 2; Sept. 24, 1898, 1–2. C. R. Runyon, "North American Conferences," ibid., Oct. 29, 1898, 1; Nov. 19, 1898, 1. "Bishop Tanner Asks: 'Where Are The Studious Brethren?'" ibid., Dec. 19, 1898, 2. "Quindaro University Bill Signed," ibid., Mar. 25, 1899, 2. B. T. Washington to W. T. Vernon, Mar. 16, 1899, ibid., Mar. 25, 1899, 1. "Quindaro's Financial Victory," ibid., Apr. 17, 1899, 2.

17. Tanner, *The Descent of the Negro* (Philadelphia: n.p., 1898), 6, 12–13, 14, 19, 20, 23. For a review, see *A.M.E. C.Rev.* 16 (July 1898): 513–28; *CR*, Aug. 25, 1898, 2.

18. Tanner, *The Dispensation in the History of the Church and the Interregnums* 1: preface, 12–14.

19. Tanner, *The Dispensation,* 18. J. H. Hubbard, "Bishop Tanner's New Book," *CR*, Aug. 24, 1899, 5. L. H. Reynolds, "Bishop Tanner's New Work," *CR*, Sept. 21, 1899, 1. W. S. Scarborough, "Dispensations in the History of the Church," *A.M.E. C.Rev.* 17 (Jan. 1900): 360–66. Tanner, *The Negro in Holy Writ* (Philadelphia: 1900), 3–5, 10, 19, 23, 25, 35, 46–47, 50, 52–55. Charles B. Copher, "Three Thousand Years of Biblical Interpretation with References to Black People," in Gayraud Wilmore, ed., *African American Religious Studies: An Interdisciplinary Anthology* (Durham and London: Duke Univ. Press, 1989), 105–28. Tanner, "Stray Thought—The Hat to Fit the Head," *CR*, Apr. 17, 1902, 1. Tanner, "Stick to the Text," *CR*, Aug. 12, 1909, 1.

20. Tanner, "Raising of Lazarus," *Western Christian Recorder,* Feb. 26, 1898, 1.

21. "Personals," *CR*, Apr. 14, 1898, 3. "40th Wedding Anniversary of Bishop B. T. Tanner," *Western Christian Recorder,* Aug. 27, 1898, 1. Jenifer, *Centennial Retrospect History,* 331–32.

22. "Personals," *CR*, Feb. 9, 1899, 3.

23. *Who's Who in America* (Chicago: A. N. Manguis, 1900).

24. "The Colorado Conferences," *CR*, Oct. 12, 1899, 1. J. T. Smith, "Colorado Conference," *CR*, Oct. 19, 1899, 3. Jesse T. Moore Jr., "Seeking a New Life in Post–Civil War Colorado," *Journal of Negro History* 78 (Summer 1993): 166–87.

25. Willard B. Gatewood, ed., *"Smoked Yankees" and the Struggle for Empire:*

Letters from Negro Soldiers, 1898–1902 (Urbana: Univ. of Illinois Press, 1971), 4–6; for Tanner's view, see *Afro-American Sentinel,* Apr. 16, 1898, 1.

26. "Bishop Tanner's Easter Poem," *A.M.E. C.Rev.* 16 (July 1898): 556.

27. *A.M.E. C.Rev.* 16 (July 1898): 556.

28. Tanner, "A Large Dose," *CR,* Mar. 1, 1900, 1.

29. *A.M.E. C.Rev.* 14 (Oct. 1896): 235.

30. Tanner, "Fair Play for the Negro," *Western Christian Recorder,* Sept. 10, 1898, 1.

31. "The Genteel Negro," *Wide-Awake,* Jan. 24, 1900, 2. *Montgomery Enterprise,* Jan. 26, 1900, 2.

32. T. W. H[enderson], "Sunday Morning at Bethel," *CR,* June 8, 1899, 3.

33. Tanner, "Saved by Grace," *CR,* Jan. 4, 1900, 1.

34. "Personals," *CR,* Jan. 18, 1900, 2; Jan. 25, 1900, 2.

35. "Personals," *CR,* Mar. 29, 1900, 2. Tanner, "Three Reasons for an Easter Thank Offering," *CR,* Mar. 29, 1900, 3. *American Citizen,* May 25, 1900, 1.

36. "The Plain Picture of a Christian Hero," *CR,* Mar. 2, 1900, 2. *CR,* Apr. 26, 1900, 7.

37. "New Bishops," *CR,* June 21, 1900, 6. *CR,* July 12, 1900, 1. *CR,* Nov. 29, 1900, 1. Levi L. Coppin, *Letters from South Africa* (Philadelphia: A.M.E. Book Concern, 1900?), 132.

Chapter 10

1. "Editor Johnson and His Brains," *Southern Recorder,* n.d., in *CR,* July 19, 1900, 3. "The Right Reverend Benjamin Tucker Tanner and the Editor," *CR,* July 19, 1900, 2; Aug. 16, 1900, 2. Bishop B. F. Lee, "Our Church Papers and Our Pastors," *CR,* Dec. 29, 1898, 1.

2. Tanner, "Our Young Men," *CR,* July 19, 1900, 1.

3. Tanner, "To The Men of the Ninth," *CR,* Aug. 16, 1900, 1. "Personal," *CR,* Aug. 16, 1900, 2. "Tanner's Calendar," *CR,* Sept. 6, 1900, 5.

4. *CR,* Sept. 20, 1900, 1; Sept. 27, 1900, 4; Oct. 4, 1900, 1; Oct. 25, 1900, 1.

5. S. D. Crutcher, "Helping Payne—A Better Way," *CR,* Nov. 22, 1900, 1.

6. Tanner, "Redemption of Payne Seminary," *CR,* Dec. 13, 1900, 1; Jan. 3, 1901, 1.

7. *CR,* Jan. 31, 1901, 1.

8. *CR,* Feb. 28, 1901, 2.

9. L. H. Welch, "Kentucky Conference," *CR,* Oct. 25, 1900, 4. H. Franklin Bray, "West Kentucky Annual Conference," *CR,* Nov. 1, 1900, 6. "Tennessee Conference," *CR,* Nov. 8, 1900, 4. Taylor S. Johnson, "West Tennessee Conference," *CR,* Jan. 24, 1901, 3.

10. Tanner, *Hints to Ministers* (Wilberforce, 1900), 9–11, 17, 50, 67, 72, 81, 83–88. Tanner, "Glory of the Ear," *A.M.E. C.Rev.* 18 (Apr. 1901): 325–33. *The Twenty-third Quadrennial Report of the Parent Home and Foreign Missionary Department of the African Methodist Episcopal Church, 1904–1908,* 16.

11. Tanner, "Notice to the Ninth Episcopal District Presiding Elders and Brethren," *CR,* Dec. 20, 1900, 1.

12. "Bishop Tanner to the Ninth District," *CR,* Feb. 21, 1901, 1.

13. James G. Martin, "Does the Church Want Our Young Men," *CR*, Mar. 21, 1901, 1.
14. "Bishop Tanner at Frankfort, Ky.," *CR*, Apr. 4, 1901, 3.
15. Tanner, "Mite Missionary Convention," *CR*, Apr. 11, 1901, 2. T. S. Johnson, "Missionary Convention," *CR*, Aug. 1, 1901, 3.
16. Tanner, "In Memoriam," *CR*, May 16, 1901, 1.
17. "Brutal Attack on Rev. Carl Tanner," *CR*, July 18, 1901, 2.
18. W. D. Chappelle, "The Bishops of the A.M.E. Church," *CR*, May 16, 1901, 1; July 4, 1901, 2.
19. "Bishop Tanner," *CR*, Oct. 24, 1901, 1, 3 (only page 3 is extant).
20. Tanner, "To the Ninth Episcopal District," *CR*, July 18, 1901, 2.
21. S. T. Tice, "The Ecumenical Conference," *CR*, July 18, 1901, 1–2. W. H. Heard, "The Ecumenical Conference," *CR*, July 18, 1901, 2 (for a complete list of A.M.E. delegates, see p. 7). "Notice from the Bishops' Council," *CR*, Sept. 19, 1901, 4. R. C. Ransom, "The Ecumenical Conference," *CR*, Oct. 3, 1901, 1. P. A. Hubbard, "A Word to the Church," *CR*, Nov. 7, 1901, 1. For mission money raised by delegates, see *CR*, July 31, 1902, 1.
22. "On the Way to Europe," *CR*, Aug. 15, 1901, 2. Tanner, "Thanks," *CR*, Aug. 15, 1901, 3. Tanner to Hallie Q. Brown, Sept. 11, 1901, in Sadie Tanner Mossell Alexander Papers, box 76, folder 79.
23. Benjamin W. Arnett, ed., *The Budget of 1904* (Philadelphia: Lampton and Collett, 1904), 256, 283, 288–89. For Walters's comment, see "Methodist Ecumenical Conference," *New York Times*, Sept. 5, 1901, 3; *CR*, Oct. 10, 1901, 1.
24. *CR*, Oct. 10, 1901, 3. Bishop Charles S. Smith, "The Third Methodist Ecumenical Conference," *CR*, Oct. 17, 1901, 1.
25. *London Times*, Sept. 13, 1901, 10. *Proceedings of the Third Ecumenical Methodist Conference Held in City Road Chapel, London, Sept. 1901* (New York: Eaton & Mains, 1901); see pp. 454–63 for Tanner's essay.
26. P. A. Hubbard, "A Word to Our Church," *CR*, Nov. 7, 1901, 1.
27. *CR*, Oct. 10, 1901, 2. Tanner to Hallie [Q. Brown], Sept. 11, 1901.
28. "Personals," *CR*, Oct. 31, 1901, 2.
29. "Personals," *CR*, Jan. 2, 1902, 2. "Snapshots of Our Bishops," *CR*, Jan. 23, 1902, 1.
30. Tanner, "To President of the Conference Mite Missionary Society and to the Women Generally of the Ninth District," *CR*, Feb. 20, 1902, 2. Bishop Levi J. Coppin, "The American Negro's Religion for the African Negro's Soul," *Independent* 54 (Mar. 27, 1902): 748–50. T. G. Steward, "The Open Sea Ahead—The Church on the Road to Success," *CR*, May 1, 1902, 1.
31. *CR*, Apr. 24, 1902, 6.
32. Tanner, "To the Ninth District," *CR*, June 12, 1902, 3.
33. Tanner, "Dear Brethren of Kentucky and Western Kentucky Conference," *CR*, July 3, 1902, 6.
34. "Address of Dr. H. B. Parks, Fraternal Delegate to the M.E. [Church, South] General Conference," *CR*, July 24, 1902, 1.
35. Tanner, "Stray Thought—Appointments," *CR*, Aug. 14, 1902, 1.
36. "The East Tennessee Annual Conference," *CR*, Oct. 30, 1902, 6.
37. "West Tennessee Annual Conference," *CR*, Dec. 11, 1902, 3.

38. "Personals," *CR*, Nov. 17, 1902, 2; Dec. 25, 1902, 2.

39. Tanner, "The Sun of Righteousness," *CR*, Feb. 13, 1902, 1.

40. Tanner, "Thy Presence," *CR*, Feb. 27, 1902, 1.

41. Tanner, "Ask of Me," *CR*, Mar. 27, 1902, 1.

42. Tanner, "A Song of Love," *CR*, July 3, 1902, 2.

43. Tanner, "Stray Thought—Ceremonies in Worship," *CR*, Mar. 13, 1902, 11.

44. Tanner, "Stray Thought—Episcopal Arrogance," *CR*, Mar. 27, 1901, 1. "Episcopal Arrogance," *CR*, Apr. 3, 1902, 2. J. W. Golden, "An Unrighteous Stroke," *CR*, Sept. 25, 1902, 1.

45. "Stray Thought—Ancient Courage versus Modern Cowardice," *CR*, Mar. 26, 1903, 1.

46. Tanner, "Stray Thought—An Example Worth Imitating," *CR*, Apr. 2, 1903, 1.

47. Tanner, "Stray Thought—Bearing Witness," *CR*, July 2, 1903, 1, 3.

48. Tanner, "Stray Thought—Through Hand Join in Hand," *CR*, July 23, 1903, 1; July 30, 1903, 2.

49. Tanner, "Stray Thought—'I Believe in the Holy Catholic Church': Apostles' Creed, What Do I Mean?" *CR*, Aug. 13, 1903, 1. For Clark's reply, see Charles S. Long, "Our Sleeves Rolled Up," *CR*, July 14, 1904, 1.

50. Tanner, "Stray Thought—Confirmation," *CR*, Sept. 10, 1903, 1.

51. Tanner, "Stray Thought Series," *CR*, Mar. 3, 1904, 1. W. E. B. Du Bois, "Of Mr. Booker T. Washington and Others," *The Souls of Black Folk* (New York: Fawcett, 1961), 42–54. Alexander Crummell, "The Attitude of the American Mind toward the Negro Intellect," Occasional Papers no. 3 (Washington: American Negro Academy, 1898), 12–16.

52. Tanner, "Stray Thought—The Holy Ghost Not Mentioned," *CR*, Mar. 31, 1904, 1, 3.

53. S. Timothy Tice, "The Election of More Bishops," *CR*, Jan. 14, 1904, 1.

54. James Dean, "A Mooted Question," *CR*, Sept. 17, 1903, 1, 7.

55. James M. Turner, "Rotation of Bishops," *CR*, Dec. 31, 1903, 1. John H. Grant, "Why Talk of Superannuating Bishop Tanner?" *CR*, Mar. 17, 1904, 1, 3. Bishop B. T. Tanner, "Stray Thought—Believed Herself Crazy," *CR*, Mar. 17, 1904, 1, 3.

56. *CR*, Apr. 21, 1904, 1, 3; Apr. 28, 1904 1; June 23, 1904, 1.

57. "Superannuation," *CR*, May 19, 1904, 2. Smith, *History of the African Methodist Episcopal Church*, 259. *CR*, May 14, 1908, 2.

58. "Negro Reject 'America,'" *Philadelphia Record*, n.d., as quoted in *CR*, May 12, 1904, 2. Tanner, "Stray Thought—Worse than Lions Loose," *CR*, June 30, 1904, 2.

59. Smith, *History of the African Methodist Episcopal Church*, 241.

Chapter 11

1. Henry O. Tanner to Booker T. Washington, Feb. 4, 1904 and Mar. 3, 1904, Booker T. Washington Papers, container 88, reel 81. "An Afro-American Painter Who Has Become Famous in Paris," n.d., in *New York Current Literature*, Oct. 1, 1908, Booker T. Washington Papers, container 88, reel 81.

2. Florence L. Bentley, "Henry O. Tanner," *Voice* [*of the Negro*] 3 (Nov. 1906): 480–82. "Henry O. Tanner," *CR*, Nov. 8, 1906, 2. "Personals," *CR*, Oct. 25, 1906, 2.

3. "Personal," *CR*, Apr. 14, 1904, 2; June 23, 1904, 2; July 7, 1904, 2; Aug. 11, 1904, 2.

4. Tanner, "Stray Thought—Roll Up Your Sleeves," *CR*, June 16, 1904, 2.

5. Tanner, "Notice, Floridians," *CR*, July 7, 1904, 1.

6. "Personal Mentions," *CR*, Sept. 8, 1904, 2; Oct. 20, 1904, 1. "Bishop Tanner at Florida's Capital," *CR*, Dec. 1, 1904, 1, 3. "Bishop Benjamin Tucker Tanner: His Administration 'in our Florida,'" *CR*, May 25, 1905, 2–3. "Bishop B. T. Tanner and His Work in Florida," *CR*, July 6, 1905, 2.

7. *CR*, Apr. 13, 1905, 1; May 11, 1905, 2.

8. Tanner, "Stray Thought—The Jim Crow Car," *CR*, May 25, 1905, 1. Tanner, "That a Race Question with Us," *Independent* 44 (Apr. 14, 1892): 505–6.

9. Tanner, "The Jim Crow Car," *CR*, Aug. 3, 1905, 2. D. W. Gillislee, "Street Car Laws—The Avery Street Car Law in Florida and Its Defeat," *CR*, Aug. 10, 1905, 1. Aptheker, *A Documentary History of the Negro People in the United States*, 2:889–93. B. T. Washington to T. Roosevelt, Mar. 23, 1908; Washington to Roosevelt, Mar. 28, 1908; Washington to William H. Taft, June 4, 1908, in *The Booker T. Washington Papers*, ed. Harlan and Smock, vol. 9:472, 478, 481–82, 550–52.

10. Tanner, "Stray Thought—'Whip Up the Left Horse,'" *CR*, July 20, 1905, 1, 3.

11. Stephen S. Steward, "Optimistic View of the Negro in America," *CR*, Jan. 4, 1906, 1. T. G. Steward, "A Trip on Vacation," *CR*, Oct. 26, 1905, 1. H. M. Turner, "Bishop Turner Returns from Mexico," *CR*, May 27, 1909, 1.

12. Aptheker, *A Documentary History of the Negro People in the United States* 2:898–915. Jenifer, *Centennial Retrospect History*, 368.

13. *Christian Index*, Mar. 19, 1908, as quoted in Aptheker, *A Documentary History* 2:896–97. Tanner, "Bethel: One Hundred Nineteenth Anniversary," *A.M.E. C.Rev.* 25 (Oct. 1908): 68–78.

14. Tanner, "Stray Thought—The Negro American—The Irish," *CR*, June 8, 1905, 1; the issues on Negro Americans and Poles and on Negro Americans and the Jew are not extant. Tanner, "A Negro Pharaoh," *A.M.E. C.Rev.* 22 (Oct. 1905): 110–15. The *Memphis Scimitar* quote was taken from Emma L. Thornbrough, "Booker T. Washington as Seen by His White Contemporaries," *Journal of Negro History* 53 (Apr. 1968): 172.

15. Tanner, "Stray Thought—Is It Wrong for Me to Dance?" *CR*, Sept. 15, 1904, 1, 4.

16. "A Minuscule," *A.M.E. C.Rev.* 21 (Oct. 1904): 127–40; for Tanner's comments, see pp. 127–31. "Shall Negro Begin with a Capital 'N'?" ibid., 192–93.

17. S. Timothy Tice, "African Methodism in New York," *CR*, Oct. 26, 1905, 5; Jan. 18, 1906, 2; Oct. 11, 1906, 1.

18. Tanner, *Joel, the Son of Pethuel* (Philadelphia: 1905).

19. R. B. Brooks, "Men and Measures," *CR*, Nov. 2, 1905, 1.

20. "Tanner's Calendar," *CR*, Oct. 11, 1906, 7. "Dr. Booker T. Washington's Address at Wilberforce Golden Jubilee," *CR*, July 5, 1906, 1, 3. Tanner, "Wilberforce Golden Jubilee Sermon," *CR*, July 12, 1906, 1, 3.

21. C. A. Whitfield, "The Florida Annual Conference," *CR*, Jan. 3, 1907, 4.
22. *CR*, Apr. 25, 1907, 2; July 1, 1907, 2; July 25, 1907, 2; Sept. 12, 1907, 2. C. M. Tanner, "A Card of Thanks," *CR*, Dec. 5, 1907, 1.
23. S. Timothy Tice, "Florida and the Next General Conference—Its Work—Wants—Needs—Demands," *CR*, Sept. 19, 1907, 2–3. For a listing of the church's educational holdings, see *CR*, Aug. 22, 1907, 1.
24. C. M. Tanner, "General Conference Work," *CR*, Jan. 30, 1908, 1.
25. J. M. Holt, "The Last Notes of Alarm to the Delegates of the Twenty-third Session of the General Conference," *CR*, Mar. 5, 1908, 4. John Q. Johnson, "The Superannuating of Bishops," *CR*, Apr. 30, 1908, 1. "The General Conference," *CR*, Apr. 30, 1908, 2.
26. S. H. Betts, "A Voice for West Florida," *CR*, May 7, 1908, 1.
27. Tanner, "Stray Thought—'If You Dance, Pay the Fiddler,'" *CR*, July 6, 1905, 2.
28. Tanner, "Stray Thought—The Supreme Test," *CR*, June 27, 1905, 1.
29. "Our Bishops," *CR*, May 14, 1908, 2. *Journal of the Twenty-third Quadrennial Session of the General Conference of the African Methodist Church Held in St. John A.M.E. Church, Norfolk, Virginia, May 4–21, 1908* (Nashville: A.M.E. Sunday School Union, 1908), 21.
30. "Our Bishops," *A.M.E. C.Rev.* 25 (July 1908): 68. *Journal of the Twenty-third Quadrennial Session,* 14–41. *CR*, May 2, 1907, 1. "Our Bishops," *CR*, May 14, 1908, 2; May 28, 1908, 2. *New York Age,* May 21, 1908, 2. Tanner, "'Thought' Series Resumed," *CR*, June 11, 1908, 4.
31. T. S. Johnson, "A Tribute to the Bishops of the A.M.E. Church," *CR*, Mar. 30, 1899, 1.
32. *CR*, May 21, 1908, 3.
33. Tanner, "'Stray Thought' Series Resumed," *CR*, June 11, 1908, 4.

Chapter 12

1. "A Happy, Half Century Union," *CR*, Aug. 27, 1908, 1.
2. Tanner, "Stray Thought," *CR*, June 18, 1908, 4.
3. Tanner, "Stray Thought," *CR*, July 16, 1908, 2. Robert Gregg, *Sparks from the Anvil of Oppression: Philadelphia's African Methodists and the Southern Migrants, 1890–1940* (Philadelphia: Temple Univ. Press, 1993), 3, 4, 5, 47, 69–71. T. G. Steward, "Some Vacation Notes," *CR*, Sept. 28, 1922, 2; Wills, "Aspects of Social Thought," 238.
4. "Personal and General," *CR*, Sept. 10, 1908, 3; Sept. 17, 1908, 3. "The Resurrection of the Recorder," *CR*, Feb. 17, 1908, 3; Apr. 1, 1909, 3. "A Great Reform," *CR*, Feb. 25, 1909, 4.
5. "Special Woman's Issue," *CR*, Oct. 28, 1909, 1. "Our Woman's Issue," *CR*, Nov. 4, 1909, 4.
6. Tanner, "The Successful Life," *CR*, June 10, 1909, 1.
7. Tanner, "The Call to Preach," *CR*, July 15, 1909, 1.
8. "Symposia of Ordination Sermon Preached by Bishop Tanner Sunday, Apr. 25, at Jersey City," *CR*, May 6, 1909, 1. Tanner, "June," *CR*, July 8, 1909, 1.
9. Tanner, "The Significance of Degrees," *CR*, June 3, 1909, 1, 2.
10. Tanner, "Papers on the Ministry, I," *CR*, Jan. 6, 1910, 1. T. G. Steward "notes on the church," 1922 scrapbook, T. G. Steward Papers.

11. Tanner, "Papers on the Ministry, V. Ministry of the Prophets," *CR*, Feb. 3, 1910, 1, 4.

12. Tanner, "Papers on the Ministry, XIII. The Character of It: Devotion," *CR*, Apr. 14, 1910, 1; "XV. Humility," *CR*, Apr. 28, 1910, 1; "XVI. Courage," *CR*, May 12, 1910, 1; "XVIII. Honesty," *CR*, May 26, 1910, 1, 4; "XXII. Hospitality," *CR*, June 30, 1910, 1.

13. Tanner, "Papers on the Ministry, XVII [mistakenly listed as XVI]. Industry," *CR*, May 19, 1910, 1.

14. Tanner, "Papers on the Ministry, XXXVIII. Subdued," *CR*, Nov. 10, 1910, 1; "XXXIX Subdued It," *CR*, Nov. 17, 1910, 1; "XL. Subdued It," *CR*, Nov. 24, 1910, 1, 4; "XLI. Subdue It, the Air," *CR*, Dec. 1, 1910, 1; "XLII. Subdue It, the Sea," *CR*, Dec. 8, 1910, 1. BTT Diary, July 22, 1860.

15. James T. Gilmore, "Praise for Bishop Tanner's Articles," *CR*, Feb. 3, 1910, 1.

16. David A. Gerber, *Black Ohio and the Color Line, 1860–1915* (Urbana: Univ. of Illinois Press, 1976), 270. J. R. Oldfield, *Alexander Crummell (1819–1898) and the Creation of an African American Church in Liberia* (Lewiston, N.Y.: Edwin Mellon Press, 1990), 116–19, 122–23. Tanner, "Discordant Notes," *CR*, June 17, 1909, 1. Carlton M. Tanner, *A Manual of the African Methodist Episcopal Church, Being a Course of Twelve Lectures for Probationers and Members* (Philadelphia, 1900), 106.

17. *CR*, July 21, 1910, 1; Jan. 26, 1911, 1; Oct. 12, 1911, 1. "Bishop Tanner's Life," *CR*, Oct. 12, 1911, 4. *CR*, Mar. 27, 1913, 1; Apr. 17, 1913, 1; Jan. 30, 1913, 1, 4. "Files of the Review," *A.M.E. Review* 29 (Apr. 1913): 384.

18. *CR*, Nov. 2, 1911, 1; Nov. 23, 1911, 4; Jan. 25, 1912, 3.

19. "Personal and General," *CR*, June 4, 1914, 5. "Mrs. Sarah E. Tanner Dead," *CR*, Aug. 6, 1914, 1. "Sarah E. Tanner—Mother," *CR*, Aug. 13, 1914, 4. "Thanks," *CR*, Aug. 27, 1914, 4.

20. *Journal of the Twenty-seventh Quadrennial Session of the General Conference of the African Methodist Episcopal Church Held in Louisville, Kentucky, May 5th Including the 21st, 1924* (Philadelphia: A.M.E. Book Concern, 1924) 388, 38.

21. Tanner to Miss Rosa [B. Stowe], n.d., in Sadie Tanner Mossell Alexander Papers, box 76, folder 78.

22. *CR*, Feb. 18, 1915, 4.

23. *CR*, May 13, 1915, 1.

24. "General Conference Proceedings," *CR*, May 4, 1916, 1; May 25, 1916, 1. "Personal and General," *CR*, Sept. 21, 1916, 5.

25. *CR*, Dec. 29, 1921, 6.

26. "Bishop Benjamin Tucker Tanner," *CR*, Jan. 18, 1923, in *Tuskegee News* Clipping File. BTT Diary, July 30, 1860.

27. Alexander Crummell, "Breathe a Prayer," fragment of unpublished 1895 poem, *CR*, July 3, 1913.

28. William P. Hunter, "Death," *CR*, Jan. 18, 1923, in *Tuskegee News* Clipping File.

29. *Journal of the Twenty-seventh Quadrennial Session*, 219.

30. "Bishop Benjamin Tucker Tanner," *CR*, Jan. 18, 1923, in *Tuskegee News* Clipping File.

31. Ibid.

Bibliography

Books

Angell, Stephen W. Bishop *Henry McNeal Turner and African American Religion in the South*. Knoxville, 1992.

Aptheker, Herbert, ed. *American Negro Slave Revolt*. New York, 1943.

———. *A Documentary History of the Negro People in the United States*, vols. 1–3. New York, 1951–1973.

Ariel. *The Negro: What Is His Ethnological Status?* Cincinnati, 1867.

Arnett, Benjamin W. *The Budget for 1881*. Xenia, 1881.

———. *The Budget: Containing Biographical Sketches, Quadrennial and Annual Reports of the General Office of the African Methodist Episcopal Church of the United States of America*. Dayton, 1884.

———. *The Budget of 1904*. Philadelphia, 1904.

Beasley, Delilah L. *The Negro Trailblazers of California*. Los Angeles, 1919.

Berry, L. L. *A Century of Missions of the African Methodist Episcopal Church, 1840–1940*. New York, 1942.

Blassingame, John, and John R. McKivigan, eds. *The Frederick Douglass Papers*. 5 vols. New Haven, 1979–92.

Bowen, John W. *An Appeal for Negro Bishops but No Separation*. New York, 1912.

Buetow, Harold A. *Of Singular Benefit: The Story of Catholic Education in the United States*. London, 1970.

Coppin, Levi J. *Letters from South Africa*. Philadelphia, 1902?.

———. *Unwritten History*. Philadelphia, 1919.

Crummell, Alexander. *The Greatness of Christ and Other Sermons*. New York, 1882.

Davis, Cyprian. *The History of Black Catholics in the United States*. New York, 1990.

Dinnerstein, Leonard, and Mary D. Palsson, eds. *Jews in the South*. Baton Rouge, 1973.

Du Bois, W. E. B. *Against Racism: Unpublished Essays, Papers, Addresses, 1887–1961*. Ed. Herbert Aptheker. Amherst, 1985.

———. *The Souls of Black Folk*. New York, 1961.

Early, Sarah J. W. *Life and Labor of Rev. Jordan W. Early, One of the Pioneers of African Methodism in the West and South*. Freeport, N.Y., 1971.

Ferris, William H. *The African Abroad*. 2 vols. New Haven, 1913.

Foner, Philip S., ed. *The Voice of Black America: Major Speeches of Negroes in the United States, 1791–1971*. New York, 1972.

Foner, Philip S., and George E. Walker, eds. *Proceedings of the Black State Conventions, 1840–1865*. 2 vols. Philadelphia, 1980.

Frederickson, George M. *The Black Image in the White Mind: The Debate on Afro-American Character and Destiny, 1817–1914*. New York, 1971.

Gatewood, Willard B. *Aristocrats of Color: The Black Elite, 1880–1920.* Bloomington, 1990.

———. *"Smoked Yankees" and the Struggle for Empire: Letters from Negro Soldiers, 1898–1902.* Urbana, 1971.

Gerber, David A. *Black Ohio and the Color Line, 1860–1915.* Urbana, 1976.

Gillard, John T. *The Catholic Church and the American Negro.* Baltimore, 1929.

Gossett, Thomas F. *Race: The History of an Idea in America.* New York, 1965.

Gregg, Robert. *Sparks from the Anvil of Oppression: Philadelphia's African Methodists and Southern Migrants, 1890–1940.* Philadelphia, 1993.

Griffin, Paul R. *Black Theology as the Foundation of Three Methodist Colleges: The Educational Views and Labors of Daniel Payne, Joseph Price, Isaac Lane.* New York, 1984.

Grossman, Lawrence. *The Democratic Party and the Negro: Northern and National Politics, 1868–1892.* Urbana, 1976.

Haley, James T., comp. *Afro-American Encyclopedia; or, The Thought, Doings, and Sayings of the Race.* Nashville, 1895.

Handy, James A. *Scraps of African Methodist Episcopal History.* Philadelphia, 1901?.

Harlan, Louis R., ed. *The Booker T. Washington Papers.* 13 vols. Urbana, 1972–84.

Higginbotham, Evelyn B. *Righteous Discontent: The Women's Movement in the Black Baptist Church, 1880–1920.* Cambridge, Mass., 1993.

The History of American Methodism. 3 vols. New York, 1964.

Jacobs, Sylvia M., ed. *Black Americans and the Missionary Movement in Africa.* Westport, Conn.: Greenwood Press, 1982.

Jenifer, John T. *Centennial Retrospect History of the African Methodist Episcopal Church.* Nashville, 1915.

Lampton, Edward W. *Digest of Rulings and Decisions of the Bishops of the African Methodist Episcopal Church from 1847 to 1907.* Washington, 1907.

Lane, Roger. *William Dorsey's Philadelphia and Ours: On the Past and Future of the Black City in America.* New York, 1991.

Lapp, Rudolph M. *Blacks in Gold Rush California.* New Haven, 1977.

Lester, Julius, ed. *The Seventh Son: The Thought and Writing of W. E. B. Du Bois.* 2 vols. New York, 1971.

Lynch, Hollis R. *Edward Wilmot Blyden: Pan Negro Patriot.* London, 1967.

Martin, Sandy D. *Black Baptists and Foreign Missions: The Origins of a Movement, 1880–1915.* Macon: Mercer Univ. Press, 1989.

Martin, Waldo E. *The Mind of Frederick Douglass.* Chapel Hill, 1984.

Mathews, Marcia M. *Henry Ossawa Tanner: American Artist.* Chicago and London, 1969.

Montgomery, William E. *Under Their Own Vine and Fig Tree: The African Methodist Church in the South, 1865–1890.* Baton Rouge, 1993.

Morse, Samuel F. B. *Imminent Dangers to the Free Institutions of the United States through Foreign Immigration and the Present State of the Naturalization Law.* New York, 1969.

Moseby, Dewey F., ed. *Henry Ossawa Tanner.* Philadelphia, 1991.

Moses, Wilson J. *Alexander Crummell: A Study of Civilization and Discontent.* Amherst, 1992.

Moss, Alfred A., Jr. *The American Negro Academy: Voice of the Talented Tenth.* Baton Rouge, 1981.

Newman, Richard, and David W. Wills, eds. *Black Apostles at Home and Abroad: Afro-Americans and the Christian Mission from the Revolution to Reconstruction.* Boston: G. K. Hall, 1982.

Ochs, Stephen J. *Desegregating the Altar: The Josephites and the Struggle for Black Priests, 1871–1960.* Baton Rouge, 1990.

Oldfield, J. R. *Alexander Crummell (1819–1898) and the Creation of an African American Church in Liberia.* Lewiston, N.Y., 1990.

Olsen, Otto H. *Carpetbagger's Crusade: The Life of Albion Winegar Tourgee.* Baltimore, 1965.

Payne, Daniel A. *History of the African Methodist Episcopal Church.* Philadelphia, 1891.

———. *Recollections of Seventy Years.* New York, 1968.

———. *The Semi-Centenary and the Retrospection of the African Methodist Episcopal Church in the United States.* Baltimore, 1866.

Peck, Dorothy A., ed. *Women on the Wing: African Methodist Episcopal Women Maximizing Their Human and Spiritual Potential.* Washington, D.C., 1983.

Penn, Garland I. *The Afro American Press and Its Editors.* Springfield, Mass., 1891.

Perry, Rufus L. *The Cushite or the Descendants of Ham.* Springfield, Mass., 1893.

Prince, W. H. *The Stars of the Century of African Methodism.* Portland, Ore., 1916.

Raboteau, Albert J. *A Fire in the Bones: Reflections on African American Religious History.* Boston, 1995.

Redkey, Edwin S. *Black Exodus: Black Nationalist and Back to Africa Movements, 1890–1910.* New Haven, 1969.

Rigsby, Gregory U. *Alexander Crummell: Pioneer in Nineteenth-Century Pan African Thought.* New York, 1987.

Seraile, William. *Voice of Dissent: Theophilus Gould Steward (1843–1924) and Black America.* Brooklyn, 1991.

Simmons, William J. *Men of Mark: Eminent, Progressive, and Rising.* Cleveland, 1887.

Simpson, Matthew, ed. *Cyclopaedia of Methodism.* Philadelphia, 1878.

Smith, Charles S. *A History of the African Methodist Episcopal Church, Being a Volume Supplemental to a History of the African Methodist Episcopal Church, by Daniel Alexander Payne.* Philadelphia, 1922.

Steward, Theophilus G. *From 1864 to 1914: Fifty Years in the Gospel Ministry.* Philadelphia, 1921.

———. *Memoirs of Mrs. Rebecca Steward.* Philadelphia, 1877.

Tanner, Benjamin T. *An Apology for African Methodism.* Baltimore, 1867.

———. *The Color of Solomon—What?* Philadelphia, 1895.

———. *The Descent of the Negro.* Philadelphia, 1898.

———. *The Dispensations in the History of the Church and the Interregnums.* Kansas City, Mo., 1899.

———. *Hints to Ministers.* Wilberforce, 1900.

———. *Joel, the Son of Pethuel.* Philadelphia, 1905.

———. *The Negro in Holy Writ*. Philadelphia, 1900.

———. *The Negro's Origin and Is the Negro Cursed?* Philadelphia, 1869.

———. *An Outline of Our History and Government for African Methodist Churchmen, Ministerial and Lay*. Philadelphia, 1884.

———. *Theological Lectures*. Nashville, 1894.

Tanner, Carlton M. *A Manual of the African Methodist Episcopal Church, Being a Course of Twelve Lectures for Probationers and Members*. Philadelphia, 1900.

Thornbrough, Emma Lou. *T. Thomas Fortune: Militant Journalist*. Chicago, 1972.

Turner, Edward R. *The Negro in Pennsylvania, Slavery—Servitude—Freedom, 1639–1861*. Washington, 1911.

Turner, Henry M. *African Letters*. Nashville, 1893.

Vexler, Robert I., comp. and ed. *Pittsburgh: A Chronological and Documentary History, 1682–1976*. Dobbs Ferry, N.Y., 1976.

Walker, Clarence E. *A Rock in a Weary Land: The African Methodist Episcopal Church during the Civil War and Reconstruction*. Baton Rouge, 1982.

White, Charles F. *Who's Who in Philadelphia*. Philadelphia, 1912.

Wilmore, Gayraud, ed. *African American Religious Studies: An Interdisciplinary Anthology*. Durham and London, 1989.

Winks, Robin. *The Blacks in Canada: A History*. New Haven, 1971.

Woodson, Carter G., ed. *The Works of Francis J. Grimké*. 4 vols. Washington, 1942.

Wright, Richard R., comp. *Who's Who in the General Conference, 1924*. Philadelphia, 1924.

———. *The Encyclopedia of the African Methodist Episcopal Church, Second Edition*. Philadelphia, 1947.

Young, Robert A. *The Negro: A Reply to Ariel*. Nashville, 1867

Articles

Beard, A. F. "The Providence of God in the Historical Development of the Negro," *Afro-American Historical Encyclopaedia* (1895): 25.

Bentley, Florence L. "Henry O. Tanner," *Voice* 3 (Nov. 1896): 480–82.

"Bermuda and African Methodism," *A.M.E. Church Review* 6 (Apr. 1890): 497–500.

"Bishop B. T. Tanner," *A.M.E. Church Review* 5 (July 1888): 1–6.

"Bishop Daniel A. Payne Symposium," *A.M.E. Church Review* 10 (Jan. 1894): 412–13.

Bixby, James T. "The Religious Genius of the Races," *Unitarian Review and Reform Magazine* 20 (July 1883): 70–78.

Blight, David W. "In Search of Learning, Liberty, and Self-Determination: James McCune Smith and the Ordeal of the Antebellum Black Intellectual." *Afro-Americans in New York Life and History* 9 (July 1985): 7–25.

Carson, Shirley J. "Black Ideals of Womanhood in the Late Victorian Era," *Journal of Negro History* 77 (Spring 1992): 61–73.

Copher, Charles B. "Three Thousand Years of Biblical Interpretation with References to Black People," in Gayraud Wilmore, ed., *African American Religious Studies: An Interdisciplinary Anthology*. Durham and London, 1989.

Coppin, Levi J. "The American Negro's Religion for the African Negro's Soul," *Independent* 54 (Mar. 27, 1902): 748–50.

———. "Fortieth Anniversary of the *A.M.E. Review*," *A.M.E. Church Review* 40 (July 1923): 3–4.

Cromwell, John W. "Our Colored Churches," *A.M.E. Church Review* 1 (Oct. 1884): 90.

Crummell, Alexander. "The Attitude of the American Mind toward the Negro Intellect." American Negro Academy occasional papers no. 3. Washington, D.C., 1898.

Dancy, John C. "Union of Methodist Bodies," *Independent* 45 (Apr. 13, 1893): 490.

Dodson, Jualynne. "Nineteenth-Century AME Preaching Women," in Darlene C. Hine, ed., *Black Women in United States History*. 16 vols. Brooklyn, 1990.

Du Bois, W. E. B. "The Conservation of Races." American Negro Academy occasional papers no. 2. Washington, D.C., 1897.

"Editorial Notes," *A.M.E. Church Review* 1 (Oct. 1884): 173; (Jan. 1885): 287.

"Files of the *Review*," *A.M.E. Church Review* 29 (Apr. 1913): 384.

Haley, James T., comp. "Colored Catholics," in Haley, *Afro-American Encyclopaedia; or, The Thought, Doings, and Sayings of the Race*. Nashville, 1895.

Holly, James T. "The Higher Criticism," *A.M.E. Church Review* 11 (Jan. 1895): 329–35.

Jackson, James H. A. "Female Preachers," *A.M.E. Church Review* 1 (Oct. 1884): 102–5.

Johnson, J. A. "African Methodism in Bermuda," *A.M.E. Church Review* 5 (Jan. 1889): 262.

Korn, Bertram W. "Jews and Negro Slavery in the Old South, 1789–1865," in Leonard Dinnerstein and Mary D. Palsson, eds., *Jews in the South*. Baton Rouge, 1973.

Lee, Benjamin F. "The Centenary of Daniel Alexander Payne, Fourth Bishop of the African Methodist Episcopal Church," *A.M.E. Church Review* 28 (July 1911) 423–29.

Lefkowitz, Mary. "Combating False Theories in the Classroom," *Chronicle of Higher Education* 40 (Jan. 19, 1994): B1–2.

"Lives of the Editors of the Review," *A.M.E. Church Review* 25 (Apr. 1909): 376–79.

Minter-Alexander, Rae. "The Tanner Family: A Grandniece's Chronicle," in Dewey F. Moseby, *Henry Ossawa Tanner*. Philadelphia, 1991.

Moore, Jesse T. "Seeking a New Life: Blacks in Post–Civil War Colorado," *Journal of Negro History* 78 (Summer 1993): 166–87.

Moseby, Dewey F. "Reflections on Race Public Reception and Critical Response in [Henry O.] Tanner's Career," in Dewey F. Moseby, *Henry Ossawa Tanner*. Philadelphia, 1991.

"No Room for the Chinese." Editorial. *The Colored American*, Dec. 28, 1901, 8; Feb. 1, 1902, 7.

"The Ordination of Women: What Is the Authority for It?" *A.M.E. Church Review* 3 (July 1886): 453–60.

"Our Book Table," *A.M.E. Church Review* 1 (Oct. 1884): 181.

"Our Colored People," *Methodist* (Nov. 3, 1860): 132.

"Our Editorial," *A.M.E. Church Review* 2 (Apr. 1886): 222.

"Our Editorial—Strikes," *A.M.E. Church Review* 3 (Aug. 1886): 98–100.

"Our Retired Bishops," *A.M.E. Church Review* 25 (July 1908): 68.

"Race Love," *A.M.E. Church Review* 4 (July 1887): 547.

Seraile, William. "Afro-American Emigration to Haiti during the American
    Civil War," *Americas* 35 (Oct. 1978): 185–200.

————. "The Struggle to Raise Black Regiments in New York State during the
    Civil War," *New-York Historical Society Quarterly* 58 (July 1974): 215–
    33.

"Shall Negro Begin with a Capital N?" *A.M.E. Church Review* 21 (Oct. 1904):
    192–93.

Smalley, E. V. "The German Element in the United States," *Lippincott Magazine*
    5 (Apr. 1883): 355–63.

Spalding, David. "The Negro Catholic Congress, 1889–1894," *Catholic Histori-
    cal Review* 55 (Oct. 1969): 337–57.

Steward, Theophilus G. "Cultured Society and the Negro," *Independent* 48
    (Apr. 16, 1896): 514.

Tanner, Benjamin T. "Bethel: One Hundred Nineteenth Anniversary," *A.M.E.
    Church Review* 25 (Oct. 1908): 68–78.

————. "Catholic Confession and the Basis It Has in Scripture," *A.M.E. Church
    Review* 14 (Oct. 1896): 179–91.

————. "Certainly Hard," *Independent* 44 (Feb. 25, 1892): 261.

————. "Columbus' Discovery and the Negro: What?" *Independent* 44 (June 2,
    1892): 753.

————. "Easter Poem," *A.M.E. Church Review* 16 (July 1892): 556.

————. "Frederick Douglass' Speech," *Independent* 27 (July 29, 1875): 5.

————. "The Fruits of Caste in the Church," *Independent* 27 (Mar. 25, 1875): 2.

————. "The Glory of the Ear," *A.M.E. Church Review* 18 (Apr. 1901): 325–33.

————. "God's Estimate of Human Life," *A.M.E. Church Review* 13 (Apr.
    1896): 482–86.

————. "The Higher Criticism," *A.M.E. Church Review* 10 (July 1893): 113–18.

————. "How the *A.M.E. Church Review* Came into Being," *A.M.E. Church
    Review* 25 (Apr. 1909): 360–62.

————. "Immortality," *A.M.E. Church Review* 12 (Apr. 1895): 521.

————. "A Methodist Confederation," *Independent* 45 (Apr. 13, 1893): 489–90.

————. "Methodist Union," *Methodist* (Apr. 16, 1870): 121.

————. "Methodist Union," *Zion's Herald* 48 (Sept. 28, 1871): 463.

————. "The Nation's Ultimatum," *Independent* 27 (Dec. 30, 1875): 7.

————. "The Negro and the Flood: A Correspondence," *A.M.E. Church Review*
    8 (Apr. 1892): 439–45.

————. "A Negro Pharaoh," *A.M.E. Church Review* 22 (Oct. 1905): 110–15.

————. "Our Latest Works," *A.M.E. Church Review* 7 (Oct. 1890): 129–38.

————. "A Prayer to Jesus," *A.M.E. Church Review* 7 (Apr. 1891): 392.

————. "The President's Power Limited," *Independent* 44 (Sept. 8, 1892):
    1246–47.

————. "A Prophecy in a Prefix," *The Independent* 27 (July l, 1875): 4–5.

————. "A Remedy Worse Than the Disease," *Independent* 27 (Sept. 30, 1875): 4–5.

————. "The Republican Defeat: A Negro's Explanation," *Independent* 44 (Nov. 24, 1892): 1658–59.

————. "Social Equality," *Independent* 27 (Feb. 25, 1875): 3.

————. "That's a Race Question with Us," *Independent* 44 (Apr. 14, 1892): 505–6.

————. "Three Suppositions," *Independent* 26 (Nov. 12, 1874): 1–2.

————. The Value of a Denominational Literature in Promoting Denominational. Success," *A.M.E. Church Review* 8 (Jan. 1892): 318–25.

"The Democratic Return to Power—Its Effect?" *A.M.E. Church Review* 1 (July 1888) 213–50.

"The Tanner Family," *Negro History Bulletin* 10 (Apr. 1947): 147–52, 167.

"Terra Incognito," *A.M.E. Church Review* 4 (July 1887): 548–49.

"Two Negro Bishops in the M. E. Church," *Competitor* 1 (June 1920): 5.

Ward, William H. "Sixty Years of the *Independent,*" *Independent* 65 (Dec. 10, 1908) 1345–51.

"What Becomes of Our Graduates," *A.M.E. Church Review* 3 (Jan. 1887): 312–16.

"What Should Be the Policy of the Colored Americans toward Africa," *A.M.E. Church Review* 2 (Apr. 1909): 360–62.

"Who Are We—Africans, Afro-Americans, Colored People or Negroes?" *Voice of the Negro.* 3 (Jan./Mar. 1906): 196.

Wright, Lawrence "One Drop of Blood," *New Yorker* (July 25, 1994): 50, 146–55.

Wynee, Lewis N. "Brownsville: The Reaction of the Negro Press," *Phylon* 33 (Summer 1972): 153–60.

Dissertations

DeBoer, Clara. "The Role of Afro-Americans in the Origin and Work of the American Missionary Association, 1839–1877," Rutgers University, 1973.

Grayson, John T. "Frederick Douglass' Intellectual Development: His Concepts of God, Man, and Nature in Light of American and European Influences," Columbia University, 1981.

Killiam, Charles. "Bishop Daniel A. Payne: Black Spokesman for Reform," Indiana University, 1971.

Seraile, William. "New York's Black Regiments during the Civil War," City University of New York, 1977.

Williams, Gilbert A. "The AME Christian Recorder for the Social Ideas of Black Americans, 1854–1902," University of Illinois, 1979.

Wills, David W. "Aspects of Social Thought in the African Methodist Episcopal Church, 1840–1910," Harvard University, 1975.

Wilmoth, Ann G. "Pittsburgh and the Blacks: A Short History," Pennsylvania State University, 1975.

Manuscript Collections

Sadie Tanner Mossell Alexander Papers. University of Pennsylvania, Philadelphia.

Black Abolitionist Papers, microfilm. Schomburg Center for Research in Black Culture, New York Public Library, New York.

John Edward Bruce Papers, microfilm. Schomburg Center.

Frederick Douglass Papers. Manuscript Division Library of Congress, Washington, D.C.

Richard T. Greener Papers. Manuscript Division. Schomburg Center.

John Albert Johnson Papers. Manuscript Division. Schomburg Center.

Theophilus Gould Steward Papers. Manuscript Division. Schomburg Center.

Benjamin Tucker Tanner Papers in the Carter G. Woodson Papers, microfilm. Schomburg Center.

Addresses, Conventions, Proceedings, and Reports

Congress of Colored Catholics of the United States: Three Catholic Afro-American Congresses. Cincinnati, 1893.

General Biographical Catalogue. The Western Theological Seminary of the Presbyterian Church, Pittsburgh, 1827–1927.

Journal of the Seventeenth Session and the Sixteenth Quadrennial Session of the General Conference of the African Methodist Episcopal Church in the United States, held at St. Louis, Missouri, May 3–25, 1880.

Journal of the Eighteenth Session and Seventeenth Quadrennial Session of the General Conference of the African Methodist Episcopal Church in the World, held in Bethel Church, Baltimore, Maryland, May 5–26, 1884.

Journal of the Twentieth Quadrennial Session of the General Conference of the African Methodist Episcopal Church, held in St. Stephen's A.M.E. Church, Wilmington, North Carolina, May 4–22, 1896.

Journal of the Twenty-third Quadrennial Session of the General Conference of the African Methodist Episcopal Church, held in St. John A.M.E. Church, Norfolk, Virginia, May 4–21, 1908.

Journal of the Twenty-seventh Quadrennial Session of the General Conference of the African Methodist Episcopal Church, held in Louisville, Kentucky, May 5–21, 1924.

Memorial of the National Convention of Colored Persons, December 19, 1873. U.S. Senate, 43rd Congress, 1st session, Miscellaneous Document no. 21.

Proceedings of the National Convention of the Colored Men of America, held in Washington, D. C., Jan. 13–16, 1869.

Proceedings of the National Conference of Colored Men of the United States, held in State Capital at Nashville, Tennessee, May 6–9, 1879.

Proceedings of the Third Ecumenical Methodist Conference, held in City Road Chapel, London, Sept. 1901.

Raymond, B. P. "A Belated Race." *Twentieth Annual Report of the Freedmen's Aid Society of the Methodist Episcopal Church for 1887*, 41–48. Cincinnati, 1887.

Report of the Proceedings of the Convention of Colored Masons held in the City of Wilmington, Delaware, May 8–10, 1878.

Roberts, Joseph Jenkins. "African Colonization." Address delivered at the Fifty-
    second Annual Meeting of the American Colonization Society, held in
    Washington, D.C., Jan. 19, 1869.
Sermons, Essays and Addresses of the Centennial Methodist Conference, held
    in Mt. Vernon Place Methodist Episcopal Church, Baltimore, Maryland,
    Dec. 9–17, 1884. New York, 1885.
Fifteenth Session of the General Conference of the African Methodist Episcopal
    Church, 1872.
The Sixteenth Session and Fifteenth Quadrennial Session of the General Con-
    ference of the African Methodist Episcopal Church, 1876.
Twenty-third Quadrennial Report of the Parent Home and Foreign Missionary
    Department of the African Methodist Episcopal Church, 1904–8.
Tiffany, Otis H. *Africa for Africans: Being the Annual Discourse Delivered at the
    Sixty-seventh Anniversary of the American Colonization Society held in
    Foundry Methodist Church, Washington, D.C., Sunday, January 13, 1884.*

Newspapers

Afro-American Sentinel (Omaha)
American Citizen (Kansas City, Kan.)
Brooklyn Daily Eagle
Christian Advocate (New York)
Christian Recorder (Philadelphia)
Cleveland Gazette
Douglass Monthly (Rochester, N.Y.)
Freeman (Indianapolis)
Freeman (New York)
London Times
Louisiana (New Orleans)
Montgomery Enterprise
New National Era (Washington, D.C.)
New York Age
New York Globe
New York Times
New York Tribune
Paul Quinn Weekly (Waco, Tex.)
People's Advocate (Washington, D.C.)
Philadelphia Bulletin
Race and Standard (Baltimore)
State Capital (Springfield, Ill.)
State Journal (Harrisburg, Pa.)
Washington Bee (Washington, D.C.)
Washington Grit (Washington, D.C.)
Weekly Anglo African (New York)
Western Christian Recorder (Kansas City, Kan.)
Wide-Awake (Birmingham, Ala.)

Index

Fire in His Heart was designed and typeset on a Macintosh computer system using PageMaker software. The text is set in Minion and the titles in ITC Officina. This book was designed by Kay Jursik, composed by Kimberly Scarbrough, and manufactured by Thomson-Shore, Inc. The recycled paper used in this book is designed for an effective life of at least three hundred years.